NINTH EDITION

DRIVE RIGHT

Authors

Margaret L. Johnson

Owen Crabb

Arthur A. Opfer

Ronald L. Budig

Reading Consultant

Robert A. Pavlik

 ScottForesman

A Division of HarperCollinsPublishers

Editorial Offices:
Glenview, Illinois

Regional Offices:
Sunnyvale, California
Tucker, Georgia
Glenview, Illinois
Oakland, New Jersey
Carrollton, Texas

ABOUT THE AUTHORS

Margaret L. Johnson is a former Supervisor of Driver, Consumer, and Health Education at Glenbrook North High School, Northbrook, Illinois. She also was an instructor of Traffic Safety and Driver Education at Northeastern Illinois University in Chicago.

Owen Crabb is Driver-Education Specialist with the Maryland State Department of Education. He also has assisted several states in developing driver-education programs.

Arthur A. Opfer has taught driver education at both the high school and college levels. He is Regional Traffic Coordinator for the Superintendent of Public Instruction at Educational Service District 105, Yakima, Washington.

Ronald L. Budig is Professor of Safety at Illinois State University, Normal, Illinois. Dr. Budig served as Supervisor of Safety and Driver Education in Missouri and taught in the state of Washington.

Robert A. Pavlik is Professor of Reading and Language Arts, Cardinal Strich College, Milwaukee, Wisconsin.

Staff Credits

Editorial: Terry Flohr, Lois Teesdale, and
     Kayla Cohen
Design: Ron Stachowiak, Paula Meyers, and
     Rosemary Hunter
Production: Barbara Albright and Francine Simon
Marketing: Edward Rock

ISBN 0-673-22464-3 (hard cover)
ISBN 0-673-22465-1 (soft cover)

Acknowlegments for quoted matter and illustrations are included in the acknowlegments section on page 392. The acknowlegments section is an extension of the copyright page.

45678910RRS0099989796959493

CONTRIBUTORS AND REVIEWERS

Contributors

Randall R. Thiel
Education Consultant
Alcohol-Traffic Safety Program
Wisconsin Department of Public
Instruction
Madison, Wisconsin

Jerry L. Gaines
Driver-Education Coordinator
Palos Verdes Peninsula Unified
School District
Palos Verdes Estates, California

Rosaria Montez-Thiel
Reading Specialist
Madison, Wisconsin

Bill Lee
Driver Education–Special Education
Los Angeles Unified School District
Los Angeles, California

James A. Tracy
Teacher and Center Director
Ray Graham Training Center
Chicago, Illinois

Beverley Whitehead
Supervising Driver Education
Teacher
Region IV Education Service Center
Houston, Texas

James Goode
Supervisor, Driver Education
Region IV Education Service Center
Houston, Texas

Reviewers

Gerald Christensen
State Specialist in Safety and Driver
Education
Kansas Department of Education
Topeka, Kansas

Patsy Collins
Driver Education-Teacher
Memphis City Schools
Memphis, Tennessee

Loretta J. Martin
Coordinator
Safety and Driver Education
Chicago Public Schools
Chicago, Illinois

Ronald E. Mauck
Department Chairperson, Driver
Education
Brooke High School
Wellsburg, West Virginia

Richard S. Pitts
Driver-Education Teacher
Menchville High School
Newport News, Virginia

David V. Sanborn
Tutor/Driver Educator
Lamoille Union High School
Hyde Park, Vermont

CONTENTS

v

THE DRIVING TASK

Chapter 1
YOU ARE THE DRIVER

Chapter 2
SIGNS, SIGNALS, AND ROADWAY MARKINGS

Chapter 3
BASIC CAR CONTROL

Chapter 4
MAKING SAFE DRIVING DECISIONS

Traffic like this might seem confusing to a beginning driver. Cars are everywhere, making turns, parking, stopping, and starting. Even on crowded city streets, though, traffic signals, signs and markings on the roadway help traffic flow smoothly. As you gain skills, you will learn to drive confidently through city streets and other parts of our nation's highway transportation system.

In this unit, you will learn about your role as a driver in the highway transportation system. You will learn about your responsibilities as a driver and about your driver's license. You also will learn what the various road signs and signals mean, and how to read and control the instruments and devices in your vehicle. Finally, you will learn an organized, thinking-doing process that will help you become a safe, responsible driver.

Chapter 1

YOU ARE THE DRIVER

You're the Driver!

Imagine you are driving in this situation. You are on one of your first sales assignments in a new job. Driving is a vital part of your job and the way you live. As a result of your good driving record and the respect you show people, you have great opportunities to get ahead.

How hard do you think you will have to work to remain a safe driver?

Why should you maintain self control, even in difficult situations?

Why is it important to know about other drivers and anticipate what they will do?

In which situations is it best not to drive?

How frequently do collisions happen and what can you do to avoid them?

This chapter introduces the highway transportation system and describes your role in it. You also will learn how you can develop the knowledge, attitudes, and skills necessary for safe driving.

Objectives

Section 1–1   You Are Part of a System
1. List and explain the three parts of the highway transportation system (HTS).
2. Explain how the HTS is regulated.

Section 1–2   Your Driving Task
3. Explain how your driving task involves social, decision-making, and physical skills.
4. Name the four steps of the IPDE process.

Section 1–3   Your Driving Responsibilities
5. Tell how your attitude can affect your driving.
6. List examples of breakdowns in the HTS.
7. Name some major causes of collisions.
8. Describe some ways our demands for transportation affect our environment.

Section 1–4   Your Driver's License
9. Tell why having a driver's license is a privilege.
10. Explain how this driver education course can help you to become a safe and fuel-efficient driver.

You Are Part of a System

The big day you have been looking forward to is almost here. The day you get your first driver's license is a special day indeed. Your license will mean many things to you. You will gain new independence. You will meet new people and do new things. And, you will have a set of new responsibilities.

The Highway Transportation System

When you drive, you will use a massive system called the **highway transportation system,** or HTS. The HTS is a complex system composed of three parts: people, vehicles, and roadways. The purpose of the HTS is to move people and cargo from one place to another in a safe, efficient, and economical manner.

Of all transportation systems, the HTS is the most complex. It has the greatest variety of users— drivers, passengers, motorcyclists, bicyclists, and pedestrians. It accepts an incredible mixture of vehicles— cars, buses, trucks, vans, bicycles, motorcycles, and emergency vehicles. And the HTS has a broad range of roadways from simple to complex.

The highway transportation system consists of people, vehicles, and roadways.

People

The people who use the HTS by walking, driving, or riding are called **roadway users.** Most roadway users are drivers and passengers of cars.

Roadway users belong to all age groups, from preschool children to senior citizens. Their physical, mental, and emotional conditions range from excellent to very poor.

Compared with other transportation systems, the HTS requires very limited training. Individuals who become airplane pilots undergo extensive training and testing. However, the training and testing requirements for drivers are much less demanding. As a result, even if you are the safest driver on the road, you might share the HTS with other drivers who are barely able to control a vehicle.

Most people use the HTS in a responsible and cooperative way. Some do not. Some people use the HTS while distracted by personal problems. Others drive when they are tired, ill, or intoxicated. You will have to compensate for others who do not drive safely and responsibly.

Vehicles

Consider the vast number and different kinds of vehicles using the HTS. The smallest and least protected is the bicycle. At the other extreme is the semitrailer truck weighing many tons. In between are motorcycles, cars, vans, buses, campers, and farm and construction vehicles.

Vehicles in the HTS represent a wide range of performance abilities. Some vehicles are older cars with many miles on them. Others are shiny new models just off the assembly line.

Roadways

Roadways of the HTS vary from dirt roads to multilane expressways. In between are congested city streets, rural highways, and mountain roadways with steep grades and sharp curves.

Traffic controls and roadway maintenance range from excellent to nonexistent. Such adverse conditions as darkness, rain, snow, fog, wind, and potholes can further complicate the driving task. As more and more people use these roadways, driving skills and cooperation become increasingly important.

Regulating the HTS

Drivers who operate their vehicles safely are the most important element in controlling the HTS. States grant individuals the privilege of driving on the HTS by issuing driver's licenses. A person earns a license by passing a state license exam. In accepting a license, you also agree to obey all traffic laws.

Many agencies and departments of federal, state, and local governments help regulate the HTS. The federal government has established the National Highway Safety Act, a set of traffic-safety guidelines. Government agencies respond to the guidelines as follows:

- Federal and state legislatures pass laws which make up the **vehicle code.**
- State and local police enforce the laws.
- State departments of motor vehicles set up rules and regulations for the control of drivers and motor vehicles.
- Courts decide whether drivers charged with violating the laws are guilty or innocent.
- Local, county, and state highway and traffic engineers maintain the roadways and traffic controls.

Review It

1. What are the parts and purpose of the HTS?
2. What element is most important in controlling the HTS?

1–2

Your Driving Task

The **driving task** includes all the skilled actions you must take to drive safely. Driving requires social skills, physical skills, and decision-making skills. To perform the driving task safely, you must:

- use visual skills and stored knowledge to interpret the ongoing traffic scene
- obey traffic laws and understand the meaning of signs, signals, and roadway markings
- judge time-space relationships that are constantly changing
- anticipate how your car will respond in normal and emergency situations
- respond with coordinated actions in a timely way to maneuver your vehicle

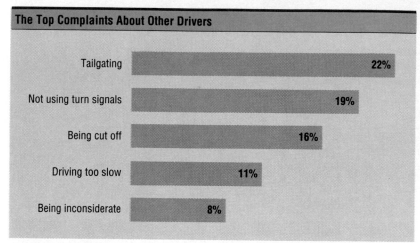

The Top Complaints About Other Drivers

Tailgating	22%
Not using turn signals	19%
Being cut off	16%
Driving too slow	11%
Being inconsiderate	8%

Results of a survey of complaints about driving mistakes.

Social Skills

Social skills make up a large part of the driving task. Like other social tasks, driving requires you to interact and cooperate with other people. Courtesy is an important part of driving. A courteous driver obeys traffic laws and is thoughtful of other roadway users—even those who make mistakes. Without courtesy and cooperation, safe and efficient driving would be impossible.

Most drivers you meet will be strangers to you. They bring their own problems and levels of skill to the immediate situation. Some roadway users might be tired; their reactions might be slower than usual. Others might be angry or distracted by personal problems. Still others, especially at night, might have been drinking. A big part of your driving task will be to apply your social skills in observing others. Then, you will be able to adjust to their mistakes earlier. The graph lists some common mistakes drivers make.

Decision-Making Skills

Safe driving is mainly a mental, decision-making task. Steering, braking, and accelerating are of little use if they are not done in the right amounts at the right time. Deciding when and where

to steer, brake, and accelerate is essential to being a safe driver.

Only after you master the decision-making skills of driving can you become a skillful driver. An organized, thinking-doing process can help you master decision-making skills.

Physical Skills

You must learn the physical skills of driving so well that they become natural habits. Then you can focus your attention on your social and decision-making driving skills.

Beginning drivers often pay too much attention to the physical part of the driving task. They might think that good driving consists only of skillful maneuvering of vehicles. Beginners might concentrate too much on how their hands turn the steering wheel and how their feet push the pedals.

Extended practice driving in simple, low stress environments is the best way to avoid trouble and build confidence during these early driving days. Once you are able to control your car without having to concentrate on how to steer, brake, and accelerate, you will start developing all the other skills that make you a safe driver.

The IPDE Process

The **IPDE process** is an organized visual-thinking-doing process you should use when driving. The four steps of the IPDE process pictured here are:

- **Identify** important information in the ongoing driving scene, especially potential hazards.
- **Predict** when and where possible points of conflict can develop.
- **Decide** when, where, and how to adjust speed and/or position to avoid conflicts.
- **Execute** the correct actions to avoid possible conflict.

With practice, the IPDE process will become a set of habits that will protect you from driving conflicts. Protecting yourself and others from dangerous and unexpected driving situations is called **defensive driving**. The IPDE process will help you to become a defensive driver so you can:

- see and anticipate the actions of other roadway users
- maintain control no matter how bad or good the driving conditions might be
- adjust to other highway users before conflicts develop.

Review It

1. How does the driving task involve social, decision-making, and physical skills?
2. What are the four steps in the IPDE process?

1. Identify the oncoming car and the driveway ahead.

2. Predict that the car might turn across your path into the driveway.

3. Decide that you will slow and be prepared to stop.

4. Execute by taking your foot off accelerator and braking gently.

Your Driving Responsibilities

Your state issues you your driver's license assuming that you are a mature person with basic driving skills. Most states make no distinction between beginning and experienced drivers. All individuals who earn the privilege to drive are expected to obey the law and avoid conflicts.

When you drive, you also assume responsibility to be a safe driver. Your responsibilities include protecting your passengers, property, and other roadway users.

Attitude

Your attitude toward driving affects your willingness to learn safe-driving habits. This attitude also influences your behavior behind the wheel.

Some drivers confuse getting attention, or "showing off," with gaining recognition as a skillful driver. Some individuals drive fast and recklessly just to get attention. Their idea of a good time might be to scare other drivers.

Other individuals drive in a safe, deliberate way day in and day out, year after year. Over time, they earn the respect of others by being good drivers under all circumstances. Getting attention is easy. Earning respect is tough and only comes over time.

Your ability to manage your relationships with others is one key to safe driving. At times, people you know might try to get you to do things you normally would not do. They might want you to drive fast or encourage you to drive when your parents have asked you not to. You will have to learn to make the right choice. Many times, you will simply have to say no—even to a friend.

Breakdowns in the HTS

A breakdown in the HTS occurs when any part of the system does not work well. Traffic tie-ups and collisions are two examples of HTS breakdowns. Your overall driving ability will be a major factor in helping you avoid being involved in these breakdowns.

Being a responsible driver sometimes might require you to say no to a friend.

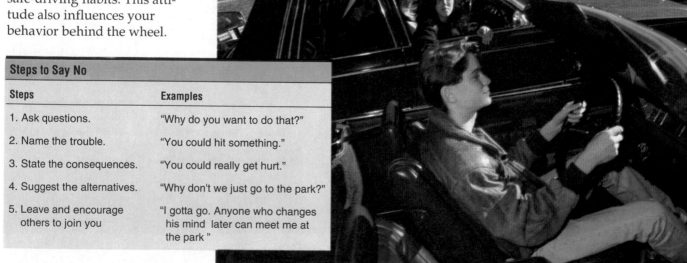

Steps to Say No	
Steps	**Examples**
1. Ask questions.	"Why do you want to do that?"
2. Name the trouble.	"You could hit something."
3. State the consequences.	"You could really get hurt."
4. Suggest the alternatives.	"Why don't we just go to the park?"
5. Leave and encourage others to join you	"I gotta go. Anyone who changes his mind later can meet me at the park"

A **collision** occurs when a vehicle hits another object. At high speeds, collisions can cause damage, injury, and death.

Collision or Accident?

Collision is a more accurate term than *accident*. The word *accident* implies something just "happened." But most collisions don't just happen; they are caused. Many causes of collisions can be eliminated. Cars can be engineered for safety, highways can be designed to prevent trouble, and programs can educate people to become better drivers.

Over the last 40 years, our nation's driving fatality rate has become lower and lower. Today, as a result of our ongoing traffic safety programs, our nation's driving record is among the best in the world. Still, we should not be lulled into a false sense of security. Compare the safety record of air, rail, and auto travel. Why do you think there is such a great difference in fatalities among these types of transportation?

Causes of Collisions Of all the possible causes of collisions, driver error is far and away the most important. Common errors include breaking various laws, not slowing in adverse weather conditions, and operating a defective vehicle. Other serious driver errors are

- following another vehicle too closely
- driving too fast for conditions
- not wearing safety belts
- driving after drinking or using other drugs.

Like most complex events, traffic collisions usually have several causes. For example, a car skids off a slippery turn and collides into a guardrail. The initial report might list the cause as driving too fast for conditions. But close inspection might also reveal that the road was abnormally slick and the tires on the car were very smooth. The slick roadway and the smooth tires probably added to the problem. Even though the primary cause of the collision was driving too fast, to really understand why the collision occurred, you must consider all the factors. If you had been the driver in that collision, what causes could you have controlled?

Age Groups in Collisions

Even though driving is a high-risk activity, people of certain age groups are at even higher risk than others. Older drivers might start to suffer from failing eyesight and slower reaction times, but younger drivers are most at risk for dying in collisions. Young drivers 16–19 years old represent less than 10 percent of the population of the United States, but they account for about 17 percent of all traffic deaths.

The chart on the next page compares traffic collisions with other major risks facing young people. Why is driving such a high-risk activity for young people? Lack of experience is a major factor in their poor driving records. Other factors include overexposure to night driving, increased risk taking, susceptibility to peer pressure, and mixing drinking and driving.

Does this mean all young drivers are bad? Absolutely not! All drivers can learn to apply the basic principles of safe driving with good results.

Your Chances of Dying on a Coast-to-Coast Trip

by Airplane

1 in 11 million

by Train

1 in 916,666

by Car

1 in 14,200

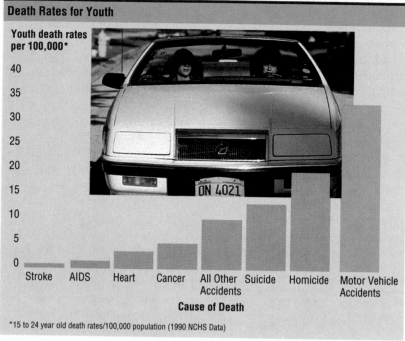

Death Rates for Youth

Youth death rates per 100,000*

40	
35	
30	
25	
20	
15	
10	
5	
0	

Stroke AIDS Heart Cancer All Other Accidents Suicide Homicide Motor Vehicle Accidents

Cause of Death

*15 to 24 year old death rates/100,000 population (1990 NCHS Data)

More young people die from vehicle collisions than from any other single cause.

Social and Economic Loss

Collisions have serious social and economic effects. Traffic collisions cost our nation billions of dollars each year in property damage, time away from work and school, medical fees, and insurance premiums. The cost of family disruption, shattered career plans, mental anguish, and physical suffering cannot simply be measured only in dollars.

Financial Responsibility

As a driver, expect to pay your share of driving-related expenses. Vehicle-related costs include buying fuel as well as maintaining and insuring your car. You also are financially responsible by law for any damage or injuries you cause.

Environmental Responsibility

Everything that surrounds us makes up our **environment**. Our nation's demands for transportation have created many threats to our environment. Some of these threats are:
- increased pollution of the air we breathe
- increased pollution of our fresh water supply
- decreasing supplies of oil

- increased frequency of chemical spills and contamination
- pollution of land caused by thoughtless disposal of used vehicle products.

How can we manage our transportation-related environmental problems? The answers rest with all of us. All drivers have the responsibility to:
- buy and maintain fuel-efficient vehicles
- use fuel-efficient driving habits
- recycle used materials whenever possible
- reduce driving trips or use public transportation whenever possible
- work for strong national, state, and local policies that reduce our fuel consumption through the use of energy efficient and environmentally clean sources of power.

If we all pitch in together, we can manage our energy needs and maintain a clean environment.

Review It

1. Is driving a right or a privilege?
2. How can your attitude affect the way you drive?
3. Why is the term *collision* more accurate than *accident*?
4. What are some of the ways we can protect our environment from the threats created by the demands of transportation?

Your Driver's License

Many people have a sincere interest in making sure that you become a good driver. Your parents have a keen interest in your well-being. Your driver education teacher cares about your driving abilities and how you apply them. Your friends have an interest in your driving skills, especially when you are the driver. Your insurance agent wants you to benefit from lower premiums as a result of a good driving record. Your state wants you to drive safely in order to keep the highways safe for everyone. In addition, if you avoid trouble you also will avoid the need for medical, legal, and other social services.

The Licensing Process

In most states, you earn a driver's license by taking examinations. You might have to take a written test, a vision test, and a driving test. You might

In some states, you sign the back of your license to become an organ donor.

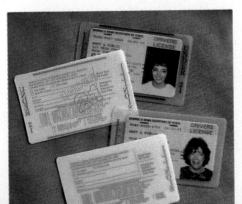

need to show that you understand traffic laws and signs, safety rules, and driving courtesy. Once you have a driver's license, you always should have it with you when you drive.

The driver's license laws and regulations in your state will determine how your early guided driving experience is combined with specific licensing requirements. When your state gives you the privilege to drive, it assumes you will obey the law and drive responsibly.

Special Programs

Many states have special programs connected with a driver's license. Your state might have one or more of these programs.

Provisional License Programs

In states with these programs, new young drivers have special licenses that put certain restrictions on them. In some states, for example, drivers under age 18 are prohibited from driving during certain nighttime hours. These programs have dramatically cut the nighttime accident rate. Other states issue special licenses to drivers younger than age 21. These licenses are designed to help prevent problems such as underage drinking.

With some provisional licenses, the state requires that young drivers fulfill a period of supervised driving. They also need to have driven without any collisions or violations for a certain period before getting a regular license.

Organ Donor Program In most states you will be given the option to donate your eyes, kidneys, or other organs in case you die in a collision. These anatomical gift programs have enabled thousands of people to live or regain health. If you agree to participate in the program, your license will state that you are an organ donor.

Implied Consent Programs In many states you may be asked to sign a statement saying that you agree to take an alcohol test on request. If you refuse to take the test, you will lose your driver's license.

Driver Education and Your License

As you begin this course, you probably are thinking of the benefits a driver's license can bring you. You are eager to learn the facts and skills needed to earn your license.

In a driver education course you will have a wide variety of experiences in the classroom and on the road. You will learn that as a result of your knowledge, attitude, and skills, you can become a safe, fuel-efficient driver. But, completing a driver education course does not guarantee that you will become a skillful driver. To do that, you will have to tell yourself every time you drive—*I am going to do my best.*

A Beginning

The *Drive Right* program is a good start toward your becoming a skillful driver. The course you are about to take is based in part on the following key driving concepts:

- Driving is primarily a decision-making process. In this program, you will learn how to use the IPDE process in your everyday driving to manage time and space. Special emphasis will be placed on speed control.
- Your driving will be greatly influenced by your attitude and what you know about driving.
- Safety belts and other restraints absolutely must be

A driver education course can help you begin to gain the knowledge, skills, and proper attitude for becoming a safe driver.

used at all times. In this program, you will learn the reasons why safety belts are vital.
- The statistics arguing against drinking and driving speak for themselves. Once you know them, we hope you will never drink and drive.

Once you pass this driver education course, you should look forward to at least one year of easing into your full time driving responsibilities. You should start gradually by working up from simple to increasingly demanding driving situations. You should ask one of your parents to go with you during your early months of driving until you gain experience. After you have driven well under a wide variety of road and traffic conditions (including driving at night and in bad weather), then you can start to think of yourself as an accomplished new driver. During your early "solo" driving trips, it is a good idea to drive

alone without the distractions of friends or loud music.

A Continuous Process

This course cannot teach you everything you need to know about safe driving. As long as you drive, you will continue to learn. Advancements in automotive technology and changes in the HTS make driver education a continuous process.

Traffic is constantly changing. In the future, new problems related to traffic conditions will arise. As a responsible driver, you will help find solutions.

Review It

1. How can a driver education program help you to become a safe and fuel-efficient driver?
2. Why is it a good idea to work gradually toward getting your regular driver's license?

DECISION MAKING

1. How will this roadway of the HTS affect your driving decision?

2. These roadway users should command your attention. How will you decide to avoid them?

3. Can the approaching vehicle make it around in time? How should you respond?

4. The IPDE process is an ongoing process. How will you apply it to this situation?

CHAPTER 1 REVIEW

Review Chapter Objectives

1–1 You Are Part of a System
1. What are the three parts of the highway transportation system (HTS)? (4)
2. How is the HTS regulated? (5)

1–2 Your Driving Task
3. How does your driving task involve social, decision-making, and physical skills? (6)
4. What are the four steps of the IPDE process? (7)

1–3 Your Driving Responsibilities
5. How can your attitude affect your driving? (8)
6. What are some examples of breakdowns in the HTS? (8–9)
7. What are some major causes of collisions? (9)
8. How can our demands for transportation affect our environment? (10)

1–4 Your Driver's License
9. Why is it a privilege to have a driver's license? (11)
10. How can this driver education course help you to become a safe and fuel-efficient driver? (12)

Check Your Knowledge

Multiple Choice   Copy the number of each sentence below on a sheet of paper. Choose the letter that best completes the statement or answers the question.

1. The purpose of the highway transportation system (HTS) is to
   (a) create greater freedom for roadway users.
   (b) replace the railroad system. (c) move people and goods in a safe, efficient, and economical way. (d) compete with other transportation systems. (4)
2. You estimate when and where possible points of conflict might occur in this step of the IPDE process:
   (a) identify (b) predict (c) decide (d) execute (7)
3. The major cause of collisions is
   (a) driver error. (b) poor weather conditions.
   (c) vehicle defects. (d) roadway defects. (9)
4. Laws require drivers to be financially responsible so that they can
   (a) have a bank account. (b) pay for car repairs.
   (c) pay for injuries and damage. (d) borrow money to buy a car. (10)
5. Saving fuel is important because
   (a) supplies are decreasing. (b) beginning drivers waste more fuel. (c) many service stations have closed. (d) the U.S. must produce all of its own energy. (10)

Completion   Copy the number of each sentence below. After each number, write the word or words that complete the sentence correctly.

6. The _____ is the group of laws that regulate the HTS. (5)
7. The driving task includes social skills, physical skills, and _____ . (6)
8. Your _____ is important in determining how safe a driver you will be. (8)
9. It is easy to "show off" driving but much harder to earn _____ for your driving skills. (8)
10. The number one cause of death for young people 15–24 is _____ . (10)
11. Agreeing ahead of time to take an alcohol test is called _____ . (11)
12. Every time you drive, you need to tell yourself I am going to _____ . (12)

Check Vocabulary

Copy the number of each definition in List A. Match the definition in List A with the term it defines in List B.

List A
13. a complex system that includes people, vehicles, and roadways (4)
14. people who use the HTS (4)
15. all the social, physical, and decision-making skills you need to drive safely (6)
16. an organized process for driving (7)
17. locate potential hazards (7)
18. judge where possible conflicts can occur (7)
19. protect yourself and others from dangerous and unexpected driving situations (7)
20. determine how to adjust speed and/or position (7)
21. perform correct actions to avoid possible conflicts (7)
22. the combined surroundings we live in are called our _____ . (10)

List B
a. decide
b. defensive driving
c. driving task
d. environment
e. execute
f. highway transportation system (HTS)
g. identify
h. IPDE process
i. predict
j. roadway users
k. vehicle code

Check Your Understanding

Write a short answer for each question or statement.

23. Describe what you can do as a driver to help protect our environment. (10)
24. Some people think of driver education as a single course. Why should you think of your driver education program as a continuous process? (12)
25. What is going on in the picture? Explain why "recycle" should be the first thought in your mind before throwing something away. (10)

Think Critically

Write a paragraph to answer each question or statement.

1. Air travel is one of the safest ways to travel. What do you think some of the reasons are?
2. Many states have adopted driver's license programs that restrict the time when young people can drive. Why do you think these programs have been so successful in reducing the number of collisions caused by young drivers? Do you think all states should adopt this type of program?

Projects

1. Take a survey of new and experienced drivers, asking what they think are common driving errors that other drivers make. Tally the top ten errors stated by the new drivers and the top ten given by experienced drivers. **Write** a report about the differences you found.
2. Collect stories on several local traffic collisions. Then report on these collisions. Did each collision have multiple causes?

Chapter 2

SIGNS, SIGNALS, AND ROADWAY MARKINGS

You're the Driver!

Driving would be next to impossible without signs, signals, and roadway markings. These controls help traffic flow smoothly.

Imagine that you are driving on the street shown here. The red traffic light is about to turn green. You want to continue straight ahead.

Have you stopped at the right place?

Are you in the best lane to continue straight?

Will you have to stop for other vehicles that plan to turn?

How might pedestrians create a problem for drivers?

What is the purpose of the two white parallel lines in front of you?

Do these traffic lights have a special signal for drivers turning left?

To be a safe driver, you must know what signs, signals, and roadway markings mean. This chapter discusses these controls and proper responses to them.

Objectives

Section 2–1   Traffic Signs

1. State the meaning of the eight shapes and eight colors used for traffic signs.
2. Describe the actions to take at STOP, YIELD, and speed limit signs.
3. List five situations where warning signs might be used.
4. Explain how guide signs and international signs help you when driving.

Section 2–2   Traffic Signals

5. Describe what to do at a red light, a yellow light, and a green light.

6. Describe the action to take when you approach a flashing red signal or a flashing yellow signal.
7. Explain how arrows and lane signals control traffic.
8. Describe the actions to take with pedestrian signals and officers' signals.

Section 2–3   Roadway Markings

9. Describe the difference between broken yellow lines and broken white lines.
10. Explain the purpose of rumble strips and raised roadway markers.
11. List six types of special roadway markings.

Traffic Signs

You will see hundreds of different traffic signs as you drive. While traffic signs serve many purposes, each traffic sign has a specific shape and color.

Shapes and Colors

Note the eight sign shapes and eight sign colors shown here. Each sign and color shape has a special meaning. By knowing the meaning of these shapes and colors, you can tell the meaning of a sign at a distance.

Each traffic sign has a special purpose. A **regulatory sign,** such as a STOP sign, controls traffic. A **warning sign,** including a signal ahead sign, alerts you to possible hazards and road conditions. A **guide sign,** such as an interstate sign, gives directions.

Regulatory Signs

Regulatory signs tell you about laws that you must obey. The most important signs, STOP and YIELD, have unique shapes. All other regulatory signs are either white squares or rectangles with red or black lettering.

Stop Sign
A STOP sign is used on a road that crosses a main highway or a

Shapes

Octagon:
Stop

Triangle:
Yield

Vertical Rectangle:
Regulatory

Pentagon:
School

Round:
Railroad Crossing

Pennant:
No Passing

Diamond:
Warning

Horizontal Rectangle:
Guide

Colors

Red:
Stop, yield, or prohibited

Yellow:
Warning

White:
Regulatory

Orange:
Construction or detour

Black:
Regulatory

Green:
Guide

Blue:
Motorist service

Brown:
Public recreation and cultural interest

through street. The STOP sign is a red octagon with white letters and a white border.

Always come to a **full stop** at a STOP sign. Once stopped, always yield the right of way to pedestrians or other vehicles in or approaching the intersection. To **yield** means to allow others to use an intersection before you do. Using the **right of way** means you accept the privilege of immediate use of the roadway. If another driver must slow or stop after you leave a STOP sign, then you have not yielded the right of way.

The location of a STOP sign or stop line helps you decide where to stop. If there is only a STOP sign, stop before entering the intersection. Stop where you can see approaching traffic, but stop before you reach any crosswalk. The picture here shows where to stop when a stop line is present. Stop just behind the stop line and before entering a crosswalk.

If your view is blocked as you approach an intersection and you cannot see cross traffic clearly after stopping, move slowly and stop again. Make sure the way is clear before driving into the intersection.

At some intersections, STOP signs are posted at all four corners. Each STOP sign might be posted with a small sign that says "4-WAY" or "ALL WAY." Follow these steps at a 4-way stop:

1. The driver who stopped first should be allowed to go first.
2. When cars stop to the right or left of each other at the same time, the driver on the right should be allowed to go first.
3. When stopped across the intersection facing oncoming traffic, the driver going straight should be allowed to proceed. A driver turning left should wait.
4. Show your intention to proceed by moving forward slowly before entering the intersection.
5. Check traffic to all sides and watch for other vehicles or pedestrians in the intersection while you drive through it.

Car colors in all traffic model pictures are as follows:

- **Yellow — action car**
- **White — other cars in motion**
- **Blue — parked cars**

You should stop behind a white stop line that is next to a STOP sign. When no stop line is present, stop before entering the intersection.

If you were driving the yellow car, you would have the right of way at this 4-way stop.

Yield Sign

Always slow or stop, and give the right of way to traffic, when you approach a red and white triangular YIELD sign. It is found where roads cross or merge.

Slowing enough ahead of time can often permit you to proceed without completely stopping. Always be prepared to stop. Proceed only when it is safe to do so, without affecting the flow of traffic in the lane you are entering.

Speed Limit Signs

Speed limit signs are used to restrict travel to safe speeds. Many experts think that collisions and fuel consumption are reduced as a result of setting 55 mph as the maximum speed limit throughout the country. However, individual states may now set the maximum speed as high as 65 mph on interstate highways in some rural areas.

Speed limits are set for ideal driving conditions. When traffic, roadway, or weather conditions are not ideal, you must obey the **basic speed law.** This law states that you may not drive faster than is safe and prudent for existing conditions, regardless of posted speed limits.

A **minimum speed limit** is set on some roadways, such as highways and expressways. This speed limit tells you not to drive slower than the posted minimum speed unless conditions are less than ideal. If conditions are bad, follow the basic speed law and drive slower than the minimum speed limit.

Advisory speed limits are set for special conditions such as sharp curves. The signs are often posted below a warning sign. They indicate the maximum suggested speed under ideal conditions. Speed should be slower under bad conditions.

Turns and Lanes

One Way

Parking and Passing

Pedestrians and Trucks

The speed limits posted on these roads tell a safe speed for ideal conditions. When conditions are bad, you must drive slower than posted speeds.

In some areas, special speed limits are set for different times of the day. For example, school zones have special speed limits when children are present during school hours only.

Other Regulatory Signs

Look at the regulatory signs at the left. These signs are used to

- direct traffic to turn or go straight.
- direct one-way traffic.
- control parking and passing.
- restrict pedestrians or truck traffic.

Red-lettered words on a white sign, or white-lettered words on a red background, usually tell what *not* to do. Black-lettered words usually tell what you *can* do. Some signs have a black symbol in a red circle and crossed by a red, diagonal slash. The red circle and slash indicate that a certain action is not allowed.

Warning Signs

A warning sign helps you avoid surprise situations. Most warning signs are diamond-shaped. Warning signs have black symbols or lettering on a yellow or orange background.

Diamond-Shaped Warning Signs

Yellow, diamond-shaped signs such as these warn you of a danger ahead. Be prepared to slow or stop when you see a warning sign.

Road Narrows
(from right)

Signal Ahead

Divided Highway
Ends

Sharp Right Curve

Side Road
(left)

Left Curve

Two Way Traffic

Slippery When Wet

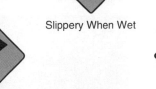

Merging Traffic
(from right)

Handicapped
Crossing

Cross Road

Fire Station

Farm Machinery
Crossing

Divided Highway
Begins

Pedestrian
Crossing

Hill

Deer Crossing

Low Clearance

21

If you intend to pass, you must complete passing before you reach a sign like this one.

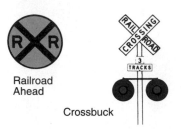

Railroad Ahead

Crossbuck

The round, yellow sign warns you that a railroad crossing is near. The white crossbuck is at the crossing.

School Zone   School Crossing

In what way is a school zone sign different from a school crossing sign?

No-Passing Sign

A yellow, pennant-shaped sign with black letters, as shown here, can be posted on the left side of the roadway. The sign appears at the start of a no-passing zone and shows you at a distance where a no-passing zone starts. A no-passing sign is used together with a solid yellow line on the roadway. If you intend to pass, you must complete your pass before reaching this sign.

Construction Signs

Orange, diamond-shaped or rectangular signs alert you to construction zones. Orange, triangular warning signs might be used on a construction vehicle to warn that the vehicle is slow moving. Be alert in a construction zone, such as in this picture. Be ready to slow, stop, or drive around workers and equipment. Follow the directions from any worker directing traffic.

Railroad Signs

A round, yellow sign, with a black X and two Rs, warns that you are approaching a railroad crossing. This sign is posted about 250 feet before a railroad crossing in a city. A railroad-crossing sign usually is posted about 750 feet before a railroad crossing in a rural area. A large X might be painted on the roadway as an additional warning.

The crossing itself is marked with a white crossbuck sign. Flashing red lights and/or crossing gates might be added to alert you when a train is coming.

School Signs

Two signs are used around schools. A school zone sign, only showing two children, is posted within a block of a school. A school crossing sign shows children in a crosswalk area. This sign is posted near intersections or crossings that children use. Notice the difference between these two signs.

Use extra care in a **school zone.** Children might dart out into the street without looking. They might ride bicycles on the wrong side of the street or take other unexpected actions. Be ready to obey a crossing guard's directions in a school zone.

At times, a construction worker might hold a warning sign.

Guide signs can provide information about city streets, state routes, and interstate routes.

The idea of a national network of roads carrying high volumes of traffic was conceived in 1938. The Federal-Aid Highway Act proposed the building of six interstate roads. With the threat of war in 1940, President Franklin D. Roosevelt called for a survey of the highways. A 75,000-mile system of highways strategic to national defense was recommended. In 1944, Congress passed an act designating a National System of Interstate Highways to connect all major population and industrial centers. Today's network of the U.S. Interstate system was born. These roads are among the safest in the world.

Guide Signs

Guide signs provide information. Guide signs mark routes, intersections, service areas, and other points of interest or information.

U.S. Route Marker

State Route Marker

County Route Marker

Interstate Route Marker

Route Signs

Local, state, U.S., and interstate routes are posted with route signs. Notice that route signs vary according to the type of roadway. State and county route markers will vary from state to state. All the signs tell you about route numbers. Notice in the photograph how route signs can be combined with information about a city's streets. Use this information to plan ahead and adjust your route as needed.

Signs indicating interstate routes are red, white, and blue shields. Notice here how a special numbering system is used for interstate routes. Study the illustrations to learn this numbering system.

An east-west route is even numbered. A north-south route is odd numbered.

A three-figured route that starts with an odd number leads into a city.

A three-figured route that starts with an even number goes around a city.

US 38	5
Greenville	40
St Louis	125

Green signs provide information on mileage to other routes or destinations.

FOOD - PHONE
GAS - LODGING
HOSPITAL
CAMPING
SECOND RIGHT

Blue signs guide you to services near the highway.

ROCKY MOUNTAIN
← NAT'L PARK

Brown signs indicate points of interest.

Other Guide Signs

You will see a wide variety of guide signs in addition to route signs. Note that green signs provide information on destinations ahead and distances to be traveled. Blue signs highlight highway services such as fuel, food, lodging, and nearby hospitals. Brown signs direct you to recreation areas or cultural points of interest.

International Signs

These international signs tell their messages with symbols rather than words. Drivers who travel from country to country can understand these signs without learning several languages. The United States has adopted several **international symbols** for use as highway signs. More and more of these symbols will be used as international travel increases.

Review It

1. What do the eight shapes and colors of traffic signs stand for?
2. What actions should you take at STOP, YIELD, and speed-limit signs?
3. What are situations where warning signs might be used?
4. What information do guide signs and international signs provide?

Stop

Falling rocks

No bicycles

Speed limit

Yield

Road narrows

Gas station

No U-turn

Traffic Signals

Traffic lights, arrows, flashing signals, lane signals, and pedestrian signals are used to help traffic flow smoothly. Each of these devices is a **traffic signal.** All traffic signals have specific colors. Each color has a specific meaning. Red means stop. Yellow means caution: you must be ready to stop. Green means go: you can proceed *if the way is clear and safe.*

Traffic Lights

Various combinations of traffic lights are placed at intersections to control traffic. Remember the following types of lights so you will be familiar with them while driving.

Red Light

The first picture shows a red light. You must come to a **full stop** at a red light. Stop behind the stop lines, crosswalk, or before entering the intersection.

Yellow Light

The second picture shows a yellow light. Make every reasonable effort to stop at an intersection for a yellow light. Sometimes you might be too close to stop safely when a yellow light appears. You then will have to go through the intersection.

Green Light

The third picture shows a green light. Cross traffic is stopped. You can proceed only if the intersection is clear of traffic. When approaching a green light, check traffic to the left, right, and ahead before entering the intersection. When approaching a light that has been green for some time, be prepared for the light to turn yellow, then red.

Traffic Light Locations

Look for traffic lights beside the roadway, over a roadway, or at an intersection the lights control. The red light in a traffic signal is always mounted on the top or to the left. The yellow light is in the center. The green light is on the bottom or to the right.

Computerized Traffic Lights

Computerized traffic light systems are often used to control the flow of traffic. A computer coordinates traffic lights at several intersections. With this system, traffic can flow for several blocks at or near the speed limit without stopping.

Traffic lights also can be set to change when traffic approaches. A sensor in the roadway detects traffic. This system can be used where most of the traffic comes from one direction, such as a left turn lane.

At a red light, come to a complete stop before the entrance to the intersection.

A yellow light means caution and prepare to stop.

Proceed at a green light only if the intersection is clear.

Before you make a right-turn-on-red, make sure no pedestrians are in any crosswalk.

The flashing red light lets drivers at a distance know that they are approaching a stop.

Be prepared to stop soon after the flashing yellow signal.

Right-Turn-on-Red

Many states have laws that allow drivers to make a right turn when facing a red light. Follow these steps when making a **right-turn-on-red:**

1. Come to a *full stop.*
2. Make sure you may legally turn on a red light. Some intersections have signs saying that a right-turn-on-red is prohibited.
3. Yield to pedestrians and vehicles (including bicycles) in or approaching the intersection.
4. Complete your right turn only if the intersection is and will be free of traffic.

Left-Turn-on-Red

Some states permit drivers to make a left turn cautiously on a red light when turning from a one-way street into a one-way street, after stopping. A few permit left turns on a red light from a left turn lane into a one-way street. Be sure state laws and local ordinances permit such turns before you make a left turn on a steady red signal after you have made a complete stop.

Laws that allow turning on red have helped reduce fuel consumption and travel times. However, pedestrian accidents have increased at some intersections where vehicles can turn when the signal is red. The intersection and crosswalk must be clear of pedestrians before you turn on a red light in places like the one shown.

Pedestrians must be especially careful at intersections where turning on red is permitted. They must recheck traffic before stepping off the curb onto the street. Pedestrians must not assume that every driver knows how to make a safe turn at a red light. *As a pedestrian, do not cross until you are sure it is safe to do so.*

Flashing Signals

A **flashing signal** is used to caution drivers or to tell them to stop. These signals are used at intersections and other dangerous locations.

Note the flashing red signal in the picture. Make a full stop when you come to a flashing red signal. A STOP sign and stop line can be used with this signal. After you stop, yield to traffic, and proceed only when the intersection is clear.

When you see a warning sign and a flashing yellow signal, as in the picture, slow down. Be cautious, and be prepared to stop at the traffic light.

Arrows

Traffic must flow in the direction that an arrow is pointing. Look at the arrows shown here. These arrows usually are used together with traffic lights. If you are driving in a lane with a green arrow pointing to the left or right, turn in that direction. Remember first to yield to other traffic and pedestrians. You may not make a turn if an arrow points straight ahead in your lane.

A yellow arrow warns you that a red arrow is about to appear. Be prepared to stop or to clear the intersection quickly.

Always stop at a red arrow. Do not proceed until the arrow changes to green.

Some cities use left-turn arrows to permit drivers to turn left before oncoming traffic proceeds. In other areas, green left-turn arrows appear only after oncoming traffic has cleared or has been stopped by a red light. Some cities use different types of signals at different intersections. You should be especially cautious if you are unfamiliar with the left-turn signals you see. Always be prepared to yield.

Lane Signals

Sometimes traffic in some lanes needs to go in one direction for a certain period of time and in the opposite direction at another period of time. The direction of these lanes is reversed on some streets and expressways to control morning and evening rush-hour traffic. In these situations, lights hanging overhead show whether or not a lane can be used at that time. Each light is a **lane signal.** These signals are different from the arrows that regulate turns.

The picture here shows that you may drive in a lane with a green arrow over it. The traffic flow should be normal.

If your lane has a yellow X over it, move to a lane labeled with a green arrow. The yellow X warns you that the lane is about to be closed to traffic going in your direction.

If your lane has a red X over it, move as soon as possible to a lane that has a green arrow over it. The red X warns you that the lane is closed to traffic going in your direction.

GO left only. Be sure that oncoming traffic does not run the red light.

GO right only. Yield to pedestrians and vehicles already in the intersection.

GO straight ahead only after yielding to vehicles and pedestrians within the intersection.

WARNING. The red arrow is about to appear.

STOP. You may not go in this direction.

The red Xs warn you not to drive in these lanes. Later in the day, one or both of these lanes might be used for traffic going in the opposite direction.

Pedestrian Signals

A **pedestrian signal** is used at an intersection with heavy traffic. These signals or symbols are mounted near traffic lights as in the picture. Pedestrians may cross at an intersection when they face a WALK signal or symbol. Pedestrians must clear the intersection or wait on a curb when the DON'T WALK signal or symbol flashes or remains lit.

Normally, the WALK signal or symbol and the green traffic light will be on at the same time for pedestrians and drivers going in the same direction. The DON'T WALK signal or symbol usually begins to flash its warning just before the yellow light appears for drivers. If you approach an intersection and see the DON'T WALK signal or symbol flashing, predict that your green light will soon change.

The pedestrian's DON'T WALK signal will remain on when a green left-turn signal is permitting a driver's path of travel to cross the crosswalk. Pedestrians must wait until their WALK signal or symbol is lit. Drivers who are turning on a green left-turn signal should be alert to pedestrians who are crossing illegally.

Officers' Signals

You must obey signals given by a traffic control officer, even if the officer's signals contradict the traffic signal. A hand held up with the palm toward you means stop. A hand waving you on means go. Signals can be given at dawn, dusk, and night with lighted wands as shown in the picture.

Review It

1. What should you do when you approach a red light? a yellow light? a green light?
2. What action should you take as you approach a flashing red signal? a flashing yellow signal?
3. How can lane-signal arrows help control traffic?
4. How do pedestrian signals and officers' signals help you when driving?

When the pedestrian signal says DON'T WALK, predict that your green light soon will change.

Always follow the signals of traffic-control officers, even if they contradict other signals.

Roadway Markings

A roadway marking gives you a warning or direction. These markings are usually lines, words, or figures painted on the roadway. Sometimes special markings are used on curbs and other surfaces.

Yellow Line Markings

The broken yellow line separates two-way traffic. It also means a driver may pass only when no traffic is coming from the opposite direction, as the driver of the yellow car in the left picture is doing.

The driver of the yellow car in the middle picture may not pass. The solid yellow line on the driver's side of the center line indicates that passing is not allowed. Passing is allowed only when the solid yellow line ends on your side of the highway. Turning left across a solid yellow line into a driveway or alley is allowed after yielding to oncoming traffic.

In the right picture, two solid yellow lines divide traffic. These double lines prohibit passing that involves crossing the solid lines. Some cities permit you to make left turns across these lines after yielding to oncoming traffic. Other cities prohibit crossing the lines if they are greater than a certain distance apart or if the area between them is painted solid or striped. If you are uncertain, do not cross solid double yellow lines.

Passing is allowed across a broken yellow line.

No passing is allowed on the side of a road that has a solid yellow line.

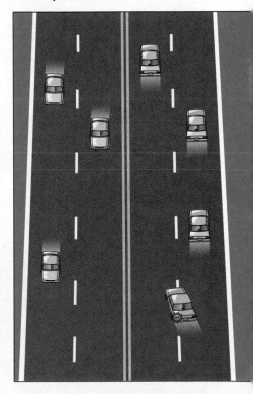

No passing is allowed if it involves crossing a double yellow line.

White Line Markings

Broken white lines separate lanes of traffic that are moving in the same direction. You may cross these broken lines when changing lanes.

Solid white lane lines keep drivers in their lanes and restrict lane changing. These lines identify locations where changing lanes is hazardous. Solid white lines generally should not be crossed. Plan ahead to prevent crossing solid white lane markings.

White arrows are used in lanes to tell you when and where to turn. If you are in a lane with an arrow and the word ONLY, you *must* continue in the direction of the arrow. You may turn or go straight if there is a curved and straight arrow in your lane.

Solid white lines also are used along the side of a roadway to mark the edge of the roadway. These lines help you to better see the edge of the roadway at night or under poor driving conditions.

Solid white lines are also used to mark pedestrian crosswalks and stop lines. Some crosswalks have diagonal or perpendicular lines between them or are painted a different color to highlight the area. You must yield the right of way to pedestrians in crosswalks. Stop lines across your lane at intersections show where to stop at a STOP sign or a traffic light.

You must turn if you are in a lane that has an arrow and the word ONLY.

Solid white lines help you see the edge of a roadway at night.

Solid white lines mark pedestrian crosswalks.

Rumble Strips and Raised Roadway Markers

Rumble strips are short sections of corrugated roadway. They alert you to approaching hazards through the noise your tires make when you drive over them. Rumble strips warn you of hazards such as a major or dangerous intersection, a tollgate, or an unexpected need to stop or reduce speed.

On some highways, it is hard for some drivers to see the driving lane at night. Raised or lowered roadway markers are used in such situations. They are raised in areas where snow seldom falls. In areas where snow may need removing, these markers may be lower than the surface of the roadway. These markers act as small reflectors. When they are struck by headlight beams, they shine and mark the driving lane.

Roadway markers are color-coded. White markers are used at the edge of a roadway or lane. Yellow markers may locate the left edge of an expressway. If you are driving and see red roadway markers, pull off the roadway immediately. These red markers warn that you are driving in the wrong direction. Safely get your car going in the correct direction.

As you drive over rumble strips, your tires make a sound to alert you of a hazard.

Roadway markers help drivers see the driving lane at night.

You may not park alongside this yellow curb marking.

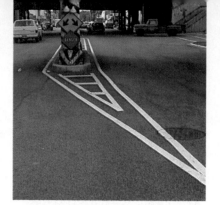

The white marking indicates an obstacle on the one-way road.

Watch for children near this school crossing.

Other Roadway Markings

Curbs alongside a road might be painted as warnings. The curb marking in the picture above, shows a No-Parking zone. The markings may be red, yellow, or white. No-Parking zones often are near fire hydrants and intersections.

Yellow lines mark obstructions on two-way roads. White lines are used on one-way roads, as shown in the picture.

Notice the marking for the school crossing . When you see this white marking, watch for children in the area.

The white roadway markings on an expressway indicate where an exit ramp starts. Do not make a last minute decision to cross this area.

White markings containing an X and two Rs indicate that you are approaching a railroad crossing. Do not pass near railroad crossings.

Signs and markings on the roadway show that a parking space is reserved for vehicles having disabled drivers or passengers. Check for signs that say DISABLED PARKING ONLY and signs with the disabled parking symbol. Check also for this symbol painted on a park-

ing space before you pull into a space. Only vehicles displaying the disabled symbol should use these spaces.

Review It

1. What is the basic difference between broken white lines and broken yellow lines?
2. What are the functions of rumble strips and raised or lowered roadway markers?
3. What are six other types of roadway markings?

Exit ramps on expressways have special white markings.

Roadway markings are one indication that a railroad crossing is near.

Before you pull into a parking space, make sure that it is not reserved for disabled drivers or passengers.

DECISION MAKING

1. What is the speed limit in this situation? What speed law might make driving at 45 mph illegal?

2. Can you use the left lane ahead? Why are lane signals located on this street?

3. The orange signs ahead are used to warn drivers about what condition? If you were driving the car that the scene is viewed from, what mistake would you have already made?

4. You want to pass the slower moving vehicle ahead. Is it safe and legal to pass here? Why?

CHAPTER 2 REVIEW

Review Chapter Objectives

2–1 Traffic Signs

1. What is the meaning of the eight shapes and eight colors used for traffic signs? (18)
2. What actions should you take at STOP, YIELD, and speed limit signs? (19)
3. What are five situations where warning signs might be used? (21)
4. How do guide signs and international signs help you when driving? (23-24)

2–2 Traffic Signals

5. What should you do at a red light, a yellow light, and a green light? (25)
6. What action should you take when approaching a flashing red signal or a flashing yellow signal? (26)
7. How do arrows and lane signals control traffic? (27)
8. What actions should you take with pedestrian signals and officers' signals? (28)

2–3 Roadway Markings

9. What is the difference between broken yellow lines and broken white lines? (29)
10. What is the purpose of rumble strips and of raised roadway markers? (31)
11. What are the six types of special roadway markings? (32)

Check Your Knowledge

Multiple Choice   Copy the number of each sentence below on a sheet of paper. After each number, write the word or words that complete the sentence correctly.

1. The color of a STOP sign is
   (a) red. (b) white. (c) blue. (d) brown. (18)
2. When you see a pennant-shaped sign, you must
   (a) stop. (b) yield right of way. (c) not pass.
   (d) watch for trains. (22)
3. When you approach a flashing yellow signal, you should
   (a) slow. (b) watch for a traffic-control officer.
   (c) pass. (d) stop immediately. (26)
4. A yellow X over a lane tells you to
   (a) drive in that lane. (b) move to a lane with a red X. (c) move to a lane with a green arrow.
   (d) pull off the roadway. (27)
5. When a traffic-control officer holds up a hand with the palm facing you, you should
   (a) go through the intersection. (b) stop. (c) back up. (d) yield the right of way. (28)

Completion   Copy the number of each sentence below. After each number, write the word or words that complete the sentence correctly.

6. The _____ of a traffic sign can tell you the meaning of the sign. (18)
7. You must come to a full stop at a _____ . (18)
8. A _____ in a red circle and crossed by a red bar prohibits a certain action. (21)
9. Lanes of traffic moving in the same direction are separated by _____ . (29)
10. A large white X with two small Rs painted on the roadway warns that a _____ is ahead. (32)

Check Vocabulary

Copy the number of each phrase below. Match the definition in List A with the term it defines in List B.

List A
11. informs you of traffic laws (18)
12. privilege to use the roadway first (19)
13. to allow another driver to go first (19)
14. requires speed to fit conditions (20)
15. alerts you to possible hazards (21)
16. gives directions and other information (23)
17. a traffic light, arrow, flashing signal, lane signal, or pedestrian signal (25)
18. flashing traffic light that indicates stop (red) or caution (yellow) (26)
19. signal that tells whether or not a lane may be used (27)
20. traffic signal saying WALK or DON'T WALK (28)
21. lines, words, and figures painted on the roadway (29)

List B
a. basic speed law
b. flashing signal
c. guide sign
d. lane signal
e. maximum speed limit
f. pedestrian signal
g. regulatory sign
h. right of way
i. roadway marking
j. traffic signal
k. warning sign
l. yield

Check Your Understanding

Write a short answer for each question or statement.

22. What pavement marking warns you of a railroad crossing? (22)
23. What is the procedure to follow when making a right-turn-on-red? (26)
24. What does a flashing DON'T WALK signal tell you as a driver? (28)
25. What should any yellow pavement marking in the center of a road tell you? (29)

Think Critically

Write a paragraph to answer each question or statement.

1. Pedestrian accidents have increased with drivers making right turns at red lights. What problems can be created for drivers and pedestrians by right-turn-on-red laws?
2. Four cars have stopped at the same time at a 4-way stop. One driver has signaled for a left turn. Which should be the sequence of drivers proceeding?
3. Imagine that the traffic signals at the intersection shown in the picture are not working. Which driver should now yield the right-of-way?

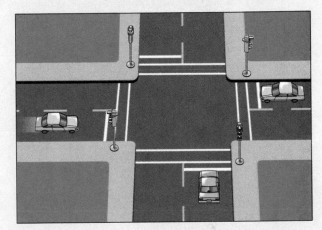

Projects

1. Observe all the traffic signs on your way home from school. On a scale of 1 to 5, with 1 being least critical, classify each sign according to how critical it is in helping drivers avoid collisions with other highway users. Give your findings to your teacher.
2. Imagine that all lane markings have been worn off on a two-lane highway. In which driving situations would you most miss having the guidance provided by the missing markings? Compare your list of situations with those of your classmates.

Chapter 3

BASIC CAR CONTROL

You're the Driver!

You are soon to become a driver like the person in this picture. Before you actually drive, you must know the location and operation of the car controls and other devices. You also must know the procedures you should follow when starting, moving, and stopping a car.

What should you check before entering the car? What should you do before starting the engine? Where is the horn? What does the odometer tell you? Does the car have an automatic or manual transmission?

This chapter explains the instruments, devices, and controls on a car. You also will learn the procedures for starting, moving, and stopping both automatic-transmission and manual-transmission vehicles.

Objectives

Section 3–1 Instruments, Controls, and Devices

1. Identify each gauge or warning light on an instrument panel and explain its function.
2. Describe the purpose of each control used to operate a vehicle.
3. Explain the use of safety, communication, and comfort devices.

Section 3–2 Preparing to Drive

4. List in order the checks you should make when preparing to drive.
5. Describe how to enter a car from the street side.

Section 3–3 Starting, Moving, and Stopping

6. Explain the use of each gear.
7. Tell the correct procedures to start, move, and stop the car.
8. Describe the correct way to leave a vehicle from the street side.

Section 3–4 Driving a Car with Manual Transmission

9. List the procedures for starting, moving, and stopping a stickshift car.
10. Define downshifting.

Instruments, Controls, and Devices

Before beginning to drive, you must know what the warning lights and gauges on the instrument panel tell you. You also must know the location and operation of the vehicle controls and devices for safety, comfort, and communication. Read the car owner's manual to learn the location and operation of the car's instruments, devices, and controls.

Instrument Panel

The location of the gauges and warning lights can vary from one car model to the next. No matter where the gauges and warning lights are located, their purposes are the same. You can make sure warning lights are working if they light when the ignition switch is turned to "On."

This instrument panel is one example of the location of the gauges and warning lights in a car. The numbers on the picture correspond to the gauges and

lights explained on this and the following pages.

Safety-Belt Light (1)   When you turn the key, the safety-belt light comes on to remind occupants to fasten their safety belts. On many cars, the light remains on for a few seconds when the engine is started, even if belts are fastened.

Speedometer (2)   This instrument tells how fast the vehicle is traveling. Speed is indicated in both miles per hour and kilometers per hour.

The instrument panel in your car might look different from this one, but all cars have similar devices to give information about the car.

Odometer (3) The **odometer** is usually located near the speedometer. The odometer shows the total number of miles the vehicle has been driven. Some cars have separate trip odometers that can be set back to zero to record the number of miles driven during a period of time.

Fuel Gauge (4) The fuel gauge shows the amount of fuel in the tank. Never let the fuel tank get below one-quarter full; you risk running out of fuel.

Try to keep the tank at least half full in cold weather to help prevent fuel-line freeze. This problem can occur when moisture condenses and freezes inside the tank and fuel line. Ice particles can block the fuel line and stop the flow of fuel.

Temperature Light or Gauge (5) This light or gauge warns you if the coolant in the engine gets too hot. If overheating occurs, stop at the nearest safe place. Turn off the engine, and wait for it to cool. Have the cooling system checked as soon as possible.

Oil-Pressure Warning Light or Gauge (6) This light or gauge warns you when the engine oil is not circulating at the right pressure. However, it does not tell you the amount of oil in the engine. Use the oil dipstick to check the engine's oil level.

Stop immediately if the light or gauge indicates trouble.

Losing oil pressure can cause serious and expensive damage to your car's engine. Have the system checked before you continue.

Alternator Warning Light or Gauge (7) Your car's electrical system is in trouble if this light comes on or the gauge shows "discharge" while the engine is running. The alternator is not generating enough electricity to run the car. If too little electricity is being generated, the engine must use stored electricity from the battery.

The **alternator warning light** or gauge warns that the battery is being drained. The more electricity used, the sooner the battery will be dead. Turn off as many electrical devices as possible, and have the system checked without delay.

Brake-System Warning Light (8) The brake-system warning light serves two purposes. First, the light reminds you to release the parking brake before moving the car. Second, should the light come on while you are pressing the foot brake, it means that part or all of the brake system is not working properly. If this light turns on, slow down, brake gradually to a stop, and have the car towed. Do not drive the car until the problem has been corrected.

Some cars have an antilock braking system. A separate

warning light indicates if a problem occurs in the antilock braking system.

Turn-Signal Indicators (9) These indicators are usually two small green arrows, each of which flashes to show the direction of the turn. The indicators stop flashing automatically when the turn signal is cancelled.

High-Beam Indicator (10) This light glows when the high-beam headlights are on. The light is off when you are using only low-beam headlights.

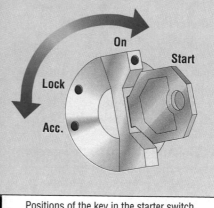

Positions of the key in the starter switch.

Devices for starting and controlling the movement of a car: steering wheel, selector lever, starter switch.

Car Controls

The characteristics and locations of car controls often vary from one car model to another. However, each control performs the same function in all cars. The numbers in the pictures on pages 40-43 match the controls explained.

Steering Wheel (11) The steering wheel controls the direction of the front wheels. The car moves right when you turn the wheel right. The car moves left when you turn the wheel left. The car's response to these turns is the same when moving forward and backward.

Some cars have adjustable steering wheels for better com-fort and control. Most cars are equipped with power steering, an option that makes the steering wheel easier to turn. If the engine stalls in a car equipped with power steering, you can still steer, but will have to use more effort to do so.

Selector Lever (12) In a car with automatic transmission, move the **selector lever** to choose forward or reverse gears. This control is located on the steering column, or on the floor to the right of the driver's seat, as shown in the picture.

Gear-Shift Lever (13) In a car with manual transmission, shift gears by moving the shift lever to the desired position. This

lever usually is located on the floor to the right of the driver. In some cars, it is located on the steering column. This type of transmission is also called a "stickshift."

Ignition and Starter Switch (14) This switch is usually located on the steering column. The picture shows all the posi-tions. Get ready to start the en-gine by putting the key into the **ignition switch**. Turn the key to the right one notch, to the "On" position. The warning lights should light, and the fuel gauge will register. Turn to the "Start" position to start the en-gine. When the switch is turned backward to "Lock," both the shift lever and steering wheel are locked, and the key can be removed. Turn to "Lock" only when the selector lever is in PARK. Turn the key to "Acces-sory" to operate the radio and other electrical equipment with-out running the engine.

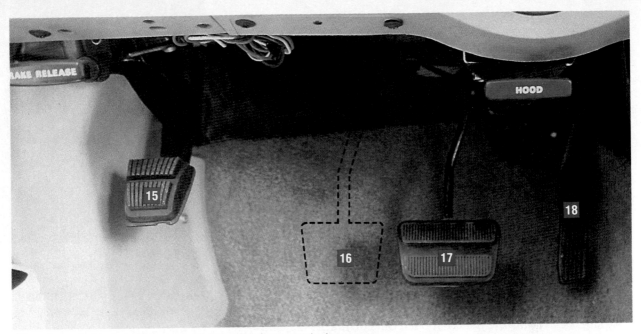

All cars have a foot-brake pedal and an accelerator pedal. Some cars also have a clutch pedal and/or a parking-brake pedal.

Parking Brake (15) The **parking brake** keeps the car in place when it is parked. If the foot brake fails while driving, use the parking brake to slow the car.

The parking-brake pedal is located on the far left in many cars. Push down on the pedal to set the parking brake. Pull the parking-brake release lever on the left side under the instrument panel to release the parking brake.

In other cars, the parking brake is a lever located on the floor to the right of the driver's seat. Pull the lever up to set the parking brake. Push the button at the tip of the lever and lower the lever to release the brake.

Clutch Pedal (16) In a stick-shift car, the **clutch pedal** is to the left of the foot-brake pedal. Pushing this pedal down lets you shift gears.

Foot-Brake Pedal (17) Pushing down on the foot-brake pedal slows or stops the car. Pushing this pedal also turns on the brake lights in the back of the car. Tapping the pedal lightly makes the brake lights flash without slowing the car.

Power brakes reduce the physical effort you must make to stop the car. However, power brakes do not shorten your stopping distance.

Accelerator Pedal (18) The accelerator controls the speed of the car. The accelerator pedal is located to the right of the foot-brake pedal. Pushing the accelerator pedal down increases speed; releasing it slows the car.

The accelerator pedal also activates the **automatic choke** in cars with carburetors. The choke adjusts how much air enters the engine when starting the car. A closed choke reduces the amount of air, making it easier to start the car when the engine is cold. To close the choke, press the accelerator pedal to the floor once, then release it. After the engine has warmed up, tap the accelerator to open the choke and reduce engine speed. Cars with fuel-injection engines do not have automatic chokes. *CAUTION:* Closing the automatic choke when the engine is warm can make starting difficult.

Devices for Safety, Communication, and Comfort

These devices are located where you can easily reach them. Locate and understand the operation of the following devices on any car you drive.

Safety Belts (19) A properly fitted safety belt helps keep the wearer from

- being thrown from the car during a sudden stop or collision
- hitting a part of the car during a sudden stop or collision.

Fasten your safety belt to a snug fit before starting the engine. Most states require drivers and front-seat passengers to wear safety belts.

Passive Restraints The term **passive restraint** describes a safety device that works without any action by the car occupants. The automatic safety belt is one type of passive restraint. This belt is connected from the door to the center of the car.

The air bag is a second type of passive restraint. In a collision, air bags inflate on impact in front of the driver and front passengers.

Head Restraints (20) Most cars have **head restraints,** padded devices on the backs of front seats. Head restraints help reduce whiplash injuries if your car is struck from the rear.

Inside and Outside Rearview Mirrors (21–22) The inside mirror (21) shows you the view through the rear window. The left outside mirror (22) shows a view of the roadway to the left and rear of your car. Each area that the mirrors cannot show is a **blind spot.** Glance over both shoulders to check these areas before changing lanes.

Horn (23) The horn usually is located on the steering wheel. Know how to use the horn on each car you drive so you will not hunt for it in an emergency.

The dark shading indicates blind-spot areas that you cannot see through your mirrors.

Emergency Flasher Control (24) This switch usually is located on the instrument panel or the steering column. When the **emergency flasher** is on, both front and rear turn-signal lights flash at the same time. These lights warn others that your vehicle is a hazard or that you are in trouble.

Windshield Wipers and Washers (25) One switch usually operates both the wiper and the washer to clean the outside of the windshield. A container under the hood of the car holds windshield-washing solution or water. Use a windshield antifreeze solution in winter to prevent freezing.

Light Switch (26) The light switch is usually a knob or switch on the left of the instrument panel. This device controls headlights, taillights, parking lights, and side-marker lights as well as the instrument panel, license plate, and dome lights.

Safety devices include the safety belt, head restraint, mirrors, horn, and emergency flashers.

Pull the knob or push the switch one notch to light the parking and side-marker lights. Pull the knob or push the switch to the second notch to light the headlights. All other lights, except the dome light, are on in both positions.

The knob or small wheel by the switch controls the brightness of the instrument-panel light. Some cars may have the light switch on the end of the turn-signal lever.

Turn-Signal Lever (27) This lever is on the left side of the steering column. Move the lever up to signal a right turn and down to signal a left turn. The turn signal stops flashing after a turn when the steering wheel is straightened. You might have to cancel a signal manually if a turn is slight. Hold the lever up or down lightly to signal a lane change.

Dimmer Switch On many cars, you change the headlights from low to high beam by moving the turn-signal lever toward the steering wheel. On other cars, the switch is a floor button.

Cruise Control (28) Use the **cruise control** to set the car's speed for highway or expressway driving. This optional device is usually a button on the end of the turn-signal lever or on the steering wheel. When cruise control is set, you can remove your foot from the accelerator pedal; the car's speed will stay constant. Tap the foot-brake pedal lightly to cancel cruise control. Use cruise control with caution. It reduces the amount of control you have over speed adjustment and might lull you into a false sense of security.

Hood Release Lever (29) Many cars have a **hood release lever**

under the instrument panel. Pull the lever to release the hood lock. This lever might be located near the parking-brake release lever. Be careful not to pull the wrong lever when releasing the parking brake.

Heater, Air Conditioner, and Defroster (30) The heating and air-conditioning systems warm or cool the inside of the car. The defroster helps keep the inside of the windshield, side windows, and rear window free of moisture. Many cars have a separate switch for a rear-window defroster.

Sun Visor The sun visor is located above the windshield. When pulled down, it helps cut glare so you can see better.

Seat Adjustment Lever The seat adjustment lever is usually at the lower front or left side of the driver's seat. In cars with bucket seats, both front seats have an adjustment lever. Adjust the seat so you are in a comfortable driving position.

Instruments for controlling windshield wipers, lights, turn signals, dimmers, cruise control, hood release, and heating and cooling.

Review It

1. What warning does the temperature gauge or light provide?
2. What action should you take if the oil-pressure warning light or gauge indicates trouble?
3. How can you check for cars in blind-spot areas?

Preparing to Drive

You should follow certain procedures and steps before you get into a car to drive.

Begin by checking both outside and inside of the car before driving. Develop a habit by practicing the procedures in the same order every time you get ready to drive.

Walk around the front and face oncoming traffic as you enter the car.

Outside Checks

1. Walk around your car and make a "circle check." Look for objects around the car and in the path you intend to take.
2. Glance at the tires to see they are inflated properly.
3. Make sure that the windshield, windows, headlights, and taillights are clean.
4. Check the back window ledge for loose objects. Remove them before driving.

Getting into the Car

1. Whenever possible, enter the car from the curb side. You lessen your risk of being struck by another vehicle.
2. If you enter from the street side, have your keys in your hand. Avoid searching for them as you stand near oncoming traffic. Walk around the front of the car. You then face oncoming vehicles and reduce your risk of being hit. Do not open the door if an oncoming vehicle is near.
3. Get in quickly and close the door.

Inside Checks

1. Lock all doors.
2. Put the key in the ignition switch. Sit with your back firmly against the seat.
3. Reach for the accelerator and brake pedals with your foot to judge a comfortable distance.
4. Move the seat forward or backward so you are within comfortable reach of all controls and devices.
5. Adjust the head restraint to reach the middle of the back of your head.
6. Adjust the inside rearview mirror so it reflects the area to the rear of the car.

Fasten your safety belt before you start the car.

7. Adjust the outside rearview mirror so you can see the area to the left and rear of the car.
8. Fasten your safety belt. Ask all passengers to fasten theirs.

Review It

1. What are three outside checks to make before entering the car?
2. Why should you walk around the front of the car when entering from the street side?

Starting, Moving, and Stopping

Learning the steps for starting, moving, and stopping an automatic transmission car is not difficult. Practice each step in the correct order so that the procedures become a habit.

Selector-Lever Positions

The **shift indicator** shows the gear positions. It is located on the steering column, on the instrument panel, or near the floor selector lever.

Park (P) This gear position locks the transmission. Always shift to PARK when you stop driving. Never shift to PARK when the car is moving. On most cars, you can remove the key from the ignition only when the lever is in PARK.

Reverse (R) Use this gear for backing. Never shift to REVERSE while the car is moving forward. Expensive damage to the transmission can result.

When you shift to REVERSE, the backup lights turn on. **Backup lights** are the white lights at the rear of the car. These lights warn others that you are backing.

Neutral (N) This position allows the wheels to roll. Shift to NEUTRAL when you are stopped in traffic for more than a few minutes. If the engine stalls while the car is moving, shift to NEUTRAL (not PARK) to restart the engine.

Be a Fuel Saver

Some cars are equipped with overdrive, shown by (D) on the shift indicator. At speeds of 40–45 mph, the car will automatically shift into overdrive. Driving in this gear saves fuel and can be used for all normal forward driving.

Drive (D) This position is for normal forward driving.

Low (L1 and L2, or 1 and 2) Both LOW positions are for slow, hard pulling and for going up or down steep hills. LOW2 also is used when driving in snow. Use LOW1 when going up or down extremely steep grades and when pulling very heavy loads.

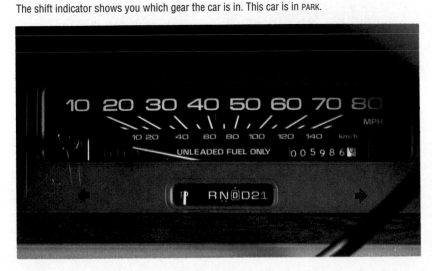

The shift indicator shows you which gear the car is in. This car is in PARK.

Backup lights are a signal to other drivers and pedestrians that your car is going to go backward.

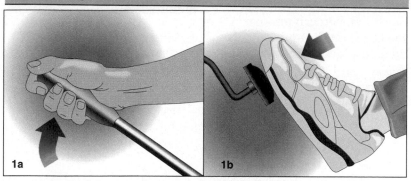

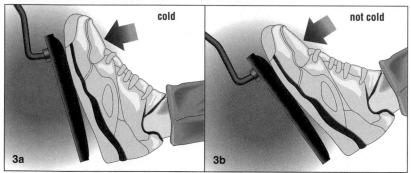

cold

not cold

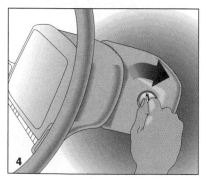

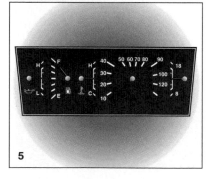

Starting the Engine

Use this procedure to start the engine. The pictures correspond to these steps.

1. Make sure the parking brake is set.
2. Make sure the selector lever is in PARK or NEUTRAL.
3. If the engine is warm, press the accelerator lightly and hold it. If the engine is cold, use one of the following procedures. If you are uncertain about the equipment in your car, check the owner's manual.

   A. If your car has a carburetor, press the accelerator to the floor *once* to set the automatic choke. Release the accelerator and then press it down lightly.

   B. If your car has fuel injection, keep your foot off the accelerator.
4. Turn the ignition switch to "On." Continue turning the key to start the engine. Release the key as soon as the engine starts.
5. With the engine running, check the gauges. Check the fuel supply. Make sure that the electrical system and oil-pressure system are working properly.

CAUTION: Never try to start the engine when it is already running. Expensive damage to the starter can result. If the engine has not started, the alternator light will be red, or the gauge will show "discharge." Press lightly on the accelerator to check whether or not the engine is running. When in doubt, turn the key to "Off" and repeat the starting procedure.

Steering the Car

Several factors contribute to proper steering of a car. Hand positions and tracking are two important factors.

Hand Positions   In order to steer properly, hold the steering wheel firmly on each side in a balanced position. Imagine that the steering wheel is the face of a clock. One very balanced position for steering control is at the 10 o'clock and 2 o'clock positions. Some drivers prefer the 9 and 3 o'clock positions. Regardless of the hand positions you find comfortable, always keep your knuckles outside the rim of the wheel. Notice the driver's hands and relaxed arm positions in the picture.

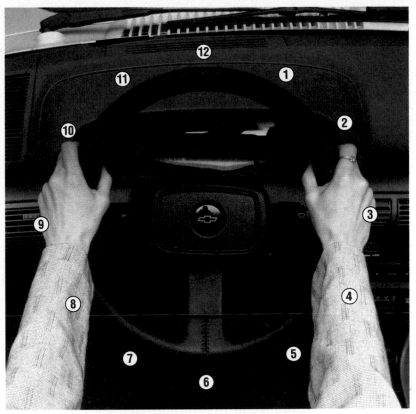

If you think of the steering wheel as the face of a clock, keeping your hands at 10 o'clock and 2 o'clock, or at 9 o'clock and 3 o'clock, gives you good steering control.

Tracking   Steering a car in its intended path of travel is called **tracking**. As you track, look well down the road ahead of you.

Make only small turns of the wheel in order to track. Beginning drivers often overcorrect steering errors by turning the wheel too much. Avoid watching the steering wheel or a hood or fender ornament as a tracking guide. Once you know how to make steering adjustments, you will make them automatically. You then can concentrate on the total driving task.

Putting the Car in Motion

After starting the engine, follow this procedure to move the car. Each numbered step is shown in the pictures.

1. With the engine idling in PARK, press down the foot-brake pedal.
2. Move the selector lever to DRIVE.
3. Release the parking brake while continuing to hold the foot-brake pedal down.
4. Check for traffic ahead and in both rearview mirrors. Glance over your left shoulder. See if any vehicle is approaching from the rear.
5. If you are going to move away from the right curb, use the left-turn signal to alert other drivers. Check mirrors again.

6. When the street is clear, you can press gently on the accelerator.
7. Quickly check again over your left shoulder for traffic.
8. Cancel the signal, if necessary.
9. As you reach your desired speed, let up a little on the accelerator. Adjust your speed to traffic conditions.

CAUTION: In a car with an automatic transmission, always press down on the foot-brake pedal and come to a full stop before shifting to any gear. This action keeps your car from moving before you are ready.

Stopping the Car

The numbers on the pictures indicate the steps to follow when stopping your car.

1. Check traffic in both mirrors before slowing down.
2. Let up on the accelerator.
3. Tap the foot brake lightly to signal for a stop.
4. Push down gradually and firmly on the foot-brake pedal. Ease up slightly on the brake pedal just before stopping. This action helps you make a smoother stop. Leave the selector lever in DRIVE if you plan to start moving again immediately. Otherwise, shift to PARK.

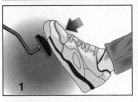

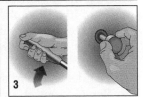

You sometimes might be parked on the left side of a one-way street. Before entering traffic from this position, glance over your *right* shoulder to see if any vehicles are approaching from the rear. Use the *right* turn signal to indicate that you are going to enter the traffic lane.

Securing the Car

This procedure for securing the car applies to cars with either automatic or manual transmissions.

Before you leave a parking place, glance one last time over your left shoulder to check for oncoming traffic.

1 Once you have stopped, continue to keep pressure on the foot brake.
2. Shift to PARK in an automatic or to REVERSE in a stick shift.
3. Set the parking brake, and turn off all accessories.
4. Turn off the ignition switch and remove the key. Release the foot brake.
5. Unfasten your safety belt.
6. Close the windows, and lock all doors except yours. If the car has electric door locks, open your door then push the door-lock button.

Leaving the Car

Leave the car from the curb side whenever possible. You avoid the risk of opening the door into moving traffic.

If you do get out on the street side, follow these steps.
1. Check both inside and outside mirrors.

2. Glance over your left shoulder for approaching traffic before opening the door.
3. Make sure you have the keys in your hand so you do not lock them inside the car.
4. When it is safe, open the door and get out quickly.
5. Lock the door. Walk around the rear of the car to the curb. You then face approaching traffic and reduce your risk of being hit.

Review It

1. What is the purpose of each gear in an automatic transmission?
2. What are the correct procedures for moving and stopping the car?
3. What should you do immediately after you turn off the ignition? Why should you leave the car from the curb side if possible?

Driving a Car With Manual Transmission

Learning to drive a car with manual (stickshift) transmission is not difficult. You must learn to coordinate the clutch, accelerator, and gear-shift lever.

Selector-Lever Positions

Most stickshift cars have either a four-speed or a five-speed shift pattern. Reverse is usually in the upper-left corner, or in the lower-left or right corner.

Fourth gear is used for highway driving, and fifth gear is used for speeds over 45 or 50 mph. These gears save fuel because they allow the engine to run slower at any particular speed.

Using Stickshift Gears

Neutral (N)   This position is the crossbar of the pattern. Have your car in this gear when standing still or when starting the engine.

First (1)   Use first gear to start the car moving up to a forward speed of 10 to 15 mph. Use first gear also to pull very heavy loads and drive up or down very steep hills.

Second (2)   Use second gear to bring the car up to a forward speed of 15 to 25 mph. Use second gear also for hills or driving on snow or ice.

Third (3)   Use third gear to accelerate to speeds in the range of 25 to 35 or 40 mph.

Fourth (4)   In a four-speed transmission, use fourth gear for highway driving. Shift to fourth gear at speeds of 35 to 40 mph.

Fifth (5)   In a five-speed transmission, use fifth gear to drive at speeds over 45 or 50 mph.

Reverse (R)   Use the reverse gear for backing. Never shift to reverse while the car is moving forward. Expensive damage to the transmission can result.

Using the Clutch

Always press the clutch pedal to the floor before starting the engine, before shifting, or before coming to a stop. Shift smoothly from one position to the next. The speeds given here for shifting are only guidelines. Read your car owner's manual; transmissions vary greatly. *CAUTION:* The term **riding the clutch** means resting your left foot on the clutch pedal while driving. This practice causes needless clutch wear.

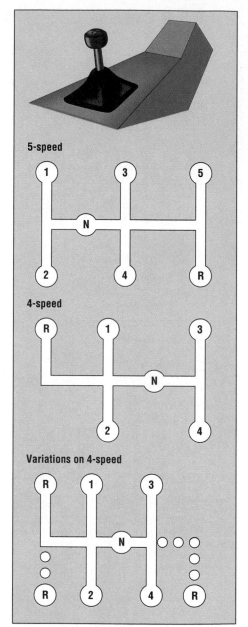

Typical patterns of gear positions for four- and five-speed transmissions. Positions might vary, especially for REVERSE.

Starting the Engine

Follow these steps to start a car with manual transmission:

1. Be sure parking brake is set.
2. Press the clutch pedal to the floor with your left foot.
3. Put gear-shift lever in neutral.
4. Depress accelerator partway and hold. (Set choke if engine is cold.)
5. Turn on ignition switch and check warning lights.
6. Turn the key forward until engine starts, and then release.
7. Check gauges.

Putting the Car in Motion

Once the engine is running, use these steps to put the car in motion. Each numbered step is pictured:

1. Press clutch pedal to the floor.
2. Move gear-shift lever to first.
3. Depress foot brake, and release the parking brake.
4. Check traffic ahead and in both rearview mirrors. Glance over your left shoulder. See if any vehicle is approaching from the rear.
5. If you are going to move away from the curb, use the turn signal to alert other drivers. Check mirrors again.

6. If the road is clear, accelerate gently and gradually and release the clutch slowly. Releasing the clutch suddenly causes the car to jerk forward. The engine can stall. The point where the engine takes hold and the car starts to move is called the **friction point.**
7. Hold the clutch momentarily at the friction point.
8. Continue gradual acceleration, and let the clutch up all the way.

Shifting from First to Second

At about 10 to 15 mph follow these steps to shift from first to second:

1. Press the clutch down.
2. Release the accelerator.
3. Move the gear-shift lever to second. Pause slightly as you go across neutral into second. This action helps you shift smoothly.
4. Accelerate gently as you slowly release the clutch. Hesitate briefly at the friction point.

Putting the Car in Motion

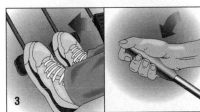
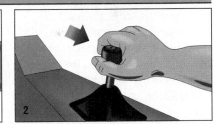

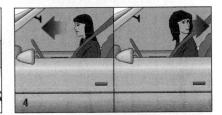

Stopping from First, Second, or Reverse

The first set of pictures corresponds to these steps:

1. Check traffic in mirrors.
2. Press the clutch pedal down while releasing accelerator.
3. Tap the brake pedal lightly to signal for a stop.
4. Press the foot brake gently.
5. Shift to neutral when stopped.

Shifting to Third, Fourth, and Fifth

Once you have accelerated to the higher-speed ranges described on page 50, follow these steps to shift gears:

1. Press the clutch down.
2. Release the accelerator.
3. Shift to the desired gear.
4. Accelerate gradually while releasing the clutch smoothly.

Stopping from Higher Gears

When stopping from third, fourth, or fifth, first use the brake to slow down before depressing the clutch. The engine helps slow the car. The second set of pictures corresponds to these steps:

1. Check the mirrors for traffic.
2. Let up on the accelerator.
3. Tap the brake lightly to signal for a stop.
4. Brake gradually to about 15 to 20 mph.
5. Press the clutch pedal down.
6. Brake to a smooth stop.
7. Shift to neutral when stopped.

Stopping from First, Second or Reverse

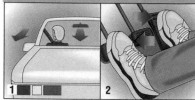
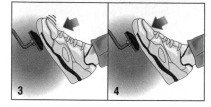

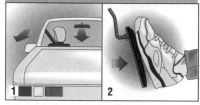

Stopping from Higher Gears

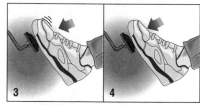
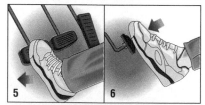
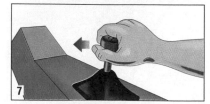

Downshifting

The term **downshifting** means shifting from a higher to a lower gear. The engine has greater pulling power in lower gears than in higher ones. If you have slowed to around 30 mph in fourth gear, you must downshift to third in order to regain speed. Follow these steps to downshift:

1. Depress the clutch and shift to third. Accelerate gradually while releasing the clutch smoothly.
2. Accelerate to 35 or 40 mph. Depress the clutch, and shift back to fourth.

You can downshift for added control, as when slowing before a sharp turn. However, be sure to complete the downshift before starting the turn. You also can downshift to gain extra pulling power when climbing long or steep hills. Use a lower gear to go down long or steep hills to save wear on the brakes. The engine helps slow the car. Let the clutch out after every downshift.

Review It

1. What are the steps for starting the engine and moving the car in first gear?
2. What is the difference between the procedures for stopping from lower gears and stopping from higher gears?
3. When might you use downshifting?

DECISION MAKING

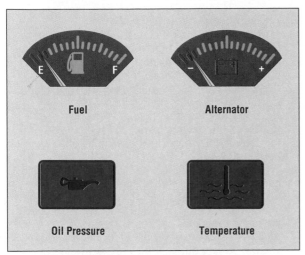

1. While you are driving at different times, four gauges or warning lights on your instrument panel might look like the pictures above. What does each gauge or light indicate? What problems might you have? What should you do?

2. This driver is going to enter the car and drive. Identify the incorrect procedure the driver is following. Explain why the procedure is unsafe. What error should the driver correct? What safety checks should the driver make?

3. What step did this driver forget while getting ready to drive? Why was this error serious? What steering problems might this driver have? How might the driver achieve more controlled steering?

4. You are preparing to turn this very sharp corner. You are driving a four-speed car in fourth gear. What should you do before entering the turn? Describe the procedure you would use.

CHAPTER 3 REVIEW

Review Chapter Objectives

3–1 Instruments, Controls, and Devices
1. What is the function of each gauge and warning light on an instrument panel? (38–39)
2. What is the purpose of each control used to operate a vehicle? (40–41)
3. For what use are safety, communication, and comfort devices? (42–43)

3–2 Preparing to Drive
4. What checks should you make when you are preparing to drive? (44)
5. How do you enter the car from the street side? (44)

3–3 Starting, Moving, and Stopping
6. What is the function of each gear? (45)
7. What is the procedure to start, move, and stop a car? (46–48)
8. What is the correct way to leave a vehicle from the street side? (49)

3–4 Driving a Car with Manual Transmission
9. How do you start, move, and stop a stickshift car? (51–52)
10. What is downshifting? (52)

Check Your Knowledge

Multiple Choice   Copy the number of each sentence below on a sheet of paper. Choose the letter that best completes the statement or answers the question.

1. A type of passive restraint is the
   (a) sun visor. (b) padded dash. (c) head restraint. (d) automatic safety belt. (42)
2. If an automatic transmission car stalls during driving, what must you do to restart it?
   (a) shift to NEUTRAL. (b) shift to LOW. (c) get a jump start. (d) set the automatic choke. (45)
3. How do you know the engine is running?
   (a) Check the exhaust pipe. (b) Try to drive. (c) Turn on the radio. (d) Press lightly on the accelerator. (47)
4. What should you do in a car with automatic transmission just before shifting to DRIVE?
   (a) fasten your safety belt. (b) press down on the foot-brake pedal. (c) engage the clutch. (d) check the fuel gauge. (48)
5. Which way should you walk around a car when you are getting out on the street side?
   (a) toward the front of the car. (b) either way. (c) toward the rear of the car. (d) neither way. (49)
6. When stopping from FOURTH in a stickshift car, which pedal do you press first?
   (a) clutch pedal. (b) accelerator. (c) foot-brake pedal. (d) dimmer switch. (52)

Completion   Copy the number of each sentence below. After each number, write the word or words that complete the sentence correctly.

7. Use the _____ to choose forward or reverse gears in an automatic-transmission car. (40)
8. When the _____ is set, you can remove your foot from the accelerator; car speed will stay constant. (43)
9. Steering the car in its intended path of travel is called _____ . (47)
10. When stopping from reverse in a stickshift car, depress the _____ first. (52)
11. Shifting from a higher to a lower gear is called _____ . (52)

Check Vocabulary

Copy the number of each definition in List A. Match the definition in List A with the term it defines in List B.

List A
12. shows miles driven (39)
13. indicates trouble in electrical system (39)
14. operated by a key to start the engine (40)
15. keeps a car in place while parked (41)
16. pedal that slows or stops the car (41)
17. pedal that controls speed of car (41)
18. controls amount of air to engine when starting the car (41)
19. safety device that works without action by the car occupants (42)
20. padded supports that help reduce whiplash injuries (42)
21. area not shown in rearview mirrors (42)
22. warns that vehicle is a hazard (42)
23. lever that unlocks hood of car (43)
24. device that shows the different driving gears and the gear being used (45)
25. white lights at the rear of the car (45)
26. driving with foot resting on clutch pedal (50)
27. point where engine begins to move a stickshift car (51)

List B
a. accelerator
b. alternator warning light
c. automatic choke
d. backup lights
e. blind spot
f. emergency flasher
g. foot-brake pedal
h. friction point
i. head restraints
j. hood release
k. odometer
l. passive restraint
m. riding the clutch
n. seat adjustment
o. shift indicator
p. parking brake
q. ignition switch

Check Your Understanding

Write a short answer for each question or statement.

28. Why is it important to press down on the foot-brake pedal before shifting to drive? (48)
29. Why do you use a different procedure when stopping from THIRD and FOURTH gears in a stickshift car than when stopping from FIRST gear? (52)

Think Critically

Write a paragraph to answer each question or statement.

1. Suppose you are driving and your brake-system warning light comes on. What would you do?
2 Imagine you are driving the camper about to go up the steep hill in the picture. The camper has a four-speed manual transmission. What action would you take before you start up the steep hill?

Projects

1. Read about the the instruments, devices, and controls in the owner's manual for your family car. If it has a stickshift, determine at what speed you shift for each gear.
2. Check several car makes and models. Which controls are located in much the same place on all cars, and which are in different places?

Chapter 4

MAKING SAFE DRIVING DECISIONS: THE IPDE PROCESS

You're the Driver!

Imagine you are approaching the intersection in this picture. You have a green traffic light. What possible hazards can you identify?

Should you predict the light will stay green? What action should you take?

What actions do you predict both oncoming drivers might take?

What would you decide to do if the person opening the car door steps out?

How can you communicate with the drivers behind you?

This chapter presents the IPDE process, an organized system for safe driving. The IPDE process will help you reduce risk. You will learn to analyze traffic situations, make wise driving decisions, and execute safe driving actions.

Objectives

Section 4–1   The IPDE Process
1. Name the four steps of the IPDE process.
2. Describe an orderly visual search pattern.
3. List the five rules of the Smith System.
4. List three elements of the HTS you should look for in every driving environment.
5. Explain how knowledge and experience help you make accurate predictions.
6. Name the three decisions you must make when applying the IPDE process.
7. List the four most important actions you can take to avoid conflict.

Section 4–2   Using the IPDE Process
8. Describe the IPDE process as a complete process.
9. Explain how you can use the IPDE process selectively.

Section 4–3   Staying in a Safe Path
10. Name the four requirements that reduce risk and maintain a safe path of travel.
11. Describe three important visibility factors that affect a safe path of travel.
12. Explain what is meant when you separate hazards, minimize a hazard, and compromise space.

The IPDE Process

Safe driving depends, to a great extent, upon your ability to correctly analyze traffic situations. Good seeing habits are most important for defensive driving. However, just being able to see well is no guarantee you will identify all critical clues or make correct responses.

The driving task is primarily a thinking task. Your hands and feet do only what your brain tells them to do. Most responsible drivers use some kind of system that deals with all the traffic possibilities they will encounter. These drivers have fewer close calls and collisions than drivers who do not use an organized system.

The IPDE process is an organized system of seeing, thinking, and responding. The four steps in the IPDE process are:

1. Identify
2. Predict
3. Decide
4. Execute

You begin by "reading" traffic situations to gather information for your decisions and actions. To process this information properly, you must identify hazards and clues and predict possible points of conflict. You then decide how to avoid conflict, and you execute the correct actions.

Identify

The first step of the IPDE process is **identify.** This step involves much more than just seeing. When you identify, you give meaning to what you see. You must know when to look, where and how to look, and what to look for.

Any part of the HTS can become a hazard. This includes the roadway, your own vehicle, other vehicles or pedestrians, and traffic controls. Clues you identify may cause you to change direction or speed, signal others, or perform any of a combination of maneuvers. The sooner you identify a possible hazard, the more time you will have to react safely.

Orderly Visual Search Pattern

You can use any of several visual patterns to help develop your own identifying process. An **orderly visual search pattern** is a process of searching critical areas in a regular sequence. To use an orderly visual search pattern, look for clues in certain areas in a systematic manner. Practice this process continually so that it becomes a habit.

Below is one example of an orderly visual search pattern for straight-ahead driving:

1. Glance ahead.
2. Check rearview mirror.
3. Glance ahead again.
4. Search the sides of the roadway, intersections, and driveways.

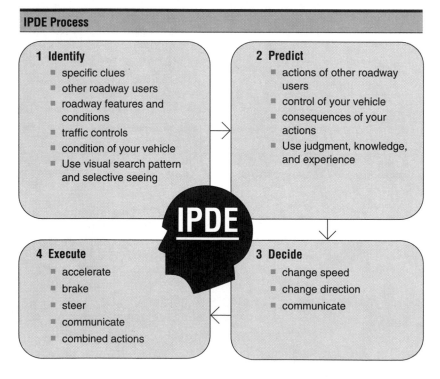

IPDE Process

1 Identify
- specific clues
- other roadway users
- roadway features and conditions
- traffic controls
- condition of your vehicle
- Use visual search pattern and selective seeing

2 Predict
- actions of other roadway users
- control of your vehicle
- consequences of your actions
- Use judgment, knowledge, and experience

IPDE

4 Execute
- accelerate
- brake
- steer
- communicate
- combined actions

3 Decide
- change speed
- change direction
- communicate

Look through curves to identify conditions and possible hazards.

5. Glance ahead again.
6. Check speedometer and gauges.
7. Glance ahead again.

All glances should last only an instant. Once your orderly visual search pattern becomes a habit, you will be able to adjust it for any maneuver or driving environment.

Where and How to Look

Different driving environments and traffic situations present a variety of visual search problems. As you gain driving experience, you will learn what kinds of traffic situations and events are most important to identify.

Use the following five rules of the Smith System to help develop your visual search habits and protect yourself from the unsafe actions of others. Not only will these rules help you learn where and how to look, they will also help you keep a safe position in traffic.

- **Aim high in steering** To "aim high" means to look far ahead as you drive. The Smith System reminds us that we do not look at our feet as we walk. We look ahead. In driving, keep your view up rather than looking down at the area in front of your car. Be a high-aim driver rather than a low-aim driver. You will then be able to analyze traffic situations and predict what might happen before you get to a point of possible conflict. In city traffic, look at least one block ahead. On highways and expressways, look as far ahead as possible. Look through curves. Identify conditions and possible hazards in the distance.

- **Keep your eyes moving** As part of an orderly visual search pattern, take selective glances. Glance near and far, right and left, in the mirrors, and at the instrument panel. Be sure to look ahead again after each glance to the sides, rear, and instrument panel.

- **Get the big picture** Getting the big picture is the mental process of putting together the critical clues that your eyes selected and identified as they scanned.

- **Make sure others see you** This rule tells you to communicate with other drivers. You can communicate your pres-

ence or intentions with lights, horn, car position, eye contact, or body movement.

- **Leave yourself an "out"** Leaving yourself an "out" means you have identified an escape path in case of a possible conflict. You constantly adjust position to keep space around your vehicle in the changing traffic conditions. If you do not have at least one available "out," adjust your position until you do have one.

What to Look For

Knowing how, when, and where to look does little good if you don't know what to look for. Develop the technique of **selective seeing** in your identifying process. Selective seeing means that you select and identify only those events and clues that pertain to your driving task.

Search for Specific Clues

Use your visual search pattern to look for specific driving-related clues. When searching parked cars on a street, you might identify an important clue, such as front wheels turned toward the street. You also might identify vapor coming from an exhaust pipe, or a driver sitting in a car. These clues indicate that a car might enter your path of travel.

As you search for specific clues, do not allow your eyes to stay too long on any one thing. Fixating on any one thing can block out your side vision for the moment. Avoid becoming a "stare" driver. Try to develop the art of **scanning**—continually glancing through your visual search pattern.

The kinds of clues you search for will change in different driving environments. In city driving, search for intersections, parked cars, pedestrians, and traffic. On open highways, search areas much farther ahead. Look for crossroads, slow-moving vehicles, and animals. During expressway driving, search the other lanes ahead, behind, and beside you.

Regardless of the driving environment, you should always look for other roadway users, roadway features, changing conditions, and for traffic controls in every situation.

Look for Other Users Search the traffic scene for other roadway users who might affect

Front wheels turned toward the street are a clue that a car might pull out into your path.

Do you think this driver is giving his full attention to the driving task?

your planned path of travel. Watch for movement of other users, especially in areas that have shadows and shade.

Look for different sizes and shapes of users, such as bicyclists, pedestrians, animals, and other vehicles.

Develop the habit of **ground viewing** as part of your visual search pattern. Ground viewing is making quick glances to the roadway in front of your vehicle. When other vehicles

are approaching, use ground viewing to see where they are headed by checking the direction of their front wheels.

Always be on the lookout for problem drivers. Problem drivers usually give clues by their driving behavior. Some fast drivers might be problem drivers. They may try to pass without enough room or in a no-passing zone. They frequently change lanes, trying to get ahead of the normal traffic flow.

The driver stopped in back of the barricades did not move to the through lane early enough and therefore had to make an unnecessary stop.

Distracted or confused drivers may also be problem drivers. Be alert for those who are driving with only one hand on the wheel while holding a coffee cup or a telephone in the other hand. While scanning the traffic scene, look for problem drivers who may present a hazard.

Look for Roadway Features and Conditions   The roadway itself is another important area to watch. Identify intersections, hills, and curves early. Be aware ahead of time that the width of your lane might be reduced. Some reasons for changes in roadway features and conditions are:

- **Change from multilane to single lane**   Multilane roadways often narrow into single-lane roadways. Identify signs warning you of this change early enough to position your car in the through lane. Roadway repair is a frequent cause of lane closure. When you see signs indicating roadway repair ahead, move into the through lane as soon as possible. Always try to avoid making an unnecessary stop in moving traffic.
- **Change in width of lane**   Standing water, patches of snow, potholes, or objects in the roadway can narrow your lane space. Identify these con-

ditions early so you have more time to plan a path around them.
- **Roadside hazards**   Your identification process should keep you looking constantly for pedestrians, bicyclists, parked cars, and animals. Watch for shopping center entrances and exits, roadside stands, and restaurants. Other users can appear suddenly from almost any location and can cause your lane space to be reduced.
- **Roadway Surface**   Identify the roadway surface and condition each time you begin to drive. Many times, the weather will change while you are driving. Roadway surfaces may be dry when you start out and then become wet and slippery with rain, snow, or ice as you are driving. Be prepared to adjust your driving for changing weather conditions that might affect the roadway surface. Roadways with a gravel surface can be a possible hazard. Gravel can cause sliding or skidding just like a wet or slippery surface. Use extra caution when driving on unpaved roads.

Look for Traffic Controls
Learn to look in different places for traffic controls. At major intersections, controls can be overhead, in the center, or on a corner. Identify traffic controls as early as possible so you are ready to make correct responses.

Predict

Once you have identified a possible hazard, **predict** how this hazard might create a conflict. When you predict, you interpret the information you have identified. You predict where possible points of conflict can occur. You try to foresee what might happen and how it might affect your planned path.

Analyzing a situation is a part of predicting. It is also a basic part of defensive driving. If you never had to face more than one hazard at a time, predicting would not be difficult. However, most of the time you will be faced with more than one possible hazard, so predicting can become a complex process.

How to Predict

Predicting involves what is happening, what could happen and, if it does happen, how it might affect you. To predict, you must evaluate the situation and make a judgment about the possible consequences. The more complex a situation is, the more difficult it is to identify and predict.

As you gain driving experience, you will become more selective about which hazards are critical. Base your predictions on those hazards that could most interfere with your safe path and cause a conflict.

Imagine you are driving the car on the right in the picture. You should predict that one of the bicyclists might swerve or

What might you predict if you were driving the car on the right?

fall. If so, predict that the oncoming car might enter your path in order to avoid the bicyclist. Your ability to predict and make sound judgments will improve as you gain knowledge and experience.

Knowledge The basic part of your driving knowledge comes from your study of traffic laws and driver education materials. Whenever you drive, you also gain knowledge by gathering more information and learning from others.

Think of storing driving knowledge as adding to your memory bank. The more you drive, the more you add to your memory bank of knowledge. This knowledge will enable you to identify and predict more quickly and accurately.

Experience In addition to knowledge, experience helps you improve your ability to predict accurately. Exposure to a variety of driving experiences provides a solid base for making sound judgments later.

Judgment Making a judgment about a traffic situation involves measuring, comparing, and evaluating. As you drive, you judge speed, time, space, distance, traction, and visibility. You make judgments about your own driving performance as well as the actions and performance of other roadway users. Make every effort to develop the ability to make sound judgments that lead to accurate predictions.

What to Predict

Nearly all predictions that you make as a driver are related to three elements in the traffic scene. You must predict
- the actions of other roadway users
- your control of your vehicle
- the consequences of your actions.

Predicting Actions of Others

Do not assume that other roadway users will always take the correct action. Instead, watch for clues to what they *might* do. The defensive driver predicts that other drivers and pedestrians will make mistakes. When you expect the worst from others, you can adjust your actions to compensate for their mistakes.

The most important types of predictions to make concerning the actions of others are:
- **Path**   Where might the other driver go? What possible paths might be taken?
- **Action**   What action will the other roadway user take?

Is more than one action possible?
- **Timing**   When will the action be taken? Where might I be then?
- **Space**   Will some of my planned space be used?
- **Point of Conflict**   Where might our paths cross?

Imagine that you are driving toward the intersection in the first picture. The oncoming driver is signaling for a right turn. Assume the worst and predict that driver will turn left across your path. You should also predict that the pedestrians will step out in front of you. By making these predictions, you will be able to slow, swerve, or stop in order to avoid a conflict.

Predicting Control of Your Vehicle   Speed is probably the most important factor in maintaining control of your vehicle. Always be prepared to adjust your speed for varying conditions and situations. Different traffic, roadway, and weather conditions can change the

amount of time and space needed for deceleration and braking control.

In the second picture, the driver identifies the wet leaves on the roadway ahead. The leaves will make the roadway slippery. Thus the driver predicts that stopping for the traffic signal will take longer than if the roadway were dry. Based on this prediction, the driver slows and brakes earlier.

At times you will need to accelerate, rather than brake, in order to avoid a conflict. With practice, you will be able to predict the time and space needed for both acceleration and braking in different conditions and situations.

Predicting Consequences

In most traffic situations you have a choice of actions to take. While there is not always one correct action, there is usually one best action. You must compare and judge the possible consequences before deciding on the best action.

What should you predict that the oncoming driver might do? that the pedestrians might do?

How do the wet leaves affect your prediction about your stopping distance?

Decide

Once you have identified a situation and predicted a possible conflict, you then **decide** upon an action to avoid the conflict. There is probably no task more important for a driver than making wise decisions in time to avoid conflict. There may be times when you fail to identify every clue in a situation. Other users will often take actions you did not predict. The decisions you make in these situations become the basic factor for your safe driving.

In some driving environments you might make over fifty decisions during each mile driven. Your decision might be to change speed, change direction, communicate your plan to others, or it might be a combination of these actions. Be prepared to change your plans to avoid a conflict.

Decide to Change Speed   Any decision you make is influenced by your own speed and the speed of other vehicles. Many drivers think that slowing down is the only way to avoid a conflict. In many situations, you will decide to accelerate rather than to slow down. Base your decision on your evaluation of the situation and the possible consequences.

The driver of the yellow car on the two-lane road in the picture judged time and space correctly. The driver avoided a conflict with the passing and oncoming cars.

Decide to Change Direction
You can change your position on the roadway. You might change lanes or swerve to the left or right.

The Smith System guideline of "Leave yourself an out" allows you to change direction when necessary. Then you will have an escape path to use in order to avoid conflict. Having an escape path gives you an area of space all around your vehicle. This area is called a **space cushion.** A space cushion lets you more easily position your vehicle where you want it. Adjust your direction to improve your space cushion.

The driver of the yellow car decided to accelerate in order to provide space for the passing driver to return to the right lane.

The shaded area is the space cushion of the yellow car in multiple-lane traffic.

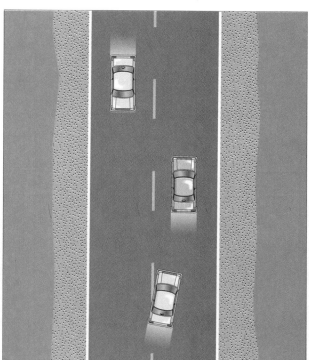

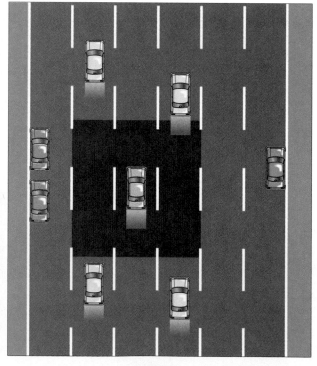

Your vehicle can be seen more easily if your headlights are on, even in daytime.

Decide to Communicate

The decision to communicate with others helps reduce a possible conflict. The Smith System rule, "Make sure others see you," tells others where you are and what you plan to do. You can communicate with others by using lights, horn, car position, eye contact, and body movement.

Lights Use lights to give messages to other roadway users.

- **Brake Lights** Brake-light messages tell drivers behind that you are slowing, stopped, or standing still. Tap the brake pedal to signal for a stop. This signal warns drivers to the rear that you intend to slow or stop.
- **Turn-signal lights** These lights give the message, "I plan to turn or change lanes."
- **High-beam and low-beam headlights** These lights inform others that you are approaching. Use low-beam headlights during poor weather conditions that reduce visibility, even in daylight.
- **Taillights** Taillights tell drivers behind where you are. Taillights stay on when headlights are on.
- **Emergency flasher lights** Flasher lights convey the messages, "I am in trouble," or "I cannot move," or "I am moving very slowly."
- **Back-up lights** White back-up lights let others know you are backing up or you intend to back up. Look for back-up lights on cars in parking lots. Not only are back-up lights a clue for a possible conflict, they also may tell you where you might find a parking space.
- **Parking lights** These lights warn other drivers that you are parked along the side of the roadway. It is illegal in most states to use only parking lights when you are moving.

Horn A light tap on the horn, when needed, lets others know you are there. In an emergency, a loud blast might be necessary.

Car Position Where you position your car in a lane can be a helpful communication to others. Moving to the right side of the lane indicates that you might turn right. Moving toward the center line indicates that you might turn left.

Eye Contact Try to develop eye contact with other roadway users. You can communicate many messages this way. If there is the possibility of a conflict, check to see if the other person is looking at you.

Do not depend on eye contact alone to communicate to other roadway users. While eye contact often helps reduce the risk of conflict, it does not guarantee against conflicts.

Darkly tinted windows interfere with communication between drivers.

Body Movement Waving your hand can tell another driver to proceed, or tell a pedestrian to cross in front of you. However, if you signal a pedestrian to proceed, you are responsible for the pedestrian's safety in the roadway.

In an emergency, raise your right hand and wave it side to side. Seeing this signal through your rear window can alert the driver behind you. Taking this action while tapping the brake pedal rapidly is a combined message for an emergency stop.

Execute

Carrying out your decision in order to avoid conflict is the **execute** step in the IPDE process. This step involves the physical skills used in driving.

In most cases you will execute routine maneuvers and actions. Many actions will be for use of defroster, heater, windshield wipers, gearshift lever, and other controls. More important actions however, involve timing and placement of your vehicle so as to avoid conflict. These important actions you will execute are:

- accelerate
- brake
- steer
- communicate.

Accelerate Executing the decision to accelerate means you have judged the speed and use of space by others. You might accelerate to get out of another driver's way or to avoid an obstruction in the roadway.

Deciding to accelerate also means that you are aware of the acceleration capabilities of your vehicle. Remember that different vehicles have different acceleration capabilities. Consider your own vehicle's capabilities before executing a decision to accelerate.

Brake When you have decided to decelerate or brake to reduce risk, you should have already considered the surface of the roadway. The amount of braking needed will vary with the situation, the speed of your car, the condition of the roadway, and the condition of your brakes. When braking suddenly, check for vehicles to the rear.

Avoid locking the brakes in an emergency stop. Locked brakes make steering impossible, since wheels must be turning to provide traction for steering. Some cars have an antilock braking system. Such a system prevents loss of steering control.

The driver in this picture has braked to avoid striking the children. The driver avoided locking the brakes so as not to lose steering control. Locking the brakes on the wet roadway could have caused the driver's vehicle to slide and result in a conflict. The roadway surface, the speed of the vehicle, and the amount of braking determine the results of the driver's response.

By using your visual search pattern, you can predict the actions of others and reduce the need for emergency braking.

If brakes lock during a sudden stop, the driver might lose control.

How is the driver of the car ahead communicating with the driver behind?

What actions should you take to avoid a conflict?

Combined Actions   You will often need to execute a combination of actions. Sometimes you might need to accelerate and steer at the same time. In other situations, you might need to brake, communicate, and steer at the same time.

If you were driving alongside the parked car in the picture, you would be in that situation. In order to avoid an open car door, you should signal, brake, and steer around it. The precision and timing with which you execute these actions determine whether or not a conflict will occur.

Review It

1. What are the four steps of the IPDE process?
2. What are the five rules of the Smith System?
3. Give an example of an orderly visual search pattern.
4. What three major elements should you always look for in any driving environment?
5. What are three elements about which you must predict?
6. What are the three basic decisions you make in the decide part of the IPDE process?
7. What are four actions you can execute to avoid conflict?

Steer   When you decide to steer away from a conflict, execute just the amount of steering needed. Oversteering can cause you to lose control of your vehicle, especially at higher speeds. Higher speeds also require more space for your maneuver. Drivers who keep a space cushion around their vehicle usually have an escape path to steer into, thus reducing possible conflict.

Communicate   In many instances your only action will be to communicate. Communicate early enough to give the other person enough time to complete the IPDE process. The driver in the stopped car in the picture is not sure the car behind will stop in time to avoid a rear-end collision. The stopped driver is communicating with both an arm signal and brake lights.

Using the IPDE Process

Of the thousands of collisions that occur every year, only a very small percentage could not have been prevented. Once you begin using the IPDE process, you will be well on the way to using the precautions that prevent tragic conflict and collision.

Learning the IPDE process does not just happen. You must practice using the process in order for it to become a habit. Once you have developed this habit, you will be able to plan and execute maneuvers to reduce hazards and avoid conflicts.

Practice is necessary to develop all skills.

IPDE Takes Practice

Practice is necessary for the development of any skill. The more practice your school teams have, the better they will perform their skills.

When you begin practicing the IPDE process, you must make a conscious effort to identify and evaluate every possible conflict. Develop your identifying skill by aggressively scanning and searching for clues. As you ride with others you can practice the first three steps of the process—identify, predict, and decide. You can then evaluate the actions taken by others. Once you have established an effective

IPDE process, you will:
- see more
- make better judgments
- make accurate predictions and correct decisions
- execute maneuvers more successfully.

Putting IPDE into Action

As you begin to develop your IPDE process, you will use the four steps in order. Once you have learned techniques and skills for identifying, you should add the predicting process. Identifying and predicting are linked together as they are put into action. You identify

the hazards or events, and then predict how they might affect you. You then perform the third step, deciding. Finally, you execute your maneuvers based on your decisions.

The decision-making step is of utmost importance in the IPDE process. It may well be the most important skill you will develop for safe driving. There may be times when you fail to identify every important clue in a traffic situation. Other users will often take actions which you did not predict. However, decisions you make for determining your own actions become the basic foundation for your safe driving.

IPDE Must Be Combined and Continual

You might learn each step of the IPDE process separately, but you cannot use the IPDE process successfully if you treat each part as an isolated step. Think of the steps being combined into one smooth process. As you continue your driving experience, make a conscious effort to use the IPDE process at all times.

Only through continual practice will your IPDE process become effective and habitual. As you ride with others, continue to practice the process. Consider different decisions for actions that you might have made. Evaluate the consequence of each possible action.

As you become a more experienced driver over the years, you may become lazy or careless with the use of your IPDE process. Guard against this by identifying, predicting, and making decisions on a conscious aggressive level. Do not allow complacency to creep into your driving performance.

Selective Use of IPDE

You will find occasions when you do not carry the total IPDE process to the execute step. You can use the IPDE process selectively. For example, you may identify a bicyclist ahead as a hazard. However, at that same moment the bicyclist may turn onto a side street out of your path. You no longer need to predict the bicyclist's actions.

The driver nearing the crest of the hill in the picture has identified the curve sign. No other vehicles are visible, but the driver predicts an oncoming car at the crest of the hill. Based on this prediction, the driver has decided on an escape path to the right. Since there was no oncoming car, the driver did not execute the escape maneuver. In this situation, the driver used IPD, but did not use E of the IPDE process.

As you become a more experienced driver you will learn the characteristic clues and trouble spots of different areas of the HTS. Residential, city, and rural areas all have their own clues and characteristics. With practice and experience you will learn to recognize the problems each area presents. You will then be able to adjust your selective application of the IPDE process for those specific areas.

Sometimes you should begin a new IPDE process cycle before completing the previous one. Imagine you are driving toward the workers in the traffic scene shown on page 70. You identify the workers as hazards, predict their actions, and begin to make a decision. At the same time you identify the truck which might enter your lane ahead. While you carry out your decision regarding the workers, you also decide what action to take if the truck enters your path.

If you were driving the car, what might you predict?

What would you identify, predict, and decide if you were driving into this scene?

What hazards does this driver face?

IPDE Takes Time

Remember that the IPDE process takes time. You must have time to identify, time to predict, time to decide, and time to execute. The more complex the traffic situation is, the longer it takes to carry out the IPDE process. The IPDE process takes more time when you must decide among several different actions.

Deciding upon the correct action depends upon the actions of the other users. Imagine you are the driver approaching the bicycle rider in the picture. You identify the driver in the parked car. You predict that the car might enter the path of the bicycle. If the rider swerves or falls, you might decide to brake. If the rider does not swerve or fall, you might decide to steer left, though the oncoming van presents a hazard. You might also decide to brake and swerve at the same time.

At times, your own feelings or condition cause you to take more time to complete the IPDE process. You might not be as alert as usual. You might be thinking of other problems and not making a conscious effort to use your IPDE process. You might be allowing complacency and laziness to creep into your driving behavior.

When you are driving, make every effort to keep your mind on the driving task. Full attention is required to use the IPDE process effectively.

Review It

1. What parts of the IPDE process can you practice while riding with others?
2. How can you combine the IPDE steps into one smooth process?
3. Explain what is meant by the selective use of the IPDE process.
4. What are four conditions that can cause your IPDE process to take more time?

Staying in a Safe Path

All activities involve some degree of risk. Activities such as participating in a sport, mowing the lawn, and driving a car all expose you to some risk. Even when you were a young child and first learned to ride a tricycle, risk was involved.

Risk Taking

Driving a vehicle in today's traffic environment can cause you to be at high risk. Sometimes, you unknowingly might take a risk because you did not use the IPDE process effectively. There also may be times when drivers knowingly take risks with little or no regard for the safety of themselves or others. Drivers who knowingly ignore stop signs or continually exceed the speed limit are taking risks and endangering other users.

Since some degree of risk is always present, try to make sure that nothing about your own condition or the condition of your vehicle raises your level of risk. Set your goal for becoming a collision-free driver by reducing risk to a minimum. Develop your IPDE process so you will be better assured of low-risk driving and a **safe path of travel.** There are four major requirements for reducing risk and maintaining a safe path of travel. These requirements are visibility, traction, space, and traffic flow.

Visibility

About ninety percent of all traffic information you gather is received through your eyes. No matter how good your vision is, limited visibility will affect your IPDE process at times.

When there is limited visibility you may not be able to identify all possible hazards in time to avoid conflict. To make up for limited visibility, drivers should reduce their speed and/or change their position. By doing this they will have more time and space which is needed for using the IPDE process. Three important visibility factors are sight distance, field of vision, and depth perception.

Sight Distance   Your **sight distance** is the distance you can see ahead. The longer this distance is, the more time you have to identify possible conflicts. Your sight distance can be shortened by curves, hills, large vehicles, weather, buildings, trees, or even a dirty windshield.

Notice the short sight-distance of the driver following the truck. By following the truck too closely, the driver has sacrificed sight distance. The driver should reduce speed to compensate for shorter sight distance and to have more time for the IPDE process.

Following too closely reduces your sight distance.

Field of Vision   Your **field of vision** is the area you can see around you while looking straight ahead. Many of us can see an area about 90 degrees to each side, for a total picture of 180 degrees. Only about 3 degrees directly ahead make up your **central vision.** This is the area you can see clearly while looking straight ahead. The area you can see to the left and right of central vision is called side vision or **peripheral vision.** The wider your peripheral vision is, the better chance you have to use the IPDE process. However, the area you see in peripheral vision is not in sharp focus. This is why it is so necessary to use the Smith System rule to keep your eyes moving.

Field of vision is most important in areas such as intersections, driveways, and other places where other roadway users might cross your path. Vehicles could enter your path before you could identify them. Reduce your speed when your field of vision is narrowed.

Depth Perception   The ability to judge the distance between yourself and other things, especially when both are moving, is **depth perception.** This ability tells you how far away the vehicle ahead is and how rapidly that distance is opening or closing. You also use depth perception, or distance judgment, when you meet or pass vehicles and when you judge stopping distance.

Parked cars can make driveways difficult to see, restricting your field of vision.

Traction

The basic requirement for controlling any vehicle is traction between the tires and the roadway. Traction is the result of friction, a force which keeps tires from slipping when they are stopped or rolling. **Traction** is actually the gripping power between the tires and the roadway surface. The more traction there is, the greater the gripping power between the tires and the roadway.

You must continually evaluate the amount of available traction and adjust speed according to conditions. Wet, snowy, icy, and bumpy or gravel roadways all reduce traction. The poorer traction becomes, the lower your speed must be. You will need more time to stop, accelerate, or make maneuvers.

Space

A safe path of travel requires space. Always try to allow more than enough space for a safe path. Think of the space cushion around your vehicle as four zones—front, rear, right, and left. Try to keep all four zones free from conflict. When a zone becomes smaller because someone has entered it, adjust your speed or position to regain the lost space. Try to open up the side and rear zones by choosing a lane where the fewest vehicles or objects can invade your space.

As a driver, you have the most control over the front zone of your space cushion. When you are stopped behind another vehicle, stay back about one car length. If someone "rear ends" your vehicle, you will more likely avoid hitting the vehicle in front of you. By controlling the space in your front zone, you can greatly reduce possible hazards and conflict.

Whenever space is limited, it is more difficult to avoid a hazard. Reduce your speed in such areas of limited space as bridges, narrow lanes with parked vehicles, or in lanes next to other traffic.

Traffic Flow

The fourth requirement for a safe path of travel is traffic flow. Adjust your speed to traffic conditions so that you keep up with the flow of traffic and avoid unnecessary stops.

The safest position in traffic is the place where the fewest vehicles or other objects surround you. Your objective is to keep your vehicle surrounded by space. Look for changes in traffic conditions. Be ready to adjust your speed and space cushion accordingly. By avoiding unnecessary stops, you reduce your risk of rear-end collisions.

Use the following techniques to manage space, time, and distance in order to maintain a safe path of travel.

The driver must separate two hazards—the pedestrians on the right and the approaching truck on the left.

Separate Hazards You might be involved in a possible conflict situation with two or more hazards at the same time. Adjust your speed in order to handle only one hazard at a time; that is, to **separate the hazards.**

The car driver in the picture should try to avoid meeting the approaching truck near the pedestrians. The car driver should adjust speed so that the truck and the pedestrians are handled separately. In this situation, the car driver should reduce speed to allow the truck to pass the pedestrians first.

The car would then meet the truck with ample space before passing the pedestrians.

Minimize a Hazard You can minimize a hazard to reduce risk by putting more distance between yourself and the hazard. Study the left picture on page 74. As the yellow car approaches the parked car, the driver predicts a door might open. To minimize the hazard, the driver steers away from the door. This action gives the driver more space and thus reduces the danger.

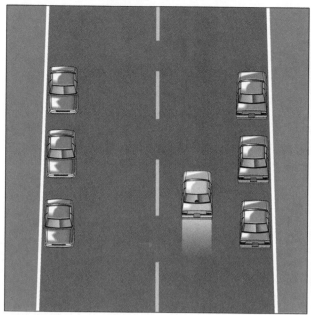

The driver of the yellow car predicts a door might open. To minimize the hazard, the driver steers away from the parked cars.

The driver of the yellow car is compromising space in order to give more space to the greater hazard.

Compromise Space Sometimes hazards cannot be separated or minimized. When this situation occurs, you must **compromise space** by giving as much space as possible to the greater hazard.

The truck in the right picture might enter the lane of the yellow car to avoid the parked car leaving the parking space. Although the cars on the right present a hazard, the driver of the yellow car should steer right as far as possible. This action gives more space to the greater hazard, the truck.

Compromising hazards is not always possible or successful. Try to handle multiple hazards by separating, rather than by compromising.

You can never be completely free of hazards in your planned path of travel. Using the IPDE process can reduce or simplify potential hazards. Develop the habit of anticipating multiple hazards. Try to have enough control over situations to prevent meeting two or more high-risk hazards at once. By doing so, you will more often be assured a safe path of travel.

DECISION MAKING

1. You are the driver approaching the slow-moving vehicle. How will you use the IPDE process? Which action will you choose? What factors might affect your safe path of travel?

2. How would knowledge and experience help the driver approaching the STOP sign execute a safe stop?

3. What do you predict will occur in the space of your front zone? What steps will you take to reduce risk?

4. The approaching car is entering your lane. What possible conflicts are there? What actions might you take? How can you communicate with a driver behind you?

CHAPTER 4 REVIEW

Review Chapter Objectives

4–1 The IPDE Process

1. What are the four steps of the IPDE process? (58)
2. What is meant by an orderly visual search pattern? (58)
3. What are the five rules of the Smith System? (59)
4. What three elements of the HTS should you be looking for in every driving environment? (60-61)
5. How can knowledge and experience help you make accurate predictions? (62)
6. What three decisions must you make when applying the IPDE process? (64)
7. What are the four most important actions you can take to avoid conflict? (66)

4–2 Using the IPDE Process

8. Why should the IPDE process be a complete process? (69)
9. How can you use the IPDE process selectively? (69)

4–3 Staying in a Safe Path

10. What are the four requirements for a safe path of travel?(71)
11. What are three important visibility factors? (72)
12. What is meant when you separate hazards, minimize a hazard, and compromise space? (73–74)

Check Your Knowledge

Multiple Choice   Copy the number of each sentence below on a sheet of paper. Choose the letter that best completes the statement or answers the question.

1. What step of the IPDE process helps a driver become aware of problems?
   (a) identify (b) predict (c) decide (d) execute (58)
2. "Leaving yourself an out" means
   (a) leaving a door unlocked in case of an emergency. (b) deciding to change direction.
   (c) parking so that your door is not blocked.
   (d) having an escape path available. (59)
3. What step of the IPDE process tells how to avoid a conflict?
   (a) identify (b) predict (c) decide (d) execute (64)
4. The area you can see to the left and right is called
   (a) central vision. (b) depth perception. (c) visual acuity. (d) peripheral vision. (72)
5. What action reduces the risk of handling two hazards at the same time?
   (a) scan (b) separate (c) track (d) predict (73)

Completion   Copy the number of each sentence below. After each number, write the word or words that complete the sentence correctly.

6. Searching critical areas in a regular sequence is called an _____ (58)
7. Your ability to predict will improve as you gain in both knowledge and _____ . (62)
8. _____ is probably the most important factor in maintaining control of your vehicle. (63)
9. Carrying out a decision is the _____ step of the IPDE process. (66)
10. Being able to judge distance between yourself and other things is called _____ . (72)
11. The gripping power between the tires and the roadway surface is called _____ . (72)

Check Vocabulary

Copy the number of each definition in List A. Match the definition in List A with the term it defines in List B.

List A
12. making quick glances to the roadway in front of your vehicle (60)
13. step in the IPDE process that tells what might happen (62)
14. path that is free of hazard (71)
15. distance you can see ahead (71)
16. area you can see around you while looking straight ahead (72)
17. the area of about three degrees that you can see directly ahead (72)
18. reduce risk by putting more space between you and a single hazard (73)
19. reduce risk by giving as much space as possible to the greater of two or more hazards (74)

List B
a. minimize
b. predict
c. central vision
d. safe path of travel
e. sight distance
f. compromise space
g. depth perception
h. IPDE process
i. ground viewing
j. field of vision

Check Your Understanding

Write a short answer for each question or statement.

20. What are the five rules of the Smith System? (59)
21. How can ground viewing help you predict the actions of other drivers? (60)
22. When communicating with others by use of headlights, which Smith System rule do you use? (65)
23. Why is locking the brakes in an emergency a dangerous action? (66)
24. How can you keep from becoming lazy or careless with the use of your IPDE process? (69)

Think Critically

Write a paragraph to answer each question or statement.

1. Suppose you have just come to a stop at a 4-way stop intersection. You see a truck approaching from the right and you believe it is slowing to stop for the stop sign. You decide to proceed through the intersection. When you are almost through the intersection, you are struck by the truck on the right rear of your car. How could better use of your IPDE process have prevented this collision?
2. Imagine you are the driver of the yellow car in the picture. You are approaching the bridge and you see the truck approaching. What actions will you take and why?

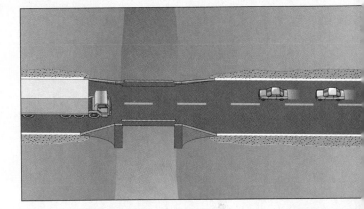

Projects

1. While you are riding as a passenger with family or friends, practice identifying, predicting, and deciding what to do in various traffic situations. Take notes on whether the drivers react the same way you would if you had been driving. Report your findings to the class.
2. Stand near a busy roadway where you can observe the performance of drivers. Notice the number of drivers who pay little or no attention to their space cushion. Discuss with the class the possible results of your findings.

CONTROLLING YOUR VEHICLE

Chapter 5
NATURAL LAWS AND CAR CONTROL

Chapter 6
PERFORMING BASIC CAR MANEUVERS

Chapter 7
NEGOTIATING INTERSECTIONS

Chapter 8
SHARING THE ROADWAY

This country road might look a bit like an amusement park ride, going uphill and downhill, with lots of gentle waves in between. The natural laws of gravity and energy of motion affect how your car performs in this, and every other, driving situation. To drive successfully on roads like this, you should be familiar with the capabilities of your vehicle and of all the other vehicles sharing the roadway with you.

In this unit you will learn how natural laws affect car control and how to maneuver your vehicle in various situations. You also will learn how to manage different types of intersections. Finally, you will learn how to interact safely with other roadway users, such as motorcyclists, bicycle and moped riders, pedestrians, and truckers.

Chapter 5

NATURAL LAWS AND CAR CONTROL

You're the Driver!

At the very instant that this photograph was taken, tremendous forces were being applied. The forces were strong enough to cause the air bag to inflate. If you had been the driver and were using your safety belt, the air bag would have prevented serious injury.

How can you control the force of impact in a collision?

Do you know how to use restraint devices to protect yourself and your passengers?

How do natural laws affect your car control?

What can you do to help protect everyone in your car?

To become a really good driver, you need to know about natural laws. Once you understand these laws, you will be able to adjust your driving for them ahead of time.

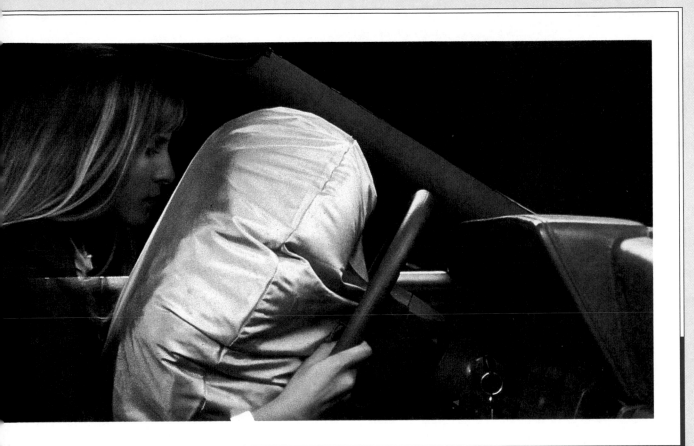

Objectives

Section 5–1   Gravity and Energy of Motion
1. Explain how gravity affects your car.
2. Describe the factors that affect energy of motion.

Section 5–2   Friction and Traction
3. Explain how traction controls your car.
4. List three factors that can reduce traction.
5. List factors that affect your car in a curve.
6. Tell why it is important to know the performance capabilities of other vehicles.

Section 5–3   Stopping Distance
7. Define total stopping distance.
8. Explain how to use the four-second rule.
9. Name six factors that affect braking distance.

Section 5–4   Force of Impact and Restraint Devices
10. List three factors that will change your vehicle's force of impact in a collision.
11. Explain the correct way to adjust safety belts.
12. Describe passive restraints for adults and safety seats for children.

Gravity and Energy of Motion

The natural laws of gravity and energy of motion work together to affect how your car performs. When you ride a bicycle, you usually can easily control these forces. But when you drive a 3,000-pound car at higher speeds, these forces are much greater. You may have a hard time maintaining control at highway speeds or in unusual situations requiring you to make an emergency maneuver.

To maintain control of your car, you must understand the effects of these forces. By staying alert and ready to act, you can apply what you know and reduce possible conflicts.

Gravity

Gravity is the force that pulls all things to earth. The lack of gravity lets astronauts float in space. Throw a ball, drop a glass, or drive a car off a curb and gravity pulls each to earth.

Driving Up and Down Hills

You can feel the effect of gravity as you drive on steep hills. When you drive uphill, your car will lose speed unless you use extra power. To maintain speed you must increase power to overcome the force of gravity pulling on your car.

You might have to shift to a lower gear in a stickshift car to increase power.

Before passing on a multilane uphill road, you need to ask yourself this question: "Do I have enough extra power to accelerate around the vehicle ahead?" If there is any doubt in your mind, do not pass.

The force of gravity can also increase your speed going downhill. In addition, you will need a longer distance to stop. To avoid trouble, think ahead. Plan to use a longer stopping distance when going down hills or mountains. Release your accelerator early. Use your foot brake ahead of time to slow or stop. On steep hills, shift to a lower gear to let your engine help slow your car.

Center of Gravity

An object's **center of gravity** is the point around which all of the object's weight is evenly balanced. For example, circus high-wire performers can use a pole to lower their center of gravity and maintain balance. As the ends of the pole bend down, the performer's center of gravity is lowered. This lower center of gravity helps the performers to keep their balance and avoid falling.

Most vehicles have a low center of gravity so they can turn and maneuver smoothly. Look at the three pictures on this page. Note how raising the vehicle's center of gravity increases its chance of turning

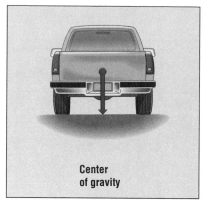

Center of gravity

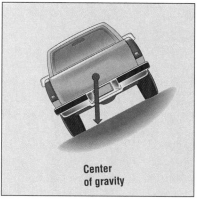

Center of gravity

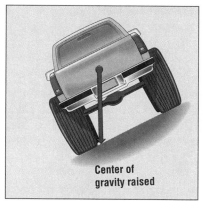

Center of gravity raised

As its center of gravity rises, a vehicle becomes less stable on curves or hills.

over on a steep hill. Imagine how a top-heavy vehicle would act in a sharp turn or hard stop.

Energy of Motion

The energy an object has as it moves is called **energy of motion** or kinetic energy. The faster your car moves, the more energy of motion it has.

The pictures show how the energy of motion increases dramatically as weight and speed increase. Note the following facts about the truck's energy of motion:

- The truck's energy of motion doubles when its weight doubles. When the truck weighs twice as much, it needs about twice the distance to stop.
- The truck's energy of motion will change in proportion to the *square* of its change in speed. When the truck's speed doubles, it needs about *four times* the distance to stop. If your speed triples, you would need *nine times* the distance to stop.

Once you understand the natural law concerning energy of motion, you can adjust to traffic situations ahead of time. Now you can see how important it is to always reduce your speed in an emergency driving situation. Every time you cut your speed in half, you can cut your energy of motion by four times.

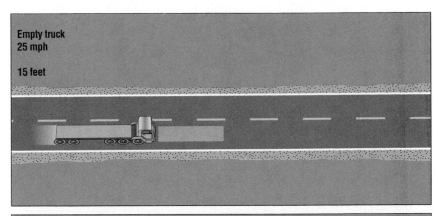

Empty truck
25 mph

15 feet

Double truck weight
25 mph

30 feet

2x

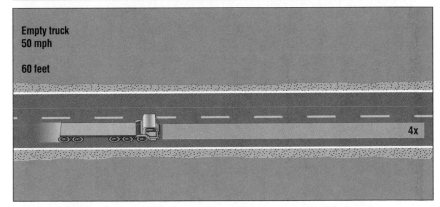

Empty truck
50 mph

60 feet

4x

A vehicle's energy of motion increases as its speed increases and as its weight increases.

Review It

1. How does the force of gravity affect a car going uphill?

2. How would a heavily loaded car-top carrier affect the performance of your family car?

3. What would you have to do to your speed if you wanted to cut your stopping distance by about four times?

Friction and Traction

You might think your car's steering wheel, brake pedal, and accelerator control your cars since you operate these controls. Actually, your tires control the movement of your car. The picture below shows the small areas where your tires actually touch the road. Each area is about as big as this page you're reading.

Friction is the force that keeps each tire from sliding on the road. You can feel friction by rubbing your hands together.

The friction created by a tire on the road is called **traction**.

Traction allows your car to grip the road so you can speed up, slow down, and turn. Push the accelerator pedal and the drive wheels turn. The traction of your tires allows your vehicle to move forward.

Push the brake pedal, and braking friction in the brakes will slow the wheels. As the tires slow on the road, traction between the tires and the road slows the car. When you turn the steering wheel, the tires provide traction to turn.

Ice, rain, snow, oil, wet leaves, and loose sand on the road will reduce the traction between your tires and the road. Your ability to control your car will be cut when traction is reduced.

Tires

Tires make a difference in the way your car handles. To get the best performance from your car, you must know about tires and how to care for them.

Tread and Traction   The grooved surface of a tire that grips the road is called **tread.** When the road is wet, the tread allows water to flow through the grooves and away from the tire. The tire can then grip the road and will not "float" on the water. This gripping action prevents skids and allows you to control your car.

The only contact between your vehicle and the road is the small areas where your tires touch the roadway.

The amount of tread touching the road will increase the gripping traction a tire can produce. For example, a snow tire's extra large, open tread grooves allow snow to escape from under the tire. More of the tread then grips the roadway.

Tire size also affects the amount of tread and traction on the road. But be careful about increasing tire size. Check your car's manufacturer recommendations for tire size.

A worn, bald tire with no tread is dangerous. A bald tire will not grip a wet or icy road well. A bald tire can be punctured easily. The tire can have a **blowout,** which results from having a sudden loss of air pressure.

Inflation and Traction   A tire works best within a range of pressures. The pictures show how too much or too little air pressure can reduce traction. The gray boxes show the areas of best traction. When you inflate a tire to the proper pressure, it grips the road evenly. Correct tire pressures also increase fuel economy by reducing your tire's rolling resistance.

If air leaks out, your tire will become underinflated. Only the outside edges of the tire will grip the road well. The outside edges of the tire will also wear more quickly.

A tire can be overinflated with too much air pressure. Only the center of the tire will grip the road well. The center of an overinflated tire will wear quicker.

Temperature changes will affect tire pressures. As outside temperatures increase, your tire pressure also will go up. If the temperature decreases, tire pressures will go down. Make a point of checking your tire pressures regularly, especially when weather conditions change dramatically. Check tire pressures when your tires are cold, before you start driving.

Split Traction   Even under ideal conditions, the amount of traction your tires can produce is limited. The way you use your traction limit is up to you.

In a straight-line braking situation, all traction is used to slow down your car. However, when you are braking and turning, you divide your traction limit. You may use some of your traction to turn and some to slow. Or, you may use some traction to turn and some to speed up. In turning-braking situations, you will have to ease up on your brake pedal to avoid skidding.

High speeds can also require more traction than your tires can produce. At low speeds you can usually avoid skids. But at high speeds, you will have to adjust your steering, braking, and accelerating ahead of time to avoid skidding.

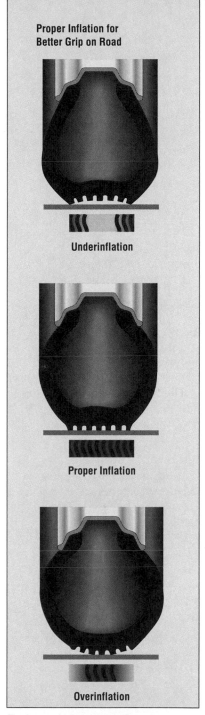

Proper Inflation for Better Grip on Road

Underinflation

Proper Inflation

Overinflation

The boxes show the areas of traction—properly inflated tires grip evenly; underinflated tires grip only by the outer edges; overinflated tires grip only in the center.

Slow before a paved road changes and your traction is reduced.

Factors That Reduce Traction

You need two things to maintain high levels of traction. First, your car must be in good condition. Second, the road you drive on must be paved, clean, dry, and level.

Car Condition   Your car will be easiest to control when it's new. But as your car ages, you must work harder to maintain it so it will perform correctly. If you allow tires, shock absorbers, or steering system parts to wear, traction and control will be reduced.

Good shock absorbers are very important for maintaining traction. They keep your tires from bouncing off a rough road as you drive. Worn shock absorbers allow tires to lose contact with the roadway. Worn shock absorbers must be replaced to maintain good traction.

Worn or bald tires do not grip the road well. If you have one or more worn tires, you might lose control in a skid. This problem usually happens in an emergency driving situation. To be sure your tires are safe, check their tread often.

Roadway Surface   When you drive on a straight, dry, flat road, traction and control are very good. But, if you drive that same car on the same road on a rainy or snowy day, your control can be reduced dramatically.

As you leave a paved road and drive on a muddy, sandy, or gravel road, traction will be cut immediately. When you see that the roadway is about to change, reduce your speed ahead of time.

Bad weather can reduce traction on even a good road. Snow, ice, and rain reduce traction. When ice is covered with water from melting snow and ice, traction is often reduced to almost nothing. Be alert for wet or icy roads on bridges, especially metal bridges, and in shaded areas. These areas can freeze *before* other roads as the temperature nears freezing.

Checking Traction   Reduce speed to maintain control when road conditions are poor. Use the following steps to see how much traction you have:

1. Make sure no traffic is near.
2. Brake *gently* to see how your car responds.
3. If your car does not respond well, reduce speed further.

Check tire tread often to make sure you have enough traction.

Curves

When you drive around a curve, two forces work on your car. These forces are energy of motion and traction.

The first force, your moving car's energy of motion, will increase as your speed increases. This force will try to keep your car going in a straight line. The higher your car's speed, the more your car will tend to go straight.

Tire traction is the second force at work. If you are going too fast, you might not have enough traction to keep from skidding straight off the road in a curve. Traction from your tires must overcome the energy of motion in your car.

Car Control in Curves

Your speed, the sharpness and bank of a curve, and your car's load affect the control you have over your car in a curve.

Speed You have no control over how sharp a curve is, but you can adjust your speed. To reduce the chance of skidding, do not adjust your speed in a curve, if you can help it. Instead, slow before you get into the curve. Remember, too, your energy of motion in a curve will change in proportion to the square of your increase or decrease in speed. If you cut your speed in half, the force pushing you off the road will be cut four times.

You would need to slow your vehicle for this turn.

How would the same vehicle handle now?

Sharpness of Curve The sharper a curve, the more traction your car needs to grip the road at any speed. Use lower speeds for sharp curves. Slow before entering any curve. Curves on newer roads, like expressways, are designed to be gradual so you can drive through them at higher speeds.

Banked Curves A curve that is higher on the outside than it is on the inside is called a **banked curve**. This type of curve helps to overcome your car's tendency to move to the outside of the curve.

Load Your car's load can affect how well your car will handle in a curve. Imagine that a lightly loaded vehicle can barely make a safe turn at 35 mph. Add a heavy load to that same vehicle, and you will have to reduce speed to avoid trouble. How would you change your driving in the two situations shown?

Vehicle Capabilities

Think about some of the skills you must have just to drive from home to a store nearby. To complete this trip, you must know how fast your car will accelerate. As you approach a STOP sign, you must know how much braking power your car has and how to use that power. If a child darts into your path of travel, you will have to know how to stop or swerve out of the way. In addition, you will have to know how your car responds at higher speeds. At expressway speeds, you must modify the way you brake, steer, and accelerate. You will have to think and act well ahead of time. In all of these situations, you must know how to adjust your driving to the capabilities of your car.

In addition to having control of your car, you must know what other vehicles and drivers can and cannot do. The better you are able to judge what others can and will do, the better you will be able to use the IPDE process to drive. Once you know how vehicles are likely to perform, you will be able to:

- **Identify** vehicles that are, or will start, moving.
- **Predict** where and when another vehicle might create a conflict with your car.
- **Decide** how to adjust your speed and position to create a space cushion.
- **Execute** a braking, steering, or accelerating action to complete this move.

Think of each vehicle as fitting into one of the four groups listed across the top of the chart on the opposite page. An example of each type of vehicle is shown below.

Small vehicle

Mid-size vehicle

Large vehicle

Recreational vehicle

Capability	Small Vehicles	Mid-Size Vehicles	Large Vehicles	Recreational Vehicles
Accelerating	Moderate to high depending on engine size	moderate	usually slow	slow in most situations; 4-wheel drive vehicles accelerate well in low-traction situations
Braking	good	ranges from slow to good; heavy loads might reduce vehicle's braking capability	slow, especially when fully loaded	slow
Turning	good for quick turns	good; possibly slower when heavily loaded	poor for quick turns	poor for quick turns; vehicles equipped with special high suspensions can be dangerous in quick turns
Total Control	good response at higher speeds; high winds might make vehicle wander in lane	good response; sluggish response when heavily loaded	slow response, especially when heavily loaded	slow response

Small Vehicles This group includes vehicles such as motorcycles, subcompact cars, and high-powered sports cars.

Mid-Size Vehicles This group includes larger cars, station wagons, minivans, sedans, and small trucks.

Large Vehicles This group includes trucks, buses, and other large, over-the-road vehicles.

Recreational Vehicles This group includes full-size vans and off-road vehicles.

Grouping vehicles will not improve control of your own car. But, it can give you an idea of how each vehicle can perform in different situations.

While driving, you must consider how another vehicle might perform. Then, you must think ahead to anticipate what the driver is likely to do. This chart shows the way vehicles can perform.

Remember, other vehicles will respond differently. If you have any doubt as to how a vehicle will respond, increase your space cushion. Give the other driver extra space to maneuver.

Review It

1. What is the purpose of grooves on tire tread?
2. What three factors can reduce traction?
3. When should you start to slow for a curve?
4. Why does it help you to know the performance capabilities of other vehicles?

5–3

Stopping Distance

When you are driving and have to stop, three things must happen. You must perceive the hazard or warning; react; brake your car to a stop.

Total Stopping Distance

The distance your car travels while you make a stop is **total stopping distance**. This distance is measured from the point you first see a hazard to the point where your vehicle stops.

Perception Time and Distance

The length of time you take to identify, predict, and decide to slow for a hazard is called your **perception time.** Perception time will vary greatly depending on visibility, the hazard, and your abilities at the time. Do you think your perception time could be lengthened if you were distracted by passengers or a loud radio? The distance your vehicle travels during this time is your **perception distance.**

You cannot consistently estimate your perception distance because your ability to perceive will change from time to time. Sometimes it will take longer to perceive a complex driving situation than it will take to brake to a stop. To help shorten your perception time, look well down the road so you will be

ready to respond to a dangerous situation.

Reaction Time and Distance

Once you know a hazard will be a problem, the length of time you take to execute your action is your **reaction time.** An average driver's reaction time is 3/4 second. Your reaction time will be longer if your abilities are impaired. The distance your vehicle travels while you react is your **reaction distance.**

Braking Distance

The distance your vehicle travels from the time you apply the brake until your vehicle stops is called **braking distance**. A vehicle's energy of motion is proportional to the square of its increase in speed. Your braking distance is also proportional to the square of your vehicle's increase in speed. If you increase your speed from 20 mph to 40 mph, your braking distance will be about four times longer. If you know you are going to be driving into a dangerous situation, why is it so important to drive at a lower speed?

Estimating Stopping Distance

The chart shows how far your vehicle will travel while you react and brake to a stop from different speeds. These distances will change depending on your ability at the time, your vehicle's condition, and the condition of the road.

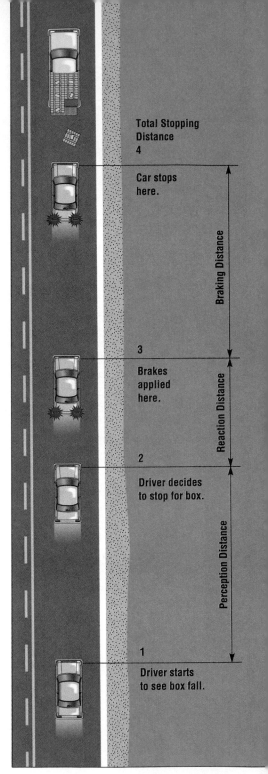

The parts of total stopping distance

Estimating stopping distance can be hard. To help, use the 4-second rule. This rule enables you to project your approximate stopping distance under ideal conditions at any speed.

Use these three steps to estimate your stopping distance while driving.

1. Pick a fixed checkpoint (a shadow or mark on the road) ahead where you think you could stop your vehicle.
2. Count off 4 seconds: "one-thousand-one, one-thousand-two, one-thousand-three, one-thousand-four."
3. Check your vehicle's position. If you have just reached your fixed checkpoint, you can assume the distance you estimated in Step 1 was the approximate distance it would have taken you to stop.

Practice estimating your stopping distance from various speeds. Keep in mind it will take you almost 300 feet, or the length of a football field, to stop if you are traveling 65 mph.

Factors That Affect Braking Distance

Just because natural laws affect all vehicles in the same way, never assume you can stop in the same distance as the vehicle ahead. The following six factors can affect your braking distance:

- **Speed**   The higher the speed, the longer the braking distance. At higher speeds, you will have a harder time controlling your car.
- **Vehicle Condition**   A vehicle with worn tires, shock absorbers, or brakes needs a longer distance to stop. If the brakes on one side of your vehicle are worn or in need of adjustment, your vehicle will pull to one side in a stop. In the end, it will take you longer to stop.
- **Roadway Surface**   Rain, snow, ice, dirt, sand, wet leaves, and gravel reduce traction on the road and increase your braking distance.
- **Driver Reaction**   If you panic and slam on your brakes, you might lose control of your car in an emergency situation.
- **Hills**   Your braking distance will increase when driving downhill and be shorter when going uphill.
- **Load**   A heavy load will increase your braking distance.

Review It

1. What three parts add up to your total stopping distance?
2. How can you estimate your stopping distance?
3. What factors can affect your braking distance?

Distances traveled at various speeds while driver begins to stop

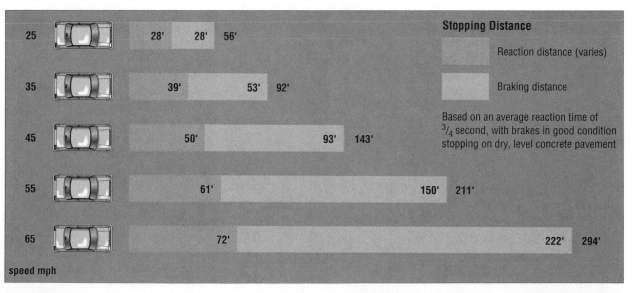

Force of Impact and Restraint Devices

As a driver, you must know about the possible forces resulting from a collision. Even more important, you need to know the steps you absolutely must take ahead of time to avoid being injured in a collision.

Force of Impact

The force with which a moving object hits another object is called **force of impact**. Three factors determine how hard a moving vehicle will hit another object—speed, weight, and distance between impact and stop.

Speed Speed is the most important factor in determining how hard a vehicle will hit another object. The force of impact is in proportion to the square of the increase in the vehicle's speed.

Study the illustrations on this page. Note that when the vehicle's speed doubles to 40 mph, it hits a solid object four times as hard as it would have if it were moving at 20 mph. When its speed triples to 60 mph, the force of impact is nine times as hard. How do you think the damage done at these different speeds would compare?

Any reduction in speed can greatly reduce the damage in a collision. Therefore, it is very important to reduce speed in any emergency situation.

Weight The heavier a vehicle is, the harder it will hit another object. A vehicle weighing twice as much will hit a solid object twice as hard. But, this fact does not mean a small car protects its occupants better than a heavier vehicle. In most cases, a larger vehicle can absorb the impact of a crash better and protect its passengers more.

Distance Between Impact and Stop The distance a vehicle covers between the instant it hits an object and the moment it comes to a complete stop can vary greatly. Imagine hitting a large, solid tree. Your vehicle will stop quickly. Damage will be great.

Now think how different it would be to hit something softer, like a hedge. The softer object helps cushion the impact. Your vehicle will slow gradually. Damage will be much less. Given a choice in an emergency, always hit the softer object.

Energy-Absorbing Features

Automobile manufacturers have included many energy-absorbing features in their vehicles. These features protect occupants in crashes.

- **Front and Rear Crush Areas** Cars now have areas, such as front ends and trunks, that crush on impact. Crush areas protect occupants by absorbing the force of impact.
- **Energy-Absorbing Bumpers** Many bumpers are designed to absorb low levels of impact under 5 mph without damage.

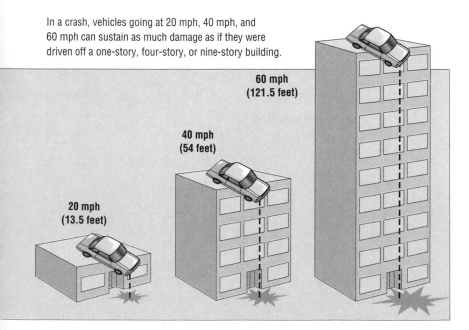

In a crash, vehicles going at 20 mph, 40 mph, and 60 mph can sustain as much damage as if they were driven off a one-story, four-story, or nine-story building.

60 mph
(121.5 feet)

40 mph
(54 feet)

20 mph
(13.5 feet)

- **Side Door Beams** Steel beams inside the doors protect occupants in side impacts.
- **Reinforced Windshield** A plastic sheet between layers of windshield glass helps protect passengers from being cut by broken glass.
- **Energy-Absorbing Steering Wheel and Column** These features absorb some of the force of impact and protect drivers.
- **Padded Dash** Metal areas are covered and cushioned. Controls are recessed.
- **Head Restraints** Padded areas on the top of front seats help protect against whiplash injuries.

Safety Belts

Two collisions occur when a car hits a solid object. The first collision happens when the car hits the object and stops. The second collision occurs when the occupants hit their restraint devices or the inside of the car.

A **restraint device** is any device that holds a car occupant in place during a crash. A safety belt you must buckle is an **active restraint device**.

How to Wear Safety Belts

Any time you are in a vehicle, you need to follow these steps for using your safety belt:

1. Adjust your seat to a comfortable upright position. Make sure your safety belt is not twisted.

2. Snap the metal fitting on the end of the safety belt into the buckle. Then, adjust the lap part of your safety belt so that it is low and snug across your hips. The bottom edge of the safety belt should just touch your thighs. By making this adjustment, any crash forces will be applied to your pelvic bones.

3. Finally, adjust the shoulder part of your safety belt across your chest. Your shoulder adjustment should be snug.

This adjustment procedure will work for all adults, including expectant mothers. In addition, a properly adjusted safety belt also will hold you firmly in your seat if you must swerve or brake violently to avoid a collision. You have a responsibility as a driver to make sure all passengers use their safety belts.

The following are some questions you might be asking about using safety belts.

- **Can't I get trapped in an accident with safety belts?**
  Answer: You might be trapped, with or without safety belts. But, you are more likely to be conscious and able to get out of your vehicle after a collision if you have been belted in.
- **Isn't it better to be thrown free in a collision?**
  Answer: No, being thrown free is much more dangerous than remaining in the vehicle.

- **Why not just wear safety belts on long trips?**
  Answer: Most collisions occur within 25 miles of home at speeds less than 40 mph. Your chance of surviving a collision increases 50 percent when wearing safety belts. Since safety belts have been proven so effective, most states require that drivers and passengers wear safety belts constantly.
- **Do safety belts ever need repair?**
  Answer: Yes, especially after collisions in which safety belts become stretched. If you have any question, do not hesitate to replace worn safety belts or safety belt parts.

Other Restraint Devices

In addition to safety belts, other types of devices restrain people in vehicles. These devices include air bags, automatic safety belts, and child seats.

Passive Restraints   A **passive restraint device** is a device that works automatically. Air bags and automatic safety belts are two examples of passive restraints. All new vehicles sold in the United States after 1991 are required to have some type of passive restraint.

Look at the picture that opens this chapter on page 80. This photo shows what an air bag looks like during the brief instant it is being used. In a collision, an air bag is inflated, provides protection, and starts deflating in the time it takes you to blink your eye. Air bags provide a tremendous amount of protection in a collision.

The following is part of an actual report of a collision involving two cars with air bags.

The investigation revealed exactly what had happened. Driver A had seen a car heading toward him on his side of the road and had virtually stood on his brakes. Then he was aware that his face was being buried in a balloon-like pillow. Driver B remembers her bag suddenly billowing in front of her nose. "It was a jolt, but not a hard jolt. Like when you were a kid and jumped on a mattress. . . ."

The Insurance Institute team established that the crash was the equivalent of each of them hitting a stationary object at 68 mph. As the cars slammed together, each driver's head was thrown forward with 1700 pounds of force. . .

By the time the hood of each car began to crumple, both bags were fully inflated and positioned directly in line with the head and torso of each driver. As their heads slammed forward, the folds of the air bag softened the impact, like a big balloon. At maximum inflation, the bags began to vent nitrogen gas to ensure the gentlest impact possible.

Thanks to air bags, both of these drivers recovered from this collision.

Air bags are designed to be used in combination with regular safety belts. Therefore, some car manufacturers refer to air bags as being a supplemental restraint system. It is important for you to know that air bags only work in front end collisions.

Automatic safety belts are also passive restraint devices. They work automatically once your car door is closed. In some vehicles, you must actively fasten a lap belt along with the shoulder strap.

Child Seats   Safety belts are not designed to protect infants and small children. You have a legal responsibility to make sure young passengers are

With many automatic seat belts, you also must fasten a lap belt.

secured in specially designed infant seats or small-child seats. Place the seats on the rear seat of the vehicle, if possible. All states now require the use of child seats.

Review It

1. What three factors can affect force of impact?
2. What is the right way to adjust your safety belt?
3. What is the difference between an active and a passive restraint device? What is an example of each?

DECISION MAKING

1. The car ahead is blocking your lane. You cannot stop. How can you reduce the force of impact?

2. You are driving the yellow car and have slammed on your brakes to avoid a head-on collision. Your wheels are sliding. You want to head for the shoulder to avoid trouble. What should you do?

3. You are approaching this curve at 40 mph. To maintain control, when should you adjust your speed?

4. The driver ahead is braking to maintain control. What two factors might increase the stopping distance in this situation?

CHAPTER 5 REVIEW

Review Chapter Objectives

5–1 Gravity and Energy of Motion
1. How does gravity affect your vehicle when it is in motion? (82)
2. How does your vehicle's speed and weight affect its energy of motion? (83)

5–2 Friction and Traction
3. How does traction help control your vehicle? (84)
4. What three things can reduce the amount of traction you will have for control? (86)
5. What factors can affect your vehicle in a curve? (87)
6. Why is it important for you to know the performance capabilities of other vehicles? (88)

5–3 Stopping Distance
7. What is total stopping distance? (90)
8. How does the four-second rule apply to your driving? (91)
9. What six factors can affect your braking distance? (91)

5–4 Force of Impact and Restraint Devices
10. What three actions could you take to cut your force of impact in a collision? (92)
11. How should you adjust your safety belt before driving? (93)
12. How do passive restraints and child safety seats protect drivers and passengers? (94)

Check Your Knowledge

Multiple Choice   Copy the number of each sentence below on a sheet of paper. Choose the letter that best completes the statement or answers the question.

1. The large open tread of a snow tire gives extra
   (a) grooves. (b) traction. (c) tire pressure. (d) strength. (85)
2. To estimate stopping distance, use
   (a) the 4-second rule. (b) reaction distance. (c) braking distance. (d) traction. (91)
3. A vehicle's speed, its weight, and the distance between impact and stop determine the
   (a) center of gravity. (b) energy of motion. (c) perception time. (d) force of impact. (92)
4. A restraint device that you must fasten is
   (a) an air bag. (b) an active restraint. (c) a passive restraint. (d) a seat lever. (93)
5. An air bag is a type of
   (a) active restraint. (b) brake. (c) passive restraint. (d) indicator. (94)

Completion   Copy the number of each sentence below. After each number, write the word or words that complete the sentence correctly.
6. Adjust power when driving on hills to overcome the effects of _____ . (82)
7. Using a roof-top carrier might raise your car's _____ . (82)
8. A _____ is a sudden loss of air pressure in a tire. (85)
9. Worn shock absorbers can _____ traction on a rough road. (91)
10. By knowing how your car and other vehicles might react in different situations, you will be better able to use the _____ . (88)
11. All states require the use of _____ . (93)
12. _____ is a force that prevents slipping. (84)
13. The _____ gives a tire its grooved surface. (84)

Check Vocabulary

Copy the number of each definition in List A. Match the definition in List A with the term it defines in List B.

List A

14. curve where the outside of the roadway is higher than the inside of the roadway (87)
15. distance it takes your car to stop from the instant you see a hazard (90)
16. time you need to identify, predict, and decide to slow (90)
17. distance your car travels during the time you perceive a situation (90)
18. time it takes you to act after perceiving a situation (91)
19. distance a car travels while you act (90)
20. distance your car travels from the time the brakes are applied until your car stops (90)
21. device designed to hold car occupants in their seats during a collision (93)

List B

a. banked curve
b. braking distance
c. force of impact
d. perception distance
e. perception time
f. reaction distance
g. reaction time
h. restraint device
i. total stopping distance

Check Your Understanding

Write a short answer for each question or statement.

22. If your car's speed increases, what will happen to its energy of motion? (83)
23. What happens to your available traction if you try to steer and slow in a curve at the same time? (87)
24. If you are approaching a curve at a high rate of speed, when should you adjust your speed? (87)
25. What will happen to your perception time when you encounter a complex traffic situation? (90)

Think Critically

Write a paragraph to answer each question or statement.

1. If you were about to collide with another car, why is it very important that you do not give up trying to reduce your speed and that you continue to maneuver?
2. What factor could have prevented a collision like the one in the picture?

Projects

1. With the owners' permission, check the tire pressure on about 10 vehicles. Use a tire-pressure gauge. How many had pressures that were within the recommended limits indicated on the sidewalls of the tires?
2. Observe at least 50 vehicles at a busy intersection. How many drivers and passengers had their safety belts on? As a result of the survey, **write** a persuasive speech for the need for passive restraints.

Chapter 6

PERFORMING BASIC CAR MANEUVERS

You're the Driver!

Suppose you are the driver approaching the intersection in the picture. From which lane would you make a left turn?

What hazards do the angle-parked cars on the left present to you? What clue tells you that a parked car might back up? How can you warn the driver?

What clues tell you that you are on a one-way street?

If you want to angle park on the left side, when would you begin to turn into the parking place?

This chapter explains how to perform basic maneuvers of steering, changing lanes, turning, and parking. You will also learn how to turn your car around and how to start and park on hills. In addition, you will learn when and where to perform these maneuvers safely.

Objectives

Section 6–1　Steering, Signaling, and Changing Lanes

1. Explain how to steer straight forward and backward.
2. Describe the correct use of hand signals.
3. List the steps for changing lanes.

Section 6–2　Turns and Turnabouts

4. Describe hand-over-hand steering.
5. List the steps for making left and right turns.
6. Describe how to back left and right.
7. Explain five turnabouts.
8. List the factors to consider when deciding which type of turnabout to use.

Section 6–3　Parking

9. List the steps for angle and perpendicular parking.
10. List the steps for parallel parking.
11. Explain how to park uphill and downhill with and without a curb.
12. Explain how to start from an uphill parking space without rollback.

Steering, Signaling and Changing Lanes

Steering control is critical to safe and successful driving. Developing steering control involves visual habits, use of space, speed control, and continual adjustments of the steering wheel.

This driver is in the correct position for backing straight.

Steering Straight Forward

Use a comfortable, balanced hand position when you steer straight ahead. Aim high with your visual search. Look far ahead toward the center of your intended path. Do not look at the center line or at the hood ornament. Avoid looking at your hands or feet. When you look down, you cannot see your planned path of travel.

Relax your arms and continually make slight steering corrections so you will drive in a straight line. Some new drivers tend to turn the steering wheel too much, or **oversteer.** When you oversteer, your car will weave from side to side rather than move in a straight line.

Other new drivers might tend to **understeer.** They do not turn the steering wheel enough to keep the car in the planned path. If you understeer, you go too far in one direction, then too far in the other direction. Correct understeering by

turning the wheel slightly and more often.

You will soon develop a feel for the space your vehicle occupies. Practice and experience will help you think of your car as an extension of yourself. You soon will be able to accurately judge the space your car uses while it is moving and the space you need to make various maneuvers.

Steering Straight Backward

Backing the car might feel strange when you do it for the first time. Before backing any vehicle, look back to make sure your path is clear. Do not use only the rearview mirrors. Follow these steps to back correctly:

1. Hold the brake pedal down and shift to REVERSE.
2. Turn your body to the right, and put your right

arm over the back of the seat. Look back through the rear window.
3. Put your left hand at the top of the steering wheel at the 12 o'clock position.
4. Release pressure on the brake just enough to allow the car to creep backward slowly. The idle speed of most automatic transmission vehicles usually allows the car to move slightly without you stepping on the accelerator.
5. Move the top of the steering wheel in the direction you want the back of the car to go. Make only small steering corrections.
6. Keep your foot over the brake pedal while the car moves back. Glance quickly to the front and sides to check traffic. Continue looking back through the rear window as you brake to a smooth stop.

Right Turn

Left Turn

Slow or Stop

Backing a Stickshift Car

You can back slowly in a stick-shift car by carefully controlling your use of the clutch pedal. Follow these steps for backing in a stickshift car:

1. Push the brake and clutch pedals down.
2. Shift to REVERSE.
3. Release the brake, and let the clutch come out slowly to the friction point.

Holding the clutch at the friction point allows the car to back at a slow, controlled speed. Releasing the clutch suddenly causes the car to jerk back quickly, or even continue backing if the engine does not stall.

Most stickshift cars can move slowly in REVERSE with the clutch at the friction point and with no acceleration. When this backing procedure is possible, keep your right foot over the brake pedal, ready for a stop.

When stopping, push the clutch pedal down and brake to a smooth stop. Continue to look back until the car is stopped.

Signaling

Signaling with turn-signal lights and arm signals is very important when you plan to turn, change lanes, enter traffic, slow suddenly, or stop. Always signal well in advance of any maneuver so other drivers have time to react.

Even though cars have turn-signal devices, a combination of turn lights and hand and arm signals will be more effective at times. Hand signals are easier to see in bright sunlight. At night, however, turn lights are easier to see. A waving arm signal gets attention during an emergency stop. Should the

turn-signal device not work, you must use hand signals.

Notice the hand and arm positions in these pictures. The first shows the left arm and hand pointing up for a right turn. The second shows the left arm and hand extended straight out for a left turn. The third shows the left arm extended downward, indicating slow or stop.

When using arm signals, use your right hand to maintain steering control. Make any arm signals well before you enter a turn. Return your left hand to the steering wheel before executing a turn. Use both hands on the steering wheel when executing a turn.

101

Changing Lanes

Drivers must be able to execute the lane-change maneuver before they learn to pass other vehicles. Changing lanes is a maneuver you will often use on a roadway with two or more lanes of traffic moving in your direction. You may also need to change lanes before turning right or left.

At times, changing lanes gives you a better position or view when driving in traffic. For example, you might want to change lanes when following a large truck on a multilane highway. By moving to a different lane you can increase your sight distance and get a broader view of the traffic flow.

Steering control is a critical factor as you learn the lane-changing maneuver. Oversteering, a common error, can cause your car to turn too sharply as you start to enter the adjoining lane. At higher speeds, this oversteering error could cause you to lose steering control.

Change lanes as smoothly as possible. Avoid sudden turns of the steering wheel. The second picture shows the safe path of travel of a car executing a smooth lane change.

Always follow the same procedure for making a lane change, regardless of your reason for making the lane change. Before changing lanes, make sure that you can see far

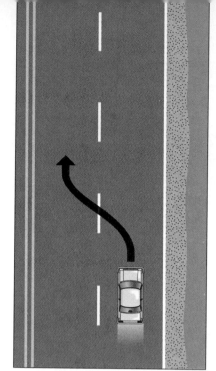

Oversteering can cause you to take an incorrect path for changing lanes.

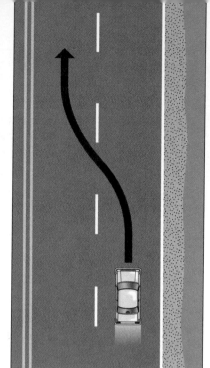

This path of travel is correct for a smooth lane change.

ahead and that no obstructions are in either lane.

Follow these steps when making a lane change to the left:
1. Check traffic ahead in both lanes and through both rearview mirrors.
2. Signal and make a blind-spot check over your left shoulder to see if any vehicle is about to pass you.
3. Steer gently into the next lane if it is clear.
4. Cancel your signal and adjust speed.

Follow the same procedure when making a lane change to the right, with one exception. After checking traffic ahead and through both mirrors, check the blind-spot area over your right shoulder. Take only a glance to make this check. Be

careful not to pull the steering wheel to the right as you turn to glance over your right shoulder. Keep steering straight as you check your blind spot. If the lane is clear, complete the lane change to the right the same way as to the left.

Review It

1. Where should you be looking when steering straight forward?
2. Describe the correct driver position for backing straight.
3. What are the three arm and hand signals for turns and stopping?
4. List the steps for changing lanes.

Turns and Turnabouts

Making turns properly depends on steering control, speed control, and good visual habits. Look far ahead as you approach a turn, then look "through" the turn you are about to make. Looking through the turn shows you where the car will go, any hazards in your path, and how much to turn.

Hand-Over-Hand Steering

You use **hand-over-hand steering** by pulling the steering wheel down with one hand while your other hand crosses over to pull the wheel farther down. The pictures match these steps for correct hand-over-hand steering for a left turn:

1. Begin the turn from a balanced hand position.
2. Place your right hand near the top of the wheel. Start pulling down to the left while releasing your left hand from the wheel.
3. Continue pulling down about a quarter turn with your right hand while crossing your left hand over your right. Grasp the wheel near the top.
4. Pull down with your left hand again as you release your right hand. Continue alternating hands until you have steered enough

Steps for steering for a left turn

1

2

3
4

to complete the turn. As a beginning driver, you might find you need to turn the wheel less than you thought.

Some cars straighten after a turn if you relax your grip and let the wheel unwind through your palms. However, always be ready to unwind the wheel hand-over-hand, especially at lower speeds and with front-wheel drive cars.

Making Left and Right Turns

Make left and right turns cautiously and only after checking the traffic situation around you.

Take these precautions:
- Look for pedestrians, oncoming traffic, and parked cars.
- Obey all traffic signs, signals, and roadway markings. Remember that you must yield to oncoming traffic when preparing to turn left.
- Plan turns well in advance so you are in the correct lane about a block before the turn.

When turning in a stickshift car, you might need to downshift to slow the car before entering a sharp turn. Downshift before the turn so you have both hands free for turning. Be sure to release the clutch before entering the turn.

A center left-turn lane in a four-lane road

Steps for making left turns (yellow car) and right turns (white car)

Procedure for Turning The numbers in the picture match the following steps for turns:

1. Position your car in the correct lane for the turn. For a right turn, be in the far right lane about four feet from the curb if there are no parked cars. For a left turn, be in the lane nearest to the center line. (On a one-way street, be in the far left lane.) Check traffic to the rear. Signal about half a block before the turn.
2. Brake gently to reduce speed.
3. Use your visual search pattern to continue to check traffic all around you. Search for pedestrians and bicyclists.
4. Slow to about 10 mph just before the crosswalk.
5. For a right turn, check to the left again before turning. Then look right, in the direction of the turn. Turn the steering wheel when your car's front wheels are even with the bend of the corner.
6. For a left turn, check traffic to the right and then look left. Turn the steering wheel just before you reach the center of the intersection. Continue looking left into the lane you will enter.
7. As you begin the turn, make a quick blind-spot check through the right side-window. Check that the intersection is still clear. Turn into the nearest lane of traffic going in your direction. Accelerate gently about halfway through the turn. Return the steering wheel to the straight-ahead position.

Some left turns into business areas can be made in midblock from a center lane. Before making a left turn from a center lane, scan for traffic and pedestrians. Follow the correct lane-change procedure to enter the center lane. Look ahead for oncoming traffic and be prepared to yield to any vehicle whose path you will cross. This type of left turn can be hazardous, especially when you meet an approaching vehicle also turning left from the center lane.

Backing Left and Right

Use hand-over-hand steering and follow these steps to make sharp turns while backing:

1. Before backing, check for traffic, pedestrians, parked cars, and low stationary objects behind you. Turn your head toward the direction you will back. Look through the rear and side windows in that direction.
2. Keep both hands on the wheel, ready for hand-over-hand steering. Pull the wheel to the left to back left. Pull the wheel to the right to back right. The back of your car will go in the direction you turn the wheel.
3. Back slowly as you enter the turn. Begin to unwind the steering wheel to finish the turn in a straight position.

When backing left, allow a wide space on the right side. The front wheels will move far to the right of the rear wheels and the front of your car will swing wide to the right.

When backing right, allow a wide space on the left side.

Turning the Car Around

In many cases, the safest and best way to turn your car around is to drive around the block. However, on dead-end streets and in some other locations, you need to use other ways to turn your car around.

A **turnabout** is a maneuver for turning your car around to go in the opposite direction. Turnabouts can be risky since you cross or back into one or more lanes of traffic. Take these precautions when you plan to make a turnabout:

- Do not make a turnabout near hills or curves or within 200 feet of intersections.
- Never attempt a turnabout in heavy traffic.
- Be sure local laws permit the turnabout.
- Select a site with at least 500 feet of clear visibility in each direction. This distance is equal to one and one-half football fields.
- Be sure you have enough space to complete the maneuver.
- Check continually for traffic and pedestrians.

You must decide which turnabout is best for each situation. Study the five different turnabouts described on the next three pages. The steps for each turnabout match the numbered car positions.

The correct driver positions for backing to the left and to the right, and the space and path the car takes during backing.

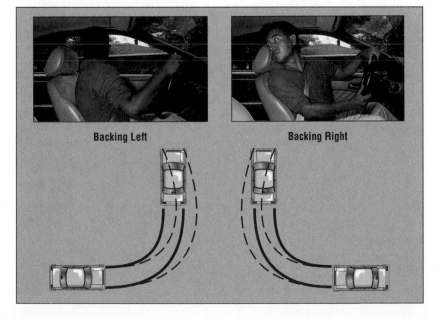

Backing Left   **Backing Right**

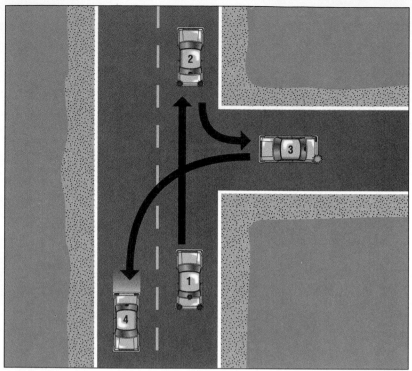

Driveway (right side)

Back into Driveway on Right Side Choose this turnabout if a clear driveway is on the right and there is no close traffic to the rear in your lane. This turnabout has the advantage of letting you reenter traffic going forward.

1. Check traffic to the rear, and signal a stop. Proceed beyond the driveway.
2. Stop two to three feet from the curb. Check traffic again, then back slowly to the right to position 3. Use hand-over-hand steering. Stop with the wheels straight when your car is completely off the street.
3. Signal a left turn. Check traffic.
4. Drive forward to position 4.

Midblock U-turn You need a wide space to make a U-turn because no backing is done. In quiet, residential areas, you usually can make a U-turn on a wide street or at an intersection. However, a U-turn at an intersection is illegal in some states. A U-turn is risky because you must cross several lanes of traffic to execute it.

1. Check traffic ahead, to the rear, and then signal right. Pull to the far right and stop at position 1.
2. From your stopped position, signal a left turn and begin moving toward position 2.
3. Check traffic ahead, to the rear, and in your left blind spot. Turn sharply left

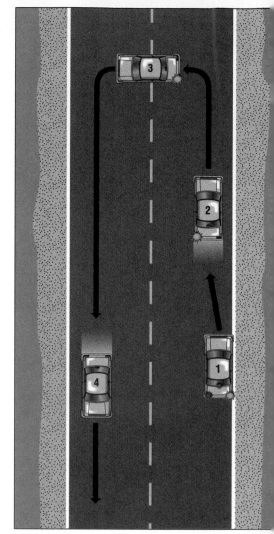

Midblock U-turn

while moving slowly toward position 3. Check the forward space you need to continue the turn. Do not stop if you have enough space to complete the turn.
4. Move slowly toward position 4. Check traffic to the rear. Straighten the wheels while you accelerate gently into the proper lane.

Pull into Driveway on Left Side You might choose this turnabout if oncoming traffic is light and a driveway on the left is available. A disadvantage of this turnabout is that you must back into the traffic flow before moving forward.

1. Check traffic ahead and to the rear. Signal a left turn and use the left-turn procedure to move to position 2. Stop with the wheels straight when your car is completely off the street.
2. Check traffic again, especially from the right. Back slowly to the right, to position 3. Look to the right rear and side while backing. Stop with the wheels straight.
3. Accelerate gently, and drive forward to position 4.

Pull into Driveway on Right Side This type of turnabout is a high-risk maneuver. To complete it, you must back across two lanes of traffic before moving forward. Avoid this turnabout whenever possible.

1. Check traffic ahead and to the rear. Signal a right turn and use the right-turn procedure to move to position 2. Stop with the wheels straight when your car is completely off the street.
2. Check traffic again from both directions. Back slowly across the street, turning left toward position 3. Look to the left, rear, and side when backing. Glance to the front, then continue looking back while stopping with the wheels straight in position 3.

Safe Driving Tips

- When backing to either the right or left, be sure to leave a wide space for the front of your vehicle to swing. When you first practice backing, you may find that the front of the car needs more space than you first thought it would.

- Be especially careful to "clear" your path when backing out of driveways. Children playing on the pavement are below your line of vision when looking out the rear window. It is a good idea to walk around the rear of your car and observe up and down the street before backing out.

3. Accelerate gently, and drive forward to position 4.

Driveway on Left Side

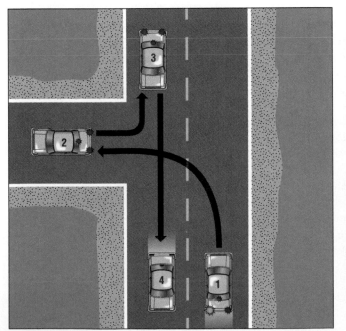

Driveway on Right Side

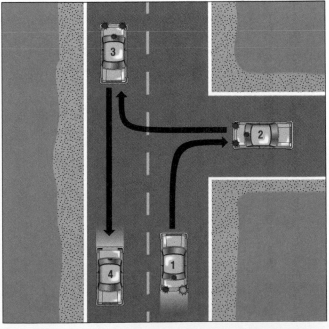

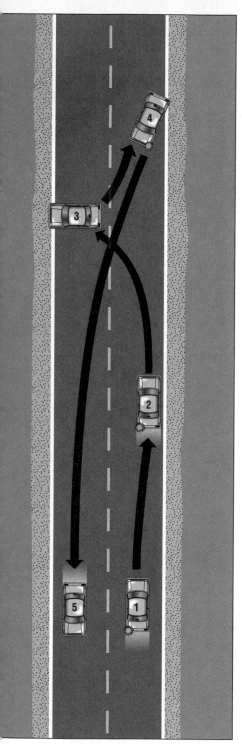

Three-point Turnabout

Three-Point Turnabout This turnabout is hazardous to perform. You not only cross traffic lanes, but your car is stopped across a traffic lane.

1. From position 1 check traffic to the rear and over your right shoulder. Signal right and stop close to the curb as in position 2. From position 2 check traffic ahead, to the rear, and over your left shoulder. Signal a left turn.
2. Turn sharply left while moving slowly to position 3. Stop with the wheels straight.
3. Check traffic again. Turn the wheels sharply right while backing slowly to position 4. Back only as far as necessary to complete the maneuver. Stop with the wheels straight.
4. Check traffic again and signal left. Move slowly forward while steering left toward position 5.

Deciding Which Turnabout to Use

Consider these factors when deciding which turnabout to use:

- legality of the turnabout
- amount of traffic
- need to enter traffic lanes forward or backward
- ample space and time to enter traffic
- number of traffic lanes to cross.

Backing into a driveway or an alley on the right side is usually the safest type of turnabout to use. You can enter traffic forward from this turnabout. This turnabout makes it easier to choose a safe space in which to enter traffic and to accelerate into that space.

Sometimes you might need to make a turnabout in light traffic. If there are driveways on both the left and the right sides to turn into, choose the left driveway rather than the right. This turnabout lets you back into your own lane rather than back across both lanes. Select a gap in traffic that gives you time and space to complete the maneuver.

A three-point turnabout is appropriate at very few times. Use this turnabout only when you are on a dead-end street or on a rural roadway with no driveways.

Review It

1. What is the procedure for hand-over-hand steering?
2. What are the steps for turning left and right?
3. What space must you consider when backing to the left and to the right?
4. What is the safest type of turnabout to use, and why is it the safest?
5. What factors should you consider when planning to execute a turnabout?

Parking

Parking your car requires you to use basic maneuvers you have learned. Use **angle parking** to park your car diagonally to the curb. Use **perpendicular parking** to park your car at a right angle to the curb. Use **parallel parking** to park your car parallel to the curb.

Parking is easier and safer if you consider these factors:

- Try to find a parking space with ample room for entering and exiting easily. The size of your car is a factor in determining the space you choose.
- Avoid spaces at the end of parking lanes and near a large vehicle that might block your view.
- Avoid spaces with a poorly parked car on either side.

The following procedures refer to entering a parking space to your right. When parking to your left, adjust your actions and visual checks for the left side. The steps in each procedure match the numbered car positions in the pictures.

Angle Parking

1. Position your car about five feet out from the row of parked cars. Signal a right turn, and check traffic to the rear. Begin to brake.

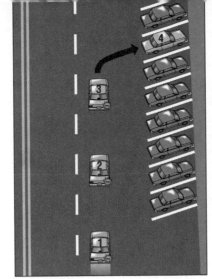

Angle Parking

2. Flash your brake lights to warn drivers behind. Continue braking. Check your right blind spot.
3. When you can see down the right line of the parking stall, turn the wheels sharply to the right. Slowly enter the stall.
4. Straighten the wheels when you are centered in the space. Stop before the wheels strike the curb.

Perpendicular Parking

1. Position your car as far to the left of your lane as possible. Signal a right turn, and check your right blind spot. Begin to brake.
2. Flash your brake lights. Check traffic to the rear, and continue to brake.
3. When the front bumper of your car passes the left rear taillight of the car to the right of the empty parking

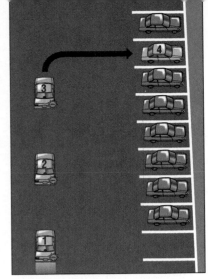

Perpendicular Parking

space, turn the wheels sharply right. Slowly enter the stall. Check your right rear fender for clearance.
4. Straighten the wheels when you are centered in the space. Stop before the wheels strike the curb.

Leaving an Angle or Perpendicular Parking Space   Your view often will be blocked as you begin to back into moving traffic. Back cautiously as you look to the rear and sides to search for other roadway users.

1. Creep straight back while you control speed with your foot brake. (Hold the clutch at the friction point in a stickshift car.)
2. When your front bumper is even with the left car's rear bumper, begin to turn right.
3. Back into the nearest lane, and stop with the wheels straight. Shift to a forward gear and proceed.

Parallel Parking

Successful parallel parking depends on steering and speed control. You must also be able to judge space and distance. Select a space that is about six feet longer than your car. During the maneuver, the front of your car will swing far to the left. Check over your left shoulder to be sure this needed space is clear. The steps match the car positions in the pictures.

1. Flash brake lights, and signal a right turn. Stop two to three feet away from the front car with the two cars' rear bumpers even. Shift to REVERSE. Check traffic. Look back over your right shoulder. Back slowly as you turn right. Aim toward the right rear corner of the space. Control speed with your foot brake (clutch at friction point in a stickshift car).

2. When the back of your seat is even with the rear bumper of the front car, straighten wheels. Slowly back straight. Look over your shoulder, through the rear window.

3. When your front bumper is even with the front car's back bumper, turn wheels sharply left. Back slowly; look out the rear window.

4. When your car is parallel to the curb, straighten wheels, and stop before your car touches the car behind. Slowly pull forward to center your car in the space.

Leaving a Parallel Parking Space You are responsible for avoiding a collision when leaving a parallel parking space. Yield to all approaching traffic.

1. Back straight until your rear bumper almost touches the car behind. Turn wheels sharply left just before you stop.

2. Signal a left turn. Check left blind spot. Move forward slowly.

3. Check right front fender for clearance.

4. Turn wheels slowly to the right when halfway out of parking space. Center car in the lane. Accelerate gently into traffic.

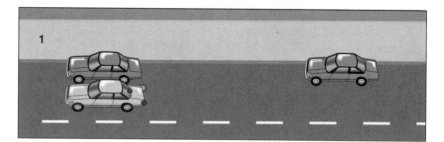

Parking on Hills

When parallel parking on a hill, you must be sure the car will not roll down into traffic. Always set the parking brake and turn the front wheels to prevent the car from rolling downhill. Procedures for uphill and downhill parking apply to parking on the right side of the street. Adjust your actions and visual checks when parking on the left side.

Uphill Parking with a Curb
1. Position your car close to the curb. Just before stopping, turn the steering wheel sharply left as shown in the first picture.
2. Shift to NEUTRAL. Let the car creep back slowly until the back of the right front tire gently touches the curb.
3. Shift to PARK (FIRST in a stickshift), and set the parking brake.
4. When leaving the parking space signal, check traffic, and accelerate gently into the lane of traffic.

Uphill Parking with No Curb
1. Pull as far off the pavement as possible. Just before you stop, turn the steering wheel sharply right, as in the second picture.
2. Shift to PARK (FIRST in a stickshift), and set the parking brake.
3. When leaving the parking space, let the car creep backward while straight-ening the wheels. Signal and check traffic. Shift to DRIVE (FIRST in a stickshift), and accelerate gently into traffic.

Downhill Parking with a Curb
1. Position your car close to the curb and stop.
2. Let the car creep forward slowly while you turn the steering wheel sharply right, as in the third picture. Let the right front tire rest against the curb.
3. Shift to PARK (REVERSE in a stickshift), and set the parking brake.
4. When leaving the parking space, check traffic and back a short distance while straightening the wheels. Signal and check traffic again. Shift to DRIVE (FIRST in a stickshift), and accelerate into traffic.

Downhill Parking with No Curb
Follow the same procedure as parking downhill with a curb. Turn the wheels sharply right as you creep as near to the shoulder as possible. Note this position in the fourth picture. Use the same steps for parking downhill with a curb to complete your maneuver, and to leave the parking space.

When you leave any hilly parking space, make sure you have a big enough gap in traffic to enter safely. Traffic coming down a hill may be approaching faster than you think it is.

Uphill Parking with a Curb

Uphill Parking with No Curb

Downhill Parking with a Curb

Downhill Parking with No Curb

Starting on a Hill

At times, you might have to stop as you are going up a hill. You must then be able to start moving forward again *without rolling back*. Starting on an uphill grade without rolling back involves timing and coordination.

Using Automatic Transmission

One method for starting on a hill without rolling back involves using the parking brake. Follow these steps when using this method:

1. While holding the foot brake down, set the parking brake firmly.
2. Accelerate until you feel the engine start to pull.

When you start on a hill after a stop, take care not to roll backward before moving forward.

3. Release the parking brake as you continue to accelerate.

A second method for starting on a hill involves using only the foot brake:

1. Hold the foot brake down with your *left* foot.
2. While still holding the foot brake with your *left* foot, accelerate gradually until the engine starts to pull.
3. Release the foot brake gently as you increase acceleration to move forward.

Using a Stickshift

One method for starting on a hill in a stickshift car involves the use of the parking brake. Follow these steps in a stickshift car:

1. Be sure the parking brake is set.
2. Shift to FIRST.
3. Use one hand to hold the steering wheel. Hold the parking-brake release with the other hand.
4. Accelerate to a fast idle. Let the clutch out to the friction point.
5. Release the parking brake slowly when you feel the engine begin to pull.
6. Increase pressure on the accelerator, and let the clutch all the way up as your car begins to move forward. Completely release the parking brake.

You might be able to coordinate the clutch and accelerator to move forward without using

the parking brake. Follow these steps:

1. Shift to FIRST while stopped.
2. Keep the foot brake down while releasing the clutch slowly, just to the friction point.
3. Move your right foot quickly from the foot brake to the accelerator. Accelerate gently.
4. Release the clutch smoothly, and accelerate gradually.

Review It

1. What are the steps for angle parking? perpendicular parking? parallel parking?
2. Which way should the front wheels be turned when parking uphill with a curb? uphill with no curb? downhill with a curb? downhill with no curb?
3. How do you use the parking brake to start on a hill without rollback?

DECISION MAKING

1. You are the driver in this picture and need to make a turnabout. What type of turnabout would you choose? Why would you choose this type?

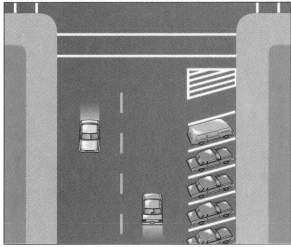

2. For what reasons should the driver of the car in the picture not choose to park in the open space at the end of the lane?

3. What procedure must the driver of the parked car follow before entering the traffic lane? If there is a collision, who is at fault? Why?

4. In which direction should the wheels be turned for the cars parked uphill? for the cars parked downhill? Why is this important?

CHAPTER 6 REVIEW

Review Chapter Objectives

6–1 Steering, Signaling, and Changing Lanes
1. How do you steer straight forward and straight backward? (100)
2. What are the hand signals for right and left turns and for slowing or stopping? (101)
3. What are the steps for changing lanes? (102)

6–2 Turns and Turnabouts
4. How do you steer hand-over-hand? (103)
5. How do you turn left and right at an intersection? (103-104)
6. How do you back to the left and to the right? (105)
7. What are five ways to turn a car around? (106-108)
8. What factors should you consider before deciding which type of turnabout to use? (108)

6–3 Parking
9. How do you angle park and perpendicular park? (109)
10. What are the steps for parallel parking? (110)
11. How do you park uphill and downhill with and without a curb? (111)
12. What is the procedure to start from an uphill parking space without rollback? (112)

Check Your Knowledge

Multiple Choice   Copy the number of each sentence below on a sheet of paper. Choose the letter that best completes the statement or answers the question.

1. To back straight, where should you place your left hand on the steering wheel?
   (a) on the bottom (b) on the left side (c) on the right side (d) on the top (100)
2. When preparing to change lanes, first
   (a) signal. (b) check traffic ahead and to the rear. (c) make a blind-spot check over your left shoulder. (d) accelerate gently. (102)
3. When preparing to make a right turn, you should be in the
   (a) left lane. (b) center lane, if there is one. (c) right lane. (d) special right-turn lane, otherwise you cannot turn right. (104)
4. The tire that rests against the curb when parked uphill on a two-way street is the
   (a) right front tire. (b) left front tire. (c) right rear tire. (d) left rear tire. (111)
5. When parking on a two-way street with no curb and your car is headed uphill, which way should you turn the front wheels?
   (a) to the left (b) to the right (c) straight (d) either left or right (111)

Completion   Copy the number of each sentence below. After each number, write the word or words that complete the sentence correctly.

6. Your vehicle can weave from side to side when you _____ . (100)
7. Holding the clutch at the _____ lets you back your car with controlled speed. (101)
8. To slow a stickshift car before turning, _____ to a lower gear. (103)
9. Turn the steering wheel to the _____ when you want to back to the left. (105)
10. In many cases, the safest and best way to turn a vehicle around is to _____ . (105)
11. Perform a _____ only when there are no driveways to use for another turnabout. (108)
12. When you use the parking brake method for starting on a hill in an automatic transmission car, you should use your _____ foot on the foot brake. (112)

Check Vocabulary

Copy the number of each definition in list A. Match the definition in list A with the term it defines in list B.

List A
13. not turning the steering wheel enough (100)
14. maneuver for turning the vehicle around to go in the opposite direction (105)
15. parking diagonally to the curb (109)
16. pulling the steering wheel down with one hand while the other hand crosses over (103)
17. parking parallel to the curb (109)
18. turn the steering wheel too much (100)
19. parking at a right angle to the curb (109)

List B
a. oversteer
b. angle parking
c. turnabout
d. parallel parking
e. turning a corner
f. understeer
g. perpendicular parking
h. hand-over-hand steering

Check Your Understanding

Write a short answer for each question or statement.

20. What is the difference between correcting for understeering and correcting for oversteering? (100)
21. How do you control your speed when backing a stickshift car? (101)
22. What are other reasons for making a lane change besides passing another vehicle? (102)
23. What area of space should you allow for when backing to the right and to the left? (105)
24. What factors should be considered when you are deciding which type of turnabout to use? (108)
25. The driver of the yellow car wants to make a left turn in midblock from the center lane in the picture. What procedure should the driver follow for making this turn safely? (104)

Think Critically

Write a paragraph to answer each question or statement.

1. Imagine you are about to make a right turn. Where should you be looking? How does this differ from where the vehicle is headed?
2. Suppose you are leaving an uphill parking space and will enter moving traffic. What procedure will you follow, and what precaution will you take to enter traffic safely?

Projects

1. Select a multiple lane intersection you can safely watch for a period of time. Make a survey of the number of drivers who start and finish the turn in the correct lane. Discuss your results with the class.
2. When riding with family or friends, note the driver's hand position on the steering wheel. Note also how many drivers use hand-over-hand steering. *Write* a report about your observations and present your findings to the class.

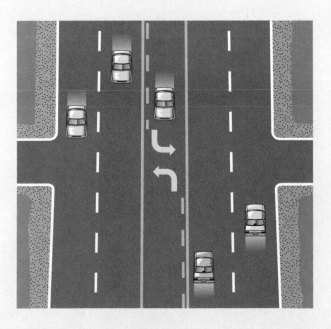

Chapter 7

NEGOTIATING INTERSECTIONS

You're the Driver!

Imagine you are driving the car waiting for the children to cross this intersection. The light is about to turn green. You plan to make a left turn. How could the pedestrians affect your left turn?

Where should you be positioned in the intersection while you wait to turn? Where should you look?

Can you turn left without waiting for oncoming traffic to clear?

Intersections can be the most dangerous locations on any roadway. Vehicles can create conflicts from several directions. Other roadway users, such as pedestrians and bicyclists, also might be present. Your decisions require both accurate identifications and predictions.

This chapter tells how to identify each kind of intersection. You also will learn how to interact safely with other roadway users at intersections.

Objectives

Section 7–1   Uncontrolled Intersections
1. Describe an uncontrolled intersection.
2. Explain the procedures to follow at an uncontrolled intersection.

Section 7–2   Controlled Intersections
3. Explain how to approach a controlled intersection.
4. Tell how to make both unprotected and protected left turns.
5. List three possible right-turn conflicts.
6. Tell how to turn right and left at a red light.
7. Tell how to move from a STOP sign when your view is blocked.

Section 7–3   Judging Time and Distance
8. Explain how to judge gaps in traffic.
9. Tell how to cross and join traffic.

Section 7–4   Determining Right of Way
10. Define right of way.
11. Describe situations in which the driver must yield the right of way.

Section 7–5   Railroad Crossings
12. Explain differences between controlled and uncontrolled railroad crossings.
13. Describe the procedures for crossing railroad tracks.

117

Uncontrolled Intersections

The chances of a collision are greater at intersections than at any other point on a roadway. Intersections are dangerous because many drivers' paths cross there. About 40 percent of all collisions and 25 percent of all fatal collisions take place at intersections.

One reason for the large number of collisions at intersections is the driver's failure to identify an intersection. Look for these clues to identify an intersection ahead:

- street signs and street lights
- parked cars on cross streets
- rows of fences and mailboxes
- tree or scrub plantings
- power lines.

Identifying Uncontrolled Intersections

An **uncontrolled intersection** has no signs or signals to regulate traffic. These intersections usually are found in areas of light traffic, such as residential areas. The picture shows how you would see an uncontrolled intersection to the left, straight ahead, and to the right. Although they are quiet, these streets can be dangerous because drivers might not be expecting cross traffic or pedestrians. Quick reactions might not protect you at uncontrolled intersections.

Sometimes a driver fails to identify an intersection as uncontrolled. The driver assumes that the other driver will stop or, on a quiet street, that no one is there. If you do not see a traffic sign or signal, assume that the intersection is uncontrolled. Reduce speed and be prepared to stop.

Approaching Uncontrolled Intersections

Look left first when you approach an uncontrolled intersection. You cross the path of vehicles from the left first.

Look right first when a building, bushes, or parked vehicles block your view to the left. Then look left when you reach a position where you have a clear view of the cross street to the left. Drive slowly, as if a vehicle is coming. You can then stop safely if a vehicle appears.

If a vehicle is coming, the driver on the left must yield to the driver on the right. However, predict the worst in each case. Never assume that the other driver will yield. The only safe action is to slow or stop. Treat an uncontrolled intersection as you would a YIELD sign.

Always let a pedestrian go first, no matter where the pedestrian is crossing. As a driver, you must protect pedestrians even if they are breaking a traffic law.

Where are the signs and signals at this intersection?

Procedures at Uncontrolled Intersections

To proceed safely through uncontrolled intersections, use the IPDE process at three critical locations. The numbers on the cars pictured in the diagram refer to locations where a set of steps are to be taken when approaching the intersection.

IPDE Process at Location 1

1. Scanning 12 seconds ahead, check roadway conditions as you approach the intersection. Check for approaching traffic straight ahead.
2. Identify whether or not the intersection is uncontrolled.
3. Identify other roadway users in or near the intersection.
4. Search the view to each side. Predict when you can see one-half block to your left and right. That view must be clear for you to proceed safely.
5. Check the rearview mirror for following traffic, then slow your vehicle. Allow yourself time to use the IPDE process at the other two locations.

You should take a series of steps at each of these three locations near uncontrolled intersections.

IPDE Process at Location 2

1. Search left first, pausing briefly as you scan. You will cross the path of a vehicle from the left first.
2. Keep your foot over the brake. Prepare to stop if a vehicle is coming from the left.
3. If no vehicle is within one-half block of the intersection, begin searching to the right.

IPDE Process at Location 3

1. Pause momentarily as you continue searching to the right. Recheck traffic to the rear, and brake to stop if a vehicle is approaching from the right.
2. If no approaching vehicle is within one-half block of you, search again to the left and right. Proceed through the intersection when your path is clear.

Review It

1. How should you identify an uncontrolled intersection?
2. What should you do at an uncontrolled intersection?

Controlled Intersections

A controlled intersection is one at which signals or signs assign the right of way. Obey all STOP signs, YIELD signs, and traffic signals when approaching a controlled intersection. Yield the right of way to through traffic.

Controlled Intersections with Signals

Traffic signals usually have three lights to each cycle—red, yellow, and green. Signals also can have a fourth or fifth light, such as a yellow arrow and a green arrow. Imagine you are stopped at the red light in the picture. Watch the whole cycle closely. Proceed, with caution, when your light turns green.

As you approach an intersection controlled by a traffic signal, check the signal to see if it is about to change. Identify any cars stopped on the cross street. If a car appears to be starting a turn on a red light, predict that the driver might pull in front of you. Cover the brake. Being ready to stop is the only way to achieve a safe path of travel in this situation.

Treat each intersection as a separate problem. Scanning 12 seconds ahead, search the next intersection to see what color the light is. Look for any traffic moving on the cross street. Before you reach the point where you must brake at an intersection, quickly check left and right. If the light is going to be red or if cross traffic is blocking the way, slow and prepare to stop.

Use the IPDE process when approaching an intersection. Proceed only when you are certain your intended path of travel will be clear. Remember always to yield the right of way to pedestrians.

Signals

Use the IPDE process to handle traffic signals. Identify the color of a signal as soon as you see it. Predict that the color might change as you come closer to the intersection.

Stale Green Light A **stale green light** is a light that has been green for some time. If the light is green and remains green when you first identify it, slow down. Predict that the light will turn yellow soon.

Fresh Green Light A **fresh green light** has just turned from red to green. A fresh green light does not guarantee that you will have a safe path of travel. Be sure that no driver on the cross street is running the yellow or red light. Look left again before you proceed.

What will you do when your signal turns green?

Yellow Light When you approach an intersection as the light turns yellow, you must decide whether to stop or proceed. There is a point of no return, where it is no longer safe to stop without entering the intersection. You must proceed. If the light turns yellow before you reach the point of no return, check traffic to the rear. If it is safe to stop, do so before you enter the intersection. Otherwise, go through the intersection.

Be very careful when completing a left turn on a yellow light. Oncoming traffic might try to hurry through before the light turns red. Wait for all oncoming traffic to stop before starting a turn.

Unprotected Left Turns

An **unprotected left turn** is made at a signal-controlled intersection without a special turn light. When you turn left, you must yield to oncoming traffic. When oncoming vehicles approach the intersection on a green light, they should not have to slow or change position to avoid you.

Procedure for Turning Left

Use this procedure to make an unprotected left turn:
1. Wait until the light turns green. Move to the center of the intersection, as the yellow car in the picture has done.
2. Keep your wheels straight until you are ready to turn. By doing so, you will not be pushed into oncoming lanes of traffic if you are rear-ended.
3. Stay close to the center line so others can pass on your right.
4. Wait until traffic is clear. Turn left into the lane nearest the center line after making a final check on traffic to the right.

Multiple-Lane Streets While waiting to turn left in multiple-lane traffic, make four additional checks, as follows:
1. **Traffic light** Watch the traffic-light cycle in case the light turns yellow. Thus, you will not miss making your turn when the light changes.
2. **Inside lane** Check speed, distance, and number of oncoming vehicles. Predict openings in oncoming traffic.
3. **Outside lane** Check for hard-to-see vehicles that might be hidden by vehicles stopped in the inside lane.
4. **Turning path** Check the exact path your vehicle will take. Look for pedestrians in or near the crosswalk. Begin your turn only when you know you can complete it without stopping. Do not block the outside lane while waiting for pedestrians to clear the crosswalk.

Make four checks when making a left turn on a multiple-lane street.

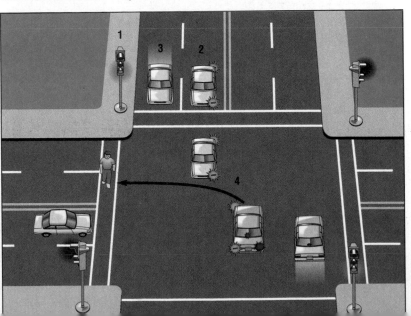

Protected Left Turns

You can make a **protected left turn** when a special left-turn light, green arrow, or delayed green light lets you turn left while oncoming traffic is stopped. The protected turn can occur before or after oncoming traffic proceeds. Left turns might be prohibited when the protected left-turn cycle ends. If the turn is allowed, respond to it as to an unprotected left turn.

Left-Turn Light   A left-turn light provides a protected left turn. The left-turn light can be mounted near the lane with a sign reading LEFT TURN SIGNAL. Some left-turn lights are located over the turn lane without using signs.

Green Arrow   A green arrow can appear with the normal red, yellow, and green cycles. The arrow can come on immediately after the red light or after oncoming traffic has proceeded. In many places the green arrow simply turns off to indicate the protected turn has ended. Other green arrows are followed with a yellow arrow as a warning.
   Watch the light carefully for the end of the protected turn. Watch for oncoming drivers who might proceed, thinking your green arrow is their green light.

The green arrow permits you to make a protected left turn.

Delayed Green   A **delayed green light** indicates that one side of an intersection has a green light while the light for the oncoming traffic remains red. This light allows traffic from one side to turn or go straight before the light for oncoming traffic turns green. Obey your signal only. Do not proceed automatically when oncoming traffic proceeds.

Right-Turn Conflicts

Although a right turn appears to be less dangerous than a left turn, three kinds of conflicts can develop. Be prepared for pedestrian conflicts, conflicts to the rear, and conflicts with oncoming left-turning cars.

Pedestrian Conflicts   As you turn right, pedestrians might step out in front of your car, creating a conflict. Check in and near the crosswalk for pedestrians well before you turn.

Conflicts to the Rear   Signal your right turn one-half block in advance to alert drivers behind you. Check your rearview mirror for following traffic. Tap the brake pedal to flash your brake lights. Recheck following traffic for reactions. Brake early, and slow gradually. If you slow or stop suddenly, cars behind you can run into you.

If you were driving the yellow car, might you have a conflict with another car at this intersection?

Conflicts with Oncoming Left-Turning Vehicles   Study the picture in which cars are turning left and right. Conflicts can develop when two cars are trying to complete turns in the same direction at the same time. Cars turning left often swing wide. Cars turning right might also turn wide. Conflicts can develop if both cars swing wide at the same time. Time your right turn so you complete it just before or after an oncoming driver has completed a left turn. Stay in your lane throughout the turn.

Turns on Red

Most states now permit turns on red. Check local laws to see if a turn on red is legal. If so, you can turn on red unless a posted sign prohibits this turn.

Right on Red   Before turning right on a red light, come to a full stop as you would at a STOP sign. Move to a position where you can see clearly. Look left, then right, then left again. You must yield the right of way to any vehicle or pedestrian in or approaching the intersection. When your path is clear, complete your turn into the nearest right lane.

Left on Red   Some states permit a left turn on red if the turn is from a one-way street onto another one-way street. A few states also permit turning on a red from a left turn lane on a two-way street onto a one-way street. Follow the same procedure as in a right turn on red, except that you look for traffic ahead and to the right. Then turn into the nearest left lane.

Before turning right on red, stop and look for pedestrians as well as vehicles.

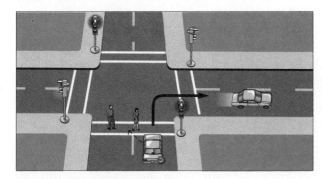

Where do you search for vehicles and pedestrians when turning left on red?

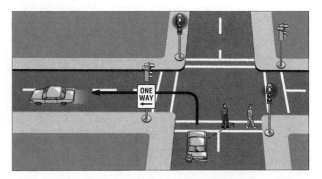

Come to a full stop and allow crossing vehicles to clear the intersection at a YIELD sign.

Controlled Intersections with Signs

Two kinds of signs control intersections. At a STOP sign, before you enter the intersection you must come to a **full stop** at a crosswalk, stop line, or sign if no line or crosswalk exists. At a YIELD sign, slow and yield the right of way to vehicles on the through street.

Signs on corners of an intersection create a through street for traffic not having signs. Drivers facing signs at controlled intersections must yield. However, drivers on through streets have no guarantee that drivers on cross streets will stop.

Blocked View at Stop Sign

Sometimes parked vehicles or other objects block your view at intersections. Follow these steps to cross intersections safely and merge with traffic after stopping. The numbers on the yellow cars refer to the car positions shown in the pictures.

Crossing Traffic   Follow this procedure when you need to cross traffic through an intersection:

Crossing Traffic

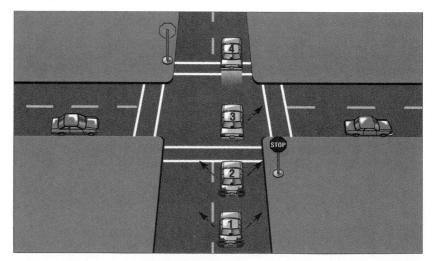

1. Look around and through the windows of parked cars. Continue to glance left, right, and ahead as you creep forward.
2. If your intended path of travel seems clear, move forward to Position 2. Here, you can still stop clear of cars from the left.

3. When the left is clear, glance right. Move to Position 3. Here, you could stop for a car from the right, if necessary.
4. When clear from the right, proceed by accelerating to the proper speed.

Joining Traffic — Right Turn

Take these steps when turning right to join traffic:

1. Search ahead and to the sides. Stop in Position 1, if traffic is approaching from the left. When clear, move forward while steering into the right turn.
2. In Position 2, glance left for traffic, then look ahead, then glance right for your turn path. Glance left once more to check for traffic.
3. When your path is clear, go. At Position 3, accelerate to adjust to traffic speed.

Joining Traffic — Left Turn

Follow these steps when turning left:

1. Glance left and right around and through windows of parked cars after checking ahead.
2. Stop in Position 2, if traffic is approaching from the left.
3. When your left is clear, move to Position 3. Stop, if necessary, for a car from the right.
4. When your path is clear, go. At Position 4, accelerate to a proper speed.

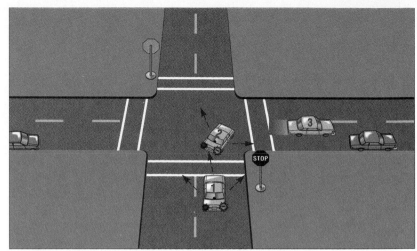

Joining Traffic–Right Turn

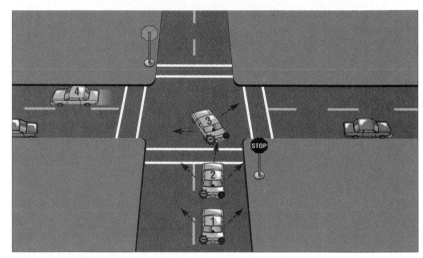

Joining Traffic–Left Turn

Review It

1. How should you approach an intersection with signals?
2. What checks should you make for an unprotected left turn?
3. How can you prevent each of the three right-turn conflicts?
4. How should you make a right turn at a red light?
5. How should you move from a STOP sign to cross traffic when your view is blocked? when joining traffic—right-turn? when joining traffic—left-turn?

Judging Time and Distance

You must be able to judge time and distance at intersections. These judgments are especially important at uncontrolled intersections or at intersections that have only YIELD or STOP signs. These judgments are essential for performing two basic skills at intersections:

- judging gaps between vehicles
- knowing how long it takes to pass through or enter intersecting traffic lanes.

Judging the Size of a Gap

A **gap** is the distance between vehicles. When you enter a through street after stopping at a STOP sign, you must judge the size of the gaps in traffic from the left and right.

You need different-sized gaps, depending on the maneuver you plan to make and the speed of traffic. Crossing a two-lane street takes about 4 to 5 seconds. Turning right and accelerating to 30 mph takes about 6 seconds. Turning left and accelerating to 30 mph takes about 7 seconds. Driver inexperience and reduced traction can increase the time needed to complete a maneuver.

Use these steps to better visualize the size gap you need at an intersection:

1. Stand at a through street, as in the diagram. Pick a car approaching from the left.
2. Start counting at "one-thousand-one, one-thousand-two," and so on.
3. Continue counting until the car passes the intersection. You will see how much time this gap would have given you to cross traffic or to merge safely.

Crossing and Joining Traffic

You need to know how long it takes to turn right, to turn left, and to cross traffic at a typical intersection. Turning right or left into lanes of other vehicles is called **joining** traffic. You must make time-distance judgments to cross or to join traffic.

Estimating Gap Size at 30 mph

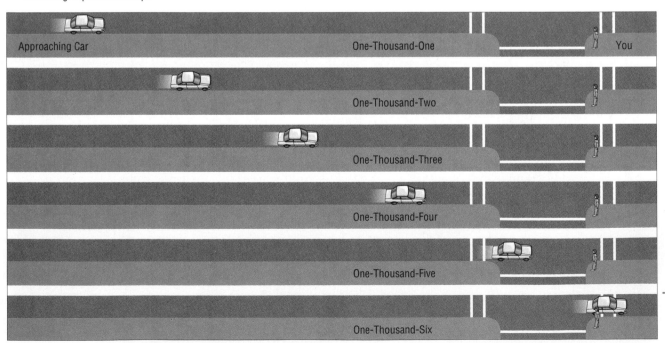

Approaching Car	One-Thousand-One	You
	One-Thousand-Two	
	One-Thousand-Three	
	One-Thousand-Four	
	One-Thousand-Five	
	One-Thousand-Six	

Crossing Traffic

Crossing an intersection takes about 4 seconds from a stop. If traffic on the through street is traveling 30 mph, you need a gap of about two-thirds of a block in each direction.

Joining Traffic–Right Turn

You need a larger gap to join traffic when turning right than when crossing. You need enough distance to reach the speed of through-street traffic without interfering with the flow of traffic.

Imagine you are driving the yellow car in this drawing. To join traffic, the white car must be far enough away so you can turn right and reach 30 mph without forcing the white car to slow. Therefore, the white car must be at least one block away from this intersection.

The faster traffic is moving, the larger the gap must be. At 20 mph, the white car should be more than one-half block away; at 55 mph, more than 3 blocks away.

Joining Traffic–Left Turn

A left turn is more dangerous than a right turn. You cross the paths of traffic from the left before entering traffic from the right.

Slowly cross the lane from the left while still gaining speed. The gap to the left should be greater than when you make a right turn. At 20 mph, you need a gap of more than two-thirds of a block in both directions. At 55 mph, you need a gap of more than three and one-half blocks.

Review It

1. How can you estimate the distance a car on a cross street would travel in 6 seconds at 30 mph?
2. Imagine traffic is moving 30 mph on a through street. How large a gap would you need to cross the street?
3. Why would you need a larger gap to make a left turn than a right turn?

Gap Selection for Crossing and Joining Traffic

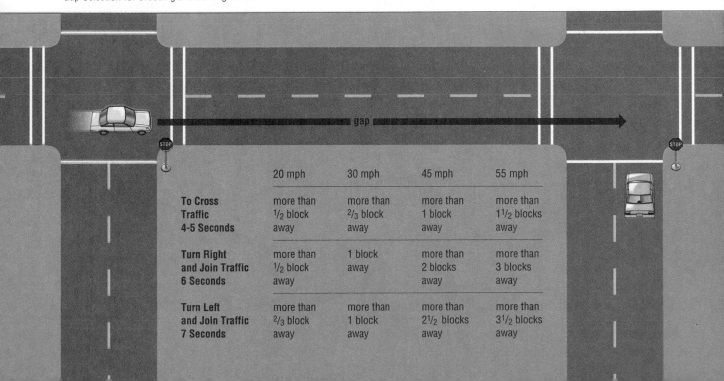

	20 mph	30 mph	45 mph	55 mph
To Cross Traffic **4-5 Seconds**	more than 1/2 block away	more than 2/3 block away	more than 1 block away	more than 1 1/2 blocks away
Turn Right and Join Traffic **6 Seconds**	more than 1/2 block away	1 block away	more than 2 blocks away	more than 3 blocks away
Turn Left and Join Traffic **7 Seconds**	more than 2/3 block away	more than 1 block away	more than 2 1/2 blocks away	more than 3 1/2 blocks away

Determining Right of Way

A defensive driver knows that conflicts often occur at intersections and is prepared to handle these conflicts. As a defensive driver, allow other traffic to go first rather than create a conflict.

What Is Right of Way?

The term **right of way** describes the privilege of having immediate use of a certain part of a roadway. You have the right of way only when other drivers give it to you.

You will often have to **yield,** let others go first, to be safe. Letting others go first is "yielding the right of way." Sometimes you must yield to prevent a collision. At other times, yielding is an act of courtesy. Most of the time, laws determine the right of way.

Situations When You Must Yield

Remember the following points in yield situations:
- Your action should not cause those to whom you should yield the right of way to slow or stop.
- Traffic signs and signals only show who should yield the right of way. They do not stop traffic for you.
- Others can give you the right of way. Never assume others will always yield to you.
- A safe action is to yield the right of way even when the law requires the other driver to yield.
- Failure to yield the right of way is one of the most frequent violations in fatal collisions.

You must yield the right of way in many situations. Knowing right-of-way laws will help you make safe decisions. These drawings show the most common situations regarding yielding the right of way. In each situation the yellow car is required to yield.

Review It

1. What is meant by "yielding the right of way"?
2. When should you yield the right of way?

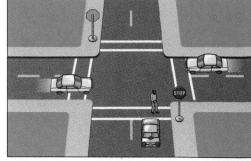

Yield at STOP signs to
- pedestrians in or near the crosswalk
- all traffic on the through street.

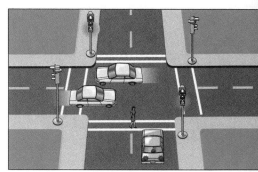

Yield at fresh green lights to
- pedestrians still in the crosswalk
- vehicles still in the intersection.

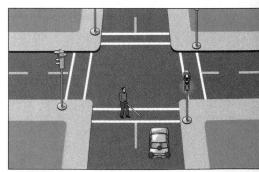

Yield to any blind person
- carrying a white cane or accompanied by a guide dog.

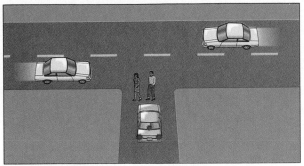

Yield coming from an alley, driveway, or private roadway to

- pedestrians before reaching the sidewalk
- all vehicles on the street. (Make two stops.)

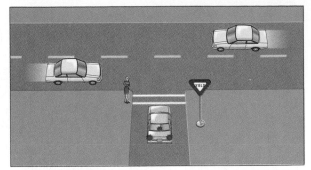

Yield at all YIELD signs to

- all pedestrians in or near crosswalks
- all vehicles on the cross street.

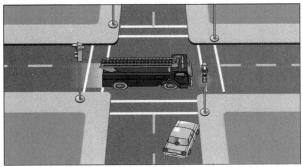

Yield to emergency vehicles

- sounding a siren or using a flashing light. Stop clear of the intersection close to curb. Wait for emergency vehicles to pass.

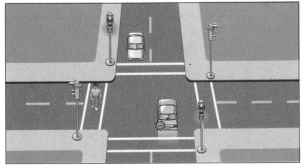

Yield when turning left at any intersection to

- all pedestrians in your turn path
- all oncoming vehicles that are at all close.

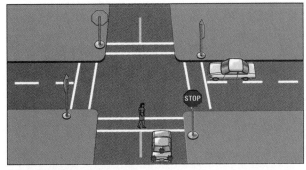

Yield at four-way stops to

- all pedestrians in or near crosswalks
- vehicles that arrive first
- a vehicle from the right if you arrive at the same time.

Yield at uncontrolled intersections to

- pedestrians in or near the crosswalk
- any vehicle that has entered the intersection
- oncoming traffic when you turn left
- a vehicle from the right if you both arrive at the same time.

Railroad Crossings

Railroad crossings are actually a type of intersection. More collisions occur at railroad crossings than most drivers realize. Over half of these collisions involve a driver who lives within two miles of the railroad crossing. A driver can become careless after crossing the same tracks day after day and seeing only an occasional train. The driver often forgets that the railroad crossing is a hazard.

Railroad crossings are nearly always marked. In towns and cities, a round, yellow railroad-crossing sign is posted about 250 feet from a crossing. In rural areas this sign is about 750 feet from a crossing. A **crossbuck**, a large, white X-shaped sign, often is located beside the crossing. Many times a large, white X is painted on the roadway near the crossing.

Controlled Crossings

A **controlled railroad crossing** usually has both red lights and crossing gates. Make a complete stop when the lights are flashing or the gates are down. Remain stopped until the lights stop flashing and the gates are raised. It is illegal to drive around the gates.

Uncontrolled Crossings

An **uncontrolled railroad crossing** does not have red lights or crossing gates. However, most uncontrolled crossings, like controlled crossings, are marked with a round, yellow railroad-crossing sign and the crossbuck shown here. Treat uncontrolled crossings the same as an intersection with a YIELD sign. Slow and be prepared to stop.

Crossing Railroad Tracks

Take these actions when approaching a railroad crossing:

1. Slow down. Check traffic to the side and to the rear as you approach the round railroad-crossing sign.
2. Turn off the radio, air conditioner, or heater fan to listen for train sounds. Open window, if the area is noisy.
3. Reduce speed to handle a possible rough road crossing. Check available sight distance. Reduce speed if the sight distance is short.
4. Stop at a safe distance before the tracks if a train is approaching, if the red lights are flashing, or if the crossing gates are down.
5. Wait for the train to clear. Then check the crossing. Be sure another train is not approaching on another set of tracks.
6. If it is safe to cross, try to keep your speed up to at

A railroad crossing is an intersection that requires special caution.

least 20 mph. Then your car can roll across the tracks if its engine should stall.

7. If you have a stickshift, shift to a lower gear before crossing to prevent stalling on the tracks.
8. Drive onto the tracks only after you have enough space and speed to clear the tracks. Make sure any vehicles ahead clear the tracks before you start to cross. Never stop on railroad tracks, waiting for traffic ahead to move.
9. When following buses or trucks hauling flammable contents, be prepared for them to stop. Some states require such vehicles to stop at all crossings.

Review It

1. What signs appear at or near controlled and uncontrolled railroad crossings?
2. What are the procedures to use at a railroad crossing?

DECISION MAKING

1. You are driving the yellow car and are approaching an uncontrolled intersection. You and the other car are the same distance from the intersection. What do you predict about the other driver? What should you do?

2. You have just stopped at a red light. You wish to turn left. Is a left turn at this intersection legal on a red light? Where should you check before turning?

3. You are driving the white car, approaching an intersection where several cars are stopped for a traffic light. Note the railroad tracks in front of you. Where should you stop? What could happen in this situation?

4. You are driving the blue car that is stopped at the STOP sign. At what speed would you assume the cars on the through highway would be traveling? How far away would the cars have to be for you to turn left?

CHAPTER 7 REVIEW

Review Chapter Objectives

7–1 Uncontrolled Intersections
1. How do you identify an uncontrolled intersection? (118)
2. What are the procedures to follow at an uncontrolled intersection? (119)

7–2 Controlled Intersections
3. How should you approach a controlled intersection with signals? (120)
4. What actions should you take when making both unprotected and protected left turns? (121–122)
5. What are three possible right-turn conflicts? (122–123)
6. How should you turn right and left at a red light? (124)
7. What steps should you take to move from a STOP sign when your view is blocked? (124)

7–3 Judging Time and Distance
8. How should you judge gaps in traffic? (126)
9. What should you do to cross and join traffic? (127)

7–4 Determining Right of Way
10. What is right of way? (128)
11. What are the situations in which you must yield the right of way? (128–129)

7–5 Railroad Crossings
12. What are the differences between controlled and uncontrolled railroad crossings? (130)
13. What are the procedures for crossing railroad tracks? (130)

Check Your Knowledge

Multiple Choice Copy the number of each sentence below on a sheet of paper. Choose the letter that best completes the statement or answers the question.

1. An uncontrolled intersection is one in which
   (a) there is no traffic. (b) there are no traffic-control signs or signals. (c) signs assign the right of way. (d) drivers do not yield the right of way. (118)
2. Where should the identification process begin at an uncontrolled intersection?
   (a) 12 seconds before intersection. (b) one-fourth block from the intersection. (c) just before the crosswalk. (d) just as the front wheels reach the crosswalk (119)
3. When you are about to cross an uncontrolled two-way street, first look
   (a) left. (b) right. (c) straight ahead. (d) at the speedometer. (118)
4. In most states, you can make a right turn during a red light when
   (a) turning onto a one-way street. (b) forcing other traffic to slow down. (c) no sign prohibits it. (d) pulling out with traffic. (123)
5. Which action takes the least amount of time at a typical intersection?
   (a) crossing an intersection. (b) turning left. (c) turning right. (d) waiting for a train to pass. (126)

Completion Copy the number of each sentence below. After each number, write the letter of the word or words that complete the sentence correctly.

6. A traffic light that is green when you first see it, but will soon turn yellow is a _____ . (120)
7. Keep your wheels _____ while stopped in an intersection waiting to turn left. (121)
8. When you have a protected left turn, oncoming drivers face a _____ . (122)
9. Crossing an _____ from a stop takes about four seconds. (127)
10. Fitting into a gap in traffic is called _____ . (126)
11. You _____ when you allow another driver to proceed first. (128)
12. At an uncontrolled intersection, the driver on the left must yield to the driver on the _____ . (129)
13. You must always yield to _____ . (129)

Check Vocabulary

Copy the number of each phrase below. Match the definition in List A with the term it defines in List B.

List A
14. intersection regulated by signs or signals (118)
15. light that has just turned from red to green (120)
16. left turn made at an intersection that does not have a special turn light (121)
17. turn made on a left-turn light or arrow while oncoming traffic is stopped (122)
18. distance between approaching cars in which to cross an intersection or join traffic (126)
19. privilege of immediate use of the roadway (128)
20. crossing with crossing gates and signals (130)
21. crossing without crossing gates and signals (130)
22. large, white X-shaped sign (130)

List B
a. controlled intersection
b. controlled railroad crossing
c. crossbuck
d. fresh green light
e. gap
f. protected left turn
g. right of way
h. uncontrolled railroad crossing
i. unprotected left turn
j. yield

Check Your Understanding

Write a short answer for each question or statement.

23. What should you *not* assume when you are to the right of another driver at an uncontrolled intersection? (118)
24. Why do you need to watch for oncoming drivers when making a left turn on a green arrow? (122)
25. Does it take a bigger gap in traffic to make a right turn and join traffic than it does to cross traffic? Explain your answer.(127)
26. Why do drivers who think they have the right of way have a greater chance of collision? (128)
27. Do you need to stop at a railroad crossing when red lights are flashing and no train is within sight? Explain your answer. (130)

Think Critically

Write a paragraph to answer each question or statement.

1. Could the vehicle crossing in front of you in the picture have had to stop at a STOP sign before proceeding? Why?

2. Two vehicles have collided at an intersection. What factors should be considered to determine which driver should have yielded the right of way?
3. What factors will determine if you will need more or less gap when crossing or joining traffic twenty years from now under the same roadway and vehicle conditions?

Projects

1. Clip two articles reporting intersection collisions from your local newspaper. Analyze each report to determine which vehicle should have yielded the right of way. **Write** a summary of your findings and compare your opinions with other classmates analyzing the same collisions.
2. Imagine that all intersections in your neighborhood are uncontrolled. Would it take less or more time to drive a mile from your home? Why?

Chapter 8

SHARING THE ROADWAY

You're the Driver!

As a driver, you will be sharing the roadway with a variety of other vehicles and pedestrians. These other users present their own special problems in your driving environment.

What problem might this motorcyclist have when he starts through the intersection?

Where should the car driver predict there might be an oncoming motorcycle?

What conflict might be caused by the open door on the right?

As a driver, you must know what actions to expect from other users. This chapter explores the problems presented by pedestrians, motorcyclists, trucks, special-purpose vehicles, buses, and emergency vehicles.

Objectives

Section 8–1   Interacting with Motorcycles
1. Tell why you have the major share of responsibility for protecting motorcyclists.
2. Tell how to use the IPDE process to protect motorcyclists while driving.
3. Describe situations where you should look for motorcyclists while driving.

Section 8–2   Motorcyclist Actions That Can Affect You
4. Compare acceleration and braking abilities of motorcycles and cars.
5. List the protective equipment a motorcyclist should use.
6. Tell how motorcyclists can help reduce conflicts.

Section 8–3 Interacting with Bicycles, Mopeds, and Motor Scooters

7. Tell how you can help prevent conflicts with bicyclists.
8. List the guidelines that moped and motor scooter drivers should follow when riding.

Section 8–4 Pedestrians and Other Roadway Users

9. Name areas where you can expect to encounter pedestrians.
10. List precautions to take when near buses and in parking lots.
11. List three steps to take to clear the way for emergency vehicles.

Section 8–5 Interacting with Trucks

12. List the guidelines you should follow when passing large trucks.
13. Describe situations in which you should not pass a truck on the right.

Interacting with Motorcyclists

You might never ride a motorcycle. However, you will be a safer driver if you understand some problems involved with motorcycles and motorcyclists.

Deaths from motorcycle crashes increased a few years ago as the number of motorcycles increased. Recently, however, the number of motorcycle registrations has declined. The death rate in motorcycle crashes also has dropped. At the same time, the use of other, lower powered, two- wheeled vehicles such as motor scooters has increased.

Injuries and deaths from motorcycle crashes result primarily from the exposed position of the rider. Unlike the driver of a larger four-wheel vehicle, a motorcyclist has little or no protection. The motorcycle's small size, instability, and handling characteristics add to its problems in traffic.

As the driver of a larger vehicle, you must accept the major share of responsibility for protecting motorcyclists as they interact within the HTS. Show cyclists the same courtesy you show other drivers. Motorcyclists are entitled to their share of the roadway. However, they too have a responsibility to follow safe driving practices. They must obey traffic laws, ride defensively, understand the problems motorcycles present, and make every effort to avoid conflict.

Using the IPDE Process to Protect Motorcyclists

Most drivers tend to be alert for other cars and larger vehicles that might cause conflicts. Motorcycles are smaller than cars and can be driven in several different positions within a traffic lane. Therefore, other roadway users must make extra efforts to be aware of motorcyclists. Other roadway users can use the IPDE process to help prevent conflicts.

The identify step is crucial for drivers because motorcycles are more difficult to see than larger vehicles, particularly in rush-hour traffic. The size and location of motorcycle taillights, brake lights, and turn signals also make motorcycles less noticeable. The small size of motorcycles also makes it difficult for car drivers to judge motorcycle speed and distance in traffic, especially at night.

Identify places where motorcycles might be hidden from view. Scanning the roadway ahead and behind for motorcyclists requires an understanding of where they might be and what they might do.

Predict the possible actions of motorcyclists by remembering the instability factor and the handling characteristics of motorcycles. Base your decisions on the problems and conditions confronting the motorcyclist. In short, think like the motorcyclist.

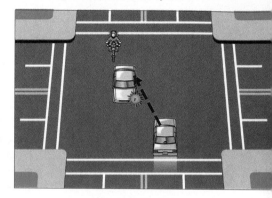

Scan through the windows of other cars to see motorcyclists or other roadway users.

Execute your actions smoothly, and avoid sudden actions that can surprise the motorcyclist. The driver in the picture has caused a possible conflict by opening the car door before checking to see if a motorcyclist is there. If the car driver had checked the rearview mirrors and left blind-spot area, this possible conflict would not have occurred.

Before opening a car door, check your mirror and blind-spot area for cyclists.

Where to Look for Motorcyclists

Cyclists can travel several places within a traffic lane and can appear suddenly if you are not alert for them. Look for motorcyclists in the following situations.

Vehicle Turning Left in Front of Motorcyclist   When you are planning to turn left across a lane of oncoming traffic, be very sure your planned path is clear. Even though the cyclist in the picture above is signaling for a left turn, the car driver should predict the cyclist might continue straight. The car driver should complete the left turn only after the motorcyclist has started in the path of a left turn. When you are turning left at night, be especially watchful for motorcycle headlights.

Vehicle Turning Right at Intersection or Driveway   Car drivers who do not check their mirrors and blind spots frequently might not be aware of traffic to the rear. Therefore, they may turn right directly in

The car driver should let the motorcyclist start the turn first.

front of a motorcyclist, as in the photograph at the left below.

Motorcyclist Turning Left
In the picture, the oncoming motorcyclist may be blocked from the view of the driver of the yellow car. That driver should be scanning through the windows of the white car in the next lane. When you cannot see the entire intersection clearly, expect smaller vehicles to appear in your path, and be prepared to act to avoid conflict.

Motorcyclist Passing Car on Right or Left   Check your rearview mirrors and blind spots frequently, anticipating that motorcyclists will pass you. The

failure of many vehicle drivers to check their mirrors and blind-spot areas can easily lead to conflict with motorcyclists. Be especially aware of being passed on either the right or left at an intersection where there is more space. Even though motorcyclists should not pass at intersections, always watch for them so you can avoid conflict. When you are being overtaken by a motorcyclist, maintain both your lane position and your speed.

Scan for small vehicles that might turn as you drive through intersections.

This possible conflict could have been prevented if the car driver had checked the right blind spot. The motorcyclist should have kept a greater following distance and stayed out of the blind spot.

Motorcyclist Meeting an Oncoming Car You are more likely to see an oncoming motorcyclist in the daytime if the motorcycle's headlight is on, as in the top picture. Many states require that the motorcycle's headlight be on at all times. Whenever you see an oncoming motorcyclist, stay on your side of the roadway until the motorcyclist has passed.

Tailgating Motorcyclist
Braking distance is about the same for cars and motorcycles under ideal conditions and with skillful use of brakes. However, if the driver of the yellow car in the picture brakes suddenly to let the car on the shoulder in, the tailgating motorcyclist could lose control. The motorcyclist does not have enough following distance to stop in time. When following another vehicle, check your rearview mirrors and increase your following distance to 3 seconds or more if a cyclist is tailgating you.

Motorcyclist Riding in Driver's Blind Spot Because of its small size, a motorcycle is often hard to see in the blind-spot areas behind your vehicle. The roof-support columns on the back and sides of vehicles add to the problem of seeing cyclists in the blind-spot areas. Always check your blind-spot areas with a glance over your shoulder before turning or changing lanes.

Stay in your lane until an approaching motorcyclist has passed.

Watch for tailgating motorcyclists if you slow or stop suddenly.

Passing a Motorcyclist

When you plan to overtake and pass a motorcyclist, stay well back until you start to pass. Do not tailgate a cyclist before passing. The appearance of a very close vehicle in the cyclist's rearview mirror could cause an unexpected action and a conflict.

When the way is clear, execute your passing maneuver. Tap your horn to alert the cyclist you are going to pass. Use the entire left lane for passing so as not to crowd the cyclist. Return to the right lane only after you can see the cyclist in your rearview mirror.

A roof-support column can hide a motorcyclist in a driver's blind spot.

Protecting Motorcyclists

Unlike a driver protected inside a car, a motorcyclist is fully exposed to dangers that might cause injury or death. For this reason, you must accept an extra share of responsibility for avoiding conflicts with cyclists. The following characteristics of motorcyclists and motorcycles can cause special problems.

Motorcyclists Can Lack Experience and Skill   Some motorcyclists ride rented or borrowed motorcycles and have not had enough practice to develop sound judgment and good control. Others, who own their own motorcycles, might not have received proper riding instruction. Be alert when approaching a cyclist. Predict judgment and control errors due to inexperience and lack of skill.

Handling Traits of Motorcycles   Help protect motorcyclists from conflicts by being aware of the handling traits of motorcycles and how they operate. Notice in the picture that the motorcyclist leans to the side when making a turn. A cyclist can have difficulty handling a motorcycle in a turn or curve on windy or rainy days or on rough roadways.

Increase Your Following Distance
Most motorcycles have only two wheels in contact with the ground and are less stable than cars. A motorcyclist's balance

Motorcyclists lean when making turns. Car drivers should watch a motorcyclist's shoulders to anticipate turns.

Increase your following distance on gravel roads where traction is poor.

and stability depend on the two small areas of tires gripping the roadway. Water, sand, oil slicks, wet leaves, potholes, or loose gravel reduce traction and can make motorcycle control even more uncertain.

Watch for a motorcyclist's balance and stability problems. Predict that the motorcyclist might maneuver unexpectedly or even fall. Give the cyclist extra space by increasing your following distance to at least 3 seconds. By doing so, you give yourself an extra margin of safety should the cyclist fall.

Make the Motorcyclist Aware of You
When you are following a motorcyclist, do not assume the cyclist is aware of your presence. Traffic noise and motorcycle noise make it more difficult for the cyclist to hear. Protective helmets worn by cyclists might

also muffle some traffic sounds. The small size of the mirrors on the handlebars and the vibration of the motorcycle can restrict the motorcyclist's view to the rear. Keep extra space in your front zone when you think a cyclist is unaware of your presence.

Review It

1. Why must a car driver accept a large share of responsibility for protecting motorcyclists?
2. How can you use the IPDE process to help protect motorcyclists while driving?
3. What are five places where you should look for motorcyclists while driving?
4. What procedure should you follow when passing a motorcyclist?

Motorcyclist Actions that Can Affect You

Although you share the responsibility for protecting motorcyclists, they have the primary responsibility for avoiding collisions. How motorcyclists ride, their protective equipment, and their special riding problems affect other roadway users.

How Motorcyclists Ride

Since motorcyclists share the roadways with others and present special problems, cyclists should develop safe riding skills. The best way to learn the skills needed to ride safely is to take a motorcycle-riding course taught by a certified instructor. Many high schools, colleges, and some safety councils offer

such instruction. Proper training and more widespread helmet use have helped reduce motorcycle fatalities.

The basic procedures for operating a motorcycle safely are even more critical than those procedures for a car. A beginning cyclist must learn to start, stop, balance, and control a motorcycle safely before riding in traffic.

Braking and Accelerating

A car driver needs only to step on the foot-brake pedal to stop a car. However, a motorcyclist must operate separate brakes for front and rear wheels. A lever on the right handlebar operates the **front brake.** This brake supplies up to 70 percent of the motorcycle's braking power. A foot pedal controls the **rear brake.** A cyclist must coordinate both foot and hand brakes carefully for maximum braking. If the front brake is applied too

hard, it can lock the front wheel and cause loss of control. This action often causes collisions with other roadway users.

A motorcyclist must coordinate the hand throttle, hand clutch, and foot-gearshift lever to accelerate smoothly. Balance problems can occur if the cyclist does not coordinate the throttle and clutch properly.

Loss of Balance

Unlike a four-wheeled vehicle, a motorcycle might have difficulty remaining upright while in motion. Be alert and anticipate that motorcyclists can lose balance due to the following:

Surface Conditions Sand, mud, gravel, oil drippings, water, and objects on the roadway can cause balance and control problems for motorcyclists.

Following Distance

Motorcyclists can increase following distance to reduce risk of collisions. They should use a 3-second following distance, since they might not be stable in a sudden stop.

Motorcyclists also must maintain a safe following distance to avoid being struck by small pebbles or dirt thrown back by the vehicle ahead. Trying to avoid the dirt or pebbles can cause motorcyclists to lose balance. As a driver, check your rearview mirrors often, be aware of following motorcyclists, and avoid making sudden stops.

The motorcyclist ahead of you might be trying to keep a 3-second following distance.

Use of Protective Equipment

Since cars can injure motorcyclists severely in a collision, it is the responsibility of motorcyclists to protect themselves. Motorcyclists can reduce or prevent injuries by using **protective equipment.** A motorcyclist's protective equipment includes such items as:

- **helmet**—the headgear worn to reduce or prevent head injuries
- eye-protection—goggles or a **face shield,** a plastic device attached to the helmet
- heavy shoes or boots
- full-length pants and jacket made of heavy material
- gloves.

Helmets are important in saving lives. In an accident, a motorcyclist who does not wear a helmet is three times more likely to suffer fatal head and neck injuries than a rider who wears a helmet.

Special Riding Problems

Weather and roadway conditions present greater problems to cyclists than they do to drivers of larger vehicles. Allow extra time and space for motorcyclists in all adverse conditions. When you are following motorcyclists who are crossing railroad tracks or carrying passengers, use extra caution.

Adverse Weather Conditions

A motorcyclist cannot cope with adverse weather conditions as well as you can. For example, a puddle might hide a pothole that jolts your car. That same hidden hole can throw a motorcycle out of control.

Just as for car drivers, the worst time for motorcyclists is immediately after rain starts. As rain mixes with dirt and oil on the roadway, traction is greatly reduced. Since balance is important for motorcycle control, reduced traction is far more critical to motorcyclists.

You can turn on your windshield wipers when it rains. When dirt splashes on the windshield, you can use the windshield washers. A cyclist has neither device. Therefore, the motorcyclist's vision is greatly reduced and can be distorted under these conditions.

Motorcyclists should use extreme care crossing railroad tracks and painted lines on roadways as they can be extremely slippery when wet. Motorcyclists can gain extra traction by riding in a vehicle's wheel tracks. This practice can help prevent a collision if the car driver needs to brake suddenly.

As a car driver, remember that bad weather makes it

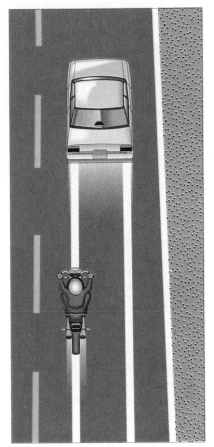

Motorcyclists can gain traction on wet roads by riding in a vehicle's tracks.

harder to see a cyclist who might be hurrying to find protection from the weather. Be extra alert and allow a much larger space cushion under adverse conditions.

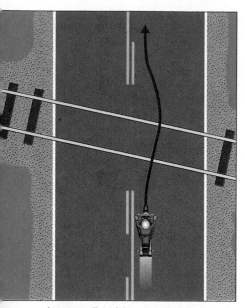

A motorcyclist might swerve in order to cross tracks as close to a right angle as possible.

Motorcyclists Crossing Railroad Tracks Railroad tracks are a special problem for motorcyclists. Motorcycle tires can get caught in the grooves of the crossing, causing the motorcyclist to lose balance. A cyclist should cross railroad tracks as close to a right angle as possible, as long as this does not cause the cyclist to enter another lane. You should predict that the cyclist might lose balance or control at a crossing.

Motorcyclists Carrying Passengers A motorcycle carrying two people calls for double caution from car drivers. Be alert for a difference in acceleration, braking, and turning when a motorcyclist is carrying a passenger.

A passenger can create balance and control problems for a cyclist. The passenger might lean the wrong way on curves and turns, or might bump the cyclist when brakes are applied suddenly. Motorcyclists should not carry passengers until they have mastered a variety of traffic situations alone.

How Motorcyclists Can Help Car Drivers

Motorcyclists can use special strategies to reduce conflicts. However, the safe-riding strategies of motorcyclists should not diminish the caution you must practice near motorcyclists.

Be Visible in Traffic Motorcyclists should position themselves in traffic so they will be seen easily. Riding in the left wheel track of the car ahead makes a motorcyclist most visible. A cyclist in the correct position is visible to the driver ahead and to oncoming drivers.

Riding on the left side of the lane also forces other drivers to use the other lane to pass. This position adds safety to the passing maneuver. It also reduces the chance that the cyclist will be forced off the roadway.

Motorcyclists should not ride between lines of moving vehicles. This practice is both illegal and dangerous for everyone.

To be most visible in traffic, a motorcyclist might try to stay in the left track of the car ahead.

When riding in groups, the cyclist on the left should be ahead of the one on the right.

The reflective tape on the cyclist's clothing and the extra reflectors on the motorcycle make this motorcyclist more visible to other drivers at night.

Riding in Groups Motorcyclists often travel in groups, especially in pairs. When you see one cyclist, be prepared to see others. Cyclists should not ride side by side in traffic. Such

When turning, motorcyclists should move into single file and turn in the correct lane.

riding can be hazardous if one cyclist loses control.

Motorcyclists' positions in the traffic lane should be staggered. The cyclist on the left should be ahead of the cyclist on the right. This position allows either rider to swerve without hitting the other.

Motorcyclists should make turns at corners in single file and turn in the correct lane. Always give motorcyclists extra space to turn in front of you.

Riding at Night It is far more difficult for car drivers to judge the speed and the position of a motorcycle at night. Because a cyclist's taillight is generally small, drivers behind may have difficulty seeing it.

Motorcyclists should take added precautions when riding

at night. They can make themselves more visible by putting reflective tape on helmets and clothing. Putting extra reflectors on the motorcycle also helps make it more visible.

Review It

1. How do a motorcycle's braking and acceleration differ from those of a car?
2. What protective equipment should a motorcyclist use?
3. How do adverse conditions and roadway problems affect motorcyclists?
4. What procedures should motorcyclists follow when riding in groups?
5. How can motorcyclists make themselves more visible when riding at night?

Interacting with Bicycles, Mopeds, and Motor Scooters

Many people use bicycles and low-powered two-wheeled vehicles for transportation. The small size and low price of mopeds and motor scooters have contributed to their popularity. The exhaust from vehicle engines is still a major source of pollution of our environment. Thus, for economy, environmental preservation, convenience, and recreation, roadway users often use two-wheeled vehicles for short trips and local errands.

Users of the smaller two-wheeled vehicles have the same rights and responsibilities as other drivers. Both larger-vehicle drivers and bicyclists are required to obey the same traffic laws. We all share the roadways. By cooperating, we can avoid conflicts. However, drivers of larger vehicles with their greater protection must accept the major responsibility for avoiding conflict.

When bicycle riding at night, wear reflective clothing and have reflective material on helmets and bicycles.

Bicyclists' Responsibilities

Bicyclists must share the responsibility for avoiding conflicts. Because of their small size and maneuverability, bicyclists can turn so quickly that they can surprise you and cause a collision. To be a responsible bicyclist, follow these safe-riding practices:

- Ride on the right-hand side of the roadway.
- Obey all signs, signals, and traffic laws.
- Walk bicycles across busy intersections.
- Wear light-colored clothing and have reflectors on bicycles used at night.
- Do not listen to music through earphones while bicycling. Wearing earphones while bicycling or driving a motor vehicle is illegal in many states.
- Keep bicycles in safe operating condition.

In some places, a bicyclist is required to have a horn or some other noise-making device. Reflective tape on the frame and fenders of your bicycle adds safety for night riding. When riding at night, you should also have a headlight that is visible for at least 500 feet.

More and more bicyclists wear helmets for increased protection. Even the best bicyclists cannot predict when they might be involved in a collision. Helmets are cheap insurance against serious head injury.

Bicycle safety programs in elementary and junior high schools help develop rider responsibility and reduce conflict between bicyclists and drivers. Increased police enforcement of bicycle riding regulations, along with greater driver awareness of bicyclists, can also reduce potential conflict between riders and drivers.

Protecting Bicyclists

As a driver of a larger vehicle, give bicyclists extra space whenever possible. Some bicyclists might not be able to control their bicycles well and might suddenly get in your path. When following a bicyclist, be aware of the possible pathways the cyclist can take. The cyclist may swerve into your path because of a variety of hazards. Scan the roadway ahead of cyclists as you search for potholes, puddles, storm drains, and railroad tracks. Predicting a possible change of direction by the cyclist usually enables you to stop in time to avoid a collision.

Use the IPDE process constantly as you encounter bicyclists. Scan wide enough to include the sides of the roadways as well as sidewalks. Whenever you identify a cyclist in a traffic situation, predict every possible action the cyclist might take. You then are better prepared to decide on the correct action to execute.

Preventing Conflicts with Bicyclists Passing bicyclists on a two-lane roadway presents a problem for both drivers and riders. Consider the position of the cyclist in traffic when you plan to pass.

Always start your passing maneuver well behind the cyclist. You should have at least one-half of a lane between your car and the bicyclist. If you do not have this space, wait for a gap in oncoming traffic and then pass.

Use these techniques to help prevent conflicts with bicyclists:

- Warn a bicyclist of your presence with a tap on the horn before you move to pass.
- Signal early when you plan to turn or stop.
- Help others identify a bicyclist by adjusting your position. At night, use low-beam headlights or a brief flick of high-beam headlights so that others can see the cyclist. Avoid shining your high-beam headlights into a cyclist's eyes. The glare could temporarily blind the cyclist.
- Reduce speed when a bicyclist presents a problem.
- Look for bicyclists before opening the street-side door. Opening a door into a cyclist's path causes many collisions.

Large tricycles have become popular in many communities, especially retirement areas.

Even though these tricycles are larger than bicycles and are more readily visible, they can become a hazard. They tend to move more slowly in the traffic scene and may tip over easily if they are turned too quickly. Be alert for and protective of riders of these large tricycles when they are a part of your traffic environment.

Large tricycles provide transportation and exercise, but they move more slowly than other vehicles.

To pass a bicyclist safely, have one-half lane of space between the bicyclist and your car.

Mopeds and Motor Scooters

The word *moped* is combined from *mo*tor-driven bicycle and *ped*al-driven bicycle. Like a bicycle, it can be pedaled and can be stopped with a hand brake. Like a motorcycle, it is powered by an engine and controlled by a hand throttle. The engine on a moped is very small and can produce only 1 or 2 horsepower.

Motor scooters are also low-powered, two-wheeled vehicles. They are more powerful than mopeds. Motor scooters are similar to small motorcycles, though most scooters require no shifting.

Moped and Motor Scooter Restrictions   Most states require moped and motor scooter operators to have a driver's license. Some states have a special moped operators' license or certificate.

Mopeds and motor scooters are restricted from certain high-speed roadways. Both the speed and the acceleration of mopeds are limited. Since they do not accelerate to traffic speed as quickly as a car or motorcycle, they may be unable to keep up with the traffic flow. Maximum speed for a moped is usually between 25 to 40 mph. With a passenger, mopeds accelerate even more slowly. Therefore, passengers should not be carried on mopeds in traffic.

Motor scooters with higher powered engines are permitted

Wear protective clothing when driving a motor scooter.

on some roadways with higher speed limits. It is important for motor scooter owners to know the local requirements and state laws that regulate the operation of their vehicles.

Responsibilities of Moped and Motor Scooter Drivers   Even though these vehicles are smaller than motorcycles, their drivers can benefit from taking a rider training course. Information about courses is available from the Motorcycle Safety Foundation.

In addition to observing laws and local requirements, moped and motor scooter drivers should follow these guidelines:
- Wear protective clothing, including helmet, face shield or goggles, long sleeved shirt or jacket, full-length heavy pants, boots, and gloves.
- Before riding, check tires, oil and fuel levels, lights and horn.

- Check the operation of the brakes each time you start out.
- Have the headlight on at all times.
- Position yourself in the lane so you can be seen by others.
- Keep a space cushion between yourself and other vehicles.
- Increase your following distance at night and when carrying a passenger.
- Be especially cautious when riding on wet or slippery surfaces. Brake carefully and avoid skidding or locking up the brakes.
- Use the IPDE process, concentrate on the driving task, and always set a good example for others.

Drivers of larger vehicles should predict possible sudden actions from drivers of mopeds and motor scooters. Since the smaller vehicles are quieter and less noticeable than motorcycles, there is a greater possibility for conflict. You must be especially alert when you are driving near a moped or motor scooter. You must take every precaution to avoid conflict.

Review It

1. What safe riding practices should bicyclists follow?
2. In what ways can you help protect bicyclists?
3. What guidelines should drivers of mopeds and motor scooters follow?

Pedestrians and Other Roadway Users

Of all highway users, pedestrians are the most vulnerable. It is the special responsibility of motorists to watch for and protect pedestrians.

Pedestrians

Many pedestrians who do not drive are not fully aware of all traffic laws and signals. Many do not know the distance needed to stop a moving vehicle. Children and older people are most at risk. Children can act impulsively and might run into traffic without thinking. Older people may take longer to cross streets. They may not be able to see or hear well and may be unaware of possible conflicts.

Never assume that pedestrians will move out of the way. In many situations you will have to stop to allow a pedestrian to cross the street safely. Try to let them know you are there. Many times a simple wave of your hand or a tap on the horn will do. Use the IPDE process continually and be ready to stop for pedestrians.

Learn where you can expect to see pedestrians and be extra alert when approaching the following areas:

Crosswalks and Intersections

Many pedestrians assume that drivers will yield the right-of-way to anyone in the crosswalk. When they cross at an intersection with a green light, pedestrians might not even look for cars.

Pedestrians waiting to cross a street often stand in the street instead of on the curb. They may even dash across the street

Safe Driving Tips

Some states have laws requiring drivers to yield the right-of-way to any pedestrian who is in a crosswalk. Pedestrian crosswalks might be painted on the street in mid-block. Know the laws for each state you are driving in and always be prepared to yield to pedestrians.

without warning. During rain or snow many pedestrians are concerned about protection from the weather. They may be hurrying and paying very little attention to the moving traffic.

Be alert for pedestrians at night. Even in well lighted areas, it is often difficult to identify pedestrians at night.

Alleys and Driveways   When leaving an alley or driveway, always stop before crossing the sidewalk, and look for pedestrians. Tap your horn as a warning. Once across a sidewalk, be prepared to stop again if traffic is coming.

Jogging Areas   Although a jogger is safer using a sidewalk or jogging path, you might encounter joggers on the street. A jogger who is coming toward you should see you. However, a jogger whose back is toward you might not hear you. In any event, be ready to slow, steer around, or stop for joggers.

Be especially alert for pedestrians as you drive out of an alley or driveway where buildings obstruct your view. Be prepared to stop.

The van is preventing the backing driver and the pedestrians from seeing each other.

The Driver as a Pedestrian

The moment you step from your vehicle, you are a pedestrian, without the protective shield of your vehicle. When you are a pedestrian in town or rural traffic situations, make an extra effort to obey all traffic rules. Because you know about driving, you are more aware of the possible problems and conflicts of pedestrians.

When you are a pedestrian at night, protect yourself by being seen. Wear something white or carry a light. Try to be where drivers expect to see you. Do not walk into traffic lanes from between parked cars. If you are a jogger, use sidewalks or jogging paths. Use your IPDE process and be as responsible as you try to be as a driver.

Parking Lots

Pedestrians as well as other vehicles present problems for drivers in parking lots. Such problems develop because drivers traveling at low speeds do not expect anything to happen. You may not realize that a vehicle, a pedestrian, or a bicyclist in a parking lot does not have to move very far or very fast to cause a conflict. Even at lower speeds many property damage collisions and injuries occur in parking lots.

Use these guidelines to lower your risk when driving in parking lots:
- Drive no faster than 15 mph.
- Follow the routes for traffic. Obey the traffic arrows on signs or on the pavement. Do not drive diagonally across a partially empty parking lot because other drivers will not be able to predict where you are going or what you intend to do.
- Watch carefully for pedestrians, especially for children.
- Avoid tight parking spaces. Try to avoid parking in end spaces where a turning vehicle might strike you.
- Do not back into an angle space. If you back in, you will be headed against the flow of traffic when you leave.
- Drive far enough into the space so the rear of your vehicle will not extend into the path of moving traffic.
- Position your vehicle properly in the parking space. Parking too far forward or too much to the right or left creates problems for others.
- When leaving your vehicle, avoid letting the door swing out and hit the next vehicle.
- Secure the vehicle properly and lock it when you leave.
- Keep looking in all directions when backing out of a parking space.
- Watch for others who may be backing out and may not be able to see your vehicle.

Parking garages and underground lots can be a source of potential conflict. Space is often limited in such areas, and turns must be very sharp. Turn your headlights on to help others see you in such areas.

Special Purpose Vehicles

Campers and house trailers towed by other vehicles require more time and space to reach highway speed. Often mobile homes will be preceded and followed by vehicles that carry the "Wide Load" sign. Use extra caution when meeting or passing such vehicles.

Mobile home trailers often have "Wide load" signs to indicate that the load might be wider than a traffic lane.

Safe Driving Tips

On some school buses amber lights flash before the red lights come on. Use flashing amber lights on a school bus as a warning signal that the bus will soon stop, and you must stop also.

Buses

Other special purpose vehicles use highways during certain seasons. Highway maintenance crews usually do road repair work in the summer. After snowstorms expect to see snow plows in all traffic lanes. In rural areas, expect slow moving vehicles such as tractors and combines to be using the highways.

Most states require traffic going in both directions on a two-way street to stop when a school bus stops to load or unload passengers. This law is for the protection of those who might not yet fully understand traffic laws. The child in the picture has just left the school bus and is darting across the street. Do not expect her to yield to traffic. At times, children may be running to catch the bus. Approach any stopped bus slowly, and always be ready to stop. In most states, if the roadway is divided by a median strip, those vehicles approaching the bus on the other side of the median need not stop.

A school bus has flashing red lights and, in some states, a STOP sign that swings out from the side of the bus. Do not proceed until the lights stop flashing and the STOP sign is withdrawn.

Use the techniques listed on the next page to protect pedestrians near buses:

All traffic on this street must stop for the school bus when the red lights flash and the STOP signal appears.

- **Look Carefully** The "big picture" extends beyond the curb to sidewalks, driveways, and cross streets. Standing cars might hide pedestrians, especially children, approaching or leaving a bus.
- **Position Car** Sometimes you might approach a place where a pedestrian is getting off a bus or running to catch a bus. If so, slow down and move over to increase the distance between you and the pedestrian. Both you and the pedestrian will have more time to see and respond to each other.
- **Communicate** Tap your horn and make eye contact with pedestrians coming from or running to a bus.
- **Control Speed** Reduce speed and cover the brake, if needed, to give yourself more time to respond.

Emergency Vehicles

Looking in your rearview mirror and seeing an emergency vehicle approaching can be a frightening experience, especially when its lights are flashing and its siren is wailing. Some drivers may simply freeze at the wheel. You must make way for emergency vehicles with sirens and flashing lights regardless of the direction the emergency vehicle is traveling.

The instant you know an emergency vehicle is approaching, pull safely out of its way and stop.

At times you might hear a siren and not know the location or type of emergency vehicle. Scan, search, and listen so you can confirm that it is close to you. Your quick response to an emergency vehicle might save a life. Take these steps to clear the way for an emergency vehicle:

1. Always be alert for emergency vehicles. The instant you identify one, find a place on the right to safely pull out of the way and stop. Follow this procedure when the emergency vehicle is a fire truck, a police vehicle, or an ambulance.
2. If you are in heavy traffic, move in the direction other drivers are moving to clear the way. Leave as much open space for the emergency vehicle as possible.
3. Once you have pulled out of the way, stay there until the emergency vehicle passes. Be sure another emergency vehicle is not following the first. Then check traffic and proceed when your path of travel is clear.

Review It

1. Why should you be particularly careful of pedestrians?
2. In what areas should you expect to see pedestrians?
3. What guidelines should you follow when you are driving in a parking lot ?
4. What precautions should you take when approaching a bus?
5. What steps should you follow to clear the way for an emergency vehicle?

Interacting with Trucks

Trucks help transport nearly everything we eat, wear, and use in other ways in our daily lives. Trucks link producers with consumers across our continent, and help make American products available to the world.

Types of Trucks

Trucks differ in speed, performance, and weight. Some kinds of trucks are smaller than some automobiles. The three main classifications of trucks are light, medium, and heavy. Most trucks, pickup trucks, for example, are light. Medium trucks, such as parcel-delivery trucks, are higher and wider than light trucks. Heavy trucks include dump trucks and tractor trailers.

Tractor Trailers

Trucks that have a powerful tractor that pulls a separate trailer are called **tractor trailers.** The tractor is the front part of the truck that includes the engine and the cab. The most common size tractor trailer is the **tractor-semitrailer.** This is a tractor that pulls one trailer and is commonly called an "eighteen wheeler." Next in size is the double trailer, two trailers pulled by a tractor. The largest trucks, triple trailers, consist of three trailers pulled by a tractor.

Following Trucks

In general, trucks take slightly longer to stop than cars. However, when stopping on wet roads, trucks might have better traction and stability than cars, allowing them to stop more quickly. When you are following a large truck, leave a greater distance than the two-second interval. The two-second interval does not allow you enough clear sight distance ahead to identify potential problems early. Also, in an emergency stop situation, you might rear-end the truck.

When you follow a truck closely, you are in the truck driver's blind spot. The truck driver might be unaware of your presence, and you will not be able to see ahead. Increase your following distance. Position your vehicle so the truck driver can see you in the rear-view mirrors of the truck. You will then have a better view of the road ahead and the truck driver can give you plenty of warning for a stop or a turn. You will have more time to react and space to stop.

By driving near the left of the lane when following a truck, you will be visible to oncoming drivers. If you meet vehicles, move to the center of your lane.

Your view of the road is limited if you follow a truck too closely.

By increasing your distance, you are able to see farther ahead.

When you follow trucks at night, always dim your headlights. Bright lights from a vehicle behind can blind the truck driver as the light reflects off the truck's large mirrors.

Meeting Trucks

You do not have much room when meeting trucks on narrow two-lane highways. When you meet a truck coming from the opposite direction, move slightly to the right side of your lane. This will reduce the possibility of a sideswipe collision. Check the position of the oncoming truck in its lane. Look well ahead and drive in a straight line. If possible, choose a meeting point where the shoulder offers an escape path.

When meeting large trucks, you may feel a wind gust. Keeping to the right in your lane will reduce the wind turbulence between the two vehicles. When meeting very large trucks, hold the steering wheel firmly to stay on course.

Passing Trucks

Large trucks can travel as fast as cars even though they do not reach highway speed as quickly. Whenever possible, plan to pass a large truck when the driver shifts gears to gain speed. Places where passing is more easily done are just over the crest of a hill or when leaving a STOP sign

or a traffic light. Do not begin to pass until you are both clear of the intersection.

Use the following guidelines when passing large trucks:
- When in a legal passing zone, check front and rear traffic, signal a lane change, and change lanes smoothly. It takes several seconds longer to pass a truck than a car.
- Position your vehicle to the far left of the passing lane and complete your pass as soon as possible. Try not to stay next to the truck any longer than necessary.
- Return to the right lane after you can see the front of the truck in your rearview mirror. If the driver blinks the truck lights after you pass, that tells you it is safe to return to the right lane.
- Signal for a lane change to the right, check over your right shoulder, and return to the right lane. Do not slow down during the return. After completing the pass, maintain your highway speed.

Passing a large truck during a rain storm increases your level of risk. You have less traction and visibility is reduced. When preparing to pass under such conditions, flash your high-beam headlights so the truck driver will know you are passing. Keep your windshield wipers on high speed. The wet spray kicked up by the truck tires can almost blind you as you begin passing.

Keep out of the open space to the right of a truck that might make a right turn.

Trucks Making Right Turns

Because the tractor-semitrailer is so long, the driver must make very wide right turns. Stay far behind a truck that has signaled a right turn, and stay out of the open space to the right of the truck. To avoid conflict, never pass a truck on the right if there is a possibility the truck might make a right turn.

Review It

1. What precautions should you take when following a large truck?
2. What guidelines should you follow when passing large trucks?
3. What factors cause higher risk when passing a large truck in a heavy rainstorm?

DECISION MAKING

1. What is the car driver's responsibility in avoiding a collision? How could the car driver above have avoided this possible conflict?

2. What is wrong with the motorcyclist's position in the traffic lane? Why is this position hazardous? What is the correct position for the cyclists in the traffic lane?

3. You are driving the car above. What do you predict the bicyclist will do? What actions will you take?

4. What protective equipment should the driver of this motor scooter wear? How could the driver make the motor scooter more visible?

CHAPTER REVIEW

Reviewing Chapter Objectives

8–1 Interacting with Motorcycles
1. Why do you have a major share of responsibility for protecting motorcyclists? (136)
2. How should you use the IPDE process to protect motorcyclists while driving? (136)
3. In what situations should you look for motorcyclists while driving? (137-138)

8–2 Motorcyclist Actions That Can Affect You
4. How do acceleration and braking qualities of a motorcycle differ from those of a car? (140)
5. What protective equipment should motorcyclists use? (141)
6. How can motorcyclists help reduce conflicts? (142-143)

8–3 Interacting with Bicycles, Mopeds, and Motor Scooters
7. How can you help prevent conflicts with bicyclists? (145)
8. What guidelines should moped and motor scooter drivers follow when riding? (146)

8–4 Pedestrians and Other Roadway Users
9. In what areas should you expect to see pedestrians? (147)
10. What precautions should you take with buses and parking lots? (148-149)
11. What three steps should you take to clear the way for an emergency vehicle? (150)

8–5 Interacting with Trucks
12. What guidelines should you follow when passing large trucks? (152)
13. Why should you not pass a truck on the right if there is the possibility the truck might make a right turn? (152)

Check Your Knowledge

Multiple Choice Copy the number of each sentence below on a sheet of paper. Match the numbers with the letter that best completes the statement or answers the question.

1. Where in traffic is a car driver most likely to have a conflict with a motorcyclist?
   (a) parking lots (b) driveways (c) express lanes (d) intersections (137)
2. Which piece of equipment best protects a motorcyclist from head injuries?
   (a) helmet (b) face shield (c) leather jacket (d) gloves (141)
3. How much space should a car driver have when passing a bicyclist?
   (a) full lane (b) twenty four inches (c) half a block (d) half a lane (145)
4. When you hear the siren of an emergency vehicle, you should
   (a) continue at the same speed. (b) slow and move to the center of the lane. (c) safely pull out of the way and stop. (d) stop immediately. (148)
5. When following a large truck, the two second interval is not enough because you do not
   (a) have enough space to stop. (b) have enough clear sight distance ahead. (c) have space to pass. (d) have an escape path. (151)

Completion Copy the number of each sentence below. After each number, write the word or words that correctly complete the sentence.

6. Major _____ must be taken by larger vehicle drivers in order to protect motorcyclists. (136)
7. Motorcyclists should cross railroad tracks as close to a _____ as possible. (142)
8. Bicyclists should ride on the _____ side of the roadway. (144)
9. _____ are restricted from higher speed roadways depending upon the power of their engine.(146)
10. Of all the highway users, _____ are the least protected. (147)
11. When you follow a truck too closely, you are in the driver's _____ to the rear. (151)

Review Vocabulary

Copy the number of each definition in List A. Match the definition in List A with the letter of the term it defines in List B.

List A

12. operated by a hand lever on a motorcycle (140)
13. operated by a foot pedal on a motorcycle (140)
14. helmet, face shield, heavy clothing, heavy shoes or boots, and gloves. (141)
15. worn to prevent injury to the head (141)
16. plastic device attached to the helmet (141)
17. combination of a motor-driven cycle and a pedal-driven cycle (146)
18. trucks that have a powerful tractor that pull a separate trailer (151)
19. the front part of the truck that includes the engine and the cab (151)
20. a tractor that pulls only one trailer (151)

List B

a. face shield
b. protective equipment
c. tractor trailer
d. tractor-semitrailer
e. moped
f. rear brake
g. bicycle
h. helmet
i. tractor
j. front brake

Check Your Understanding

Write a short answer for each question or statement.

21. For what reasons might roadway users choose two-wheeled vehicles? (144)
22. What are reasons for pedestrian actions that might cause conflict? (147)

Think Critically

Write a paragraph to answer each question or statement.

1. In the picture below, the motorcyclist and the moped driver plan to turn left when the light changes to green. What hazards does each cycle driver face? What problem might the semitrailer cause?

2. Imagine you are following a semitrailer in a heavy rainstorm on a multilane highway. Describe the procedure you would use to pass the truck.

Projects

1. Visit your library to research newspaper accounts of pedestrian, bicycle, and motorcycle fatalities in your community. **Write** a report about your findings and share it with the class.
2. Spend 30 minutes at a busy intersection in your community. Compile lists of the types of trucks that pass through the intersection during that time. Discuss with your class the results of your survey and the impact the trucking industry has on your community.

DRIVING IN DIFFERENT ENVIRONMENTS AND SITUATIONS

At some time, you might have to drive through a mountain environment like this one. The road is winding, with many sharp turns. If snow starts to fall, or if darkness sets in, the environment becomes more threatening, and driving risks increase.

In this unit you will learn how to drive safely in various environments and conditions. You will learn how to drive in cities and towns as well as on rural roads and high-speed expressways. You will not always drive in ideal conditions of quiet roads and sunshine. The unit will teach you the skills you will need for driving during adverse conditions and for handling emergencies.

Chapter 9

DRIVING IN URBAN AREAS

You're the Driver!

Welcome to this great city! These words ring in your ears as you drive into the situation pictured here. As you drive here, or in any other urban area, you will encounter many types of vehicles and numerous pedestrians. Streets are crowded with people who are in a hurry and are not attentive to traffic. You will need to drive and park your car on unfamiliar streets.

Where should you predict points of conflict? How do uphill and downhill streets affect your control? How far ahead should you look for hazards?

This chapter will show you how to use special skills for sharing a limited amount of space with many users. By using these skills, in combination with a positive attitude for others, you will be able to drive safely in any urban area.

Objectives

Section 9–1 Adjusting to Urban Traffic
1. Name two factors that can make driving difficult in urban areas.
2. Describe how to use the IPDE process for urban driving.

Section 9–2 Following and Meeting Traffic
3. Tell how you would use a 2-second following distance.
4. List the actions you can use to manage a tailgater.
5. Describe how you can avoid conflicts with oncoming traffic.

Section 9–3 Techniques for Driving in Traffic
6. Explain how far ahead to look in urban traffic.
7. Tell what you must avoid doing when covering your brake.
8. Explain how to select the proper lane for driving on multilane streets.

Section 9–4 Situations You Might Encounter
9. Tell how to identify a one-way street.
10. Describe the proper lanes for turning left and right from a one-way street.

Adjusting to Urban Traffic

Once you can maneuver your car, you are ready to start learning how to drive in urban areas. Some urban situations are harder to manage than others.

Complex Traffic Situations

If you drive on a rural road in good weather with light traffic, you might encounter few hazards. Your driving task should be an easy one. The same would be true if you were to drive at low speeds on a suburban street with a few more hazards.

Two added factors can make driving in cities more difficult:

- Urban traffic has more hazards than suburban or rural roads.
- You will have to deal with hazards more frequently in urban areas.

In the rural and suburban situations described above, you were driving at a high speed with a few hazards or at a lower speed with just a few more hazards. You had time to adjust for both situations. However, if you had to react to several hazards while traveling at a higher speed, the difficulty of the situation would increase dramatically.

The number of hazards at the same location in a city can differ from time to time.

Number of Hazards Mile for mile, urban roads have the highest number and variety of hazards. Cars, trucks, pedestrians, bicycles, and other hazards demand your attention. Compare the two pictures on this page of the same location at different times. Decide which situation is harder to handle. Why?

Time, Distance, and Speed As you drive, remember that it takes time to use the IPDE process. If a hazard, such as another car, is threatening you at a given distance, slowing down is the best way to increase your distance and gain *time* to think and respond. When the number of hazards increases, you must decrease your speed—sometimes drastically.

City driving presents a variety of distractions and problems for drivers.

Using the IPDE Process

Driving in heavy urban traffic will test your driving skills to the limit. Your best course of action to avoid conflicts is to focus your attention exclusively on driving. Avoid distracting activities such as drinking a soft drink or coffee, eating, listening to very loud music, or being irritated by other drivers or passengers. You can do your best when your attitude is upbeat and when your attention is undivided.

Think of the IPDE process skills you would need to use as you drive down the street in the picture. When driving in urban situations, focus on the IPDE process in these ways.

- **Identify** Be more aggressive in using your visual skills. Look ahead to gain more time to use the IPDE process.
- **Predict** Be prepared to predict possible points of conflict earlier.
- **Decide** Always be ready to reduce speed and change your vehicle position.

- **Execute** Be prepared to use your car's controls in an instant.

Review It

1. What two factors can make driving in urban areas difficult?
2. How should you use the IPDE process for urban driving?

Following and Meeting Traffic

To be a safe driver in any environment, you need to maintain an ample space cushion between your vehicle and possible hazards. Managing the space cushion, or distance, between your vehicle and the car ahead is the first step.

Following Others

A long following distance has these major advantages.
- You are better able to see farther down the road.
- Other drivers will be able to see you better.

- You have more time to use the IPDE process.
- You are in a better position to avoid the vehicle ahead if it stops suddenly.

2-Second Following Distance

Using a set procedure is the best way to measure your following distance. A 2-second following distance is considered a safe space cushion for most normal driving conditions. Use these steps to measure your 2-second following distance:

1. Pick a fixed checkpoint on the road ahead. Road marks or shadows make good checkpoints.
2. When the vehicle ahead of you passes your checkpoint, count: "one-thousand-one, one-thousand-two," for your 2-second count.

3. Check to see whether or not your car is short of the checkpoint after you complete your 2-second count.

If your car is still short of your checkpoint, your following distance is correct under normal driving conditions. If you pass your checkpoint before your 2-second count is done, you are too close behind the vehicle ahead. You do not have an adequate following distance. Slow and check your following distance again.

Imagine that you are driving the car shown on this page. Do you have a 2-second following distance?

This 2-second technique works well at all speeds for measuring a normal following distance. As your speed increases, so does the distance your car travels during your 2-second count. Thus, when you count off 2 seconds, your following distance will be greater at higher speeds than at lower speeds.

This 2-second distance is not the total stopping distance you need to avoid hitting a stationary object. A 2-second following distance only protects you from colliding with vehicles you are following.

Increase your following distance to *3 or more seconds* under adverse conditions, or if you need more time to complete the IPDE process. Maintain extra distance in the following situations:

The 2-second rule helps you maintain a good following distance. Here you would start counting as the rear of the car ahead passes your checkpoint.

End your count as the front of your car reaches the checkpoint. If you reach the spot before you count "one-thousand-two," you are following too close.

A high-mount brake light is easy for following drivers to see and cannot be mistaken for any other light.

Advancements in Traffic Safety

Since September 1, 1985, all new cars in the United States have been required to have a high–mount brake light. (The official term for this light is a Center High-Mounted Stop Lamp.) These lights are designed to give following drivers an added warning that you intend to slow or stop. These lights are effective for the driver to your immediate rear and for those farther back. A 1987 evaluation sponsored by the U.S. Department of Transportation reported the following:

- Cars with a high-mount brake light were 17% less likely to be hit in the rear while braking.

- When all cars on the road have these lights, 80,000 non-fatal injuries will be prevented each year.

- You are first learning to drive. Your ability to use the IPDE process is not yet fully developed.
- You are following a tailgater or are being tailgated.
- Traction or visibility is poor.
- You are carrying a heavy load or pulling a trailer.
- You are driving downhill.
- The driver ahead seems unsure of the next action to take.
- You are following a motorcycle.

Looking Ahead of the Car Ahead

The 2-second rule is only one technique for following other cars in traffic. When following another car, look over, through, and around the car ahead. You can even use the reflection of brake lights on wet pavement. Be alert for brake lights, like the high-mount brake light shown. Try to anticipate what the driver ahead will do. Is there a pedestrian or something else in the road that will cause the driver ahead to stop?

Areas for Sudden Stops

Knowing where sudden stops might occur can help you predict where high-risk areas are located. Four common high-risk areas are:
- unmarked intersections
- intersections with signal lights
- lanes next to parked cars
- parking lot entrances and exits.

Looking Away Safely

Imagine you are checking your mirrors or are looking for a house number. Suddenly, the driver you are following slams on the brakes while you are looking away. By the time your eyes return to the road, it could be too late to stop. Take the following precautions to prevent this type of collision:
- Make sure the situation ahead has no immediate hazards before you look away.
- Lower your speed in close situations.
- Take several split-second glances rather than one long look.
- Ask a passenger to help look for a street name or house number.

Being Followed

You are in a high–risk situation when someone is following too closely, or is **tailgating**. You can take several steps to lower the risk in this type of situation.

Why Tailgaters Are Hazards

A tailgater is a hazard because if you suddenly brake hard, the tailgater might hit you from the rear. Imagine you are driving the yellow car in the first picture. You are applying the 2-second rule as you follow car A. But, car B is tailgating you. Suddenly the driver in car A brakes hard for an emergency. You brake hard to keep from hitting car A. Car B might then hit you in the rear.

Car B is tailgating. If the yellow car stops suddenly, the tailgater would be responsible for any collision that might occur.

Managing Tailgaters If you are being tailgated, take these actions to avoid being hit from the rear:

- Increase your following distance to 3 seconds or more. If you have to slow or stop for the driver ahead, you can do it more gradually and give the tailgating driver more time to react.
- Move slightly to the right to give the tailgater a better view ahead. Imagine you are the driver in the car ahead in the second picture. How has your car position helped the tailgater to see better?
- Signal early for turns, stops, or lane changes.
- Flash your brake lights ahead of time to warn a tailgater that you plan to slow or stop.
- In extreme situations, change lanes or pull out of the traffic flow to avoid the tailgater.

The car ahead has moved slightly to the right to allow the tailgater to see farther and be warned of cars that have slowed or stopped.

A long vehicle making a turn might cross a center line into your path.

Responding to Oncoming Traffic

If a driver crosses the center line toward you, you must react instantly. Knowing how to respond to this type of situation ahead of time may give you enough time to avoid a collision.

Reasons for Crossing A Center Line

A driver might cross into your path of travel for these reasons.

- **Driver impairment** A driver might be sleepy, distracted, confused, intoxicated, or sick.
- **Poor judgment** A driver might misjudge speed or distance.
- **Poor visibility** Direct sunlight, blinding headlights, or bad weather can reduce a driver's ability to see.

- **Reduced space** A snowbank, narrow bridge, or an object in or near the road might force a driver across the center line.
- **Sudden moves by others** Children, cycles, pedestrians, animals, or a car door opening might force a driver to make a last-second move.
- **Vehicle failure** A driver might lose control of a vehicle due to mechanical failure.
- **Turning buses and trucks** Long vehicles, like the one in the picture, need extra room just to make normal turns. Cars pulling trailers can create the same situation.

Avoiding Conflicts

If a car comes at you, take these actions to avoid a collision:

- Slow so the other driver can return to the normal lane. You can also slow so that you meet the other driver at a point where there is more room to pass.
- Turn on or flash your headlights and blow your horn.
- Move to the right and give the oncoming driver more room, as the driver in this picture has done. Swerve sharply to an open space on the right, if necessary.

Review It

1. How many seconds should you use for a normal following distance?
2. What can you do to manage a tailgater?
3. How can you avoid a conflict with an oncoming vehicle in your lane?

9–3

Techniques for Driving in Traffic

When you drive in an urban area, you must respond to a wide variety of traffic situations. Unfamiliar streets, signs, vehicles, and pedestrians make your driving task more complex. Use your best driving skills and maintain a positive attitude toward others to drive safely.

Looking Ahead While Staying Back

How far ahead should you look while driving in a town or city? In addition to looking around your car, you need to look regularly at the traffic scene a block or more ahead. By looking around and ahead, you are better able to spot a problem in time to adjust your speed and/or position to avoid trouble.

Imagine you are the driver in these two pictures. To have a good view of the road ahead, you must maintain a safe following distance. By keeping a 2-second following distance, you can see farther down the road. At this distance, you have more time to react. You also would be unlikely to collide with the vehicle directly ahead of you if it should stop suddenly.

View of the road ahead with a 2-second following distance.

With a following distance of less than 2 seconds, your view of the road is very limited.

Approaching Traffic Signals

Check traffic signals down the road by looking at least a block ahead. By doing so, you will have more time to react.

If the light is red, slow and prepare to stop. If the signals on your street are synchronized and the light turns green, you should be able to drive for several blocks without stopping.

If the light is green when you first see it, predict it will change soon. A traffic light that has been green and will soon turn yellow is called a **stale green light**. Watch for a DON'T WALK pedestrian signal that has started to flash. This signal warns you that the traffic light is about to turn yellow. If the pedestrian signal is flashing, you must decide if you have enough time to safely drive through the intersection before the light turns yellow. Your decision will depend on your distance to the intersection and your speed.

Never speed up to get through a green light before it changes. At any speed, you will reach a point-of-no-return, or a point where you must have started to brake if you are going to stop before the intersection. If you were the driver in the second picture, could you stop before the light turns red? Should you be alert for cross traffic that might jump into the intersection? Could a tailgater either ram you or force you to have a collision?

Even though your signal is green, the flashing DON'T WALK pedestrian signal is a warning that your signal is about to turn yellow.

When you approach a yellow light, you must consider your present speed, your distance to the intersection, the position of vehicles following you, and the locations of other vehicles near the intersection.

Covering the Brake

You can maintain a normal speed if you are driving into a stable, hazard-free traffic scene. But, if you are driving into a scene like the one in the first picture, you might have to stop fast. To be ready to stop, you need to use a technique called **covering the brake**. Take your foot off the accelerator, and hold it over the brake pedal so that you are ready to stop quickly. You can use this technique whenever you sense trouble.

Take these actions to identify and react to the hazard of parked cars:
- Look for drivers by glancing through rear windows created by parked cars.
- Look for parked cars' brake lights, exhaust, or wheels turned out.
- Cover your brake.
- Tap your horn, if necessary.
- Be ready to stop or swerve.

While driving past parked cars, also watch for a car door that might open unexpectedly, as in the second picture. Drive at least one car door's width away from parked cars if your lane is wide enough to do so.

When you cover your brake, make sure you do not rest your foot on the brake pedal. This mistake is called **riding the brake**. When you ride the brake, your brakes wear faster and your brake lights stay on. Drivers behind you might become confused. They might assume you are going to slow or stop when you are unsure. Only flash your brake lights to warn drivers behind you when you know you are going to slow or stop.

Be prepared to stop fast on city streets with many hazards.

Be alert for a door opening suddenly as you approach parked cars.

Adjusting Speed

Imagine you have been driving for an hour in the country. You are just coming into the town shown in the picture on the next page. The speed limit is 25 mph. However, traffic conditions should tell you to adjust your speed, and drive even slower.

Blending into traffic is one of the most common skills in good urban driving. Use these guides when selecting the best driving speed.
- Drive with the traffic flow.
- Stay within the speed limit.
- Adjust ahead of time for other drivers who might block your way.

Driving 5 mph faster saves only a second or two per city block. This chart shows how the amount of time saved gets progressively smaller as speeds increase.

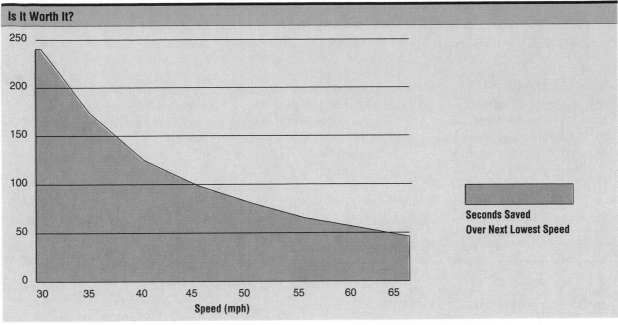

Is It Worth It?

Speed (mph)

You do not save very much time if you travel over the speed limit.

Adjust your speed as you enter a town after driving in the country.

Selecting the Best Lane

When two or more lanes of traffic are going in your direction, select the best lane for your purpose. You will use different lanes at different times. You should select the lane with the fewest number of immediate hazards.

The left lane is usually for faster traffic. But at times, traffic can be held up by drivers waiting to turn left. These left-turning drivers can be a problem when only two lanes are going in your direction.

If your street has three lanes going in your direction, choose the lane where the traffic flow is the smoothest. Imagine you are driving the yellow car in the picture. Why is the center lane the best for drivers going straight?

Lane Positioning Use these techniques to position your car safely in multilane urban traffic:

- Increase your following distance to more than 2 seconds when you are in heavy traffic.
- Adjust your speed and/or position to stay out of other drivers' blind-spot areas.
- Move to an opposite lane if you encounter another hazard.
- Center your car in your lane and be prepared to slow or stop if you encounter more than one hazard at the same time.

Changing Lanes

Once you start driving in a lane, try to stay in that lane. If you must change lanes, follow these steps:

1. Check traffic in both lanes and in your mirrors.
2. Signal your lane change early.
3. Look into your blind-spot area by quickly checking over your shoulder.
4. Change lanes without slowing.
5. Cancel your signal.

Repeat this procedure if you need to change more than one lane.

If you want to go straight ahead on this three-lane street, choose the center lane. You would not have to stop while cars wait to turn left, nor slow for cars turning right.

Overtaking and Passing

At times, you will want to **overtake**, or pass, a vehicle ahead. To overtake another vehicle, use the lane changing procedure just described and drive past the slower vehicle.

Passing in an urban area can be dangerous. You must be alert for pedestrians, cross traffic, signals, and oncoming traffic.

If you have to overtake another moving vehicle on a two-lane, two-way street, make sure you can do so legally. It is illegal to pass at intersections or over double yellow center lines. Follow these steps to reduce your risk when overtaking another vehicle:

1. To be sure you can see ahead clearly, start your pass when you are following at a safe distance.

This lane is reserved for buses. Cars cannot use it.

2. Check your mirrors for traffic behind you.
3. Signal your lane change and, if needed, tap your horn to alert the driver ahead.
4. Look over your shoulder to check your blind-spot area.
5. Check traffic once more as you accelerate to pass. If you have any doubt, do not pass.
6. Signal briefly and return to your lane when the front of the car you have passed appears in your inside rearview mirror.

Special Traffic Lanes

To improve rush-hour travel, many city streets now have special lanes for bus traffic, as shown here. Many cities also have carpool lanes. Drivers who travel alone must use other, slower lanes. With these special lanes, people can ride together to save time and fuel, reduce pollution, and avoid parking problems.

Review It

1. How far ahead should you look when driving in the city?
2. What should you avoid doing when you cover your brake?
3. What must you consider when selecting the best lane while driving on a multi-lane street?

Environmental Issues

As more and more drivers try to squeeze onto the same highways, more conflicts develop. Pollution from cars is increased. There are increased occurrences of "gridlock"—the urban situation in which cars cannot move at all because heavy traffic blocks all intersections.

As early as the late 1800's, the streets of London were clogged with traffic. One part of the solution was the creation of a subway system, a network of tunnels carrying trains throughout the city. For many people today in London and other European cities, subways are the best and fastest way to get around.

In the United States, subways are expanding. The "metro" in Washington, D.C. is a modern engineering wonder. Started in 1969, more than 300,000 passengers now use this system daily. In other cities such as New York, Chicago, Atlanta, Boston, and San Francisco, thousands of people who might drive or ride at street level now travel underground.

When you travel in or into an urban area, always remember—driving might not be the best way to get around.

Urban Situations You Might Encounter

As you drive in urban areas, you will encounter a wide variety of situations. By using the IPDE process, you will be ready to adjust to each situation ahead of time.

Driving on Two-Way Streets

Most city streets are two-way streets with one lane going in each direction. Other streets are multilane and have two or more lanes going in the same direction.

Many urban intersections do not have traffic controls. You cannot be sure what other drivers will do as you approach an uncontrolled or blind intersection. Therefore, slow and be prepared to yield or stop when you approach an uncontrolled intersection.

Some intersections have special left-turn lanes. If you turn left at an uncontrolled intersection, you must yield to oncoming traffic.

Many clues tell you that this is a one-way street.

Driving on One-Way Streets

One-way streets can move a greater volume of traffic than two-way streets, and with fewer conflicts. One-way streets generally are less congested than two-way streets, so fewer conflicts occur. Usually, one-way streets are safer to drive on.

Identifying One-Way Streets
When you come to an unfamiliar street, you must determine if it is a one-way street. These clues can help you identify a one-way street:

- ONE WAY signs are posted on most one-way streets.
- All moving traffic and parked cars point the same way.
- Broken white lines are used as lane lines.
- Most traffic signs will be facing the same direction. If you are driving on a street and the signs are facing the other direction, you probably are going the wrong way on a one-way street.

Imagine you are approaching the intersection pictured here. Even if you did not see the DO NOT ENTER sign, you should be able to identify this as a one-way street. All the cars are facing you.

To turn right onto a one-way street, turn from the right lane into the first available right lane.

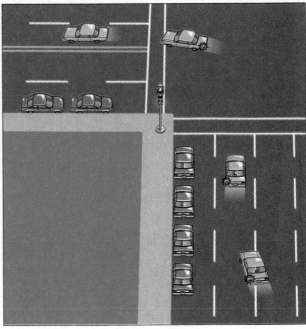

To turn left from a one-way street, turn from the left lane and enter the first available lane going in your direction.

Entering One-Way Streets

Imagine you are driving the yellow car in the first picture. To enter the one-way street, you turn from the right lane into the first available right lane.

To enter a one-way street going left, position your car in the first available left lane. Make a sharp left turn into the first lane going left. Signs are used to alert you when your street is about to become a one-way street.

Lane Choice on One-Way Streets

If you plan to drive on a one-way street for a distance, try to avoid any lane that is next to parked cars. If a clear center lane is available, use it to reduce possible conflicts.

When you plan to turn, position your car ahead of time. Move into the right or left lane at least one block before your turn.

Leaving One-Way Streets

Imagine you are driving the yellow car in the second picture. To turn left from your one-way street, you need to position your car in the far left lane ahead of time. To turn right, position your car in the far right lane ahead of time. Complete your turn by entering the first available lane going your way.

On some one-way streets, the outside lane may be for turns only. On other one-way streets, you can turn onto a multilane street from more than one lane. Road markings or overhead signs will direct you.

You might be forced to leave a one-way street when it turns into a two-way street. Your lane might end, or you might be forced to turn. Signs or lights will warn you when a one-way street is about to change to a two-way street.

Signaling Wrong-Way Drivers

If you encounter a car headed the wrong way on a one-way street, slow, steer right, and sound your horn. If there is time, flash your headlights to warn the other driver.

On a narrow, two-way street, be prepared to stop for a car that might suddenly pull out, leaving you little room to maneuver.

You might not be able to see a pedestrian in front of a car that is stopped at a green light.

Unexpected Situations on Crowded Streets

As you are driving along, a car suddenly emerges from an alley and is about to enter your path of travel. In addition, a bus is coming toward both of you. The street is so narrow that you have little room to maneuver.

Your only choice to maintain a safe path of travel and an adequate line of sight is to slow or stop. In such crowded urban driving situations, with no space to the right or left, cover your brake and be ready to respond. When necessary, let traffic clear before you move ahead.

When driving on a city street, continuously scan the road for any vehicles that might be stopped in unusual places. Even though the drivers might have a green light, they must stop for pedestrians. Many times, stopped vehicles will hide pedestrians or drivers waiting to go. When in doubt, slow and be ready to stop.

Angle or parallel parking often is allowed along streets. When driving close to parked cars, be alert for possible conflicts. At the first sign of movement from a car or pedestrian, slow, stop, or move to another lane.

Review It

1. What lanes should you select to make a left or right turn off a one-way street?
2. What can you do if another driver comes at you from the wrong direction on a one-way street?

DECISION MAKING

1. You are about to drive around the car ahead. What other hazard should you have identified? How will you respond?

2. You are driving the red car at 25 mph. The car on the right wants to turn left at the intersection one block ahead. What should you do?

3. You have been driving for two blocks where parking has been prohibited on the right. How could you have improved your lane position?

4. You are driving the red car on this narrow street. How can you reduce the conflict between the yellow van and you?

CHAPTER 9 REVIEW

Review Chapter Objectives

9–1 Adjusting to Urban Traffic
1. What two factors can make driving difficult in urban areas? (160)
2. How can you use the IPDE process for urban driving? (161)

9–2 Following and Meeting Traffic
3. How can you use a 2-second following distance? (162)
4. What actions can you take to manage a tailgater? (164)
5. How can you avoid conflicts with oncoming traffic? (165)

9–3 Techniques for Driving in Traffic
6. How far ahead should you look in urban traffic? (166–167)
7. What must you avoid doing when covering your brake? (168)
8. How should you select the proper lane when driving on a multilane street? (170)

9-4 Situations You Might Encounter
9. How can you identify a one-way street? (172)
10. What are the proper lanes for turning left and right from a one-way street? (173)

Check Your Knowledge

Multiple Choice Copy the number of each sentence below on a sheet of paper. Choose the letter that best completes the statement or answers the question.

1. To use the IPDE process in a difficult situation you will need more
(a) speed. (b) hazards. (c) time. (d) acceleration. (161)
2. The point beyond which you can no longer stop without entering an intersection is called the
(a) fixed check point. (b) point-of-no-return. (c) stopping point. (d) backing point. (167)
3. Broken lane lines on one-way streets are colored
(a) red. (b) yellow. (c) white. (d) orange. (172)
4. If you encounter a car headed the wrong way on a one-way street, you should immediately
(a) call the police. (b) make a sharp left turn into the first available left lane. (c) park and flash your headlights. (d) slow, steer right, and sound your horn. (173)
5. If you drive into a narrow crowded situation with no room to the left or right, you should
(a) slow and cover your brake. (b) blow your horn. (c) brake hard. (d) signal with your headlights. (174)

Completion Copy the number of each sentence below. After each number, write the word or words that complete the sentence correctly.

6. An increased number of _____ can make urban driving more difficult. (160)
7. You need to always try to maintain at least a _____ second following distance. (162)
8. If you are being tailgated, move slightly to the _____ (164)
9. When driving in a town or city, you should look at least one _____ ahead. (166)
10. The _____ lane of traffic often flows the smoothest on a street with three lanes going in the same direction. (170)
11. Look over your shoulder to check your _____ when changing lanes. (170)
12. If you are driving alone, you may not use a _____ lane. (171)
13. If all traffic and street signs are pointing in one direction, you can assume you are on a _____ street. (172)

Check Vocabulary

Copy the number of each definition in List A. Match the definition in List A with the term it defines in List B.

List A

14. a traffic signal light that has been green and will soon change to yellow (167)
15. placing your foot over the brake so you are ready to stop (168)
16. passing the vehicle ahead (171)
17. resting your foot on the brake pedal while driving (168)
18. someone following you too closely (164)

List B

a. all-clear signal light
b. covering the brake
c. overtake
d. riding the brake
e. stale green light
f. tailgating

Check Your Understanding

Write a short answer for each question or statement.

19. What actions should you avoid while using the IPDE process in heavy urban traffic? (161)
20. What conditions in the picture might encourage you to use a following distance of more than 2 seconds? (162)
21. As a driver, describe precautions you can take before looking away from the traffic scene ahead. (163)
22. Compare the time saved at different speeds and describe the total time savings when driving 10 miles at various speeds.(169)
23. List those actions you can take to position your car safely in urban multilane traffic. (170)
24. Describe those steps you need to take when overtaking another vehicle. (171)
25. List those steps you can take when approaching an uncontrolled or blind urban intersection. (174)

Think Critically

Write a paragraph to answer each question or statement.

1. The better you understand the relationship between time, distance, and speed, the better driver you will become. Describe the relationship and how it will affect your driving.
2. You know how important it is to have time to use the IPDE process. Why should you look ahead of the car ahead when using this process?

Projects

1. Choose a busy intersection that is controlled by a traffic light. Over a period of time, count the number of drivers who drive through on a yellow light. **Write** a summary of what this tells you about the risk of an accident at busy intersections.
2. Position yourself back and away from a busy pedestrian crosswalk. Observe other drivers as they approach this situation. How many slow or adjust position for the pedestrians? **Write** about how you would respond in this situation as a driver or pedestrian.

Chapter 10

DRIVING IN RURAL AREAS

You're the Driver!

Even if you live in an urban area, you will drive in rural areas often during trips. Some rural roads are multilane and some are two lane.

What problems might occur along this rural road? How does it differ from a city street? Where are the traffic controls?

How has the tractor affected how far ahead you can see? How might you safely pass this slow-moving vehicle?

This chapter discusses some problems you might encounter while driving on rural roads. It also explains how to use the IPDE process during rural driving. You also will learn how to safely handle some rural hazards.

Objectives

Section 10–1   Characteristics of Rural Traffic
1. Describe rural roadways.
2. Describe the conditions of a rural road and how they affect a driver's determination of a safe speed.
3. Explain how traffic controls help you travel safely on rural roads.

Section 10–2   Using Basic Skills in Rural Areas
4. Explain the use of the IPDE process in rural areas.
5. List the steps in a visual search pattern.
6. Describe how to approach a curve on a two-lane road.

7. List rural situations that require increased following distance.
8. Explain how to enter a multilane rural road.

Section 10–3 Passing and Being Passed on Rural Roads

9. Explain checks to make before passing another vehicle.
10. List steps for passing on two-lane roads.
11. List situations and conditions where no passing should be done.

Section 10–4 Rural Situations You Might Encounter

12. Tell how to pass a slow-moving vehicle.
13. Explain how to separate hazards when meeting traffic.

Section 10–5 Special Driving Environments

14. Describe safety precautions for mountain driving.
15. Describe safety precautions for desert driving.

Characteristics of Rural Traffic

Wide open spaces are characteristic of rural areas. Because of this space, you might think that rural roads are safer to drive on than city streets. However, statistics show that rural roads can be quite dangerous. Almost twice as many traffic deaths occur on rural roads than on urban ones. Higher speeds on rural roads result in more serious injuries. When a collision occurs on a rural road, medical help might not be able to reach the scene quickly.

Roadways

Rural roadways may be made of concrete, brick, asphalt, gravel, macadam (tightly packed crushed stone), or dirt. Lane widths can be wide or narrow. The roadway shoulders can be wide, narrow, low, or almost nonexistent. The surface might be smooth or in poor condition with many potholes or grooves.

Lighting on rural roads might be inadequate for safe night driving. Traction can vary from excellent on dry, clean pavement to poor on wet, muddy, snowy, or icy roads.

Rural roads carry light traffic. Where can you expect to meet vehicles on this rural road?

You must be alert to identify problems and adjust quickly to changing roadway conditions. On rural roads, roadway conditions can change abruptly. What is the condition of the road in the picture? What good features of this rural highway can you identify? Where might conflicts occur? What features might be changed to improve the safety of this roadway?

Speed

Determining safe speed is the most important decision you can make in rural driving. Speed affects
- how far ahead you must look
- stopping distance
- vehicle control
- the amount of damage and injury, as well as survival rate, in a collision.

A 55-mph speed limit applies to most rural highways. Rural interstate highways might have a speed limit of 65 mph. Posted speed limits will be lower where traffic or other conditions make it necessary. Weather conditions such as rain or snow, and road conditions such as curves, hills, and narrow lanes require lower speed. Always follow this basic rule in regard to speed: *Do not drive faster than road or traffic conditions permit.*

Rural roadways often have a lighter traffic load than urban roadways. Therefore, posted rural speed limits are often higher than urban speed limits. Always consider other traffic when choosing your speed.

This sign warns you to prepare to stop soon beyond the hill.

Even in rural areas, major highways can intersect. They might have pavement markings and traffic signals.

Traffic Controls

Traffic controls consist of signs, signals, and roadway markings. They help you to travel safely by providing advance information and warnings in these situations:

- location of hazards you cannot yet see
- areas of high-speed cross traffic
- unusual and unexpected highway features, such as sharp curves
- channeling of traffic into reduced space, such as a detour around a construction zone or a lane ending.

The STOP AHEAD sign in the picture is an example of a warning sign. The sign informs you that a STOP sign, not yet visible, is just beyond the crest of the hill. This stop might be so close beyond this point that, without the warning, you might have difficulty stopping.

Traffic controls can be quite complex if they govern several lanes of traffic. Notice the intersection on the multilane highway. At such an intersection, a red light is used with a green arrow and turn lane. Traffic stops so vehicles in the turn lane can turn left and cross several lanes safely. Signs and roadway markings can specify certain turns, as shown.

Roadside Hazards

Rural roadways, especially older ones, can have many hazards. Signposts located on the road shoulder might be close to the pavement. They can block use of the shoulder in an emergency. Shoulders might be narrow or rough. Guardrails, bridges, bushes, trees, and fences might be near the edge of the road. Consider these hazards when deciding on a safe speed.

Businesses along the roadside can create hazardous situations. Vehicles enter and leave areas with service stations, stores, small factories, and restaurants. Vehicles might slow down to turn right or be stopped waiting to turn left. Drivers attempting to enter the roadway can be a hazard to others. The driver who makes a last-second decision to stop along the roadside is especially hazardous. You must look far ahead to identify these hazards so you can have enough space and time to avoid a collision.

Review It

1. What roadway conditions must a driver consider while on a rural road?
2. How does the basic speed law compare with posted speed limits?

Using Basic Skills in Rural Areas

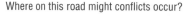

After driving a distance on a rural road with light traffic, you might feel that no conflicts will occur. However, collision-free driving comes from thinking ahead in a constantly changing traffic scene. You might encounter problems with little or no warning.

Applying the IPDE Process

Traveling at high speeds on rural roads increases the chance of a collision. The faster you drive, the less time you have to use the IPDE process. Take these precautions as you use the IPDE process at higher speeds:

- **Identify** hazards farther away than when you drive at low speeds because you reach the hazard more quickly. The sooner you identify hazards, the more time you have to make a decision and execute a safe maneuver. Keep your eyes moving, constantly scanning the road. Since the number of eye movements tends to decrease as a person looks farther ahead, you must make a conscious effort to scan.
- **Predict** conflicts. You must predict much farther ahead and determine what to do before you arrive at an area of possible conflict. You might not have much time to make safe predictions. Making early predictions gives you more time to make safe decisions.
- **Decide** what to do while you still have enough time. Decide where to position your car and how fast you want to go.
- **Execute** your decision. Give yourself ample time to act.

Where on this road might conflicts occur?

Controlling a car at higher speeds is more difficult than at lower speeds. You might not be able to stop or swerve in time to avoid a collision. Hard braking or sharp turns can cause a skid and total loss of control. Give yourself ample time to maintain control of your vehicle.

Drive at a speed at which you can stop or swerve in time to avoid a collision. A proper, safe speed is an important protection in all traffic situations.

Imagine you are driving along the rural road in the picture on page 182. How would you and the other drivers apply each step of the IPDE process in this situation?

Visual Search Pattern
The process of searching and scanning critical areas in a regular sequence is an **orderly visual search pattern**. A visual search pattern, such as in the guidelines described below, helps you adjust to any unusual events in rural areas.

- Look well ahead as well as to the sides of the road. This wide field of vision brings into your line of sight hazards along the roadside and at intersections.
- Check for safety features such as wide shoulders, shallow ditches with gentle slopes, and traffic controls. Think of how a lack of these features will affect your decisions.

- Note the roadway surface. Mud or gravel can cause loss of traction. Potholes and ruts can affect vehicle control.
- Glance in rearview mirrors often. See if a driver behind you is starting to pass or is tailgating you.
- Check your speed and the warning lights in your car after you make visual checks of the roadway and of traffic.
- After completing the checks, return your attention to the roadway ahead. Repeat these checks from time to time. You can take quick glances away from the traffic scene only when you have determined that the scene is not changing.

What can you expect of the road after the crest of the hill?

Driving on Two-Lane Roads

Much of your rural driving will be on two-lane roads with a 55-mph speed limit. Know the characteristics of two-lane roadways and the techniques to drive safely on them.

Curves A warning sign usually marks a sharp curve on a two-lane road. An **advisory speed sign** often appears below the warning sign if the curve is very sharp. This square yellow sign informs you of the maximum safe speed for the curve under ideal conditions. If you were driving on the road in the picture on page 183, both signs would be important to you. As you come to the top of the hill, you would not be able to see the curve ahead.

When you approach a curve, take the following steps:
1. Take quick glances across the curve to identify oncoming traffic. Be alert for any driver who might enter the curve too fast and cross the center line into your lane. You could be forced to take evasive action.
2. Maintain proper lane position by glancing ahead at your intended path of travel. If your lane is wide enough, stay to the right of it while driving around the curve.

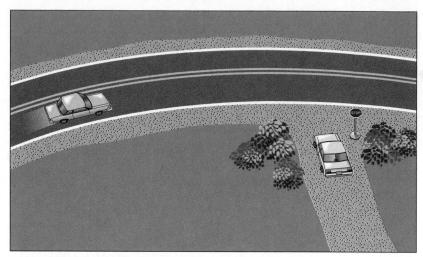

What problems do the two drivers face at this intersection?

3. Identify the advisory speed sign. Evaluate the sharpness of the curve. Slow to a suitable speed before entering the curve.
4. After entering the curve, accelerate gently.
5. Once out of the curve, resume a safe speed.

Hills A hill generally is not marked with a warning sign unless it is unusually steep or long. On two-lane roads, the uphill lane is usually a no-passing zone. Your **sight distance,** or how far ahead you can see, becomes shorter as you near the top of a hill. You cannot see far enough ahead to pass safely. Slow to a speed that allows you to check for traffic coming over the hill. Keep to the right side of the road.

Intersections Rural intersections can vary greatly. Traffic signals probably will control busy intersections on two-lane roads. Identify traffic signals early so you can predict what color the light will be when you arrive. If the light is green when you first see it at a distance, predict that it will be red by the time you arrive. If the light is red, adjust your speed so that you might arrive when the light is green.

A common rural intersection is one in which a side road crosses a main road. The side road usually will have a STOP sign. Trees, bushes, and crops can obscure the view at the intersection. Drivers on the main road and on the side road might have difficulty seeing one another. Drivers on the side road can have difficulty entering the main road if the main road has a hill or a curve.

Imagine you are the driver of the yellow car in the picture on the opposite page. You might have difficulty identifying the hidden car. When you see it, you should predict that the driver of the white car might pull out in front of you. Be alert for drivers who misjudge the time and distance needed to enter and accelerate to highway speed.

Following Traffic

Vehicles cover great distances in a short time at rural road speeds. When following a vehicle on a rural road, use the 2-second rule. When you use the 2-second rule at a fast speed, the distance between vehicles is greater than on city streets where speed limits are lower.

At high speeds, a hazard can quickly develop into a conflict. The 2-second following distance provides you space and time to prevent conflicts under normal conditions. In special situations, you should increase your following space to a 3- or even 4-second distance.

Longer following distances are necessary when you are
- being tailgated
- on a steep downhill slope
- following a motorcycle
- pulling a trailer
- following a truck or bus
- driving on wet pavement.

Adjust speed and position to keep a space cushion around your car. If a vehicle cuts into your 2-second following distance, gradually drop back. Reestablish a 2-second following distance between your car and the vehicle ahead.

Sometimes the car following you is so close that your braking could cause the tailgater to hit the rear of your car. If you release your accelerator and slow gradually, a tailgater usually will pass you. Always have an **escape path** ready, though. You can move into such an opening to avoid a collision with another vehicle. Sometimes you can maneuver to the left or right, or onto the shoulder, as an escape path.

Where can you find an escape path in this situation?

185

A wide median strip safely separates high-speed traffic moving in opposite directions.

Driving on Multilane Roads

Some rural roads have four or more lanes. They have the high speed limits typical of rural roads. They also might have intersections. At some large intersections, two or more major roads might cross. At smaller intersections, a two-lane road might cross a multilane one.

Multilane Roadways With Center Lines   Roadways with two or more lanes in each direction might have only a double, solid yellow center line to separate high-speed traffic. You should never cross double yellow lines, except to turn left. Passing is legal only in the lanes on your side of the center line.

Divided Roadways   On divided roadways, lanes going in opposite directions are separated in some way. The two-way traffic might be divided by a guardrail or a **median strip**, which is an area of ground. Some median strips are only a few feet wide; others are wider, like the one in the picture.

Cross each half of a multilane divided roadway as though it were a one-way street. Turn left or right into a multilane road as though you were entering a high-speed, one-way street.

Lane Choice   Whenever possible, drive in the right-hand lane of a multilane highway. The left lane usually is for passing or turning left. In many states, the law requires that you drive in the right-hand lane for normal driving.

Turning at an Intersection When leaving a multilane roadway, turn right from the right lane. Make left turns from the lane closest to the center line or median strip.

Some intersections have special lanes for right and left turns. Signal your intentions far in advance. If there are no turning lanes, watch your rearview mirror for vehicles while you wait to turn. A vehicle could hit you from the rear before you turn. Keep

To make a left turn from a side road onto a multilane highway, a median strip provides a safe place to wait for a gap.

your wheels straight while waiting to turn. If you are struck from behind, your car would go straight rather than into the path of oncoming traffic. If you see a vehicle approaching from behind at high speed, accelerate rapidly across the intersection. Continue straight ahead without turning.

Entering a Multilane Road

Use the following procedures to enter a multilane roadway from a side road:

- For a right turn, first look for a 6-second gap in traffic. Enter the nearest lane that is going in your direction. Accelerate promptly to the prevailing speed. Change lanes only after clearing the intersection.

- For a left turn, first cross the lanes on the near side of the roadway. Choose a time when no traffic is approaching in the lane just across the center line. Turn into the near lane. Accelerate more promptly to roadway speed than you would for a right turn. Left turns require gaps considerably greater than for right turns.

Entering the roadway from a driveway presents the same problems as entering from a side road. Other drivers might not know you are there. At side roads, warning signs might alert drivers on the main road of possible conflicts. However, such signs might not be present at driveways. Look for a larger gap in traffic than when entering from a side road.

Review It

1. How should you use the IPDE process during rural driving?
2. What procedures should you use when approaching a curve on a two-lane rural road?
3. What are the steps in an orderly visual search pattern when driving in rural areas?
4. How can you make turns from and onto a multilane road?

Passing and Being Passed on Rural Roads

Is passing safe in this situation?

Passing another vehicle on a two-lane rural road is a potentially dangerous maneuver. When you pass a vehicle on a two-lane road, you will be in the same lane as oncoming traffic for a few seconds. To pass safely, you must know the proper procedures. You must make critical decisions quickly.

Passing

Passing another vehicle is a three-stage procedure. You decide to pass, prepare to pass, and execute the maneuver.

Deciding To Pass

Before deciding to pass, you must be able to answer "yes" to these questions:

- Is passing here legal?
- Is passing here safe?
- Is passing worthwhile?

The major responsibility for passing safely belongs to the driver who is passing.

Preparing To Pass

Take these actions when preparing to pass:

- Realize that you are rapidly closing the distance between your car and the car ahead. Determine if the car ahead is going slower than the posted speed. If so, you might decide that passing would be to your advantage.
- Check the roadway and signs ahead. Make certain that passing is legal in the area.
- Determine whether there are other reasons why you should not pass. For example, the sight distance ahead might be limited.
- Check traction conditions ahead. You need a longer distance to pass safely when traction is not ideal. Under poor conditions, accelerate gradually while changing lanes. Keep a firm grip on the steering wheel.
- Look ahead of the car you intend to pass. You must have room to return to your lane after passing.
- Check the roadway shoulders ahead. Make sure that no hazards could cause the driver ahead to swerve to the left.
- Check the rearview mirrors for fast-approaching vehicles. Delay passing if another car is about to pass you.
- Glance over your left shoulder to see if a vehicle is in your blind spot. If you have been regularly checking mirrors, you probably know whether or not a vehicle is nearby. Check again to make sure.
- Check the oncoming traffic lane. Make sure you have plenty of space to pass safely. *If you are uncertain, do not pass.*
- Check driveways and intersections ahead to make sure that no vehicle will be entering the roadway.

After you have determined that your path is clear, you are ready to pass. If your checks indicate a problem, slow down and follow the car ahead. Use the 2-second following distance rule. Prepare to pass again when conditions permit. Repeat all the checks. With practice, you can make these checks in just a few seconds.

Executing a Pass on Two-Lane Roads

Use these steps to pass on a two-lane road.

1. When it is safe and clear to pass, tap the horn gently to warn the driver ahead that you are going to pass. When you pass at night, quickly flash the headlight beam from low to high and back to low.
2. Signal for a lane change to the left. Check the blind spot over your left shoulder.
3. Change lanes smoothly.
4. Cancel the signal.
5. Pass at a speed at least 10 mph faster than the car you are passing. *All passing must be done within the speed limit.*
6. At this point, you can still change your plans. You can return to the right lane if any unexpected problem occurs ahead. If all is clear, continue to accelerate to the proper speed.
7. Maintain speed. Remain in the left lane until you can see in your inside rearview mirror both headlights of the car you have passed.
8. Signal for a lane change to the right. Check the inside mirror again. Check over your right shoulder.
9. Return smoothly to the right lane. Do not slow down during the return.
10. Cancel the signal. Adjust your speed.

No-Passing Situations

No-passing areas are marked by solid yellow lines. Signs also can indicate no-passing zones. Passing is illegal and unsafe under these general conditions:

- Sight distance ahead is limited.
- Space is narrow. Escape routes do not exist.
- Cross-traffic is a hazard. In these situations, passing is unsafe even if no warning signs or lines are present.

How do the general conditions apply to the following specific situations?

No passing on roads going uphill   Passing is not allowed in the last 700 to 1,000 feet before the crest of a hill. Notice that the driver of the yellow car in the picture cannot see oncoming traffic in time to pass safely.

Some states with mountains and steep hills have special uphill-passing lanes. Passing while driving downhill is legal where visibility is good and there is no solid yellow line.

No passing at intersections Passing is illegal within the last 100 feet before an intersection. Slow down when approaching an intersection. Why is passing at an intersection dangerous?

The solid yellow line means that drivers in the right lane must not pass. They would not be able to see vehicles coming over the hill.

Passing at an intersection is dangerous. A driver turning from the crossroad might enter your lane.

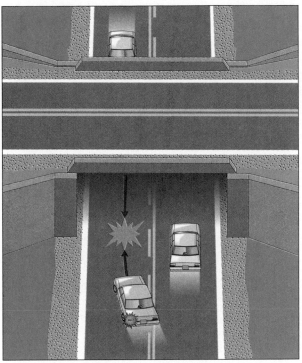

Do not pass on bridges and underpasses, since they might not have shoulders to provide escape areas.

Passing is illegal in both lanes around this curve.

No passing at railroad crossings Passing is illegal within the last 100 feet before a railroad crossing. You should slow at railroad crossings, but passing requires a steady speed or even acceleration.

No passing on bridges or underpasses Passing is unsafe within the last 100 feet before a 2-lane bridge or an underpass. As the picture indicates, the roadway on or under a bridge might not have a shoulder.

No passing on curves Passing on curves is illegal because you do not have enough sight distance to see around curves. The driver of the yellow car in the picture cannot see the oncoming car. Stay in your lane on any curve, out of the way of oncoming traffic.

Other No-Passing Conditions Do not attempt to pass in these situations that might not be marked by no-passing lines:
- The car ahead is traveling at or near the speed limit.
- Sight distance is limited by fog, snow, or rain.
- The roadway surface is slick.
- Several vehicles are ahead of you.
- You cannot complete passing before a no-passing zone begins.
- Oncoming traffic is too close.
- You will stop or turn soon.

Passing on Multilane Roads

On divided roadways, oncoming vehicles present little danger for a driver who is attempting to pass. On a multilane roadway with a center line, a passer should be more cautious. On all multilane roads, check all lanes going in your direction before you pass. If you are in a center lane, check both left and right lanes. Check all lanes on the passing side. Be sure no one is about to enter your passing lane from another lane. The car you are going to pass should be traveling several mph slower than you.

In general, all passing should be done in the left lane. Passing on the right is often illegal. Sometimes, though, it might be necessary to pass a vehicle that is in the left lane on a multilane road. That vehicle might be preparing for a left turn, for example. In such a situation, if passing is legal in the area, check to the right to be sure your path of travel is clear. Signal for a right turn, check the blind spot over your right shoulder, change lanes smoothly, and complete the pass with extra caution.

Being Passed

The driver who is passing has the major responsibility for passing safely. If you are the driver being passed you have certain responsibilities as well.

You should be aware that another car is passing, even without a warning horn or flashing headlights. Regularly glance in the rearview mirror to see if cars are approaching. Stay to the right side of your lane to give the other driver a better view ahead and more room to pass.

Determine if the passing driver is having difficulty completing the pass. If so, help the other driver by slowing down. It is illegal to speed up while being passed. Sometimes the passing driver decides not to pass and drops back. If so, accelerate slightly to open up space behind you.

Review It

1. In what general situations should you not pass another car?
2. What checks must you make when preparing to pass?
3. What are the steps for passing on a two-lane road?
4. How does passing on a multilane roadway differ from passing on a two-lane roadway?
5. What procedures should you follow when being passed?

Glance regularly into your mirror to see if a car is about to pass you.

10-4

Rural Situations You Might Encounter

In rural areas you might come across vehicles and animals that you would not see on city streets. However, you can apply the same safe-driving techniques described below in urban as well as rural areas. For example, you might encounter a tractor only in a rural area. In the city, though, you might find yourself driving behind a slow construction truck or delivery van. You will meet oncoming traffic in urban as well as in rural areas.

Slow-Moving Vehicles

A slow-moving vehicle is one that is unable to travel at highway speed. For example, most tractors or other large farm machines can travel only at 15 to 25 mph.

You need to identify a slow-moving vehicle as early as possible. Notice the orange and red triangular sign on the rear of the tractor in the picture. This sign identifies the tractor as a slow-moving vehicle.

Your car will approach a slow-moving vehicle rapidly. Be cautious, slow down, and be ready to change lanes to pass. Check for oncoming traffic. After you have checked traffic and roadway conditions, decide

The driver of this farm machine has pulled partly off the road. Should you pass in this situation?

quickly when and where to pass. Your lane might be narrowed because the slow-moving vehicle takes more than half of the roadway. Slow down before passing.

Animals

Wild and tame animals are often a problem on rural roads. They are unpredictable and can easily become frightened and run into your path or freeze still.

When a dog, cat, deer, or other animal moves onto the roadway, you might be tempted to brake hard or to swerve sharply. Do not forget that other traffic might be nearby. Before you brake or swerve, be sure that another more serious collision will not occur as a result of your action.

Large animals are an even greater menace to drivers. If

Drive slowly and cautiously around people on horseback. Frightened animals might cause a collision.

you were to hit a cow or horse, you could be injured as well as the animal. Watch especially for people riding horses. Slow down and drive around large animals to avoid a collision. Do not frighten the animals by sounding your horn. Frightened animals might bolt into your path.

Other Hazards   Watch also for a pet on a leash, a blind person with a seeing-eye dog, and livestock being herded across or alongside a roadway.

In areas where large wild animals such as deer are present, scan a wider area than usual. If you see a deer, expect others. A deer bounding into your path can cause serious damage and injury. Look for animal-crossing warnings, and reduce speed in animal-crossing areas.

Adjust your speed so that you deal with only one hazard at a time.

Meeting Oncoming Traffic

Meeting oncoming traffic on two-way roads can be dangerous. Often, only a small space separates you from oncoming vehicles. On roadways with 55-mph speed limits, a head-on collision can cause serious injury or death.

Expect that the driver of an oncoming car has the same problems that you do on a narrow road. Carefully choose the place where your vehicles will approach each other, especially on older, narrow roads. Use these guidelines for selecting a place to meet.

- Separate the hazards in or next to your path. Adjust your speed so you deal with only one hazard at a time. Whenever possible, slow down or speed up to control where you will meet another hazard. Suppose a parked car is on your side of the road,

Adjust speed so that you meet another vehicle where you have the most space.

as in the picture. Slow down so that you will meet the oncoming car before passing the parked car. If you are approaching a narrow bridge and an oncoming car is closer to it, slow to let the other vehicle cross the bridge first.

- Meet where the most space is available. If you are on a narrow road, meet where you will have space to swerve. Avoid places with bad pavement edges. If the roadway is not wide enough for two cars to meet, pull off the road and stop. Proceed when the other car has passed.

- If you are meeting a line of vehicles, drive near the right edge of the roadway. In this position, your car will be more visible to oncoming drivers. Some drivers might be anxious to get ahead in the line. Look for drivers who might pull out to pass without checking for oncoming traffic.
- Meeting vehicles at the top of a hill can be dangerous. An oncoming driver might be passing a vehicle and will be in your lane as you top the hill.

Oncoming drivers might cross the center line into your lane for other reasons, such as:

- a blowout, a pothole, rocks on the road, or a strong wind
- unexpected loss of traction due to rain, snow, mud, ice
- driver impairment due to intoxication, illness, fatigue, or distractions
- vehicle failure.

Meeting Slow-Moving Vehicles

Watch carefully when meeting a slow-moving or a standing vehicle with an oncoming car close behind it. The driver of the oncoming car might not see you and might swerve around the slow vehicle into your lane. If the driver of the car sees you but is unable to stop in time, that driver might hit the slow-moving vehicle. The debris from that collision could slide into your path before you could react to avoid it. Be prepared to take evasive action to avoid a collision.

Be alert for an oncoming driver who might want to pass.

Meeting at Night

Some drivers have poor night vision. Be especially alert when driving at night. Be aware of cars far in the distance. Make sure your windshield is clean.

At night, headlights shining over a hill can warn you of an approaching vehicle. If you are using high-beam headlights, dim them early when you see a car approaching. Do not look directly into the oncoming car's headlights. Glance instead to the right edge of the roadway. You and the other driver can be momentarily blinded even if both vehicles are using low-beam headlights. You should identify this problem early to give yourself enough time and space to avoid a collision.

Railroad Crossings

About 75 percent of railroad crossings do not have complete controls, such as flashing lights and gates. At many rural crossings, trains travel at high speed. Be watchful for round railroad-crossing signs and pavement markings. Slow down, check traffic to the side and rear, and follow the steps for crossing tracks safely.

Review It

1. What type of sign identifies a slow-moving vehicle?
2. Explain how you would separate hazards when meeting an oncoming vehicle.
3. Why should you drive to the right side of your lane when meeting oncoming traffic?
4. Why might an oncoming car suddenly cross the center line into your lane?

195

Special Rural Environments

Driving through mountains and desert can offer challenges to your patience, energy, and skill. Pay special attention to speed limit and warning signs in these areas, and watch your gauges.

Mountain Driving

Mountain driving presents more problems and special situations than driving in flat areas. You constantly must consider the effects of gravity. Gravity pulls down on a car, causing it to pick up speed when traveling downhill. Gravity also slows a car's forward motion when it is traveling uphill.

Mountain roads often zigzag across the face of a mountain through a series of sharp turns. In a very sharp turn called a **switchback,** the road bends back in the opposite direction. The sign in the picture warns that a switchback is ahead.

Driving Up a Mountain

Steady acceleration is necessary to maintain speed when driving uphill. If the slope is steep, downshift in a car with manual transmission. An automatic transmission will downshift by itself. If you need more power on a steep incline, you can shift an automatic transmission to a lower gear. At a high elevation, the amount of power available to the engine might be reduced.

Stay to the right and tap your horn when you cannot see oncoming traffic around mountain curves. An oncoming car can cross into your lane because the driver is going too fast for the curve. Driving too fast on curves is a leading cause of collisions in the mountains.

Loaded trucks, recreational vehicles, and cars pulling trailers move slowly up mountain roads. Follow at their speed and at a safe following distance. The picture shows a **pull-out area**, a place where slow-moving vehicles can pull over and stop. Faster traffic following behind can then proceed.

Driving Down a Mountain

Gravity pulls you faster and faster downhill unless you resist it. Downshift before starting downhill, whether the car has an automatic or manual transmission. Never coast downhill in NEUTRAL, with the clutch disengaged, or in OVERDRIVE, because the car will speed up and you might lose control. In fact, coasting downhill is illegal in some states.

At the switchback this mountain road curves so sharply that it reverses direction.

Drivers can stop at a pull-out area so they can enjoy the view or let faster traffic proceed.

Adjust speed with occasional use of the brakes. Do not apply the brakes steadily; the power of the brakes can fade from overheating. If you are braking often, shift to a lower gear. Keep your speed low enough so that you can stay in your lane. You must keep the car under your control at all times.

Large trucks can experience braking problems going downhill on long, steep grades. Some mountain roadways have runaway vehicle ramps, like the one shown. This ramp provides a place for a runaway vehicle to safely stop when brakes no longer are effective.

Sometimes two vehicles meet on a narrow mountain road. Neither vehicle can safely pass. The vehicle heading downhill must back up until the vehicle going uphill can pass, because it is more dangerous for a vehicle to go in REVERSE down a hill than up a hill.

How can an escape ramp help stop a runaway vehicle on a long downhill grade?

Weather in the Mountains

Early morning fog, snow, and ice can make mountain driving difficult. Many mountain roads become blocked by snow. If weather conditions are poor, call the state police or highway department to find out about roadway conditions before setting out on a trip. Weather conditions can change quickly, so listen to weather reports on your radio during a trip.

Effects of Altitude on Drivers

High altitude can affect the driver, causing shortness of breath, faster heartbeat, and headache. Lower oxygen content in mountain air can reduce concentration and cause drowsiness. Effects are worse for tired drivers. Do not drive if you are tired or feel these effects. If traveling with others, take turns driving.

Effects of Altitude on Cars

Thin mountain air also affects car engines. Climbing power is reduced. Acceleration is sluggish. Liquids boil and evaporate easier. If the temperature light comes on or the gauge registers hot, pull over to the shoulder, stop, and let the engine cool. You can cool the engine somewhat by turning on the heater to circulate some of the heat built up in the engine coolant.

Engines can get hot during mountain driving. Gasoline can vaporize in the fuel line near the engine when you shut off the engine. A condition called **vapor lock** develops. The engine will not start because fuel cannot be pumped into the engine in a gaseous state. Allow the engine to cool, then restart it.

If you do a great deal of mountain driving, try to prevent most of these problems. Have a mechanic adjust the engine for better performance at higher altitudes. A computer engine management system adjusts automatically to different conditions.

Desert Driving

Desert areas are larger and hotter than most drivers realize. Desert driving is hard on the driver, on the car, and on the roadway.

Effects on Drivers

Driving long distances under intense daytime heat causes great stress on drivers. You can experience a false sense of security because of the sameness of scenery. Sun glare can reduce your vision, so it is important to wear good quality sunglasses. Change drivers often. If you are driving alone, plan frequent rest stops. Carry a water supply for passengers and for the car. The desert is a harsh place to stay if you have difficulties with your vehicle.

Effects on Cars

The car needs more service for desert driving than for other environments. If you drive several hours a day, check the radiator fluid level at every fuel stop. Unless the battery is sealed, check the battery fluid level daily.

CAUTION: Never remove the cap from a hot radiator. Steam and hot fluid can burn you. Check the fluid level in the coolant recovery tank. Otherwise, wait for the radiator to cool before removing the cap.

Check tire pressure daily before you begin driving. Tire pressure will increase as you drive, but do not reduce the

Visibility can be very limited in a sandstorm.

pressure to below its normal level. Reducing air pressure causes tires to run even hotter. Tire failure can result.

The Desert Roadway

Well designed highways with gentle curves invite high speeds. However, roadside shoulders can be sandy. Wheels sink quickly into sand. If you need to park beside the roadway, choose an area that is firm. Tire tracks show that the area has been packed down.

Sandstorms and Dust Storms

Do not drive during a sandstorm or dust storm if you can avoid it. If you are caught in a storm like the one shown, slow down immediately. Carefully drive off the roadway and pull well onto the shoulder or other parking area. Turn off your lights. Turn on emergency flashers. Wait until the storm has passed.

If you must drive, go slowly enough to see clearly. Use low-beam headlights to see and be

seen. As soon as possible after the storm, change oil, oil filter, and air filter.

Flash Floods

A flash flood is a sudden rush of water from heavy rain. A flash flood can develop quickly and unexpectedly. This situation is especially dangerous in the desert because the normally dry ground washes away easily. If a flash flood occurs, drive or climb to high ground and wait for the water to recede. Stay away from creeks or natural drainage areas.

Review It

1. How does gravity affect mountain driving?
2. How does high altitude affect the driver and the car?
3. What special hazards does desert driving pose to you?
4. How should you service the car during desert driving?

DECISION MAKING

1. What hazards do you see? How can you avoid these possible hazards?

2. You are driving the yellow car. You are being passed by another car. You see the oncoming car getting close. What should you do to help the passing driver?

3. You are approaching a curve where your view of the roadway ahead is reduced. What procedures do you follow? What do you identify and predict?

4. You are driving the yellow car. You and the oncoming truck are going to meet on the bridge. The wide truck takes up part of your lane. What should you do?

CHAPTER 10 REVIEW

Review Chapter Objectives

10–1 Characteristics of Rural Traffic
1. List the characteristics of rural roadways. (180)
2. How do rural road conditions affect a driver's determination of a safe speed? (180)
3. How can traffic controls help you travel safely on rural roads? (181)

10–2 Using Basic Skills in Rural Areas
4. How would you use the IPDE process in rural areas? (182)
5. What are the steps in an orderly visual search pattern? (183)
6. How would you approach a curve on a two-lane road? (184)
7. What are some rural situations in which you should increase following distance? (185)
8. What is the procedure for entering a multilane rural road? (186–187)

10–3 Passing and Being Passed on Rural Roads
9. What checks should you make when preparing to pass? (188)
10. List the steps for passing on two-lane roads. (189)
11. Under what conditions and in what situations should you not pass? (190)

10–4 Rural Situations You Might Encounter
12. How should you pass a slow-moving vehicle? (193)
13. How can you separate hazards when meeting traffic? (194)

10–5 Special Rural Driving Environments
14. What safety precautions should you take for driving in the mountains? (196)
15. Describe safety precautions for desert driving. (198)

Check Your Knowledge

Multiple Choice   Copy the number of each sentence below on a sheet of paper. Choose the letter that best completes the statement or answers the question.

1. The single most important decision in driving on rural roads is
(a) the road surface. (b) weather. (c) speed.
(d) roadside hazards. (180)
2. As you approach a hill, your sight distance
(a) becomes shorter. (b) becomes longer.
(c) stays the same. (d) is affected only by curves.
(184)
3. When meeting a line of cars, you should
(a) drive near the center line. (b) drive near the right edge of the road. (c) drive on the shoulder of the road. (d) accelerate. (194)
4. Which action is illegal when being passed?
(a) speeding up (b) maintaining your speed
(c) slowing down (d) staying in your lane (192)
5. What does a solid yellow line on your side of the road mean?
(a) passing permitted (b) do not pass (c) do not exceed 45 mph (d) do not stop (190)

Completion   Copy the number of each sentence below. After each number, write the word or words that complete the sentence correctly.

6. On a rural two-lane road, an intersecting side road will usually have a _____ . (184)
7. When following traffic on rural roads, use the _____ rule. (185)
8. _____ following distances are necessary when you are being tailgated. (185)
9. Most often, you should drive in the _____ lane. (186)
10. The major responsibility for passing safely belongs to the driver _____ . (192)

Check Vocabulary

Copy the number of each definition in List A. Match the definition in List A with the item it defines in List B.

List A

11. a place for runaway truck to stop (197)
12. an area of ground separating lanes of traffic (186)
13. a series of sharp turns on a mountain road (196)
14. a warning sign of a maximum safe speed (184)
15. a vehicle that can travel at only 15 to 25 mph (193)
16. a sudden rush of water from heavy rain (198)
17. the process of searching and scanning critical areas (183)
18. fuel in gaseous form that prevents the engine from starting (197)
19. a place where slow vehicles can leave a mountain road (196)
20. opening into which you drive to avoid a collision (185)
21. slow down or speed up to control where you will meet another hazard (194)

List B

a. orderly visual search pattern
b. advisory speed sign
c. escape path
d. median strip
e. slow-moving vehicle
f. switchback
g. truck escape ramp
h. vapor lock
i. flash flood
j. pull-out area
k. separate hazards

Check Your Understanding

Write a short answer for each question or statement.

22. Why is executing a pass on a two-lane rural road so critical? (184)
23. Why is the use of the IPDE process so important in safely driving on rural roadways? (182)

Think Critically

Write a paragraph to answer each question or statement.

1. You are driving among other vehicles on a multi-lane rural road with a 55-mph speed limit. The car behind is tailgating and appears about to pass you. How can you assist the passing driver and at the same time increase your safety?
2. You are following the truck below on a flat, two-lane highway. The truck is traveling 20 mph below the posted speed limit. You want to pass the truck. What conditions should you consider?

Projects

1. Select a place where you can safely view an area of highway. Keep a record of how many times you see tailgating, improper passing, and failure to properly signal a lane change. Note how long you observed at this location, and *write* a report about your observations.
2. Some states that have open-range lands have rules regarding the right of way for cattle and sheep. Suppose you are traveling in one of these states. **Write** a story that describes the countryside and your experiences during your trip.

Chapter 11

DRIVING ON EXPRESSWAYS

You're the Driver!

Imagine you are driving the car behind the motorcycle on the entrance ramp to this expressway. Traffic is heavy and is moving fast.

What do you predict the motorcyclist in front of you might do? What actions should you take as you approach the acceleration lane?

How can you communicate with the driver behind you?

What should drivers on the expressway do as they approach acceleration lanes?

In this chapter, you will learn the necessary skills for entering, driving on, and exiting expressways. You also will learn how to handle special problems in expressway traffic.

Objectives

Section 11–1   Characteristics of Expressway Driving
1. List five reasons why expressways have lower collision rates than other highways.
2. Tell how to be a safe expressway driver.

Section 11–2   Entering Expressways
3. Tell how to enter an expressway.
4. Describe four possible entrance problems.
5. Explain why entering an expressway from the left is more hazardous than entering from the right.

Section 11–3 Driving on Expressways

6. Explain how to use the IPDE process to achieve a safe path of travel.
7. Explain the importance of reading signs ahead of time on an expressway.
8. Explain why a safe following distance is very important on an expressway.
9. Describe two actions that should be automatic when changing lanes.

Section 11–4 Exiting Expressways

10. List the steps for exiting an expressway.
11. Describe three possible exiting problems.

Section 11–5 Situations You Might Encounter

12. Tell how to avoid highway hypnosis and velocitation.
13. Tell what to do if your vehicle becomes disabled.

Characteristics of Expressway Driving

Driving on expressways is one of the most common and efficient ways to travel. Expressways include interstate highways, freeways, and toll roads. An expressway is a limited-access or **controlled-access highway.** Vehicles can enter or leave an expressway only at interchanges.

Traffic usually moves at high speeds on controlled-access highways. To keep traffic flowing smoothly, many expressways have minimum, as well as maximum, speed limits.

Advantages of Expressways

Expressways are designed to protect you while driving at high speeds. They carry more traffic and are safer than other highways. Despite the high speeds and heavy traffic, you are safer on expressways than on other highways. Collisions and fatality rates are far lower on expressways than on other roadways.

Five reasons why expressways have fewer collisions are:
- Cross traffic is eliminated since there are no intersections.
- Expressways have a median strip or barrier between opposing lanes of traffic.

Cloverleaf Interchange

- Pedestrians, animals, and slow-moving vehicles are not permitted on most expressways.
- The design of expressways helps prevent vehicles from hitting fixed objects.
- Expressways are designed to help drivers anticipate conditions ahead.

Expressway Interchanges

The pictures show the most common types of expressway interchanges. These interchanges have two basic features:
- Vehicles can cross over or under an expressway.
- Vehicles can enter and leave an expressway without interfering with the flow of traffic.

Cloverleaf Interchange
A cloverleaf interchange eliminates left-turn and cross-traffic conflicts for all movements.

Diamond Interchange
A diamond interchange is used when a street that has little traffic crosses a busy expressway. A complete cloverleaf is not needed because left turns can be made easily on the less busy street.

Trumpet Interchange
A trumpet interchange is used where a side road forms a T intersection with an expressway. The trumpet enables traffic to enter and leave the expressway without crossing traffic.

Directional Interchange
A directional interchange is used in complicated intersections with a high volume of traffic. From this type of interchange, traffic is channeled in several different directions.

Diamond Interchange

Trumpet Interchange

Directional Interchange

Strategies for Safe Driving on Expressways

Although expressways have advantages over other types of roadways, collisions on expressways are often more serious. Higher speeds on expressways often place greater demands on both drivers and vehicles. Expressway drivers must keep themselves alert and keep their vehicles in good condition.

When driving on expressways, you should travel at about the same speed as the other vehicles. If you drive too slowly, you can block the smooth flow of traffic and become a possible hazard. Driving faster than other traffic may cause you to be constantly passing other vehicles. Use the following strategies to help you become a safe expressway driver.

Until you gain experience, avoid driving on expressways during heavy rush-hour traffic times.

Prepare Yourself and Your Car

The constant high speeds on expressways can easily put a strain on both you and your vehicle. Make every effort to stay alert and use your IPDE process vigorously when you drive on expressways.

Have a travel plan before driving on any expressway, regardless of trip length. For a short trip, know the name, route, or number for both the entrance and exit you will use. For a long-distance trip, such as through another state, plan stops for food, fuel, and rest.

Once on an expressway, concentrate fully on the driving task. Boredom and fatigue can occur easily when driving on an expressway. You cannot make the decisions and actions necessary for safe expressway driving when you are tired. Always be alert for the actions of other drivers.

Mechanical failure can occur even during a short trip. Keep your vehicle in top condition to guard against mechanical failure when driving on expressways.

Build Experience Gradually

When you first drive alone on an expressway, choose a time when traffic is light. Avoid driving in heavy rush-hour traffic. Practice entering and exiting several times before driving in heavier traffic. When you are driving in lighter traffic, practice lane changes, even when there are no vehicles to pass. Once you have developed self-confidence by driving in light traffic, you will be better prepared to drive in heavier traffic.

Concentrate on the Driving Task Traffic conflicts can develop more rapidly at higher speeds, especially on multilane expressways. Give your full attention to the driving task. Try not to think about other matters. Concentrate strictly on the changing scene and use your best defensive driving strategies.

Cooperate with Other Drivers You must be willing to cooperate with others on an expressway. Cooperating might be difficult when someone cuts you off or moves into the space cushion ahead of your car. Resist the urge to challenge other drivers for any reason. The mature, responsible driver cooperates with other drivers instead of competing with them.

Review It

1. Why do fewer collisions occur on expressways than on other roadways?
2. What are four different types of expressway interchanges?
3. What strategies can you use to help become a safe expressway driver?

Entering Expressways

Before you enter an expressway, make sure you are using the correct entrance ramp. Guide signs mark most entrances and give the route number, direction, and name of a city located in that direction. Many drivers have mistakenly tried to enter an expressway by using an exit ramp. To prevent this error, most states post signs saying WRONG WAY or DO NOT ENTER.

If you start to enter at an entrance you do not want, go ahead and get on the expressway. You can then exit at the first opportunity.

Expressway Entrances

Most expressway entrances have these three parts:

- The **entrance ramp** gives you time to evaluate traffic as you prepare to merge onto the expressway.
- The **acceleration lane** is usually long enough so you can accelerate to the speed of traffic on the expressway. However, accelerating to expressway speed in the acceleration lane is determined by the volume of traffic both on the expressway and in the acceleration lane. Sometimes it is impossible to accelerate to expressway speed.

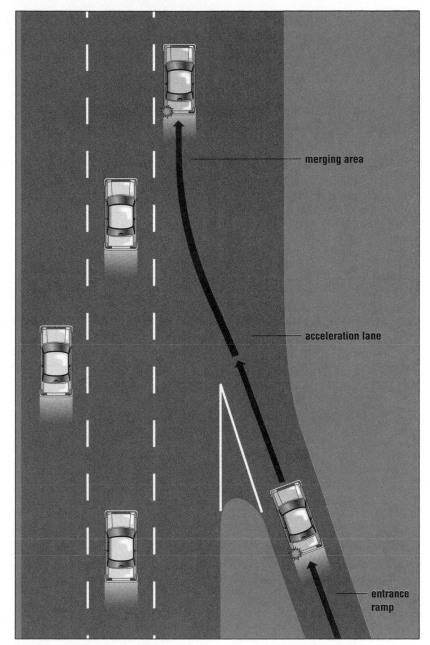

The parts of an expressway entrance

- The **merging area** is the third part of an expressway entrance. Try to enter the expressway from the merging area at about the same speed as the cars in the first lane. Once on the expressway, adjust your speed to the flow of traffic as soon as possible.

merging area

acceleration lane

entrance ramp

Steps for Entering

Follow these steps to enter an expressway smoothly and safely:

1. Be sure the entrance is the one you want and that the ramp is an entrance ramp. Look for a WRONG WAY or DO NOT ENTER sign.

2. Once on the entrance ramp, be alert for vehicles ahead and behind. Take quick glances through your left outside rearview mirror and over your left shoulder to find a gap in traffic that your car will fit into safely. Signal your intention to merge well in advance.

3. Once in the acceleration lane, adjust your speed to the flow of the traffic. Continue to glance quickly in the mirror and over your shoulder to decide the time and place to enter a gap.

4. Before entering the merging area, decide which vehicle to follow in the traffic flow. As you enter the merging area, adjust your speed to match the traffic flow. Position your car at a safe interval behind the car you plan to follow. Merge smoothly.

5. Once in traffic, cancel your turn signal and adjust to the speed of traffic. Keep a safe space cushion around your car.

On the entrance ramp, look for vehicles ahead and behind. Find a gap.

In the acceleration lane, decide where to enter the gap.

Merge smoothly into traffic.

Possible Entrance Problems

Entrance mistakes cause many conflicts and collisions on expressways. Heavy traffic, short entrance ramps, short acceleration lanes, and high dividing walls also can cause entrance problems.

Use the IPDE process at all expressway entrances:

- Make all visual checks quickly. Identify possible problems on each part of the expressway entrance.
- Predict possible actions of other drivers and decide how to adjust and execute your entrance actions safely.

Entrance Ramp Know which expressway entrance ramp you want to use. If you make a mistake and enter a ramp you do not want, continue onto the expressway. Drive to the next exit. *Never back up on an entrance ramp or on an expressway.*

When you are on an entrance ramp, look for other traffic. If traffic is on the ramp, adjust your speed immediately to avoid conflicts. Some ramps, particularly ramps with sharp curves, have signs posting a speed limit. Check your speed and stay within the speed limit. Exceeding the speed limit makes controlling a vehicle difficult, especially in a curve.

Begin looking immediately for a gap in traffic if the entrance ramp is short or there is no acceleration lane. Watch cars ahead of you and behind you. Maintain a safe space cushion.

Gaps can be difficult to find in heavy traffic. If there is no gap, you must slow or even stop before entering the acceleration lane or the expressway. Flash your brake lights to warn the driver behind you in such cases. Avoid stopping whenever possible. Try to adjust your speed so you can continue moving rather than stopping, since stopping can cause a rear-end collision. In the event you have been unable to merge by the end of the acceleration lane, drive straight ahead onto the shoulder. Wait for a safe gap, signal left, and accelerate into the flow of traffic.

If the ramp you have entered has no acceleration lane, adjust your speed on the entrance ramp so your entrance onto the expressway matches your chosen gap.

The vehicle ahead of you can present a problem for you if it slows or comes to a full stop. Give the driver time to find a gap. Make sure the driver merges safely before you accelerate. Again, try to adjust your speed so you can continue moving rather than stopping.

Some entrance ramps have high walls that divide expressway traffic and entering traffic. In this case, you will be far along the entrance ramp before you can see the traffic. Begin checking your left mirror and looking over your shoulder as

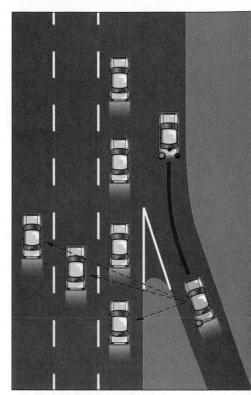

If the vehicle ahead on an entrance ramp slows or stops, give the driver time while you keep observing traffic in all lanes.

soon as you can see traffic on the expressway.

Entrance Ramp Signal Lights Sometimes signal lights regulate traffic entering an expressway. Signal lights often are used during rush hours to space the vehicles entering the expressway

Timed signal lights provide intervals at which vehicles enter the expressway. The lights are red and green in most cases. You must wait for a green light before entering the expressway.

Acceleration Lane   Once you are on an acceleration lane, try to adjust your speed to that of the expressway traffic. The amount of traffic both on the expressway and in the acceleration lane determines your safe speed in the acceleration lane. During rush hours, the large number of vehicles entering and on the expressway can make it impossible to accelerate to expressway speed.

Some entrances have short acceleration lanes. In such cases, you usually do not have the space to accelerate to the speed of expressway traffic. You need a longer gap to enter traffic and accelerate to the traffic speed.

Make every effort to enter an expressway without stopping. Time your entrance and adjust your speed properly. Stopping is extremely hazardous. A driver who is behind you might be looking for a gap, and not realize that you have stopped. If you must stop, take these precautions:

1. Flash your brake lights to warn drivers behind you. Drive the entire length of the acceleration lane.
2. Pull onto the shoulder at the end of the acceleration lane or merge area.
3. You are now in an emergency situation. Wait for a safe gap, signal left, and accelerate quickly as you join traffic.

Sometimes you might follow a driver who seems unsure

Entering an expressway on the left can be more difficult than entering on the right.

about joining traffic. If so, slow down and leave more space between your car and the vehicle in front of you. Be prepared for the driver to stop suddenly.

Merging Area   Time your entrance in order to blend smoothly and safely into expressway traffic. Adjusting your speed is critical as you enter expressway traffic. The drivers ahead of you may cause you to adjust your speed and even to select a new gap. Once you are on the expressway, accelerate to expressway speed when traffic permits. Stay in your lane until you are adjusted and accustomed to the expressway speed.

Entrance Ramp on Left   Not all entrance ramps enter at the right of an expressway. In some cases, the entrance ramp is to the left of the expressway. The acceleration lane merges into

the far left lane of the expressway. Since this lane is used for high-speed traffic, the potential for conflict is greater than when you enter from the right.

Checking fast-moving traffic over your right shoulder can be more difficult than checking to the left. Your vehicle's roof supports can obstruct your view of oncoming traffic. You might have particular trouble seeing an oncoming motorcycle. When you see a gap, accelerate as close to the speed of traffic as possible and merge into the traffic lane.

Review It

1. What are the steps for entering an expressway?
2. What problems might make entering an expressway difficult?
3. Why is the chance for conflict greater when entering an expressway from the left than from the right?

Driving on Expressways

Once you are on an expressway, stay alert and be prepared to adjust to the changing traffic scene. Vehicles are moving at high speeds; be ready to use all your driving skills and knowledge. You must know what to look for, where to look, and how to interpret the information you receive. Use this information to predict and decide accurately.

Applying the IPDE Process

Using the IPDE process on an expressway can help you maintain a safe path of travel. However, higher speeds, multiple lanes to watch, and heavier volume of traffic make the identify step more difficult.

When driving at higher speeds, you should increase the distance for looking ahead to identify and predict possible conflicts. Even though expressways are designed to give drivers a long sight distance, multiple lanes increase the amount of visual information you must gather. Keep these points in mind:

- Identify the volume of traffic in different lanes. Watch for brake lights in all lanes.
- Note signs, signals, and roadway markings.
- Be aware of roadway conditions. Under adverse conditions, stopping distances increase for all vehicles.

A predictable traffic flow is one safety feature of an expressway. However, always watch closely for drivers who make sudden stops or attempt to back up. At a distance, a car backing up might still look like a car going forward. Continually predict the actions of others around you. Be especially alert for sudden lane-change maneuvers.

Execute your decisions smoothly. Avoid making sudden, unexpected decisions or changes in direction. Signal your maneuvers early. Maintain a safe space cushion.

Lane Choice

On the expressway, decide on a lane in which to drive. The volume of traffic, type of traffic, speed of traffic, and your exit plans are all factors you should consider. Generally, it is safer to drive in the right lane and to pass on the left. Reserve the center and left lanes for drivers who are passing, and for faster traffic.

The far right lane has frequent possible conflicts from vehicles entering the expressway. During rush hours, consider using the center or left lane to avoid conflicts in the far right lane. Both the drivers entering and those already on the expressway share responsibility for protecting each other from conflicts.

Trucks, buses, and vehicles towing trailers are required to use only the right lanes on many expressways. Sometimes you will be using these same lanes. If so, make every effort to avoid driving between two large vehicles. If you become surrounded by large vehicles, slow down and make a lane change as soon as possible.

Avoid straddling lane lines. This action prevents other drivers from passing and maintaining their lane positions.

The driver of this car has a short sight distance and limited side vision because of the large vehicles surrounding the car.

If you are in the exit lane, you must exit or move out of the lane safely.

You may not enter all the express lanes, but the green arrows indicate open lanes.

Signs, Signals, and Roadway Markings   Part of your decision on lane choice is based on information from expressway signs, signals, and roadway markings. You are better able to maintain a safe path of travel and avoid making sudden last-second decisions if you

- know your destination
- read signs and roadway markings
- always think ahead.

Sometimes several overhead signs are posted above the roadway at the same place. One sign might say EXIT, another might warn of the NEXT EXIT, and yet another might show route numbers and names of distant cities. In some states, an overhead sign with a yellow panel indicates the exit lane.

Since signs differ from place to place, some might be con-fusing to drivers who are not used to certain expressways. Signs that give drivers the name of the immediate exit as well as the next exit help you plan ahead.

Overhead signals tell you if lanes are open or closed to traffic. A yellow X gives an early warning that the lane will be closed farther ahead. A red X appears farther down that lane to alert you of a closed lane. If you have not changed lanes by the time you reach the red X, you might become trapped in that closed lane. A green arrow means the lane is open for traffic.

Many expressways into and out of cities have express lanes. In most cases, these lanes have only one entrance; traffic moves without conflict from merging vehicles. Express lanes have few exits. These exits are near or in the center of the city. The same lanes are used for morning rush hours into the city and are reversed for the evening rush hours leaving the city.

The right edge of the expressway should be marked with a white line. The left edge should have a yellow line. These lines help you position your car especially at night or during limited visibility.

Speed Limits   The maximum speed limit on most express-ways is 55 mph; it is 65 mph in most rural areas. Some states have a lower speed limit for trucks and other large vehicles. When weather and roadway conditions are good, most vehicles travel at the speed limit.

These speed limits are for good driving conditions. You should drive slower than the minimum speed limit during adverse conditions.

A **minimum speed limit** is posted on many expressways to keep traffic from moving too slowly. The minimum speed limit is the slowest legal speed you can drive under good conditions. The sign in the picture shows a maximum speed limit of 55 mph and a minimum speed limit of 45 mph. During adverse conditions of rain, fog, snow, or slippery roadways, driving under the minimum speed limit is both legal and wise.

During good conditions, driving too slowly can be dangerous and is a potential cause of rear-end collisions. Other drivers might not realize how slowly you are driving until they are too close to you. Use the far right lane if you are driving at the minimum speed limit.

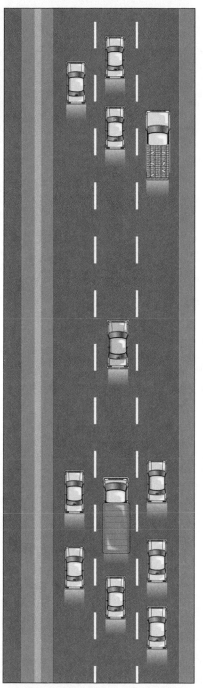

The driver of the yellow car in the center lane wisely decided to be a loner by driving between the two wolf packs.

Safe Driving Tip

When you are driving in the right lane on an unfamiliar expressway, keep looking far ahead for the yellow EXIT ONLY sign. The right lane often becomes an exit ramp, and in heavy traffic you might not have time to change lanes.

Common Speed   If you drive at the **common speed**, the speed used by most drivers, you can better blend with expressway traffic. Sometimes the common speed is above the maximum speed limit. Resist the temptation to increase your speed to keep up with the faster vehicles. Drivers who exceed the speed limit are likely to weave in and out of traffic to pass other vehicles. This practice is dangerous not only to the driver exceeding the maximum speed limit, but also to other drivers on the expressway.

Wolf Packs   An experienced, responsible driver avoids a group or bunch of vehicles known as a **wolf pack.** Reduce your chances of being involved in a conflict by being a "loner" on the expressway. A driver traveling in the middle of a wolf pack is more likely to have trouble with lane changes than a loner. Reduce your speed temporarily to get out of a wolf pack or to let a wolf pack pass.

Following

Keeping a safe following distance is most important on an expressway. Following too closely reduces your sight distance, leaves you little room to maneuver, and is the major cause of expressway collisions.

Applying the 2-second following distance rule on the expressway is a safe plan under ideal conditions. The black car in the center lane in the picture has a good space cushion and a safe following distance. However, the vehicle behind the black car is following too closely and does not have enough space in the front zone. Keeping an ample space cushion around your vehicle gives you both time and space for an "out."

Constantly scan the traffic scene around you to be aware of any situation that may affect your safe path of travel. If a driver cuts into the space ahead, slow down to reestablish a safe following distance.

When the roadway is wet or slippery, reduce your speed and increase your following distance to 3 or 4 seconds. Increasing your following distance is especially important when you are

- following a truck or bus that is blocking your vision
- following a motorcyclist
- driving in bad weather
- driving in heavy traffic
- being tailgated
- driving a heavy vehicle or pulling a trailer

How has the white car created a dangerous situation?

- operating a motorcycle
- entering or exiting an expressway.

Increasing your following distance during limited visibility is critical. Under such conditions as very dense fog, rear-end crashes of up to one hundred vehicles have occurred on expressways. If the drivers of those vehicles had increased their following distance and decreased their speed, these collisions probably would not have occurred.

Blind Spots Remember that you have a blind spot at each rear corner of your vehicle. Check your blind spots often to be alert for other drivers. If you are behind a vehicle in the next lane, keep far enough behind so you are not in that driver's blind spot. Reduce speed, or accelerate and pass in order to stay out of a blind spot.

Being Followed

Many drivers think that they have no control over the space cushion to the rear. The best action to take to get rid of tailgaters is to reduce speed slightly. This action might encourage the tailgater to pass. If a driver continues to tailgate, change lanes if it is safe to do so. Frequently check traffic behind you to stay aware of tailgaters.

The driver in the right lane should slow down or accelerate to get out of the truck driver's blind spot.

Lane Changing

Avoid changing lanes too often. Any change from the regular traffic pattern can cause conflicts. Unnecessary weaving from one lane to another can lead to a collision. Take these steps to change lanes:

1. Change lanes one at a time. Signal *every* lane change, regardless of whether or not other vehicles are present. Do not expect signals to clear the way. Signals only alert drivers of your intention to move.
2. Check traffic in both rearview mirrors. Check the blind-spot area in the direction you want to move.
3. If the way is clear, move to the next lane.
4. Cancel the signal after you have changed lanes.

Once you have made a lane change, establish your position in that lane before moving to another. Drive at the speed of traffic in that lane if it is within the speed limit.

Changing lanes on an expressway is more complicated when three or more lanes are moving in the same direction. Many times a problem occurs when two drivers want to use the same space at the same time. A quick glance over the shoulder lets you check the lane to see if it is open.

If you are not sure of another driver's intentions, make this additional check: See if another

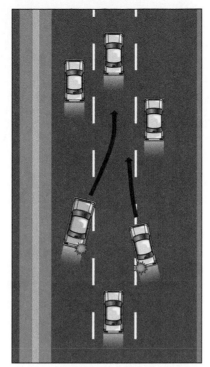

What might happen if two drivers decide to move into the same lane at the same time?

driver opposite you is speeding up or signaling to move into the gap you have chosen. If so, delay your lane change until it is safe to make your move.

Sometimes you will change lanes so entering traffic can merge safely. Remember that some expressways have entrance ramps on the left as well as on the right. If you are driving in the left lane and see a driver entering from the left, change lanes just as you would for traffic entering from the right. If you cannot change lanes, slow down or accelerate to open a gap.

Lanes are often closed during construction or repair. When a lane is closed, drive only in the lanes open for traffic. It is both illegal and hazardous to use the shoulder or median as a driving lane when traffic is backed up. Drivers who drive illegally on the shoulder are also preventing emergency vehicles from having a clear path of travel. Thus, people's lives could be at risk.

During any type of lane narrowing or closing, travel only in the open lanes.

Passing and Being Passed

Passing other vehicles on an expressway usually is safer than passing on a two-lane highway. Since you do not encounter oncoming traffic on an expressway, a head-on collision is not a threat. However, expressway speeds and a higher traffic volume demand caution, concentration, and the constant use of the IPDE process when passing. Always be sure conditions are safe for passing before you begin your maneuver. If you have any doubt about passing a vehicle safely, do not begin to pass.

Passing on the left is usual on expressways. However, passing on the right usually is permitted if a slower driver is in the left lane.

Choose a lane that allows others to pass you on the left. Try not to be a victim of the slogan, "When you're passed on the right, you're wrong." If you are continually being passed on the right, take the tip and move to the lane on your right. Slower drivers who constantly use the center lane usually cause faster drivers to pass on both sides. When you are being passed on both sides, you have diminished the space in both your left and right zones.

When passing another vehicle, follow the procedure for making a lane change to the left. Identify any other users in a lane who might conflict with your passing maneuver. Make

sure the driver you will pass knows that you are passing. If there is any doubt, tap the horn to alert the other driver of your intention to pass. After passing,

Use signals and constantly check traffic when passing on an expressway.

return to your original lane by making a lane change. Throughout your maneuver, keep an adequate space cushion between you and the vehicle you are passing.

Make these two actions automatic when you pass:
- Signal your lane change.
- Check traffic behind with rearview mirrors and traffic to the sides with one or more quick glances to the left or right, as necessary.

When you are being passed, be aware of the position of the vehicle passing you. If you do not have enough space cushion to the side, move away from the passing vehicle. Continue to check the vehicle that is passing you. Keep your speed steady and do not accelerate. Blending into the flow of traffic is just as important during passing as it is when entering or exiting an expressway.

Review It

1. How can using the IPDE process help you maintain a safe path of travel on expressways?
2. Why should you read signs ahead of time on expressways?
3. Why is a safe following distance especially important on expressways?
4. What two actions should be automatic when changing lanes to pass on an expressway?

Exiting Expressways

Leaving an expressway can be a smooth procedure when you know in advance which exit to take. Most expressway exits provide a **deceleration lane,** an added lane in which to slow down without blocking vehicles behind. In some instances, deceleration lanes are made of a different-colored pavement to let drivers know they are *not* through lanes.

The deceleration lane leads into the **exit ramp**, the ramp leading off the expressway. If you do not slow down enough in the deceleration lane, you might enter the exit ramp at too high a speed. Identify the regulatory sign that shows the exit-ramp speed limit.

Most exits are at the right. Sometimes, though, an exit is at the left. If your exit is from the left, get into the correct lane early to avoid cutting across lanes at the last minute.

If you miss the exit you want, go on to the next exit. *Never stop or back up if you go past your exit.*

Applying the IPDE Process

Use the IPDE process and plan your exit well ahead. Use the IPDE process as follows:

1. Identify the expressway signs showing the distance to your exit. Determine if the exit is from the right or left side.
2. Predict actions of other drivers who might be using the same exit.
3. Decide on the safe speed for exiting.
4. Execute your maneuver smoothly and blend with slower traffic.

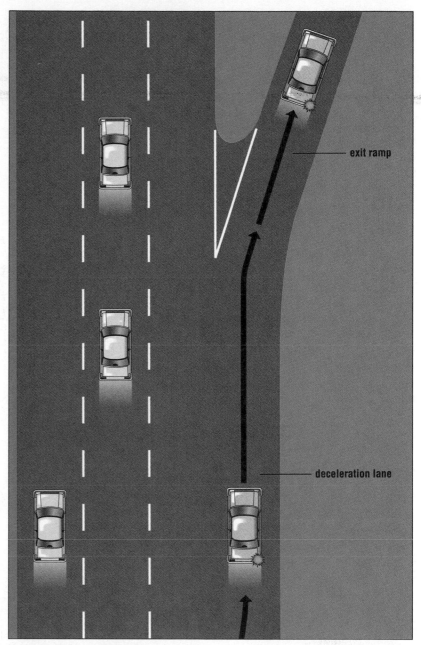

exit ramp

deceleration lane

The parts of an expressway exit

Steps for Exiting

Follow these four steps to exit an expressway:

1. About one-half mile before the exit, signal and move into the lane that leads into the deceleration lane. Avoid last-second decisions and sudden moves.

2. Move into the deceleration lane. Do not slow down until your car is out of the expressway traffic flow.

3. Cancel your signal. Flash your brake lights to warn drivers behind that you are slowing down. Check rear-view mirrors so that you know the speed of following traffic. Slow down gradually to keep a space cushion ahead and behind you.

4. Identify the exit-ramp speed sign. Check your own speed, and adjust to the exit-ramp speed limit.

   Be alert when entering traffic on a local highway or street after leaving the expressway. Anticipate two-way traffic, pedestrians, intersections, and the need for lower speeds. Expressway drivers often find it difficult to slow down to lower speeds after they leave the expressway. Check your speedometer frequently and be alert for the typical hazards of two-way streets and roads.

Identify your exit well in advance.

Move into the deceleration lane.

Adjust your speed to the exit-ramp speed limit.

Possible Exiting Problems

Leaving an expressway should be a smooth operation. However, problems such as those discussed below can occur.

If the same lane is used for entering and exiting, drivers' paths might cross.

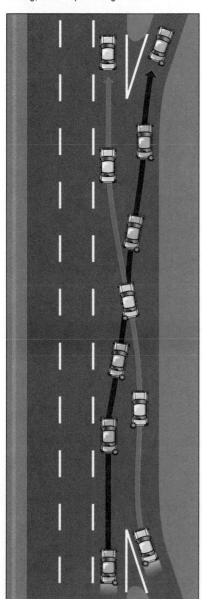

Crossing Paths   On some expressways, like the one shown, the same lane is used as both an entrance and an exit. In this situation, one driver might accelerate to enter the expressway while another might decelerate

How can you exit if traffic is backed up at an exit ramp?

to exit at the same time. Both drivers must watch out for the other to avoid conflicts. In most cases, it usually is safer to let the entering driver go first. However, when you are the entering driver, do not count on an exiting driver yielding to you.

Ramp Overflow   Traffic can back up from an exit ramp into the expressway. Rather than joining the overflow and risking a rear-end collision, go past the exit and use the next exit. Start slowing early if you must use a backed-up exit. When you see vehicles backed up near the exit ramp, flash your brake lights to warn traffic behind you. Check traffic to the rear to see if it is slowing. If it is not slowing, try to pass the exit area smoothly, and drive to the next exit.

Short Deceleration Lane   Slow more quickly if a deceleration lane is short. Being aware of traffic behind you is extremely critical in such situations. As you enter a deceleration lane
- judge the lane's length
- identify the exit-ramp speed
- check speed while braking
- watch traffic to the rear.

Review It

1. What steps should you follow when exiting an expressway?
2. What are three possible exiting problems?

219

Situations You Might Encounter

Expressways can provide the safest type of driving. Even so, driving on these highways does have certain hazards.

To help avoid highway hypnosis, stop occasionally at rest areas to exercise and to get a drink of water.

Driver Condition

Driving for long periods of time can affect drivers. Be alert for problems that can affect you and other drivers on the road.

Highway Hypnosis

Staying alert can be a problem when you travel long distances on expressways or interstate highways. You drive mile after mile at steady speeds with few hills, curves, or interchanges. A driver can be lulled into an in-attentive, drowsy state known as **highway hypnosis**. Some drivers have actually fallen asleep while driving because of highway hypnosis. Other drivers might sit back in a less-than-alert state, becoming spectators rather than attentive drivers.

When you first notice that you are becoming drowsy or that your attention is shifting, take these actions to stay alert:

- Sit up straighter, open a window, or change a radio station.
- Stop at the next rest area and stretch, take a walk, or eat a light meal. Even walking around your vehicle several times can be enough exercise to make you more alert.
- If you need more rest, stop at a safe place and get some sleep.

These actions can help you avoid highway hypnosis:

- Avoid eating heavy meals before or during a trip.
- Wear comfortable clothes.
- Sing or talk with passengers.
- Avoid driving for very long periods of time.
- If you are using cruise control, turn it off for a while so you must pay more attention to your speed.
- Keep your eyes moving, scanning the roadway ahead. Make an extra effort to use your visual search pattern systematically. Include frequent and regular checks to your mirrors.
- Maintain constant interest in traffic signs, signals, roadway markings, and the changing traffic conditions.
- Let someone else drive.
- If you are alone, sing, talk to yourself, whistle, or chew gum. These actions will help keep your wits and your reflexes alert.

Velocitation

Hours of driving can fool you into thinking your car is traveling slower than it really is. You might then unconsciously drive too fast. This condition, called **velocitation,** can be especially hazardous when you exit an expressway.

The roadways you drive on after exiting usually have a lower speed limit than the expressway. If you are "velocitized," you might continue to drive at expressway speeds after making your exit. To correct this condition, check your speed often when exiting and after joining other traffic off the expressway. Take time to adjust to lower speeds.

Road Conditions

You need to be aware of the characteristics of certain expressways in order to drive safely on them. Roadway problems also can arise.

Expressways Through Cities

Even though expressways move traffic efficiently through cities, city expressways tend to carry a high volume of traffic. City expressways have many more entrance and exit ramps than rural expressways. More ramps increase merging traffic conflicts and also give late decision-makers opportunities to make sudden moves.

Remember these points when driving through a city, especially during rush hours:

- In most cases, drive in the center or left lane to avoid merging vehicles.
- Know well in advance where you want to exit. Get in the correct lane early. A high volume of fast-moving traffic can make lane changing difficult and dangerous.
- Look constantly for signs, signals, and roadway markings.
- Predict that other drivers might be less aware and less alert than you are. Try to predict other drivers' sudden actions and driving errors. Be prepared to react correctly to avoid conflicts.

Disabled Vehicle

Take these steps at the first sign of trouble with your car:

1. Signal and pull as far as possible onto a safe place on the shoulder or median.
2. Turn on your emergency flasher lights. Get everyone out of the car and away from traffic.
3. When safe to do so, raise the hood and tie a white cloth to the antenna or door handle.
4. Set out **emergency flares** or reflectors if you have them. Place them at least 500 feet behind your disabled car. Both devices warn approaching drivers of your disabled car.

Roadway Repair

Be alert for roadway repair zones. Watch for orange construction signs and begin to slow as soon as you identify the first one. Follow the directions of the workers.

If your car becomes disabled, raise the hood and tie a white cloth to the left door handle or antenna.

Drive slowly and very cautiously around roadwork zones.

Rural Interstate Highways

Driving long distances on interstate highways can become monotonous. Check your speed frequently, and look as far ahead as possible. Use hill crests and curves to scan far ahead to determine your safe path of travel.

Some drivers tend to drive faster on rural interstates. Do not increase your speed even though you are passed. Larger vehicles and tractor-trailer trucks on rural interstates might pass you. Wind gusts from these vehicles can make car control more difficult. As such a vehicle starts to pass you, reduce your speed a little. Grip your steering wheel firmly.

Remember that larger vehicles cannot stop as quickly as you can. Try not to let these vehicles tailgate you. Pass a larger, slower-moving vehicle only when it is safe to do so.

Tollbooths

Tollbooth areas are located along some expressways. You stop at a tollbooth and pay a fee, or toll, for driving on the expressway. On some expressways you may be given a toll ticket that lists the exits on that expressway. You then pay the toll as you exit.

Tollbooth areas can create special problems. Some drivers make last-second lane changes and quick stops as they approach a tollbooth.

Rough sections of roadway, called **rumble strips,** are built

If you do not have exact coins, which tollbooth should you use?

into the approach lanes of many tollbooth areas. Rumble strips warn drivers of the tollbooth area ahead.

When approaching a tollbooth area, look for a green light above a tollbooth. A green light indicates that the tollbooth is open for traffic. Do not enter a booth with a red light overhead; that booth is closed.

Most toll areas have two types of tollbooths. One type is machine-operated or automatic. A second type is operated by an attendant. Traffic usually moves more quickly through automatic tollbooths. If you select an automatic tollbooth, make sure you have the exact change ready before you enter the tollbooth. In most cases, attendant-operated tollbooths collect tolls from drivers without exact change, drivers of large vehicles, and drivers of vehicles towing trailers.

As you leave a tollbooth, watch the vehicles leaving the booths on both sides of you.

Other drivers might want to enter the same lane as you. If you are in doubt as to who goes first, yield to the other drivers.

Using Expressways Safely

Three key factors contribute to safe driving on expressways:
- cooperation among drivers
- concentrating on the driving task
- continual use of the IPDE process.

Keep these factors in mind as you gain experience and appreciation of expressways.

Review It

1. How do you avoid highway hypnosis or velocitation?
2. What are the special problems of driving on an expressway through a city?
3. What should you do if your car becomes disabled?
4. What are three key factors that can help you drive safely on expressways?

DECISION MAKING

1. The yellow car is about to enter the merge area. What should Car 1 do? How can Car 2 help? What should Car 3 predict?

2. What problems does a lane straddler cause on an expressway? What can you do to reduce the hazard of this situation?

3. What should the approaching driver already have identified in this situation? What should the driver predict and decide? What actions should the driver take?

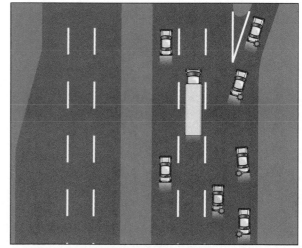

4. The driver of the yellow car plans to exit the expressway. The same lane is used for exiting and entering. What should the driver of the yellow car do? Why is this decision wise?

CHAPTER 11 REVIEW

Review Chapter Objectives

11–1   Characteristics of Expressway Driving
1. What are five reasons why expressways have lower collision rates than other highways? (204)
2. How can you become a safe expressway driver? (206)

11–2   Entering Expressways
3. What are the steps for entering an expressway? (208)
4. What are four possible entrance problems? (209)
5. Why is entering an expressway from the left more hazardous than entering from the right? (210)

11–3   Driving on Expressways
6. How can you use the IPDE process to achieve a safe path of travel? (211)
7. Why is it important to read signs ahead of time on an expressway? (212)
8. Why is a safe following distance very important on an expressway? (214)
9. What two actions should be automatic when changing lanes? (216)

11–4   Exiting Expressways
10. What are the steps for exiting from an expressway? (218)
11. What are three possible exiting problems? (219)

11–5   Situations You Might Encounter
12. What actions can you take to avoid highway hypnosis and velocitation? (220)
13. What should you do if your vehicle is disabled? (221)

Check Your Knowledge

Multiple Choice   Copy the number of each sentence below on a sheet of paper. Choose the letter that best completes the statement or answers the question.
1. Expressways differ from other highways because they have
(a) traffic signs. (b) controlled access. (c)short sight distances. (d) no shoulder on the right. (204)
2. Entering an expressway from the left
(a) takes more time. (b) is safer than from the right. (c) reduces traffic volume. (d) has greater potential for conflict. (210)
3. The major cause of expressway collisions is
(a) construction. (b) following too closely.
(c) passing. (d) exiting. (214)
4. If you are being passed continually on the right, you should
(a) stop. (b) speed up. (c) move to the lane to your right. (d) move to the left lane. (216)
5. Where should you begin to slow down when exiting an expressway?
(a) in the merge lane (b) in the deceleration lane (c) on the ramp (d) in the acceleration lane (217)
6. When can velocitation be especially hazardous?
(a) when driving on an expressway (b) when passing (c) when changing lanes (d) when exiting an expressway (220)

Completion   Copy the number of each sentence below. After each number, write the word or words that complete the sentence correctly.
7. A ramp leading onto an expressway is an ____ . (207)
8. The left edge of an expressway's traffic lanes should be marked with a ____ . (212)
9. A group of vehicles traveling in a bunch is called a ____ . (213)
10. Rough areas built into a roadway are called ____ . (222)
11. To avoid a conflict, ____ to other drivers moving into the same lane as you after leaving a tollbooth. (222)
12. ____ is a major key to safe driving on an expressway. (222)

Check Vocabulary

Copy the number of each definition in List A. Match the definition in List A with the term it defines in List B.

List A
13. permits traffic to enter expressway only from interchanges (204)
14. area where you join expressway traffic (207)
15. where you try to accelerate to the speed of expressway traffic (207)
16. slowest legal speed allowed under ideal conditions (213)
17. speed used by most drivers (213)
18. group or bunch of vehicles (213)
19. lane used for slowing down after leaving expressway traffic (217)
20. ramp leading off the expressway (217)
21. condition lulling a driver into drowsiness (220)
22. condition of unconsciously driving too fast (220)
23. used to warn others of a disabled vehicle (221)

List B
a. acceleration lane
b. common speed
c. controlled-access highway
d. deceleration lane
e. emergency flares
f. exit ramp
g. highway hypnosis
h. merging area
i. minimum speed limit
j. rumble strips
k. velocitation
l. wolf pack

Check Your Understanding

Write a short answer for each question or statement.

24. What actions should you take if you are unable to merge by the end of the acceleration lane? (210)
25. Under what conditions could you legally drive under the minimum speed limit? (213)
26. When is driving at the common speed not a wise decision? (213)
27. What can you do to get rid of a tailgater? (214)

Think Critically

Write a paragraph to answer each question or statement.

1. How would you compare the difference in fuel saving between driving on expressways and driving in cities?
2. Imagine you are driving on an expressway and are being lulled into a feeling of drowsiness. Explain how this condition might develop into velocitation.
3. Compare the conditions under which you might choose the right lane of an expressway to those when you would choose the center or left lanes.
4. Both the drivers of Car A and Car B are entering an expressway in the picture. You are the driver of Car B. Why is the potential for conflict greater for you than for the driver of Car A?

Projects

1. Choose a spot where you can observe an entrance ramp onto an expressway from a safe place. Study the actions of drivers who enter the expressway. **Write** a report on how drivers handle merging situations in heavy traffic.
2. Measure the 2-second following distance when riding with other drivers on expressways. Compare their following distances during ideal conditions to those during adverse weather conditions.

Chapter 12

DRIVING IN ADVERSE CONDITIONS

You're the Driver!

Imagine you are driving your relatives to the airport on this snowy night. Traffic is heavy, and your passengers are in a hurry to catch their flight.

What precautions can you take to make sure you can see clearly in situations like this?

What can you do to help other drivers see you and predict what you're going to do?

How can you make sure that all drivers near you have time to use the IPDE process on this night?

If needed, could you use the controlled braking technique on this road?

To make sure you will drive safely in adverse situations like this, you need to plan ahead. You need to take precautions and be ready to respond in unexpected situations.

In this chapter, you will learn how to improve your ability to see and respond while driving in adverse conditions. You will learn special techniques to help you avoid conflicts.

Objectives

Section 12–1 Reduced Visibility

1. Explain how you can gain a clear view around your car in bad weather.
2. Summarize techniques you can use for safe night driving.
3. State what you can do to help others see you in reduced visibility situations.
4. Describe special ways for using the IPDE process in bad weather.

Section 12–2 Reduced Traction

5. Describe what happens to traction during rain and snow.
6. Explain how to check traction on icy roads.

7. Summarize how to drive safely on other slick road surfaces.
8. Describe how to regain control of your car in a sideways skid.
9. Tell how to use the controlled braking technique.

Section 12–3 Other Weather Conditions

10. Explain how to control your car in windy conditions.
11. List precautions for driving in extremely hot and cold weather.
12. Summarize steps for maintaining car control during winter driving.

Reduced Visibility

To use the IPDE process effectively, you must have a clear view ahead of and to the sides and rear of your car. Your chances of having a collision increase if your view is restricted because of darkness, weather, or any other reason.

Your Car Windows

Moisture can build up on the inside of your windows when it rains or when humidity levels are high. Steamy windows will reduce your ability to see ahead and around your car. The instant your visibility starts to be reduced, use your front window defroster, rear window defogger, air conditioner, or open the side windows to remove this moisture.

In cold weather, snow, ice, or frost can build up on the outside of your windows. Clear all your windows *before* driving. Also, remove any snow from your roof, hood, and trunk lid. After your windows are clear, use your front window defroster and rear window defogger to keep them clear.

Windows and headlights get dirty very quickly in bad weather. Be sure to clean them often. Smoking and the vapors

The glare of early morning sunlight can interfere with your vision.

from plastics used in your car's interior can create a thin film on the inside of your windows. Take the time to clean your windows often with a moist towel. You'll be able to see better, especially at night.

Sun Glare

Bright sunlight in the early morning or late afternoon can create glare. Using sunglasses along with the sun visor can cut glare and eyestrain.

If the sun is behind you, other drivers might not see you. Turn

on your low-beam headlights to become more visible. Predict the problems glare can cause for drivers facing you. Mistakes can range from something as simple as not seeing your turn signal to something as serious as not seeing you at all.

Dawn and Dusk

The low level of sunlight just before the sun rises at dawn or sets at dusk can mislead drivers. Cars, motorcycles, and even trucks without headlights can be hard to see.

Just before sunrise and after sunset, try to make your car more visible to others. Turn on your low-beam headlights, even though it might not seem dark enough to use lights. Do not drive with your parking lights only. Other drivers might think that you're parked. In some states, it is illegal to drive with only parking lights on.

Night

Low levels of light at night severely limit your ability to use the IPDE process. You can see more and farther in daylight. Look at the nighttime scene in the picture and ask yourself these questions: "Are all the other drivers sober and alert?" "Could a pedestrian from the right or left stumble across my path?"

Headlights   When driving with headlights on at night, keep these points in mind:

- Use high-beam headlights to see farther ahead, but use them only when no vehicles are in front of you. Switch to your low-beam headlights the instant you see the headlights of an oncoming car, the taillights of a vehicle you are approaching, or the taillights of a car that has just passed you. This precaution prevents the temporary blinding of the other driver.
- Use low-beam lights in bad weather. If you use your high-beam lights in snow, heavy rain, or fog, more light from your headlights will reflect back into your eyes and you will see less.

Meeting Other Vehicles   If an oncoming driver fails to use low-beam headlights after you switch to your low-beam lights, be ready to take these actions:

1. Be sure the oncoming driver is far enough away to be able to react to your actions. Briefly flick on your high-beam headlights to remind the oncoming driver to use low-beam lights.
2. If the oncoming driver still is using high-beam headlights, slow down and glance at the right edge of the road as a guide for your lane position.
3. To avoid being blinded by the oncoming headlights, look ahead with frequent

quick glances to check oncoming traffic. Do not stare directly into the oncoming high-beam headlights.

Compare this daytime scene with the same location at night.

Note how much less area is visible after dark.

Overdriving Headlights The term **overdriving headlights** means driving at a speed that makes your stopping distance longer than the distance lighted by your headlights. It is your responsibility to make sure you do not overdrive your headlights, especially when driving in bad weather, in fog, or on a slick road.

Use the 4-second rule to find out if you are driving within the range of your headlights. Follow these steps to make sure your speed is correct:

1. Pick a fixed checkpoint ahead of your car the instant the checkpoint appears in the area lit by your headlights.
2. Count off four seconds.
3. Once again observe the location of your checkpoint. If you reach the checkpoint after four seconds, your speed is correct. Your stopping distance under normal conditions is within the range of your headlights.

Fog

The small particles of water in fog reflect light. When your headlights shine into fog, some light is reflected back at you, reducing your ability to see. If you use your high-beam headlights, more light will be reflected back, limiting your vision even more. To see better when driving in fog, always use low-beam headlights.

In fog, oncoming vehicles might be closer than they seem.

Fog also reduces your ability to judge distances. Oncoming vehicles may be closer than you think. To avoid trouble, maintain a safe path of travel by adding an extra large space cushion between your car and others.

Before you enter a patch of fog, slow down. Be alert and be prepared to slow even more or pull off the road, if necessary. If you stop at the side of the roadway, use your emergency flashers to warn other drivers that you are not moving.

Rain

Heavy rain reduces your ability to see and be seen. Turn on your windshield wipers to clear the windows, and use your front window defroster and rear window defogger to keep your windows from getting steamy.

Turn on your low-beam headlights to help others see you, even in daytime. Just remember, when your wipers go on, your headlights should go on too. Reduce your speed. Look hard for others who might not have turned on their headlights. Heavy rains at night can literally blind you. If you are blinded by rain, pull off the road until the rain lets up. Don't forget to use your emergency flashers.

Rain also creates problems for cyclists and pedestrians. Cyclists might have trouble controlling bicycles and mopeds on wet, slippery pavement. These roadway users also will be anxious to reach their destinations and get out of the bad weather. In these situations, they might take chances and make mistakes. Stay alert and be ready to avoid them.

How can wind-driven snow affect your vision?

When weather is bad, give yourself extra time to respond to hazards.

speed to maintain control and to give others time to respond to you. If snow covers the roadway, do not crowd the center. This action has the effect of narrowing the roadway and could lead to a head-on collision.

Applying the IPDE Process

When your visibility is reduced for any reason, you need more *time* to use the IPDE process. You, and all other drivers, will need more time to see, think through, and act in bad weather situations. To maintain a safe path of travel in situations such as these, you need to

- slow down
- aggressively search the traffic scene for problems
- build an extra space cushion between you and others so you can maneuver.

Review It

1. What can you do to help others see you at dawn and dusk?
2. When should you switch from high-beam to low-beam headlights at night?
3. Which headlights should you use in foggy weather?
4. What extra measures should you take for applying the IPDE process in bad weather?

Snow

Wind-driven snow can block your vision and cover roadway markings. Heavy snow can pile up and block your rear window, reducing visibility. Slush or ice can also build up on your windshield wipers. If snow, slush, or ice builds up, pull off the roadway and clean your wiper blades. Do not forget to clear your headlights, taillights, and other parts of your car if they need it.

Use low-beam headlights when it snows, even during daylight hours. Reduce your

Reduced Traction

Traction allows your tires to grip the road so that you can control your car. Rain, snow, ice, leaves, loose sand, and gravel on the road can reduce your traction. Reduced traction combined with poor visibility can result in a dangerous driving situation.

Wet Roadways

Rain-slick roads affect more drivers than any other reduced traction condition. The combination of low visibility and standing water can create a high-risk situation.

When Rain Starts   When rain first starts falling, it mixes with dust and oil on the roadway, making the surface slippery. Traction is greatly reduced until additional rain washes this mixture away.

The driver will lose control if a car is hydroplaning.

Your tires will not grip a wet road as well as a dry road. Reduce your speed on wet roads. You can get a little better traction by following in the slightly drier tire tracks left by the car or truck ahead of you.

Hydroplaning   When roads are wet, braking, steering, or even driving into a sudden gust of wind can be difficult. A car might be **hydroplaning**—its tires ride the surface of the water rather than grip the road. In an instant, steering and braking control could be lost.

Hydroplaning is caused by a combination of standing water, speed, and tire condition. If tires are new and inflated properly, their deep treads will cut through water and grip the road. However, even with good tires, hydroplaning can start at about 50 mph. Worn, bald, underinflated tires can start to lose their grip at less than 30 mph. Slushy snow in standing water can increase your chance of hydroplaning.

To avoid hydroplaning, take the following precautions if you must drive through water:
- Reduce speed, especially if standing water is deep enough to have raindrops "splash" on the water's surface.
- Use properly inflated tires with good tread.

Deep Water   Avoid driving through deep water whenever possible, especially if you are

unsure of the quality of the roadway. If you cannot avoid deep water, take these steps to prevent stalling:
1. Check the water depth by watching other cars and looking at objects such as fire hydrants, fence posts, and parked cars. If the water is up to the bottom of your car, *do not enter the water*. Turn around and use another route even if you must drive several miles out of your way. Moving water, even if it is less than two feet deep, can be very powerful.
2. If the water is lower than the bottom of your car, but over the rim of your tires, drive slowly in a low gear. Avoid using the road's soft shoulder. Try to drive in the higher center of the road.
3. When driving through water, use light pressure on your accelerator. At the same time, brake gently with your left foot to build friction on the brake pads. Friction heat will help to dry your brakes and keep them working.
4. After leaving the water, tap your brake pedal lightly to check if your brakes are wet. If your car pulls to one side or does not slow, drive for a short distance, applying light pressure on your brake pedal. The added friction from the brake pressure will generate heat to dry your brakes.

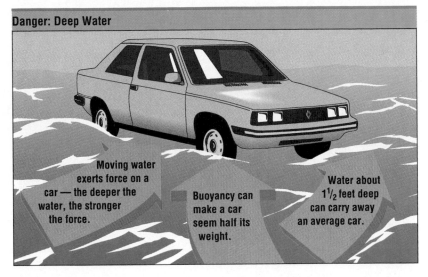

Danger: Deep Water

Moving water exerts force on a car — the deeper the water, the stronger the force.

Buoyancy can make a car seem half its weight.

Water about 1½ feet deep can carry away an average car.

Snow

Different types of snow can produce different levels of traction. When fresh snow falls at low temperatures, traction can be fairly good. When traffic packs the snow down at places such as intersections, traction is reduced. In subzero weather, even the exhaust from cars can freeze into ice on the pavement at intersections. Skids can occur very easily.

Some of the worst traction conditions occur near freezing temperatures (32°F) when snow starts to turn to watery slush. The combination of snow and water can create very slippery surfaces.

Driving Techniques on Snow

Gentleness is the key to maintaining car control in snow. Gentle acceleration, slight steering, and light braking produce the best results. Put your car into motion gently to best use the limited amount of traction between your tires and the roadway. If your drive wheels start to slip while moving forward, release your accelerator. Start again gently.

To improve traction on snow, use snow tires on the wheels that power your car. To improve traction even more, many states allow the use of **tire chains.** They are placed over the tire tread to increase traction on snow- or ice-covered roads.

Rocking a Car   You often can move your car out of snow by **rocking the car.** If your car is stuck in deep snow (or mud or sand), you can usually rock it free by following these steps:

1. Turn your front wheels straight to reduce the added resistance of turning.
2. Gently accelerate to move forward. *Do not spin your wheels.*
3. Let up on your accelerator the instant your car stops moving forward. Pause just long enough to let the engine slow. Shift to REVERSE, and move backward. When you stop moving backward, let up on your accelerator and shift to DRIVE to move forward.
4. Continue this backward-and-forward movement until your car has cleared tracks that are long enough to drive out of the deep snow.

With help from neighbors, the driver is about to move forward in tracks cleared by rocking the car.

Ice

Be especially cautious if temperatures are falling during rain, or if sleet falls. Rain falling on cold roads can freeze without any visible change on the road surface. When ice begins to form, expect roads to get slippery. Ice and sleet make driving extremely dangerous.

Temperature can change the amount of traction on ice. At very cold temperatures (near 0°F), traction is somewhat better than at slightly warmer temperatures. When ice is at or near the freezing point (32°F), traction can be very poor. If water forms on the ice, your control can be reduced to almost nothing.

To check traction in icy areas, tap your brakes lightly. Perform this check only at low speeds, away from traffic. If your car starts to slide, let up on your brake and slow down gradually.

Windows and windshield wipers can also ice up in severe weather. If you cannot keep your windows ice-free with wipers and defrosters, pull off the road and clear them by hand. Under these conditions, it might be best not to drive at all. If you must drive, be alert for the following icy situations.

- **Ice on Bridges** The roadway surfaces of bridges tend to freeze before the surfaces of roads leading to them. Cold air circulates above

Ice has formed on the bridge even though the street has not yet frozen.

and below the roadway on bridges and overpasses. As a result, ice and snow form first on these structures.

- **Ice in Shade** When driving on a sunlit road, be alert for ice forming in the cool, shaded part of the same road. Water from melting snow and ice can freeze in shaded areas.

- **Ice in Tire Tracks** Snow can pack and turn to ice in the normal tracks of travel in your lane. You can avoid these slippery tracks by moving a little to the right in the

unused portion of your lane. You might increase your traction by driving on loose snow, sand, or gravel on the edge of the road.

Other Reduced Traction Surfaces

All low-traction surfaces will increase your stopping distance. When driving on these surfaces, you must anticipate that you will need a longer stopping distance.

How can loose gravel on a roadway affect your control of a vehicle?

If these leaves are wet, they could reduce your traction.

Watch for loose material on the road near construction sites.

Gravel Roadways Loose gravel on some roads can act like marbles under your tires and cause skids. Well-packed wheel paths can form on heavily traveled gravel roads. Drive in these paths for better traction and control. If you need to move out of the wheel paths, slow down, hold your steering wheel firmly, and be prepared to steer for control. Also be alert for unexpected rough stretches of roadway.

Leaves During the fall, wet leaves on the road can reduce traction and change your stopping and steering control. If you have to drive on wet leaves, slow ahead of time. Though leaves may appear to be dry, they can be wet underneath. Steer and brake gently as needed.

Construction Areas In construction areas, trucks and other equipment can leave mud, dirt, or sand on the road. Slow, steer gently, and obey workers' directions. Be especially careful for workers and construction drivers who do not see you. Use an extra space cushion to protect them.

If your car skids to the right. . .

you see something like this. . .

If your car skids to the left. . .

you see something like this. . .

and you steer this way.

and you steer this way.

Skidding

Your car can skid on snow, ice, or smooth, dry pavement. Different combinations of traction and speed can produce a skid. Be alert to your level of traction and adjust your speed *ahead* of time. Avoid sudden, hard braking and accelerating.

Skidding can be frightening. Many drivers who skid panic and freeze at the wheel. To avoid trouble like this, you need to be able to respond quickly the *instant* you sense a skid. In any skid, remember: *Do not give up.* Always try to drive out of any one of the following skids.

Power Skid If your tires start to spin when you accelerate, you are experiencing a **power skid.** Ease off your accelerator. Sometimes your tires can spin because of the fast-idle setting on your engine. If you are trying to make a very gentle stop on a very slick road, shift to neutral and slow to a stop by gently pushing your brake pedal.

Braking Skid Your car can skid if you lock your wheels by braking too hard. This type of skid is called a **braking skid.** The *instant* you sense a braking skid, let up on your brake pedal to unlock your wheels. *Locked wheels provide no steering control.*

Sideways Skid If the rear of your car skids to the right or left, you are experiencing a **sideways skid.** Again, the *instant* you sense a skid starting, do the following:
1. Ease off your accelerator or brake. You must keep your wheels rolling to maintain steering control.
2. Steer precisely in the direction that the rear of your car is skidding. Or, in other words, steer in the direction you originally wanted to go. Steer just enough so that your car continues in a straight line. *Do not overcorrect for the skid by steering too much.*
3. Your car may continue to skid a little from side to side, or fishtail, after you have corrected for the initial skid. If so, steer in the direction of the other skids as they occur until you have gained control. As your speed drops, your control will increase. Steering actions should be done with a precise, smooth, continuous motion.

Imagine you are the driver in the situation shown. As the rear of your car skids to the right, you steer right. If the skid is to the left, you steer left. You can see how your smooth corrective actions have enabled you to regain control of your car.

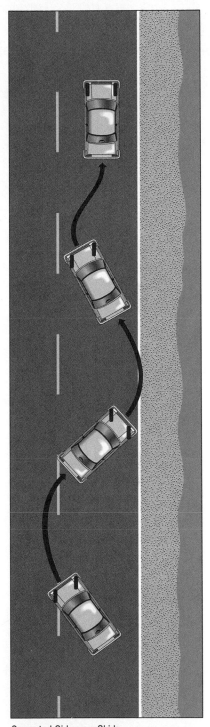

Corrected Sideways Skids

237

This driver might have prevented the skid by reducing speed before entering the curve.

Skidding in a Curve

If you enter a curve too fast, your tires might not have enough traction to hold you in the curve. You might be able to drive through a curve at a modest speed on dry, smooth pavement. But, if the curve has ice and snow, you might not be able to maintain control.

If the rear of your car skids to the outside of a curve, you need to know what to do ahead of time. Follow these steps to regain control from a skid in a curve:

1. Ease off your accelerator or your brake. Keep your tires rolling to maintain steering control.
2. Steer in the direction the rear of your car is skidding.
3. Once you correct the skid, continue to reduce your speed. Center your car in your lane once you have gained control.

If you are correcting a skid in a curve and must leave your lane, keep on trying to regain control. You might have to slip off the edge of the road to bring your car under control. But, slipping off the road is better than losing control of your car.

To prevent skidding in a curve, you only need to remember one thing: reduce your speed *before* you enter the curve.

Controlled Braking

Even though you drive defensively, you might have to make a quick stop to avoid a conflict. A quick panic stop can lock your wheels, causing a skid and loss of steering control. Remember, *locked wheels provide no steering control.*

To reduce your speed as quickly as possible while maintaining control of your car, use **controlled braking.** Controlled braking is a technique of applying your brakes to slow or stop quickly without locking your wheels. Follow these steps for controlled braking:

1. Squeeze your brakes. You must squeeze hard enough to slow your car rapidly, but not hard enough to lock your wheels. You must keep your wheels rolling to maintain steering control.

2. If your wheels lock and your car starts to skid, ease up on your brakes until your wheels start rolling. Then squeeze your brakes again.

3. Keep squeezing your brakes (and releasing them briefly as needed) until you have avoided the hazard.

Applying the right amount of brake pressure is the difficult part of controlled braking. If you squeeze too hard, you will skid. If you do not apply enough pressure, you won't stop as fast as possible. Squeezing with the right amount of pressure is especially difficult in a curve. A computer-controlled **antilock braking system**, or "ABS" was developed to help drivers use controlled braking while maintaining control of their vehicles.

The chart below shows how long it takes to stop from 20 mph. Notice how various surfaces and tires can make a difference in stopping distances. Remember, even with controlled braking or an antilock braking system, you must slow ahead of time to maintain control on slippery surfaces.

Review It

1. What happens when a vehicle hydroplanes?
2. Where can you expect ice to form first on a roadway?
3. Why must you keep your wheels rolling when braking in a curve?
4. How can you prevent skidding in a curve?

Braking Distances at 20 mph

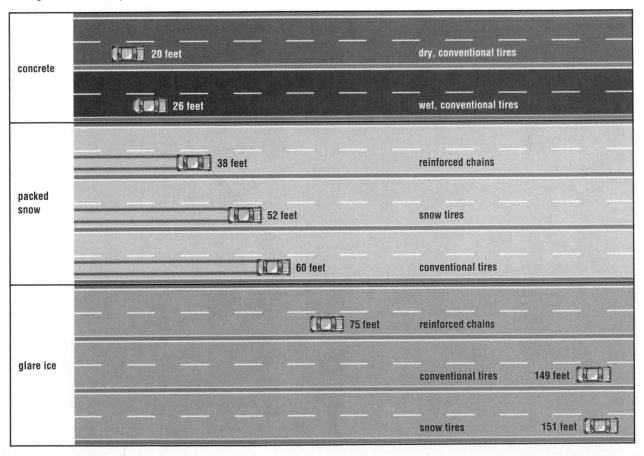

concrete	20 feet	dry, conventional tires
	26 feet	wet, conventional tires
packed snow	38 feet	reinforced chains
	52 feet	snow tires
	60 feet	conventional tires
glare ice	75 feet	reinforced chains
	149 feet	conventional tires
	151 feet	snow tires

Other Weather Conditions

Under normal weather conditions, you sometimes might drive into a difficult situation. That same situation can be even tougher if you are driving in extreme weather conditions.

Wind

Strong winds can reduce your control of your car. Imagine that a truck is passing you at 55 mph. In addition, a very strong crosswind is blowing from the left. What should you anticipate? How can you maintain control?

First, anticipate a wind blast from the truck. A strong blast will push your car to the right. Second, be ready to slow and steer slightly into the wind to the left to maintain a straight path of travel.

You might have a similar problem when you drive out from under a bridge, underpass, or tunnel. You might suddenly feel a strong crosswind. Use the IPDE process. Slow down, and keep a firm grip on your steering wheel as you steer to maintain control.

Head and tail winds can also cause problems. You might have to accelerate a little harder when driving into a strong head wind. A tail wind pushes your car forward, making it build speed. In a tail wind, you need to slow ahead of time and anticipate that it will take longer to come to a stop. In all high-wind situations, steering can be difficult. Be alert and ready to slow down. Hold the wheel firmly and steer carefully to maintain control.

Each vehicle handles differently in high winds. Small, light cars and motorcycles will be difficult to hold in a lane. Vans, campers, and cars pulling trailers may also have handling problems, especially at highway speeds. A car-top carrier can make a car harder to handle in high winds. The instant you sense that another driver ahead of you is having trouble, slow down and give the driver extra space to maneuver.

Expect to feel a blast of wind as a fast-moving truck passes you, and on a windy day the effect will be even stronger.

You might feel a strong wind gust as you drive out from under a bridge.

Hot Weather

Your car is designed to operate in a wide range of temperatures. It has a system to keep the engine cool in hot weather. However, in extreme conditions, your engine can develop problems.

Gasoline is a liquid when it is pumped to your engine. During very hot weather, the gasoline might boil and turn to a vapor. A condition called vapor lock develops. Your engine cannot use vaporized fuel, and if it receives fuel in this form, it stops running or "locks." If your engine becomes vapor-locked, turn it off. Let it cool, so the fuel in the fuel line from your gas tank will cool as well. Once the vaporized gasoline cools and returns to its liquid state, you should be able to restart your engine.

Your temperature light will warn you when your engine is too hot. Your temperature light might go on when you are
- pulling a heavy load uphill
- using a bad thermostat
- in stop-and-go traffic
- using your air conditioner in very hot weather.

If your temperature light appears, turn off your air conditioner if it is on. If the light does not go out after a few moments, turn on your heater. The added heat will be uncomfortable, but this action will help cool your engine.

If your temperature light still stays on, park your car and turn off your engine. Let your engine cool and then check for leaks in your cooling system. To avoid being scalded, do *not* open your radiator when your engine is hot.

Cold Weather

Very cold weather can also create problems. During extremely cold weather, take certain precautions, as follows:
- **Be Alert for Exhaust Leaks** You probably tend to keep your windows shut in cold weather. If you have a small exhaust leak, the deadly gas carbon monoxide can seep into your car. You cannot smell this gas. To prevent the gas from building up, open a window slightly when driving. If you are stuck in snow, make sure your exhaust pipe is not blocked.
- **Do Not Race a Cold Engine** Racing a cold engine can increase engine wear. Do not run a cold engine at high speeds.
- **Do Not Set the Parking Brake** After driving through icy or slushy conditions, do not set your parking brake when you park your car. The parking brake could freeze. Use the PARK gear position with an automatic transmission or REVERSE with a manual transmission.

How would you interpret what happened in this scene?

Clear snow off your car roof, hood, and trunk so it will not blow off and block your vision.

Suggestions for Winter Driving

Using the IPDE process in winter will take the best of your driving skills. You will need to use an extra effort to maintain an adequate line of sight, path of travel, and space cushion on snowy or icy roads. You can help yourself by following these guidelines for winter driving:

- **Listen to Radio Traffic Reports**   Adjust your travel plans accordingly.
- **Keep Windows Clear**   Remove snow and ice before driving. Make sure your windshield wipers are clear and work properly.

    Clear snow off your roof, hood, and trunk, so it does not blow off and block your own or others' vision. Make sure you also clear your headlights and taillights so others can see these lights as clearly as possible.

- **Reduce Speed According to Conditions**   Go as slow as necessary until you are sure you have control of your car. Test your brakes by tapping them gently at low speeds to know how much traction you have.
- **Keep a Safe Following Distance**   Allow much more room for a space cushion between you and the car ahead.
- **Keep Moving in Snow**   If you have to be out in a blizzard, be prepared for drivers who are stalled, disabled, or are moving extremely slow. Try to avoid getting stuck behind them. Slow down and maneuver ahead of time to avoid others and keep moving. The energy of motion created by your car will carry you through many snowy situations.
- **Leave a Window Partly Open**   This practice helps keep your windows from fogging and gives you a fresh supply of air at all times.
- **Watch for Danger Spots Ahead**   Roads over bridges and in shady areas might freeze first.
- **Use a Lower Gear on Slippery Roads**   To maintain control, use a lower gear when slowing on an icy or slippery roadway. Keep your tires rolling.
- **Avoid Cruise Control**   Do not use cruise control on slippery roads. You could skid if you had to press your brake pedal suddenly to release your cruise control.

Review It

1. What actions must you take to maintain car control in strong winds?
2. What can you do to cool an overheated engine?
3. Why should you try to keep moving at low speeds in heavy snow?

DECISION MAKING

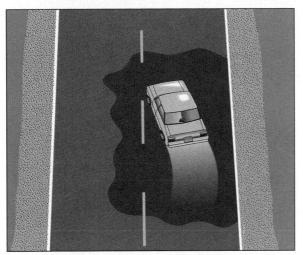

1. What actions should you take in this skidding situation?

2. In this winter situation, what problem could the road over the bridge present? What precaution should you take when approaching this bridge?

3. What visibility and traction problems could you have in this situation?

4. What actions should you take to avoid being blinded by the headlights from the oncoming car?

CHAPTER 12 REVIEW

Review Chapter Objectives

12–1 Reduced Visibility
1. How can you gain a clear view around your car in bad weather? (228)
2. What are some of the techniques you can use for safe night driving? (229)
3. What can you do to help others see you in reduced visibility situations? (230)
4. What are some of the special ways you can use the IPDE process in bad weather? (231)

12–2 Reduced Traction
5. What happens to traction during rain and snow? (232–233)
6. How can you check traction on icy roads? (234)
7. What are some of the things you can do to drive safely on other slick road surfaces? (235)
8. How can you regain control of your car in a sideways skid? (236–237)
9. How can you use the controlled braking technique? (238–239)

12–3 Other Weather Conditions
10. What can you do to control your car in windy conditions? (240)
11. What are some precautions you can take for driving in extremely hot and cold weather? (241)
12. What steps can you take to maintain car control while driving in the winter? (242)

Check Your Knowledge

Multiple Choice Copy the number of each sentence below on a sheet of paper. Choose the letter that best completes the statement or answers the question.

1. To help others see you better while driving at dawn or dusk, use your
(a) high-beam headlights. (b) brake lights. (c) low-beam headlights. (d) emergency flashers. (228)
2. To clear moisture from the inside of your windshield you should use your
(a) heater. (b) wipers. (c) rear window defogger. (d) defroster. (228)
3. When driving in fog, use your
(a) high-beam headlights. (b) low-beam headlights. (c) emergency flashers. (d) parking lights. (230)
4. After driving through deep water, check your car's
(a) acceleration. (b) brakes. (c) oil. (d) lights. (232)
5. Dry out wet brakes by
(a) speeding up and letting them air dry.
(b) parking and letting them air dry. (c) braking lightly at low speeds to let heat dry them.
(d) having a mechanic service them. (232)
6. In cold weather, ice forms first on
(a) hilltops. (b) gravel roadways. (c) bridges and overpasses. (d) driveways. (234)
7. Locked wheels cause a loss of
(a) space cushion. (b) gear-shift ability. (c) lights. (d) steering control. (239)
8. The best corrective action when skidding is to
(a) steer in the direction the rear of your car is skidding. (b) steer straight. (c) steer in either direction. (d) do not steer; let your car come out of the skid by itself. (237)
9. A strong tail wind
(a) requires more acceleration than normal.
(b) makes stopping more difficult. (c) decreases speed. (d) increases fuel consumption. (240)

Completion Copy the number of each sentence below. After each number, write the word or words that complete the sentence correctly.

10. Switch to _____ when meeting an oncoming vehicle at night. (229)
11. Use the _____ to see if you are driving within the range of your headlights. (230)
12. Drive in the tracks left by the vehicle ahead to get better _____ in rain. (232)
13. Snow tires provide _____ traction for driving on snow than regular tires. (233)

Check Vocabulary

Copy the number of each definition in List A. Match the definition in list A with the term it defines in List B.

List A
14. stopping distance exceeds the area lit by headlights (230)
15. computer controlled system to help drivers to use controlled braking (239)
16. tires riding on the surface of standing water (232)
17. devices to increase traction (233)
18. maneuver to free your car from snow, mud, or sand (233)
19. slowing or stopping quickly without locking your wheels (238)

List B
a. antilock braking system
b. controlled braking
c. hydroplaning
d. overdriving headlights
e. rocking the car
f. stopping time
g. tire chains

Check Your Understanding

Write a short answer for each question or statement.

20. If you were driving in the situation in the picture at the right, what actions could you take to gain much needed time to use the IPDE process? (231)
21. Describe the actions you can take to drive through water that is not up to the bottom of your car. (232)
22. Compare the difference in traction between cold and warm wet ice. (234)
23. Explain how you would stop on a very slick road in a car that has a fast idle. (237)

Think Critically

Write a paragraph to answer each question or statement.

1. Throughout the *Drive Right* program, a special emphasis is placed on having enough time to use the IPDE process. Describe the precautions you can take in bad weather so you can gain more time to use this process.
2. Why is it important to know how to control a sideways skid (or any other skid) ahead of time?

Projects

1. To find out how well other new and experienced drivers might handle a sideways skid, conduct this brief survey. Ask 15 new or student drivers and 15 experienced drivers how they would handle this type of skid. Compare the results and report to your class.
2. Post yourself for 20 minutes along a rural highway at dawn or dusk. Count cars with and without headlights on. **Write** a brief report about whether or not most drivers take full advantage of their headlights.

Chapter 13

HANDLING EMERGENCIES

You're the Driver!

Imagine that you are driving into this situation. The car on your right pulls out in front of you. What should you do?

Why should you not swerve to the left?

What action should the driver on the right take to help reduce the impact of the collision?

What should you do if a collision does occur?

Vehicle malfunctions, driver errors, or roadway hazards can cause emergencies. In all cases, you must be prepared to act quickly to avoid or minimize a collision.

In this chapter you will learn how to handle different kinds of emergencies, and what steps to take if you are involved in a collision.

Objectives

Section 13–1   Vehicle Malfunctions
1. List actions to take if a tire blows out.
2. List the steps to follow if the brakes fail.
3. Explain what to do if the accelerator sticks.
4. Tell what to do if the engine fails or if it overheats.
5. Explain what to do in case of steering failure.
6. List actions to take if a raised hood blocks your forward vision.
7. List the steps to take if the car catches fire.
8. Explain what to do if your car stalls on railroad tracks.

Section 13–2   Driver Errors

9. Explain how to return to the roadway if your car runs off the roadway.
10. Explain when to use an emergency swerve.

Section 13–3   Collisions

11. Explain how to avoid or minimize head-on, side-impact, and rear-end collisions.
12. List both immediate and follow-up steps to take if a collision occurs.

Section 13–4   Roadway Hazards

13. Describe how to minimize damage caused by potholes.
14. Tell how to escape a car that is sinking in water.
15. Tell what to do if you enter a curve too fast.

Vehicle Malfunctions

Good maintenance can prevent most vehicle malfunctions. A vehicle often gives warning signs before real trouble occurs. When you notice any warning signs, make the necessary repairs promptly.

Vehicle equipment sometimes will malfunction with no warning. A sudden malfunction in a moving vehicle can create an emergency. You can handle emergencies more successfully if you prepare your responses in advance. If you are prepared for emergencies, you also will reduce your risk of serious trouble in traffic.

Tire Failure

Tires wear, even under ideal driving conditions. All tires eventually need replacing. Many tire failures occur when tires are very worn.

Tires wear more quickly under unfavorable driving and poor maintenance conditions. Long trips, high speeds, and hot roadway surfaces increase wear. Hard, abrupt braking and fast, sharp steering shorten tire life. Bumps, potholes, and poor roadway surfaces add to tire stress and can cause sudden damage to the tires. Unbalanced wheels and poor wheel alignment can cause tires to wear unevenly. Underinflation is also a major cause of tire wear.

Blowouts

A **blowout** occurs when a tire loses air pressure suddenly while you are driving. In tubeless tires, the sudden air loss often occurs around the rim of the wheel. A blowout might occur if the tire hits an object on the roadway or a pothole. Older tires or badly worn tires are more likely to blow out.

When a front tire blows out, the car pulls strongly in the direction of the deflated tire. Therefore, you must steer firmly against the pull of the car to keep the car on its intended path. A left-front blowout is especially dangerous. In such a blowout, the car might pull left toward the lane of oncoming traffic.

When a rear tire blows out, the back of the car can fishtail. When **fishtailing** occurs, the rear of the car swerves first in one direction, and then in the other, until steering is controlled. The fishtail movements are often irregular and abrupt. Handle a rear blowout like a skid. Steer in the direction that you want to go.

Take these actions when a tire blows out:

1. Grip the steering wheel firmly.
2. Ease up on the accelerator to slow the car. *Do not brake.* Braking can cause the car to swerve more. Let the car slow gradually.
3. Check traffic as you gain control of the car.
4. Drive off the roadway slowly, braking gently.
5. Turn on emergency flashers. Drive on the flat tire until you find a safe and suitable place to stop. You might ruin the tire, but stopping suddenly in traffic could cause a collision.

If a left front tire blows out, the car might pull toward oncoming traffic.

Changing a Tire

Even though you might be an auto club member, you should know how to change a tire. Tire-changing instructions often are included in the owner's manual. Instructions also might be found in the spare-tire compartment or inside the trunk lid. Practice following the instructions before a blowout occurs.

You need a jack in order to change a tire. A **jack** is a hand-operated device to lift and hold one corner or side of the car. It is always possible that an elevated car might slip off a jack. Never put yourself in a position where the car could fall on you.

Follow these steps to change a tire:

Rock the spare tire into position as you mount it.

1. Park on a level spot away from traffic. Turn on the emergency flashers. Set the selector lever in PARK; use REVERSE in a stickshift car.
2. Set the parking brake.
3. Block the wheel that is diagonally opposite the flat tire. Carry two blocks of wood or two bricks in your trunk for this purpose. Otherwise use rocks or whatever else is available. Place one block firmly in front of the wheel and another block firmly behind the wheel. Blocking keeps the car from rolling when it is raised on the jack.
4. Ask your passengers to get out of the car and move to a safe place away from the roadway. They should not block other drivers' views of the emergency flashers.
5. Take out the spare tire, jack, and lug wrench.
6. Assemble the jack. Position it under the car according to the instructions.
7. Jack up the car partway. The flat tire should still touch the ground firmly enough so that the wheel cannot turn.
8. Remove the wheel cover, if one is on the wheel. Loosen the **lug nuts**, the devices that hold the wheel onto the car.
9. Jack up the car until the tire completely clears the ground.
10. Use the lug wrench to remove the lug nuts. Place them in the wheel cover or other safe place.
11. Remove the wheel with the flat tire. Place the wheel to the side.
12. Mount the wheel with the spare tire. Rock the wheel gently into position.
13. Replace and tighten the lug nuts.
14. Lower the car and remove the jack.
15. Use the lug wrench to check tightness of all the lug nuts.
16. Leave the wheel cover off as a reminder to fix the flat tire. Put the wheel cover, flat tire, and tire changing equipment into the trunk. Remove the blocks from the wheels.

Replace or repair the flat tire as soon as possible. If your spare tire is a temporary or compact tire, drive on it only as long as necessary until you can replace or repair the regular tire. Check warnings on the temporary tire for other conditions of its use.

Brake Failure

Cars are required to have a two-part braking system. Each part controls two wheels. If one part fails, the other part still brakes two wheels. The brake warning light comes on to signal the partial failure. If both parts fail at the same time, your foot brake will have no braking power at all.

Total Brake Failure

Total brake failure rarely happens. When total brake failure does occur, the driver is usually braking hard for a stop.

If your brakes fail, follow these steps immediately:

1. Pump the brake pedal fast and hard. Pumping might temporarily restore enough brake-fluid pressure to slow or stop your car. You will know after three or four pumps if your brakes are going to hold.
2. Downshift to the lowest gear. Downshifting uses the braking power of the engine and transmission to help slow your car.
3. Apply the parking brake hard. While applying the parking brake, pull and hold the parking-brake release lever out or hold the button at "off." By doing this, you can quickly release the parking brake for a moment if the car begins to skid. The parking brake, a separate braking system, brakes only the two rear wheels.
4. Scan for a safe place to slow. You can still steer the car. If necessary, rub the wheels against a curb to reduce speed. You also might steer into something soft, such as bushes, to reduce speed. If a collision is unavoidable, steer for a sideswipe rather than colliding head-on into something solid.

Power Brake Failure Brake "failure" with power or power assisted brakes is usually the loss of power that helps you brake. The power stops if the engine stops. The brakes have not failed. You simply must push the brake pedal harder than when the engine is running. Restarting the engine returns the power assistance.

Other Brake Failures

When brakes overheat, they can lose some of their effectiveness. This condition, called **brake fade**, occurs after long, continuous, hard braking. To regain full braking ability, stop the car and let the brakes cool. Overheating can warp the rotors on disk brakes. As a result, braking becomes uneven, and the car might surge forward as you brake. To restore smooth braking, you might need to have the rotors reground.

Driving through water also can cause temporary brake failure. Apply your brakes gently after you leave the water. Friction can generate enough heat to dry the brakes.

You might not get the full effect of your brakes if you cannot press the brake pedal all the way down. Objects stored under the driver's seat could move forward during sudden braking and stop under the brake pedal. A wadded floor mat can interfere with the brake pedal. Never reach down to pull out objects while you are driving. Stop your car in a safe place as soon as possible and remove the object.

If your brakes fail, apply the parking brake, but hold the button at OFF or hold the release lever out.

Accelerator Malfunctions

You can lose control of your engine's speed when the accelerator malfunctions. Some problems can cause your car to accelerate more than you intend, and other problems can keep your car from accelerating at all.

Broken Spring

A broken accelerator spring is a serious problem. If the spring breaks, the accelerator is not usable. The accelerator pedal might be flat on the floor. You can no longer control engine speed with the accelerator. Your engine speed might run wild or return to idle.

If you have this problem, shift to neutral. Put on your emergency flashers, check traffic, and brake safely to the side of the road. Do not drive the car until the spring is repaired.

Stuck Accelerator

The accelerator is stuck if the engine does not return to idling speed when you release the accelerator. One cause of a stuck accelerator is a wadded floor mat around or over the pedal.

A stuck accelerator is a critical emergency. While driving at a steady speed, you have no warning that the accelerator is stuck. You discover that there is a problem when you need to turn or stop. You must quickly bring your car under control.

Take these actions should the accelerator stick:
1. Apply the brakes. This step is the normal action that you are already prepared to take for a stop or turn.
2. Choose an escape path that leads to a safe place off the roadway. Continue braking.
3. Shift to NEUTRAL. Depress the clutch in a manual shift car. The engine will race faster, but power is removed from the wheels.

You might damage the engine or transmission in an automatic transmission car, but might avoid a collision.
4. Follow your escape path to your chosen place safely off the roadway.
5. Turn off the ignition when you are off the roadway and no longer need to change direction.

Freeing a Stuck Accelerator

If you are in a low-traffic area, you might try to free a stuck accelerator while driving. Put your toe under the accelerator pedal and lift. A passenger might also try to help you. Do not tap the accelerator while driving. It might stick farther down and cause the car to go even faster. Never reach down with your hand to lift the pedal while driving. You cannot drive safely from this position.

After stopping safely, take these actions:
- Remove any obstructions that are around, under, or over the accelerator.
- Tap the accelerator repeatedly to clear it.
- Put your toe or hand under the accelerator and lift.

After freeing the accelerator, test it with the engine running and the car parked before you drive again. If a broken spring is the problem, do not drive until it is repaired. You cannot fix a broken spring by lifting the accelerator pedal.

If you have any accelerator problems, first apply the brakes.

Engine Failure

Usually you have little warning that your engine is going to sputter or stop due to ignition or fuel system failure. When engine failure occurs, move out of traffic to a safe place.

Follow these steps if your engine stops suddenly:

1. Shift to NEUTRAL to keep moving when the engine first sputters or stops.
2. Begin moving out of traffic toward the right shoulder. Turn on the emergency flashers. Do not brake. Use hand signals for slowing and changing lanes.
3. Try to restart the engine while you are moving. If the engine starts, shift into a forward gear and proceed. If it does not start, move safely onto the shoulder or to the curb before stopping, if possible. Try again to start the engine.
   If you cannot move onto the shoulder or to the curb, stop on the roadway. Use your emergency flashers while trying to start the engine.
4. If the engine still fails to start, raise the hood and leave emergency flashers on to signal a breakdown. You and your passengers should get out of the car. Stand safely off the roadway to wait for help.

If your car becomes disabled in such risky locations as over

If your engine fails, turn on the emergency flashers, move safely off the roadway, and raise the hood to signal that you need help.

the crest of a hill or on a curve, set flares or other warning devices to alert other roadway users.

You can move some stalled stickshift cars a short distance. Turn the ignition switch to the "start" position with the clutch pedal out and the transmission in FIRST gear.

Engine failure also affects the performance of power steering and power brakes. You need more effort to steer and brake when the engine is not running.

Flooded Engine

An engine floods when too much fuel and not enough air reach the engine. You can flood the engine if you pump the accelerator repeatedly when trying to start the car. You might smell fuel when the engine is flooded.

Follow these steps to start a flooded engine:

1. Hold the accelerator pedal to the floor to let air in and to clear excess fuel from the engine.
2. While holding the accelerator down, turn the ignition switch on steadily for about 5 seconds. If the engine does not start within that time, wait several minutes, and try again.
3. When the engine starts, release the accelerator gradually to help clear excess fuel from the engine.

Engine Overheats

Sometimes even a well maintained engine overheats in hot weather or in stop-and-go traffic. Driving up long hills with the air conditioner on can cause overheating.

Take these steps if your engine overheats:

1. Turn off the air conditioner if it is on. This action helps lighten the load on the engine.
2. Turn on the heater to draw off heat from the engine.

You might be uncomfortable, but often this one action will lower engine temperature. Open the windows to cool the car's interior.

3. During stops, shift to NEUTRAL. Press the accelerator gently to speed up the engine slightly, but do not race the engine.

    Shifting to NEUTRAL lightens the load on the engine. Accelerating increases fan and water-pump speeds for cooling the radiator. This acceleration also increases coolant flow through the heater.

4. If the temperature light stays on or if the gauge points to *hot*, move to a safe place. Stop, turn off the engine, and let the engine cool. Do not attempt to add coolant to the radiator until the engine has cooled.

Steering Failure

Complete failure of the steering system seldom occurs. However, a complete steering failure is extremely serious.

Total Steering Failure
Take these actions if your steering fails completely:
1. Use your horn and emergency flashers to communicate your emergency to other drivers.
2. Stop as quickly and safely as possible. Lift your foot

If your hood flies up, look through the space below the open hood and steer to a safe place.

from the accelerator. Do not brake. Braking could cause the front wheels to turn sharply. Instead, use the parking brake. To avoid a skid, hold the parking brake release "off" to allow a quick on-off action with the parking brake.
3. Shift to a lower gear.

Power-Steering Failure
A failure in the power-steering system is the most common type of steering "failure." A power-steering failure occurs when the engine dies, when the power-steering fluid in the system is low, or when a drive belt slips or breaks. The steering mechanism still works, but you must exert much more effort to steer.

Loss of Forward Vision

If you have lost forward vision, you must act promptly to regain visibility. Do not swerve.

Continue to drive in the path you remember.

The Hood Flies Up
This emergency usually occurs because the hood is not securely latched. Stop the car in a safe place if the hood is down but vibrating, or it is not even with the top of the fenders. Release the hood and close it again. Be sure that the hood is latched securely.

Take these actions if the hood flies up while you are driving:
1. Look through the crack below the open hood.
2. If you cannot see under the hood, quickly roll down the window. Look in the direction that you are driving.
3. Continue to drive. Turn on the emergency flashers. Pump the brakes gently to warn other drivers of your emergency.
4. Slow down, and drive off the roadway to a safe location.

Headlights Fail

If you are driving at night and your headlights start to flicker, move quickly and carefully off the roadway to a safe place.

Follow these steps if your headlights fail entirely:

1. Slow down, and then continue to drive in the path you remember.
2. Try the dimmer switch, parking lights, emergency flashers, and the turn signals. Try switching the headlights from low to high. Some circuits might still work. If so, use whatever lights are available to help you drive off the roadway to a safe location.
3. Use the light from street lights, lighted signs, buildings, or other vehicles to help you see. Move off the roadway to a safe place when the car has slowed.

Splashed Windshield

Your windshield might be splashed with slush or mud from other vehicles. Snow from a snow removal machine might also cover your windshield.

Immediately turn on your windshield wipers to clear your windshield. Slow at once, and try to remember your path until you regain visibility. Use your windshield washers as needed.

Car on Fire

A car fire can be dangerous and hard to extinguish. The fire can involve fuel, oil, grease, ordinary combustibles, electrical equipment, or a combination of sources. Carry an A-B-C type fire extinguisher that is designed to control such fires. Notify the fire department of any vehicle fires.

Engine Compartment Fire

Many vehicle fires start in the engine compartment. Take these actions in case of fire:

1. Quickly steer the car out of traffic and off the roadway to a safe, open area. Stay away from buildings and service stations. Turn off the ignition to cut off the engine's electrical supply.
2. Have passengers get out of the car immediately and move at least 100 feet away from the car.
3. Estimate how serious the fire is. You might see flames and smoke around the hood. The hood might be hot to the touch. In both cases, do not try to put out the fire. Leave the hood closed. Move away from the car while waiting for the fire department. The fuel tank could explode.

If you estimate that the fire is small enough to control and you have an A-B-C type fire extinguisher, take these steps:

Do not open a hood if smoke is coming from under it.

If no train is approaching, try to push a stalled car off the tracks.

1. Use a rag to protect your hands. Lean away from the car. Turn your face away to protect yourself from the heat and flames. Carefully open the hood. Once the hood is up, the fire will burn freely as it gets more air. You must react quickly.
2. Direct the fire extinguisher on the area of the fire. Water will not put out oil and fuel fires.
3. Never try to disconnect the battery or work with your hands under the hood while it is still hot.

Fire is possible in any collision where the engine compartment is smashed. Turn off the ignition, and get passengers out and away from the car. Loose electrical wires, leaking fuel and oil, and a hot engine could combine to create a fire.

Passenger Compartment Fire

A passenger compartment fire usually is caused by a carelessly handled match, lighter, or burning tobacco product. Such fires smoulder, but rarely flame up. Pull safely off the roadway. Use water or a fire extinguisher to put out the fire. Make sure that the fire is completely out. Upholstery fires often restart.

Car Stalls on Railroad Tracks

An anxious driver might slow too much and stall the engine while crossing railroad tracks. Take these actions if your car stalls on the tracks:

1. If no train is coming, try to restart the car. It will probably start. If you hurry too much, you might flood the engine. If the engine floods, hold the accelerator to the floor as you restart the engine. Watch for trains.
2. If you cannot restart the engine, have passengers leave the car immediately. Have one passenger watch for trains, and ask some others to help you.
3. Shift to NEUTRAL and push the car off the tracks.
4. With some stickshift cars, you can make the car move a short distance. Shift to FIRST or REVERSE, let the clutch out, and turn the ignition to "start."
5. If a train is coming, abandon your car. Quickly move away from the tracks in the direction the train is approaching. This precaution helps you avoid injury from flying fragments.

Review It

1. What actions should you take if a tire blows out?
2. What should you do if the brakes fail?
3. What actions should you take if the accelerator sticks?
4. What should you do if the engine fails or overheats?
5. What actions should you take if the steering fails?
6. What should you do if a raised hood blocks your vision?
7. What actions should you take if the car is on fire?
8. What procedure should you follow if your car stalls on railroad tracks?

Driver Errors

Driver errors cause many more emergencies than vehicle malfunctions do. Errors due to inexperience, lack of attention, or poor decisions often create driving emergencies. Any driver can be put in an emergency situation by the unpredictable act of another driver.

Identifying an emergency, predicting its consequences, making correct decisions, and executing decisions quickly will help you avoid a collision. Developing automatic responses to emergencies is a critical part of the total driving task.

Driving Off the Road

When a front wheel leaves the edge of the roadway, returning to the roadway can be easy if the shoulder is paved and in good condition. However, many times the shoulder is lower than the roadway or is not paved. Many fatal one-car collisions result when drivers brake and return suddenly to the highway. In such a situation, a car might roll over. Other collisions can occur when drivers quickly return to the roadway and suddenly cross the center line into oncoming traffic.

Straddle the roadway edge.

Turn sharply to get back onto the pavement.

Countersteer when the front tire reaches the roadway.

Off-Road Recovery

Avoid quick steering to get back on the roadway when a front wheel leaves the pavement. Regain control of your car before returning to the normal lane of travel. Know ahead of time the actions you should take for a safe off-road recovery:

1. Hold the steering wheel firmly. The greater the drop-off between roadway and shoulder, the greater amount of steering control you need. Keep your car heading straight.

2. Let up on the accelerator, and brake gently to 5 or 10 mph. Avoid hard braking.

3. Position your car so it straddles the roadway edge.
4. Select a place to return to the roadway where the shoulder is nearest the level of the roadway.
5. Check for traffic. Signal and return to the roadway when no traffic is close.
6. Steer sharply toward the roadway to start your recovery. If the drop off is severe, you might need to turn very sharply to get back onto the pavement.
7. Countersteer sharply the instant the front tire comes back on the roadway. You **countersteer** when you steer in the opposite direction.
8. Center your car in your lane. Cancel your signal. Accelerate to match the flow of traffic.

If traffic is heavy when you go off the roadway, drive entirely off the roadway. Stop and wait for a large opening in traffic.

Sometimes an obstruction, such as a bridge or guardrail, might be on the shoulder ahead. In this case, make a recovery quickly. You have neither time nor space to slow down properly or to look for a level spot. Grip the steering wheel firmly as you return to the roadway. Countersteer *immediately* when the front wheel touches the roadway.

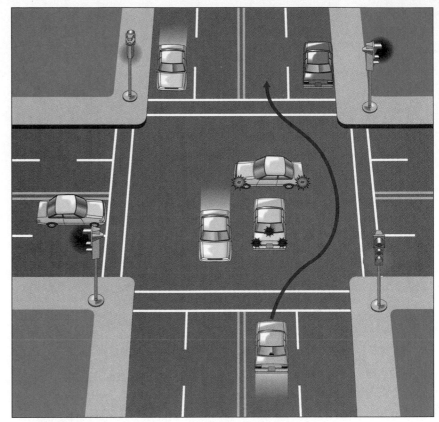

Should the driver of the yellow car stop or swerve?

Emergency Swerving

Swerving is a last-second emergency means of avoiding a collision. Swerve only when you judge that braking will not prevent a collision. At speeds over 30 mph, you can sometimes swerve to a new path in less distance than the distance you need to stop.

The Stop-Swerve Decision

This picture shows a dangerous situation. The driver of the yellow car might hit the brakes to stop. In some situations, this action will be the only choice. However, if the driver hits the brakes, the car might slide into the car ahead. When moving at 30 mph or more, the traction created by the car's tires can turn the car sideways faster than braking traction can stop it.

Make this check when deciding to swerve around an object: Be sure that no other vehicle is in the lane that you will enter.

The stop-swerve decision is not an easy one to make. Swerve only as a last resort. If a pedestrian steps in front of you at the last second, you might be forced to make a stop-swerve decision.

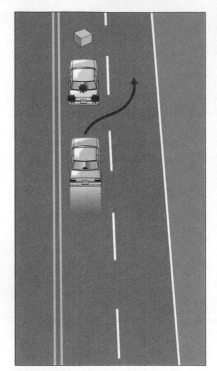

You must swerve sharply around a close object...

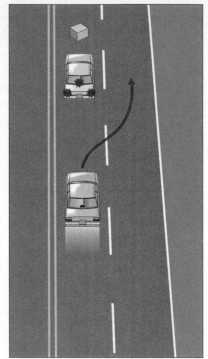

and less sharply when the object is farther away.

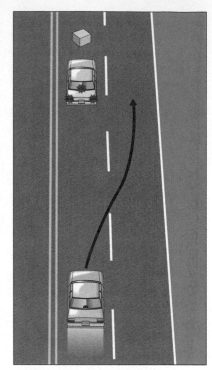

At a greater distance, the swerve is less sharp.

Use the IPDE process to protect yourself and possibly reduce the number of stop-swerve situations you encounter. In addition, allow an adequate space between yourself and the vehicle ahead.

Executing an Emergency Swerve

Follow these steps if you decide to swerve:

1. Identify possible escape paths. Choose the best escape path.
2. Grip the steering wheel firmly.
3. Turn the steering wheel sharply in the direction of the swerve.
4. In the same rhythmic motion, countersteer to

stabilize your car. Straighten the wheel, and continue to steer in your path.

How Sharply to Swerve?

The amount of time available to swerve determines how sharply you must swerve. Consider two factors—distance and speed—when determining how much time you have to swerve. Maintaining a safe following distance and traveling at a reasonable speed are critical.

The distance to the object is the first factor that determines how sharply to swerve. When the stopped car is farther away, as in the far right drawing, the swerve will be less severe and will be easier to execute.

Speed is the second factor that determines how sharply to swerve. As speed increases, the amount of time in which to swerve is reduced. You must swerve more sharply to get around a stopped vehicle at 40 mph than at 20 mph.

Review It

1. How should you safely return to the roadway if your car runs off the roadway?
2. Under what conditions should you make an emergency swerve?

Collisions

Many drivers are never involved in a collision. However, collisions sometimes are unavoidable. If you know in advance how to react, you can lessen the effects of a collision. If you are involved in a collision, you need to know the correct procedures to follow.

Minimizing Effects of a Collision

Suddenly, a vehicle emerges from a driveway and directly enters your path of travel. You know that you will have a collision that you cannot avoid. What can you do? If a collision is about to occur, act as follows:

- Above all, do not give up. Keep control of your car. Any change of speed or direction that lessens the impact also lessens the damage.
- Steer for something "soft" if you leave the roadway. Look for bushes, a snowbank, or an open field.
- Steer for a sideswipe collision rather than a head-on collision. In a sideswipe collision, only the sides of the cars touch each other.
- Avoid objects, such as trees and parked vehicles, that will stop your car suddenly.

Steer to the right if a head-on collision like this one seems about to occur.

- Act quickly after a collision. Get passengers out and away from your car if there is a threat of a fire.

Threat of a Head-on Collision

A head-on collision produces the highest force of impact of any collision. Serious injuries and death are more likely to occur in head-on collisions than in sideswipes. Try to avoid a head-on collision at all costs. Take these steps if you are threatened with a head-on collision:

1. Maintain driving control. Slow down as much as possible, but do not lock the wheels when braking. Slowing down lessens the force of impact and also gives the other driver space and time to recover control.

2. Blow the horn and flash the headlights. These actions might alert an inattentive or sleepy driver who is driving toward you in your lane. Continue braking and move to the right if the driver does not heed your warning.

3. Steer right toward the shoulder. Do not steer left. The other driver likely will try to steer back into the proper lane. Prepare to drive entirely off the roadway to the right, if necessary. Look for a soft impact spot, such as a bush, if you do not have a clear escape path.

If you want to swerve to avoid a collision, be aware of traffic so you do not cause a worse collision.

Threat of a Side-Impact Collision

The driver of the red car crossing the road in the picture might find it difficult to avoid being hit from the side. However, by accelerating, the driver might avoid having the passenger compartment crushed. An impact to the passenger compartment often causes a second collision between the passengers and the inside of the car.

Take these steps to avoid or lessen the effect of a side-impact collision:

1. Brake or accelerate quickly. Do whichever seems more likely to prevent or lessen the collision. Try to avoid a collision directly into the passenger compartment.
2. Blow the horn to alert the other driver.
3. Change lanes or swerve away from the impact. Be aware of the constantly changing traffic situation around you. Your swerve should not cause a more severe collision.

Threat of a Rear-End Collision

You are quite defenseless while your car is standing still. You might realize at the last moment that a car approaching from the rear is coming too fast. The car might not be able to stop in time.

Take these actions if you are threatened with a rear-end collision:

1. Flash your brake lights early to alert the driver approaching from behind.
2. As the car nears, release your brakes and move forward, if possible. This precaution gives the driver approaching from behind more stopping distance.
3. If the intersection is clear, accelerate across the intersection. You give the driver approaching from behind more space to stop. If your lane is not clear, turn right promptly, if possible.
4. If a collision is unavoidable, release your brakes just before the collision occurs. This step helps soften the impact. Brake immediately after the collision to avoid sliding into another car or another traffic lane.

Maintaining a safe following distance while you are driving, and keeping adequate space between your car and other vehicles ahead when stopped are good habits. These actions can often give you the space needed to maneuver in order to avoid being hit from behind.

What would you do if you saw this car approaching from the rear?

If You Have a Collision

If you should collide with another vehicle, a pedestrian, or someone else's property, you must be prepared to follow certain procedures.

Your First Steps

Each state has specific procedures that you must follow immediately when involved in a collision. All states require you to take the following five steps.

1. Stop Immediately. If you are in a collision, you must stop immediately. Failure to stop is a serious offense. If possible, move your car to the side of the roadway, out of traffic. Do not leave your car where it can block traffic unless your car is so damaged it cannot be moved under its own power. However, negligence may be difficult to establish if your car is moved. If you damage a parked vehicle even slightly, try to find the owner. If you cannot, write your name, address, and phone number on a note to the driver. Leave the note under a windshield wiper or attach it to the car so the driver will see it. Notify police even if the damage is slight.

2. Aid the Injured. Send for paramedics if anyone is seriously injured. *Do not move an injured person unless there is danger of fire or another collision.* Administer basic first aid for injuries such as severe bleeding, shock, and stoppage of breath-

ing *if you have completed a certified first-aid course.* Use a first-aid kit or manual if one is available.

Most states have what is known as a "Good Samaritan Law." These laws help protect people giving first aid in good faith at a collision scene.

3. Prevent Further Damage. Turn off the ignitions of the damaged vehicles to reduce the risk of fire. Warn oncoming traffic with flares or reflectors placed at least 100 feet ahead of and behind the collision site (500 feet away in high-speed traffic). If you do not have such devices, another person might stand in advance of the site and wave a flashlight or light-colored cloth to warn other drivers.

4. Send for Police. You must call the police if anyone is injured or killed. Some states require you to call the police for any collision, regardless of injuries.

Important People

When a collision occurs, a telephone call to a 911 emergency number often brings help through a statewide network known as an Emergency Medical Services (EMS) system. Along with police and fire fighters, specially trained emergency care providers respond to aid injured people before they are transported to hospitals by ambulances or helicopters.

Emergency care providers might be paid professionals or volunteers. They might be paramedics or emergency medical technicians (EMTs). In any case, they have successfully completed courses involving instruction and testing. The aid these prehospital workers provide is crucial during the "golden hour"—the critical first hour after an injury occurs.

What procedures should you follow in a collision, even before help arrives?

Exchange information with all drivers involved in a collision.

5. Exchange Information. Get the following information from others involved in the collision: names, addresses, driver's license numbers, license plate numbers, and insurance company names and addresses.

Note the names and addresses of passengers, the positions in which they were sitting, and the extent of their injuries. Getting this information, and giving information about yourself and your passengers, is your responsibility.

Additional Steps
Take these additional steps following a collision:

Record Witnesses' Names and Addresses Note the names and addresses of any witnesses to the collision. Make a sketch of the collision scene. Record such important facts as time, date, location, weather, and driving conditions, as the drivers in the picture are doing.

Note the name of the hospital to which the injured persons were taken. Note the name and badge number of the police officer at the collision scene.

Give Police the Facts Give the police honest and accurate facts. Do not argue with the other driver or the police over who was to blame. Stay at the scene until all information has been noted. Take your car to a repair shop for any needed repairs. Keep all towing and repair bills for future reference.

See a Doctor Have a doctor examine you if you were shaken up or injured, even if you do not notice any special ill effects of the collision. Serious complications might develop, even from an injury that appears minor.

File Necessary Reports Each state requires drivers involved in a collision to file a written report if someone was killed or injured, or if the property damage exceeds a set amount. Some states require a report to be filed within 24 hours of the collision; other states allow more time. The report usually is sent to the state's department of motor vehicles or licensing.

In addition, you must produce proof of financial responsibility by showing a card that lists current insurance coverage, or you must show a bond card. Finally, notify your insurance agent promptly. If you fail to notify your insurance company within the time specified in your policy, the company might refuse to pay your claim.

Review It

1. How can you minimize the impact of a head-on collision? a side-impact collision? a rear-end collision?
2. What steps should you take immediately if you are involved in a collision?
3. What additional steps should you take following a collision?

Roadway Hazards

Unusual and unexpected roadway hazards can cause you to lose control of your car. An emergency situation will result. Driving into deep water, sharp curves, and objects on the roadway also can result in emergencies.

Potholes in the Roadway

Potholes develop as water collects in cracks in the roadway. The water freezes and thaws, causing the cracks to expand. As vehicles drive over these water-filled cracks, they break up the roadway even more, and potholes develop and grow.

Drive slowly through potholes to prevent damage to tires.

Potholes often have sharp edges that can severely damage tires. You can lose control of your car when you hit a pothole at a high speed.

Watch for potholes and avoid them whenever possible. Drive carefully around a pothole, not over it. Stay in your own lane as you try to avoid potholes in the roadway.

If you must drive through a pothole, drive slowly to prevent tire damage. By driving slowly, you can keep better control of your car.

Car in Deep Water

If you see deep water on the roadway, do not attempt to drive through. Turn around or take another road.

In an emergency situation, however, your car might get into deep water. Act quickly if you drive or plunge into deep water. A car often will float for just a few minutes. The engine end of your car is heavier and might sink first.

Take these actions if your car goes into deep water:

1. Unfasten your safety belt. Check your passengers, and have them unfasten theirs.
2. Open the window that is farthest out of the water. Power windows might short circuit in the water, so open these windows immediately.
3. Exit promptly through the open window.

If the windows will not open, exit through a door. Do not panic if the door is slow to open. Pressure will equalize as water from outside the door enters your car. You then can open the door.

When your car is underwater, some air will be trapped for a brief time toward the highest point of the car. Try to get a full breath or two of air while locating a window or door that is facing up. Open the window or door and leave your car.

If you become trapped in your car underwater, turn on your headlights. This step can help rescuers find your car more quickly. Also, unfasten safety belts to better prepare for rescue.

Might a sharp rake be buried in this pile of leaves?

Sharp Curve

You might unintentionally go into a curve too fast on a strange roadway, especially at night. The standard warning sign does not indicate exactly how sharp the curve is. Also, the warning sign might not give you a suggested safe speed.

Take these actions if you enter a curve too fast:

1. Brake as soon as you realize your problem. If you are not yet in the curve, brake firmly. If you are in the curve, brake, but do not lock the wheels.
2. About halfway through the curve, accelerate gently to help stabilize your car.

Going around a curve at a high speed is dangerous. A bad spot in the roadway or driving over the center line might lead to a collision.

Object on the Roadway

An object on the roadway creates a hazard, whether it is a box, leaves, or an animal darting onto the roadway. A cardboard packing box in the street might not appear to be dangerous. Neither does a pile of leaves that were raked from a yard. However, avoid these and other objects on the roadway. You might not be able to identify the contents of the box. You cannot see a rake or other object in the leaf pile. In addition, both empty boxes and leaf piles attract children as places to play.

First check traffic, and then decide whether to go around, brake, straddle, swerve, or drive over the object. Choose to straddle the object only if your car can clear it and you are not able to safely steer around it. Avoid swerving left across the center line because you could encounter oncoming traffic. *Drive over an object only as a last resort.*

Review It

1. What should you do if you see a pothole in your path of travel?
2. How should you escape a car that is sinking in deep water?
3. What actions should you take if you enter a curve too fast?

DECISION MAKING

1. The white car has just had a left front tire blow out. What steps should the driver take to handle this emergency situation?

2. You are traveling at 30 mph. You brake for the stop ahead, but then realize that your brakes do not work. What should you do to stop the car?

3. You were just involved in a collision. No one was injured. What procedures should you follow?

4. You are driving the white car. Both you and the driver in the gray car are traveling 30 mph. The other driver is not aware of your car. What can you do to prevent a collision or keep the collision from being too serious?

CHAPTER 13 REVIEW

Review Chapter Objectives

13–1   Vehicle Malfunctions

1. What are the procedures to follow if a tire blows out? (248)
2. What actions should you take if the brakes fail? (250)
3. What should you do if the accelerator sticks? (251)
4. How should you respond if the engine fails or overheats? (252)
5. What should you do in case of steering failure? (253)
6. What steps should you take if a raised hood blocks your forward vision? (253)
7. What are the procedures to follow if the car catches fire? (254)
8. What should you do if your car stalls on railroad tracks? (255)

13–2   Driver Errors

9. What actions should you take to return to the roadway if your car runs off the roadway? (256–257)
10. When should you use an emergency swerve? (257)

13–3   Collisions

11. How can you avoid or minimize head-on, side-impact, and rear-end collisions? (259)
12. What are the immediate and follow-up steps to take if a collision occurs? (261)

13–4   Roadway Hazards

13. What can you do to minimize damage caused by potholes? (263)
14. What should you do to escape a car that is sinking in water? (263)
15. What actions should you take if you enter a curve too fast? (264)

Check Your Knowledge

Multiple Choice   Copy the number of each sentence below on a sheet of paper. Choose the letter that best completes the statement or answers the question.

1. If a rear tire blows out, the car can
   (a) stop. (b) fishtail. (c) pull to the right. (d) pull to the left. (248)
2. What type of location do you need to safely change a tire?
   (a) level (b) wet (c) uphill (d) busy (249)
3. Which gear position should you use to keep the car moving when the engine suddenly stops?
   (a) LOW   (b) DRIVE (c) NEUTRAL (d) PARK   (252)
4. To start a flooded engine, you should
   (a) pump the accelerator pedal. (b) turn the ignition switch without pushing the accelerator pedal. (c) open the hood so more air can reach the engine. (d) push the accelerator pedal to the floor and turn the ignition switch. (252)
5. Which type of collision is the most damaging?
   (a) sideswipe (b) head-on (c) rear-impact (d) side-impact (259)
6. What should be your first step if you are involved in a collision?
   (a) Stop immediately. (b) Aid injured. (c) File report. (d) Exchange information. (261)
7. When you realize you have entered a curve too fast, you should
   (a) brake gently. (b) brake firmly. (c) counter-steer. (d) steer toward the shoulder. (264)

Completion Copy the number of each sentence below. After each number, write the word or words that complete the sentence correctly.

8. When total brake failure occurs, use the _____ to help slow the car. (250)
9. If your car stalls on railroad tracks, try to _____ it if no train is coming. (255)
10. When a _____ drops off the roadway onto the shoulder, keep the car going straight. (256)
11. You should _____ only when you determine that braking hard will not prevent a collision. (257)
12. When faced with an oncoming vehicle in your lane, steer to the _____ . (259)

Check Vocabulary

Copy the number of each phrase below. Match the definition in List A with the term it defines in List B.

List A

13. occurs when a tire on a moving vehicle loses air pressure suddenly (248)
14. device that lifts a corner or side of the car for changing a tire (249)
15. small pieces of hardware that hold the wheel onto the car (249)
16. condition that occurs from long, continuous, hard braking (250)
17. to turn the steering wheel in the opposite direction (257)

List B

a. blowout
b. brake fade
c. countersteer
d. jack
e. lug nuts
f. wheel cover

Check Your Understanding

Write a short answer for each question or statement.

18. Why should you not reach down with your hand to free a stuck accelerator while driving? (251)
19. What generally causes an engine to flood? (252)
20. Why does driving off the roadway often result in a fatal collision? (256)
21. Why does a head-on collision result in more serious injuries than does a side-impact collision? (259)
22. What driving factors may cause a driver to enter a curve too fast? (264)

Think Critically

Write a paragraph to answer each question or statement.

1. You are traveling 45 mph on a four-lane divided highway. The driver behind you passes on your left. The driver then cuts in front of you and brakes hard. You brake hard, but skid to the left. How can you recover from this emergency?
2. Imagine that you are the driver of the disabled car in the picture. The engine failure you experienced is described in the text as a vehicle malfunction. However, how could you have made an error prior to this situation?

3. Many driving emergencies will not occur in driver education class nor in your family vehicle while you are learning to drive. They may happen for the first time at a most unexpected time. What can you do to be prepared for most emergencies?

Projects

1. Clip at least two newspaper articles reporting local collisions. Determine which events probably resulted from improper actions while responding to a driving emergency. **Write** a three-paragraph essay describing what the driver should have done to better control the situation.
2. Check for roadway hazards that may exist between your home and school. Are there situations where you may encounter potholes? deep water? sharp curves? objects on roadway? What do you conclude from this exercise?

UNIT 4

BEING A
RESPONSIBLE DRIVER

Chapter 14
EFFECTS OF DRIVER CONDITION ON
RISK TAKING

Chapter 15
ALCOHOL, OTHER DRUGS, AND DRIVING

Chapter 16
RESPONSIBILITIES OF OWNING A VEHICLE

Chapter 17
MAINTAINING YOUR VEHICLE

Chapter 18
PLANNING YOUR TRAVEL

Expressways like these are safe and efficient travel
environments. The risks of collisions are lower
than on other types of roads. To keep these risks
low, all drivers have responsibilities for keeping
themselves and their vehicles in top condition.

This unit discusses how a person's physical and
emotional condition can affect the risks involved
in driving. You will learn how alcohol and other
drugs can seriously affect a driver's abilities and
influence driving risk. This unit also describes the
responsibilities of vehicle owners for maintaining
safe roadways and a healthy environment. Finally,
you will learn how to plan your travel so that it is
safe, economical, and enjoyable.

Chapter 14

EFFECTS OF DRIVER CONDITION ON RISK TAKING

You're the Driver!

Imagine that you have just been bicycle riding like these people. Riding a bicycle involves taking some risks. Driving involves some risk, too. You can keep your risks low if you are mentally alert and feel physically healthy. You rely on your senses to keep you in touch with things going on around you.

If you were going to drive this car, which physical sense would help you the most?

If you were in a traffic jam, what techniques could you use to control your emotions?

How do you protect yourself from the effects of carbon monoxide while driving?

This chapter discusses your physical and emotional abilities as they relate to driving. You can learn how to lower the risks associated with driving. You also can learn how your senses can help lower these risks.

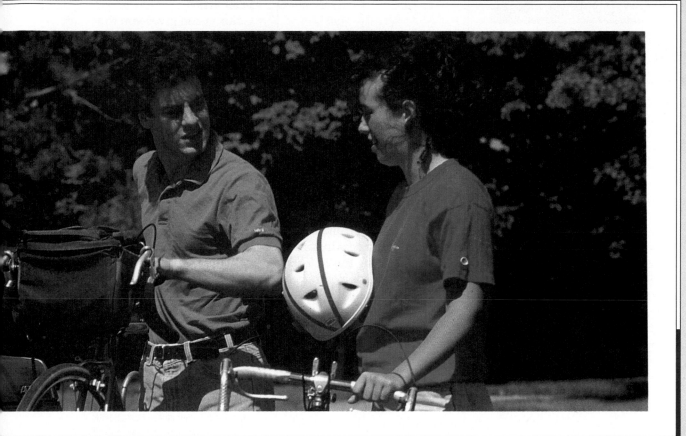

Objectives

Section 14–1   Physical Senses and Driving
1. Define field of vision and central vision.
2. List the actions you can take to compensate for poor depth perception.
3. Explain how the senses of seeing, hearing, smelling, and feeling motion help you drive.

Section 14–2   Emotions and Driving
4. Tell how anger can affect your ability to drive.
5. Explain how passengers can help a driver.

6. Tell how you can control your emotions while driving.
7. Describe the influence of emotions on your willingness to accept risk.

Section 14–3   Physical Disabilities
8. Tell what you can do to fight fatigue.
9. Explain what to do to avoid carbon monoxide exposure and how to deal with its effects.
10. Explain why drivers with permanent disabilities do not take unnecessary chances.

Physical Senses and Driving

Your senses are important when using the IPDE process. You use your ability to see, hear, smell, and detect motion to know what is occurring around your car.

Driving a car, like other activities such as sports and mowing the lawn, exposes you to some risk. You increase or decrease your risk by changing the level of control you have over your car. As you drive, your senses keep you alert and aware of changing situations. If you are constantly alert, you will maintain control over your vehicle and keep your driving risks low.

Seeing

Most of the driving information you gather is received by your eyes. You must be able to see clearly and quickly to be a safe, responsible driver.

Your brain directs your eyes to focus on objects in and around your path of travel. Information is sent to your brain and is combined with stored information. As a result, you can identify hazards, predict conflicts, decide how to adjust your speed and position, and execute your decisions.

IPDE

You have 20/20 vision in each eye if you can read these letters with each eye from 20 feet away.

Visual Acuity

You must be able to read gauges on your instrument panel, and in the next instant identify oncoming traffic. This ability to see things clearly near and far away is called **visual acuity.**

A person with normal visual acuity is said to have 20/20 vision. A person who has 20/20 vision can read letters 3/8 of an inch high on an eye chart that is 20 feet away. Estimate your visual acuity by placing this page 20 feet away. You should be able to read the term IPDE in the block on this page.

You must pass a visual acuity test in order to obtain a driver's license. Most states require a minimum visual acuity of 20/40 to drive. A person with 20/40 vision must be twice as close to an object to see it clearly as a person with 20/20 vision must be to the object. If you must wear glasses or contact lenses to pass the vision test, then you must wear them whenever you drive.

Color Vision

Color vision gives you the ability to distinguish one color from another. Not being able to distinguish colors is **color-blindness.** Being able to see the colors red, green and yellow is important since these colors give the messages stop, go, and slow or caution.

Males inherit color-blindness more often than females. The most common type of color-blindness is difficulty in distinguishing red and green.

Even though the picture below is not an actual color-blindness test, it shows what a part of a test for color-blindness might look like. A person with normal color vision sees the number 8, but a color-blind person might not be able to see it.

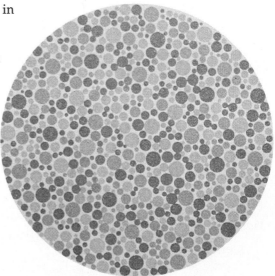

Tests for color-blindness contain patterns like this one. What do you see in this figure?

A color-blind driver can compensate by using the following strategies:

- Remember the order of the lights in a traffic signal. If the lights in a signal are vertical, the red light is at the top. If the lights are horizontal, the red light is on the left.
- Know what traffic signs mean by their shapes.
- Read all signs that appear with traffic signals.
- Check all traffic, especially cross-traffic, before proceeding at traffic signals.
- Take cues from other drivers.

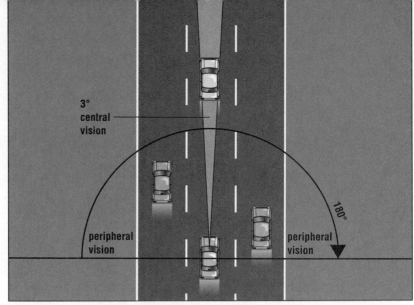

Although you see most clearly in the area of central vision, the peripheral vision area is important to the driving task.

Field of Vision

Your **field of vision** is all the area that you can see around you while looking straight ahead. From a stopped position, most people can see about 90 degrees to each side. This width is a half circle, or 180 degrees, as shown. However, you can see clearly only in your area of **central vision.** This straight-ahead part of your field of vision is a small, 3-degree, cone-shaped area. As you learn to drive, your brain begins to direct your central vision toward events that pertain to your driving task.

The vision area left and right of central vision is called side vision or **peripheral vision.** Good peripheral vision is sensitive to light and movement. It attracts your attention to possible hazards, which your central vision then identifies as you look at the hazard. A narrow field of peripheral vision (140 degrees or less) is called **tunnel vision**. A driver with tunnel vision must compensate with more frequent head and eye movements. The picture shows how objects to the side might look at expressway speed to a driver with tunnel vision.

Objects recognizable but blurred   Area of central vision, objects in sharp focus   Objects recognizable but blurred

Depth Perception

The ability to judge distance between yourself and other objects is **depth perception**. Distance judgments in driving involve your moving car and other vehicles and objects. When you are in a moving car, you have more difficulty judging the distance of another moving object.

A driver can compensate for poor depth perception by:

- using a following distance greater than 2 seconds.
- allowing for additional clear distance ahead before passing.
- using known distances, such as city blocks or the space between utility poles, to judge distances.
- allowing greater distances at night than at daytime, because darkness hides many guides you use in the daytime.

Night Vision

The ability to see at night varies from person to person. Some people who see clearly in the

When you are in a moving car, you have more difficulty judging distances of moving objects than when you are standing.

daytime have poor night vision. Not being able to see well at night is **night blindness**.

All people see less at night than in daylight. Colors are harder to identify. Details of objects do not appear as sharp as in daylight.

Your vision at night is limited to the area lighted by headlights, streetlights, and other lights. In rural areas, you might be in total darkness except for the area that is lighted by your headlights.

You might not be able to see anything to the sides, and might be less able to read signs and roadway markings. Compare the two pictures that show the same situation. The only difference is that one picture was taken during the day and the other one was taken at night. Notice that you cannot see as much at night. Your ability to judge distances accurately also decreases.

Use these guides to improve your ability to see at night:

You can see nearby objects and distant ones clearly in daylight.

Your ability to see objects and judge distances is limited at night.

- Travel at slower speeds, beginning at sunset.
- Use a following distance greater than 2 seconds.
- Glance to the shoulder of the roadway to avoid looking directly at bright lights.
- Keep the instrument panel lights on.
- Drive at night only if your eyes are rested.
- Keep the windshield and the headlights clean.
- Keep the interior car lights turned off.
- Do not wear sunglasses at night.
- Use high-beam headlights in rural areas, but switch to low-beam near other vehicles.

Glare

Glare occurs in the daytime when you look at shiny surfaces that reflect bright sunlight. Sun-roofs and convertibles let in additional sunlight that can produce glare. At night, glare occurs when you look directly at bright lights or shiny surfaces that reflect bright lights. The

Open sun roofs can result in glare.

term **glare resistance** describes the ability to continue seeing when looking at bright lights. Glare resistance varies from person to person.

Sudden glare can temporarily blind a person, especially at night. Headlights turn toward you at intersections. Bright lights appear from over hills and around curves. A car with high-beam lights on approaches from behind. The pupils of your eyes open wide at night to let in light. When your eyes are suddenly exposed to bright lights, the pupils become small. You might be temporarily

blinded before your pupils become larger again after the bright lights pass.

The term **glare recovery time** describes the time your eyes need to regain clear vision after being affected by glare. Often your pupils take five to ten seconds to open fully. At 40 mph, your car will travel almost 300 feet in 5 seconds.

Take these precautions to avoid or recover from glare:
- Avoid looking directly at bright lights. Focus on the right edge of the roadway.
- Anticipate glare situations and glance away.
- Use side vision rather than central vision to check your position and the location of oncoming cars.
- If you are impaired by glare, slow until your vision clears.
- Wear sunglasses and use your car's visor in bright sunlight.
- Use high-beam lights in rural areas when no vehicles are approaching or when you are not following a vehicle.
- Adjust your rearview mirror for night use.

You might become temporarily blinded if bright lights suddenly approach at night.

When you drive at higher speeds, your side vision is less clear.

Deeply tinted windows restrict vision of drivers who must look beyond that car.

Car Speed and Vision

As car speed increases, the need for accurate vision also increases. Yet, at higher speeds, you have less time to see clearly. Your field of vision is also narrowed. When you drive at 55 mph, your clear side-vision area is less than half as wide as when you drive at 20 mph.

Objects on the sides become blurred and distorted as your speed increases. This blur, or **speed smear**, as shown here, has an effect much like tunnel vision. Your eyes tend to focus far ahead where the roadway appears to come to a point. You see less and less of what is happening on the sides. At higher speeds, increase the number of times you glance to the sides.

Car Design and Vision

Parts of cars can sometimes block your vision. Learn to look around these areas to get a clear view of everything around you.

Roof Supports and Mirrors Roof supports and your rearview mirror can block part of your vision. Develop the habit of looking around these blocked areas as you drive. Do not hang objects from the rearview mirror or place objects either on the dashboard or on the rear window ledge where they could block your view. In a collision, these objects could hit the car's occupants.

Tinted Windows Vehicles with deeply tinted side and rear windows restrict driver vision. The darker the window, the more restricted the vision.

The dark windows also reduce a means of communication between drivers. If other drivers cannot communicate with you, it is harder for them to predict your actions. Dark windows also restrict the vision of drivers who must look through your windows to see vehicles beyond yours. Some states restrict the amount of window tint permitted.

Other Senses and Driving

Sometimes you will have to depend on senses other than vision to avoid trouble. In complex driving situations you might have to use more than one sense at a time.

Hearing

Your sense of hearing can alert you to the sounds of honking horns, train whistles, emergency-vehicle sirens, and the engines and brakes of trucks and buses. You can also get an early warning of mechanical problems with your car by listening for unusual noises.

Drivers who have sounds blocked from them can be dangerous to themselves and to others. Driving with closed car windows and with radio, head-set, air conditioner, or heater on might make a driver unaware of critical traffic sounds.

Deaf drivers know that they must see what they cannot hear. They compensate by using their eyes more than drivers who are not deaf. In general, the driving records of deaf drivers are among the best.

Smell

Your sense of smell can identify an overheated engine or something burning in the car. Pure carbon monoxide has no odor. However, other gases in car exhaust do have odors. You get an early warning of the presence of deadly carbon monoxide gas if you smell exhaust fumes inside your car.

Sense of Motion

Certain sensations can give you clues to the movement of your car. You can sense whether you are veering right or left or changing speed. Your sense of balance reminds you that you are going around a curve. A sudden vibration of the car or jerk of the steering wheel might warn you of a mechanical problem, a flat tire, or a change in roadway surface.

Your sense of motion and balance gives you clues about the movement of a car.

Risk Management

The probability of being involved in a collision determines the amount of risk in driving. You increase or decrease your risk by changing the level of control you have over your car. Likewise, other roadway users can increase or decrease your chance of having a collision. People who take unnecessary chances demonstrate **risk-taking behavior.**

Your physical senses affect your perceptions of the risk involved in each driving situation. If your vision is not clear or is blocked, you might inaccurately assess the risk of a driving situation and respond with an action that will expose you to a greater risk.

Inadequate senses of hearing, smelling, and motion will affect your management of driving risks. If you are not aware of your impaired senses, you are at an even greater risk of being involved in a collision. Being aware of how sharp your senses are is a big step in managing the risks of driving. People who know that their senses are impaired tend to take fewer risks than people who are unaware of their limitations.

High-Risk Situations

Drivers sometimes create high-risk situations like the one shown. By pulling around the car making a left turn, the driver of the yellow car risks causing a collision. If you were driving one of the other cars approaching this intersection, your keen vision would help you maneuver to lower your risk of a collision.

The driver of the yellow car has created a high-risk situation. Other drivers must react quickly to avoid a collision.

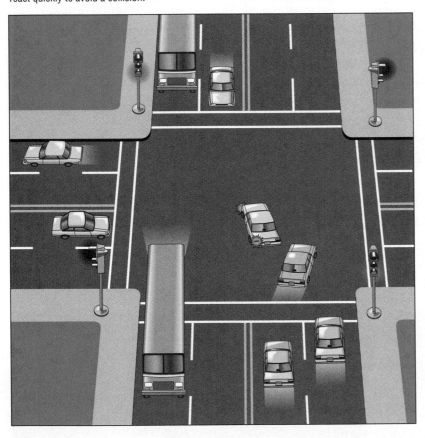

Review It

1. What is your field of vision? What part of your field of vision provides your clearest vision?
2. What can you do to compensate for poor depth perception?
3. How do your senses of seeing, hearing, smelling, and motion help you assess driving situations?

Emotions and Driving

The word **emotion** is used to name a strong feeling. Anger, fear, and joy are examples of emotions. Emotions add a special quality to life.

How Emotions Affect Driving

Emotions influence the way you think and act. When emotions affect your thoughts and actions, they can change the way you normally assess risk and make driving decisions.

Mental Effects of Emotions

Strong emotions can interfere with your ability to think and reason. When strong emotions affect you, your ability to make wise decisions is reduced. Your chances of making a mistake increase. The effect that an emotion has on your ability to drive depends upon the strength of the emotion and the effort you make to resist the effects of the emotion. Emotions can affect the way you judge the risks involved in a driving situation.

In some situations, a strong emotion can cause you to fix your attention on one event. You might miss other important events in the driving scene. In other situations, you might experience several strong emotions in a short period of time. One emotion can lead to another.

In the picture, the driver in front has just cut over to the right lane and started to slow. This action could startle following drivers. During this difficult driving situation, strong emotional feelings could turn to anger. The following drivers might become angry and not pay enough attention to other parts of the driving scene.

These drivers need to control their emotions. They should increase the space between themselves and the car ahead.

Physical Effects of Emotions

Strong emotions also can cause changes in your bodily functions. Under emotional stress, your heartbeat increases, your breathing quickens, your digestion slows, and your palms sweat. Your body prepares itself for the stressful event.

You can expect some emotional stress in your everyday life. However, continued emotional stress can exhaust you. Imagine you are driving in the expressway situation shown in the picture. You should be on the alert for the way rush-hour traffic can cause stress and fatigue in you and other drivers. You should be aware that the risks involved in this driving situation are different from those on rural roads.

How would you feel if this driver suddenly cut into your lane?

Driving in rush-hour traffic is stressful for most drivers.

Anger While Driving

When you drive, you usually rely upon a set of assumptions or expectations. You assume that others will drive and act in a safe, responsible manner. When you must change your expectations, you might be tempted to react angrily.

In normal driving, other drivers will interfere with your planned speed or path of travel. They will slow in front of you or change lanes improperly. Sometimes you might think that everyone is trying to irritate you. As a result of these and other unplanned actions, you might become angry. Anger occurs more often to drivers than any other emotion. Anger can range from mild irritation to furious rage.

The driver in the picture is angry at the people who are talking and blocking his way. The driver is angry because he might be late for an appointment. If the driver is not able to maintain emotional control, he might remain angry long after the people have cleared the street.

Anger can impair your ability to brake, steer, and accelerate smoothly. You might take risks you would not take if you were calm. If you are angry, you might not see everything you should see. You might force other drivers to stop or swerve abruptly. These last-second actions can cause conflicts and added stress not only for you, but for other drivers as well.

Other Emotions and Driving

Sorrow, depression, and anxiety are other emotions that can adversely affect driving. These emotions slow body processes and reduce mental alertness.

Anxiety differs from anger. You might be anxious if you are driving in an unfamiliar, difficult situation. You might have trouble identifying hazards when you are confused. Sometimes, you might feel panic-stricken. As a responsible driver, you can work to recognize anxiety and try to avoid it. You can realize that you are in a difficult situation, and try your best to cope.

Excitement and happiness are emotions that also can prevent you from fully concentrating on your driving task. A happy, excited driver can be just as impaired as an angry driver. After an intense event, such as a football game, be sure that strong emotions do not impair your driving ability.

The driver might remain angry long after the people have cleared his path.

Emotions and the IPDE Process

The successful use of the IPDE process requires total concentration on the driving task. Your emotional condition can drastically affect your driving ability. The event triggering the emotion might not be related to your driving. Emotions such as apathy, sorrow, or depression tend to lessen your mental alertness and distract you from driving well. Since emotions can cause you to focus your concentration on a single event, you might be unable to concentrate fully on the driving tasks.

Look at the picture, and think how emotions could affect your driving if you were beside the truck. The car ahead has been slowing and forcing you to slow. The truck driver has just decided to pass the car. You are not sure what the driver ahead is going to do. Another truck is behind the truck that is passing. The driver ahead and the truck drivers could cause you to make these mistakes when using the IPDE process:

- **Identify** If the emotional stress is strong enough, your attention could be focused on the trucks. You might not identify a sudden change in speed by the car ahead.
- **Predict** If you are unsure of the drivers around you, you will not be able to make accurate predictions.
- **Decide** Under such emotional stress, you probably have not been able to think of your decision options. In this tight situation, your best option might be to move toward the shoulder to the right.

- **Execute** When emotional stress reduces your ability to identify, predict, and decide, you might have a hard time executing the right decision. You need time to use the IPDE process. In a tight, high-stress situation, you need even more time to use the IPDE process effectively.

You would need to have your emotions under control if you were driving into this situation.

Effects of Emotions on Risk Taking

Your emotions have a big influence on the level of risk you are willing to take. If you are angry, you will probably be more willing to take risks than if you are happy. When a driver cuts you off after passing, you might want to get even by taking chances that you would not take under normal times.

Realize that mature, responsible drivers do not let their emotions make them take unnecessary chances in low- or high-risk situations. Taking chances in a situation where a mistake will not hurt you is usually safe. But, taking a chance while driving a car can be deadly. Before driving, you must be mature enough to adjust your behavior so that you do not drive into or create high-risk situations. You also must be mature enough to refuse to take part when other people suggest activities that create high-risk situations.

Your emotions might cause you to take chances at different times on the same roadway. For example, if you were driving an injured friend to the hospital, your concern might cause you to drive quickly and take some risks. An hour later, you probably would not drive home in the same manner. You would drive more cautiously.

Even when it seems quiet ahead, you must keep alert for mistakes other drivers might make.

Beware of potential risk although you drive on the street every day.

On the other hand, you sometimes might be apathetic while driving. You might be so uninterested in your trip that you fail to give your complete attention to the driving task. Driving the same way over and over again on the same roadway is a trap that an experienced driver can fall into.

Imagine that you are driving toward the yellow car in the picture. If you drive on this one-way street day after day, you might think that the yellow car could not turn toward you. If you assume that the yellow car will not turn, you could create a high-risk trap in a situation that seemed to have a low risk.

Passengers and Emotions

Peer or group pressure, a very strong force, can be good or bad, depending upon the situation. In a baseball game, team spirit can help win the game. In school, pride can help students achieve their goals. In a car, your friends can strongly influence the way you feel, think and drive.

In most group situations, one or more people need to assume responsibility and lead the group. When you are driving, you must be the leader and take control. You are the one responsible for protecting your passengers.

In this picture, the championship game has just ended. Everyone is going to a celebration party. The driver in this situation will be under special pressures. Emotions will be running high. It might be hard for the driver to concentrate on the driving task. Friends might encourage the driver to hurry. To make sure that nothing goes wrong, the driver must be the leader. The driver must constantly maintain control of the situation.

Passengers can help the driver maintain control while driving. Listed here are actions you can take to assist a driver.

Safe Driving Tips

- Always use your safety belt, no matter what your physical or emotional condition. Strongly encourage your passengers to also use their safety belts.

- When fatigued or under emotional stress, you need more time to think and act. To gain more time while driving, slow down and increase your space cushion.

- Avoid saying or doing anything that might upset the driver. Refrain from heated discussions.
- Discourage the driver from taking reckless actions. Do your best to prevent others from encouraging dangerous driving behavior. Be prepared to intervene if the driver is endangering others by reckless driving. Encourage the driver to let someone else drive, or refuse to ride in the same car. Do what you must do to protect yourself and others.
- Do not hesitate to thank a driver for doing a good job of driving in a difficult situation. Next time, you might need the same support.

Spirits might be high after winning a game, but drivers must maintain control.

How to Control Emotions

During a school assembly, you are asked to hold your applause until a certain point. You should not interrupt the program, and must control your emotions until the proper time. In driving, you must develop this same type of emotional discipline. You must not let emotions interfere with your driving ability.

Techniques for Coping with Emotions
High-stress driving situations can cause emotions to surface. The techniques below can help you to control your emotions while driving in a variety of situations.

- Drive in an organized manner. Learn and use correct driving procedures until they become habits. You then will be more likely to execute the correct action, even under emotional stress.
- Anticipate situations that produce strong emotions, and adjust your expectations. Say to yourself, "I know there will be delays during rush hour, so I will adjust the amount of time that it will take me to get home. I will not let the actions of others bother me."
- Make a self-check. If you are emotionally upset before you enter your car, tell yourself, "I am angry, but I will not drive angrily."
- Only drive when you are in control.

- Adjust your route or time of travel to avoid irritating traffic situations.
- If you are tired, make a special effort to control your emotions. A tired person can become upset easily.
- Analyze your mistakes. Decide whether or not emotions might have interfered and caused you to take more risks. Plan ahead so that the same mistakes will not be a problem in the future.

Goal of Emotional Control
Emotions are complicated and powerful forces. Learning about emotions and how to control them is something most individuals work at throughout their lives.

Maintaining an attitude of "I will always work to control my emotions" is a big step toward actually mastering your emotions. If you can control your emotions and maintain your driving ability, you will keep the risks of driving low. You will also earn the respect of others.

You earn the respect of others if your emotions do not interfere with your driving ability.

Review It

1. How can anger affect your ability to drive?
2. How can you help a driver when you are a passenger?
3. What can you do to control your emotions while driving?
4. How do your emotions affect the risks of driving?

14-3

Physical Disabilities

Experienced drivers learn how to respond to temporary and permanent disabilities. Many times driving is possible with a moderate to severe disability.

Temporary Disabilities

Sometimes you must drive even though you are not at your physical best. You can compensate for some temporary disabilities. With other disabilities, you should not drive.

Fatigue

Fatigue lessens your fitness to drive. Mental or physical work, emotional stress, or loss of sleep can cause fatigue. Fatigue dulls your senses and slows both mental and physical processes.

If you are fatigued, you will need more time to identify hazards. You might delay and make inaccurate predictions. Your actions are often abrupt and uncoordinated when you are tired. You might drive faster or slower than normal.

Fatigue can also cause drowsiness. Drivers who fall asleep at the wheel cause many collisions.

Rest is the only safe remedy for fatigue. However, people often need to drive when they are tired. If you are tired after

Drowsiness can interfere with a person's driving abilities.

work or school, take a break for a few minutes before you drive. Choose a quiet, less congested route home.

Take the following actions to compensate for fatigue on long drives.
- Rest before you start.
- Change drivers often.
- Stop regularly for light refreshments. Walk or jog.
- Open a window for fresh air.
- Wear sunglasses in bright sunlight and to shield against snow glare.
- Use your orderly visual search pattern to keep your eyes moving.
- Listen to the radio, sing, or talk with your passengers, but do not allow yourself to become distracted from the driving task.
- Stop in a safe place if you feel drowsy. Lock the car and take a nap.

- When you need to stay long in a parked car with the engine running, open windows slightly.

Temporary Illness or Injury

Any illness, even a cold, can impair driving to some extent. A temporary physical injury, such as a broken bone or a sprained ankle, can also impair your driving. These temporary conditions can cause discomfort and pain, limit physical movement, lessen endurance and strength, dull your senses, or cause a combination of these disabilities.

Take these actions if you must drive when you have an illness or injury.
- Choose a quiet route.
- Use reduced speeds.
- Drive within your abilities.

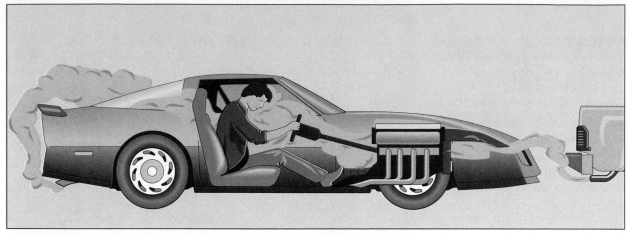

In heavy traffic, your intakes might draw in carbon monoxide from the exhaust of the car ahead.

Effects of Medicines

Many medicines have side effects that can interfere with your driving ability. A medicine to reduce headache pain or relieve hay fever, for example, might also cause drowsiness, dizziness, or reduced alertness. These situations increase the risk involved in driving.

If you take medicine, consider these points before you drive.

- Read the label. Learn the possible side effects. Ask your physician or pharmacist about side effects.
- A medicine can affect you differently at different times.
- If possible, drive home before taking the medicine.
- If you must drive after taking medicine, choose a quiet route.
- Compensate for any side effects. Do not drive if your driving ability is seriously affected.

Effects of Carbon Monoxide

Part of the exhaust fumes from your car is **carbon monoxide**, a colorless, odorless, and tasteless gas. Carbon monoxide is present in all exhaust gases from gasoline engines.

You can sometimes detect carbon monoxide in a car because it is mixed with other exhaust fumes that have an odor. However, you cannot tell how concentrated carbon monoxide is by the odor of the exhaust fumes.

Small amounts of carbon monoxide can cause drowsiness, headaches, muscular weakness, mental dullness, and nausea. Too much carbon monoxide can cause death.

Be alert for the danger of carbon monoxide in heavy traffic and in such enclosed areas as tunnels and underground parking facilities. Your heater or air conditioner intakes might draw in exhaust fumes from the car ahead, as shown

here. Having an open rear window of a station wagon or hatchback might create a slight vacuum that pulls in exhaust fumes.

Take these actions to prevent carbon monoxide exposure and combat its effects.

- If your car is parked in a garage at home, open the garage door before starting the engine.
- Avoid running the engine inside a garage. Move your car outside after starting the engine.
- In stop-and-go traffic, keep a car length or more between yourself and the vehicle ahead of you.
- In traffic jams, especially in enclosed areas, turn off the engine when possible.
- Check your exhaust system regularly.
- Move a person who is overcome by carbon monoxide into fresh air. Get medical help immediately.

Smoking

Be aware that smoking while driving is dangerous. Besides distracting the attention of the driver from the driving task, smoking also raises the carbon monoxide level in a driver's blood. Smoke residue accumulates on windows and affects vision.

Discourage your passengers from smoking. Carbon monoxide from tobacco smoke can affect even nonsmokers in an enclosed area such as a car. If someone does smoke in your car, open a window to provide fresh air.

Directions: Adults and children 12 years and over—One tablet in the morning and one tablet in the evening, not to exceed 3 tablets in 24 hours.

Warnings: May cause drowsiness. May cause excitability, especially in children. Do not take this product if you have asthma or glaucoma, or give this product to children under 12 years. Avoid driving a motor vehicle or operating heavy machinery. Avoid alcoholic beverages while taking this product.

Many commonly used medicines can affect your driving ability.

Effects on Risk-Taking

Temporary illness can affect a driver's risk-taking decisions.

Because an illness is temporary, many drivers do not recognize the illness's influence on chances they may be more willing to take. Drivers who are sick might be more willing to, and often do, take chances that they would be unlikely to take if they were well.

Being tired or under the influence of medicines can increase your chances of being in a collision or having a near miss. Be aware of the side effects of medicines. Compensate for them by using an extra space cushion and taking even fewer chances.

Permanent Disabilities

Many people have permanent disabilities. Special car equipment and controls can help many of these people compensate for their disabilities. Still other people are able to drive because they can control their disabilities with medication. Certain impairments make it impossible for some disabled people to drive.

Special equipment in cars helps physically disabled people gain independence.

Physical Disabilities

State agencies license drivers with many types of physical disabilities. Each case is considered on an individual basis.

Special equipment can allow a disabled person to operate all car controls. Some adaptive controls are quite simple, while others are options already available on a car. For example, a person who does not have the use of his or her right leg can drive an automatic-transmission car equipped with a left foot accelerator.

Older Drivers

As a nation, we are healthier and living longer. More and more older drivers are using our roadways. Some older drivers might have physical limitations. However, they can more than compensate for these limitations by adjusting their driving based on prior experience.

Chronic Illnesses

A **chronic illness** is an ailment that lasts over a period of years. Some chronic illnesses, such as high blood pressure, have little effect on driving. Other illnesses, such as heart disease, could seriously impair a person's ability to drive.

Certain chronic illnesses require regular medications that can have side effects that interfere with driving. Some people have medical conditions that result in sudden loss of consciousness or muscular

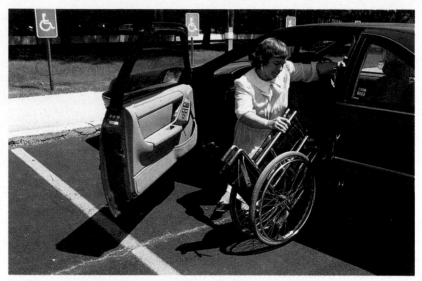

Special parking areas and license plates help disabled drivers to reach their destinations safely.

control. Before these individuals receive a driver's license, they must provide medical proof that their chronic illness is under control.

Stress worsens some chronic illnesses. Persons with these illnesses should not drive in heavy traffic or in other stressful driving situations.

Effects on Risk-Taking

Most drivers with permanent disabilities do not take unnecessary chances with driving decisions influenced by their handicaps. These drivers understand that their disability itself may put them at a higher level of risk.

Whatever the illness or disability, everyone who can perform the driving tasks safely and successfully has the privilege of being licensed to drive

when all other requirements are met.

Some drivers with permanent disabilities have special license plates or window cards with the disabled symbol. The symbol also appears on license plates or window cards of drivers who often transport disabled people. Cars with these plates can be parked in specially marked areas in parking lots and on streets.

Review It

1. How can you compensate for the effects of fatigue?
2. How can you avoid and combat exposure to carbon monoxide?
3. How can a chronic illness affect your driving?

DECISION MAKING

1. Where should you be directing your clear central vision in the next few seconds of driving?

2. What is causing this driver to be impaired for a few seconds? What actions could the driver have taken to prevent this impairment? What can the driver do now to minimize the danger?

3. These people are having an argument. How could the argument affect the driver's ability to drive?

4. How are these passengers affecting the driver? What should they be doing to help?

CHAPTER 14 REVIEW

Review Chapter Objectives

14–1 Physical Senses and Driving

1. What is field of vision and central vision? (273)
2. What actions can you take to compensate for poor depth perception? (274)
3. How do the senses of seeing, hearing, smelling, and motion help you drive? (277)

14–2 Emotions and Driving

4. How can anger affect your ability to drive? (280)
5. Why do emotions influence your willingness to accept risk? (282)
6. What can passengers do to help a driver? (283)
7. How can you control your emotions while driving? (284)

14–3 Physical Disabilities

8. What can you do to fight fatigue while driving? (285)
9. What can you do to avoid carbon monoxide exposure and how can you deal with its effects? (286)
10. Why do drivers with permanent disabilities generally not take unnecessary chances? (288)

Check Your Knowledge

Multiple Choice Copy the number of each sentence below on a sheet of paper. Choose the letter that best completes the statement or answers the question.

1. The sense that drivers use most is
   (a) hearing. (b) seeing. (c) smelling. (d) motion. (272)
2. Most drivers can see to each side approximately
   (a) 180 degrees. (b) 90 degrees. (c) 360 degrees. (d) 45 degrees. (273)
3. What temporary disability dulls your senses and lowers your ability to drive?
   (a) a minor cut (b) fatigue (c) a sprained ankle (d) a rash (285)
4. Under sudden, strong emotions, your body
   (a) prepares for a stressful event. (b) cools down. (c) is tired. (d) does not change. (279)
5. When using the IPDE process in a high-stress situation, you need
   (a) less time. (b) more time. (c) no additional time. (d) half the time. (281)

Completion Copy the number of each sentence below. After each number, write the word or words that complete the sentence correctly.

6. The person with _____ cannot see well to the sides. (273)
7. The side-vision area to the left and right of your central vision is your _____ . (273)
8. The ability to continue seeing when looking at bright lights is _____ . (275)
9. The blur and distortion of objects on the sides as speed increases is called _____ . (276)
10. The _____ of medicine might decrease your driving ability. (286)
11. Your blood's carbon monoxide level can increase due to _____ . (286)
12. A strong _____ can reduce a driver's thinking ability. (282)
13. The emotion that occurs more often to more drivers than any other emotion is _____ . (280)
14. A driving situation's _____ can be measured by the probability of collision. (278)
15. In high-risk situations, drivers might take _____ that they would not normally take. (278)

Check Vocabulary

Copy the number of each definition in List A. Match the definition in List A with the term it defines in List B.

List A
16. ability to see clearly (272)
17. inability to tell colors apart (272)
18. all the area you can see around you as you look straight ahead (273)
19. area you see clearly straight ahead (273)
20. ability to judge distances (274)
21. inability to see well at night (274)
22. time needed to regain clear vision after being blinded by glare (275)
23. deadly, colorless, and odorless gas (286)
24. an ailment that lasts for years   (288)
25. taking chances (278)

List B
a. carbon monoxide
b. central vision
c. chronic illness
d. color-blindness
e. depth perception
f. field of vision
g. glare recovery time
h. night blindness
i. risk-taking behavior
j. tunnel vision
k. visual acuity

Check Your Understanding

Write a short answer for each question or statement.

26. How can a driver compensate for poor depth perception? (274)
27. Why might a driver with normal hearing abilities who has the car windows rolled up while listening to the radio be in more danger than a deaf driver? (277)
28. How can a driver compensate for color-blindness? (273)
29. What are four emotions that could affect your driving? (280)
30. How can you learn about the possible side effects of a medicine? (286)

Think Critically

Write a paragraph to answer each question or statement.

1. Put yourself into the driver's seat of the truck to your left in the picture below. Why might your emotions have made you take risks to pass the car?

2. Your visual abilities will change as you grow older. How will you know that they have changed?
3. What has occurred in the past to permit more physically disabled people to drive?

Projects

1. Observe the drivers you ride with. How do you judge their attitude behind the wheel? Do you generally feel safe riding with them? What driving habits do they have that you feel especially good about? **Write** a summary of your observations.
2. After a school sporting event, check drivers as they leave the parking lot. List examples of emotions you observe that might encourage more risk-taking driving behaviors.

ALCOHOL, OTHER DRUGS, AND DRIVING

You're the Driver!

As you drive by, you notice that many people are having picnics before the game. At parties like these, refreshments might include alcoholic beverages. After the game, almost everyone will drive away.

What driving abilities are impaired when a person uses alcohol? What can drinkers and nondrinkers do to avoid the risk of alcohol-impaired driving?

What tests might a driver need to take if arrested for driving while intoxicated?

This chapter discusses the effects of alcohol and other drugs. Information here will help you see why you should not drink and drive.

Objectives

Section 15–1   Effects of Alcohol on Driver Performance
1. Explain how alcohol affects mental and physical abilities needed for driving.
2. Define blood-alcohol concentration.
3. Explain factors that affect blood-alcohol concentration.
4. Explain six myths about the use of alcohol.

Section 15–2   Other Drugs and Driving
5. Explain how depressant, stimulant, and hallucinogenic drugs can affect a driver.
6. Describe the effects of combining alcohol with other drugs.

Section 15–3 Traffic Laws Governing Alcohol and Drug Use

7. Explain what is meant by implied-consent laws.
8. Explain levels of intoxication and how these levels can be measured.
9. Explain what a driver should do when signaled to stop by a police officer.

Section 15–4 Peer Pressure and Drugs

10. Tell how peer pressure might affect one's decision about drinking and driving.
11. List steps to follow when faced with peer pressure to use alcohol or other drugs.
12. Tell why everyone should share the responsibility of preventing friends from driving after drinking.
13. Explain ways to keep drinking friends from driving.

Effects of Alcohol on Driver Performance

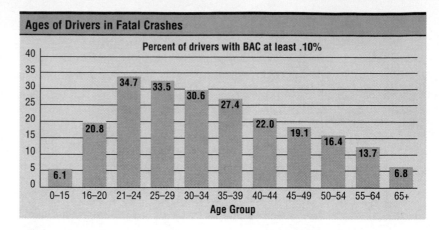

Ages of Drivers in Fatal Crashes

Percent of drivers with BAC at least .10%

Age Group	Percent
0–15	6.1
16–20	20.8
21–24	34.7
25–29	33.5
30–34	30.6
35–39	27.4
40–44	22.0
45–49	19.1
50–54	16.4
55–64	13.7
65+	6.8

The use of alcohol and other drugs has been a major problem in our society for many years. This problem is greatly compounded when someone who uses these drugs also drives. For several years, a growing number of collisions involved drivers who used alcohol or other drugs.

During more recent years, however, the rate of alcohol-related fatal crashes has declined. All states now enforce a minimum drinking age of 21. Laws against underage drinking and driving are stricter and are enforced, and alcohol-related educational programs have increased. Nevertheless, alcohol- related crashes are still a top safety problem.

Alcohol Facts

Many people who use alcohol do not realize that it is a drug. The word *alcohol* is the commonly used term for the chemical substance ethanol, grain alcohol, or ethyl alcohol.

The effects of alcohol vary from person to person. Equal amounts of alcohol affect different people in different ways. Even though the severity of its effects vary, alcohol affects everyone who uses it. One of the most serious problems of alcohol is that of the drinking driver. The demands of the driving task are so great that every driver needs to be in the best condition possible. A person cannot afford to increase the risks of driving by having his or her skills reduced by alcohol.

Consider these facts about alcohol and driving:

- Alcohol is a major factor in nearly 50 percent of all traffic deaths.
- The highest rates for intoxication are found in drivers in their early 20s.
- Over 40 percent of drivers ages 21 through 24 involved in fatal crashes had been drinking.
- Of drivers ages 16 through 20 involved in fatal crashes, about 21 percent were intoxicated.
- Drivers ages 16 through 20 are more likely to be alcohol-impaired than any other age group.
- Nearly half of those killed in alcohol-related collisions had not been drinking, but were victims of drunk drivers.
- Between 10:00 PM and 3:00 AM on Friday and Saturday nights, at least one of every ten drivers is legally drunk.
- For drivers of all ages involved in fatal crashes, about one in four is intoxicated.
- Nearly 60 percent of all fatalities during holidays are alcohol related.

Everyone needs to know how alcohol affects the mental and physical abilities needed for safe driving. Nondrinkers will interact with intoxicated drivers on the roadways. People who drive need to know the importance of not drinking.

Mental Abilities and Alcohol

Alcohol begins to affect a person's abilities almost the moment it enters the body. Alcohol is not digested. It is absorbed directly and quickly into the bloodstream through the walls and linings of the stomach and small intestine.

Once alcohol enters the bloodstream, it quickly reaches the brain because of the brain's large blood supply. Alcohol has its greatest effect on the parts of the brain that control judgment and reasoning— the most critical skills needed by drivers. Physical abilities become impaired soon afterward.

Judgment and Reasoning A driver affected by alcohol has a decreased ability to reason clearly and make sound judgments. However, the driver actually feels as though thinking and judging abilities are sharper and quicker than usual.

In addition, alcohol quickly diminishes the ability to concentrate. A decrease in the ability to concentrate greatly increases a driver's level of risk. After only one drink, such as one beer or one glass of wine, a person's driving ability can be reduced. As the amount of alcohol in a person's body increases, that person's driving ability decreases even more.

After only one drink, alcohol can

- affect judgment, reasoning, and concentration
- reduce coordination
- distort depth perception
- alter moods and emotions.

The IPDE process is affected when judgment and reasoning abilities are reduced. An alcohol-impaired driver is less able to interpret correctly what he or she sees. This driver tends to stare in one direction and fails to use a visual search pattern effectively. He or she makes errors in judging distance, speed, and shape. Alcohol-impaired drivers are very likely to make poor decisions.

Alcohol also weakens a driver's **inhibitions**, which are inner forces of personality that hold back or restrain one's impulsive behavior. As alcohol content in the body increases, a driver's inhibitions weaken. The person might drive too fast, take needless risks, and even drive into emergency situations without knowing or caring.

Physical Abilities and Alcohol

As more alcohol enters the bloodstream, the area of the brain that controls muscular movements and body control begins to slow down. Even after the driver recognizes danger, the brain takes longer than normal to process the information and react to the danger. Messages the brain sends to different parts of the body might become confused.

Reaction Time and Coordination The muscular reactions of a driver who has been drinking can become slow and clumsy. Steering and braking movements can become uncoordinated. The driver might oversteer, brake late, or not brake at all. The driver might not be able to negotiate turns properly and safely. Such actions cause drinking drivers to be involved in serious crashes.

Alcohol is more likely to affect the actions of a beginning driver than the actions of a more experienced driver. A beginning driver lacks experience, and his or her skills are less automatic. A beginning driver is more likely to be seriously affected by alcohol.

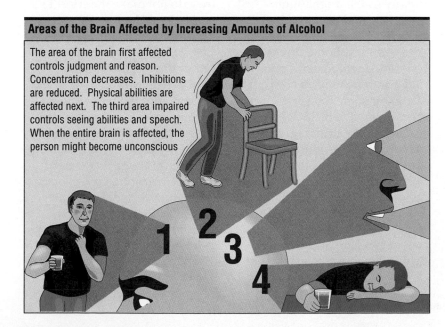

Areas of the Brain Affected by Increasing Amounts of Alcohol

The area of the brain first affected controls judgment and reason. Concentration decreases. Inhibitions are reduced. Physical abilities are affected next. The third area impaired controls seeing abilities and speech. When the entire brain is affected, the person might become unconscious

Pedestrian as seen by a driver at night

The blurring and diminishing of what the drinking driver sees is a result of impaired visual acuity.

Seeing Abilities Alcohol affects a driver's ability to see clearly. Night vision, peripheral vision, color vision, and depth perception are all impaired.

Because alcohol distorts vision, it reduces the effective use of an orderly visual search pattern. A drinking driver's eyes are more likely to fixate in a stare, thus reducing the scanning and searching process. In addition, both visual acuity and peripheral vision are reduced.

After one or two drinks, a person's eyes need more light to see dimly lit objects. At night, a driver who has not been drinking can see the pedestrian pictured here. The visual acuity of a drinking driver becomes impaired. The drinking driver might not even see the pedestrian at all.

Alcohol also affects the reflex action of the eyes. At night, this impairment can be critical. As headlights of oncoming vehicles come closer, the pupils of the eyes normally become smaller to shut out excess light. This reflex keeps you from being blinded by the glare of the headlights. When the lights have passed, the pupils enlarge again to let in all available light. The ability of your eyes to continually make this change is extremely important.

After only a few drinks, this reflex action is impaired. The pupils do not become small rapidly as the bright lights approach, and they are slow to open after the bright lights pass. As a result, the driver can be blinded temporarily, and may continue to have blurred vision for some time after meeting each vehicle.

After heavy drinking, a person might see blurred or multiple images. Each eye normally picks up a separate image of an object. The brain quickly coordinates these two images so that the person sees only one image. After several drinks, however, coordination of the images becomes impaired. The person might see several images, such as numerous center lines on the roadway. An oncoming car might even appear to be on both sides of the roadway at the same time.

Alcohol also impairs depth perception. A drinking driver might perceive something as being far away when it is actually very close. Accurate depth perception is needed to judge

- distance and speed of oncoming vehicles
- distance from vehicles ahead
- distance from signs and signals
- distance needed for stopping safely.

Peripheral vision is also impaired by alcohol. When peripheral vision is narrowed, a driver must turn and look to the sides for potential problems. After a few drinks, though, drivers are usually not aware of restricted side vision. Therefore, they do not make the effort to aggressively look to the sides. They are creating a hazard.

Other Physical Problems
As a person continues to drink, the center of the brain might become impaired. This center, called the medulla, controls breathing and heartbeat. Death can occur if large amounts of alcohol, consumed over a very short time period, reach the medulla. Usually, a person becomes unconscious and stops drinking before this point.

Amount of Alcohol in Standard Drinks

	Drink volume		Percentage of alcohol		Amount of alcohol
	12 ounces beer	×	5%	=	.60 ounces
	5 ounces wine	×	12%	=	.60 ounces
	1½ ounces whiskey (80 proof)	×	40%	=	.60 ounces

Long-Term Effects Alcoholism, an addiction to alcohol, can result from alcohol use. The liver, brain, and other organs might become damaged. Problem drinkers continue to use alcohol even though drinking causes problems in their lives. Alcoholism and problem drinking can result in trouble not only for the individual, but for the family and community as well.

Behavior and Alcohol

As judgment and reasoning become affected, a person's actions and behavior change. Just one drink can affect a person's behavior. The same amount of alcohol does not affect all people the same way. Alcohol does not even affect one person the same way in all situations. A person might be affected by alcohol more at one time than at other times.

One common effect of alcohol on behavior is a feeling of well-being. This feeling is known as **euphoria**. Some people with this euphoric effect think they can do anything. They believe they are more intelligent, funnier, and more skilled than they actually are. This feeling is only a state of mind, because alcohol depresses, or slows down, the working of the nervous system.

Alcohol-induced euphoria can cause people to take chances they normally would not take. This behavior can be deadly behind the wheel of a vehicle.

Alcohol can also change other types of behavior. People who drink often become angry or sad. Many become silly and even rude. Some of this resulting behavior depends on the person's personality as well as the mood they are in when they begin to drink. The best way to avoid these changes in behavior is to decide not to drink.

Amount of Alcohol in a Drink

People who drink and drive can be a hazard to themselves and to other roadway users. Even a small amount of alcohol can increase the "driving risk. How much is a "small amount?"

The chart shows the standard sizes of "one drink" of three different drinks. Each contains about the same amount of alcohol. The term "proof" describes the strength of liquor. Divide a liquor's proof number by two to determine its approximate percentage of alcohol. The chart shows that 80-proof whiskey is about 40 percent alcohol. A 100-proof liquor is about 50 percent alcohol.

The 12 ounces of beer and the 5 ounces of wine contain about the same amount of alcohol as the 1½ ounces of liquor. Drinking 12 ounces of beer can impair a person's abilities as much as 5 ounces of wine or 1½ ounces of liquor in a cocktail.

Alcohol in the Body

The amount of alcohol in a person's bloodstream can be measured by chemical tests. A chemical analysis of the blood can determine a person's **blood-alcohol concentration** (BAC). The BAC tells the percent of alcohol in the bloodstream, and thus indicates the level of intoxication.

The small chart shows BAC standards. Each drink adds about .02 to .03 percent to the person's BAC. The average person needs only to consume about two drinks in an hour to reach .05 percent and become an unsafe driver. However, to base drinking and driving decisions only on a BAC chart is dangerously misleading. A BAC of only .04 percent can have a great effect on the driving task.

The Effects of Alcohol

The higher the BAC, or percent of alcohol in the blood, the more affected a person will be. The following factors can affect the blood-alcohol concentration:

- The amount of alcohol consumed. The more a person drinks, the higher the BAC.
- The amount of time over which a given amount of alcohol was consumed. A person's blood-alcohol concentration rises more rapidly if only short periods of time elapse between drinks.
- The person's body weight. If all other factors are equal,

BAC Standards	
(percent alcohol in bloodstream)	
BAC	**Condition**
.01–.04%	Affected
.05–.09%	Impaired
.10%	Intoxicated

a heavier person may be affected less by a given amount of alcohol than a lighter person would be. Heavier people have more blood and other body fluids to dilute the alcohol, so their BAC level could be lower.

- The amount of food in the stomach at the time of drinking. Food in the stomach actually does very little to

slow or reduce the effects of alcohol. Even with food in the stomach, the absorption rate of alcohol into the bloodstream is rapid. When alcohol is mixed with carbonated beverages like club soda, the absorption rate is even faster.

A person can avoid alcoholic beverages at a social gathering by choosing soft drinks or other beverages rather than alcohol-based drinks. A person can also set down an unwanted drink and walk away from it.

Some people do decide to drink, but responsible friends can keep them from making additional mistakes.

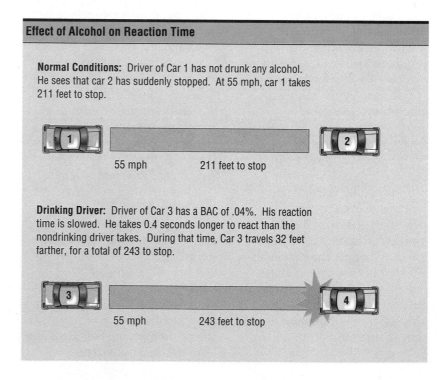

Effect of Alcohol on Reaction Time

Normal Conditions: Driver of Car 1 has not drunk any alcohol. He sees that car 2 has suddenly stopped. At 55 mph, car 1 takes 211 feet to stop.

55 mph   211 feet to stop

Drinking Driver: Driver of Car 3 has a BAC of .04%. His reaction time is slowed. He takes 0.4 seconds longer to react than the nondrinking driver takes. During that time, Car 3 travels 32 feet farther, for a total of 243 to stop.

55 mph   243 feet to stop

Effects of Alcohol on Behavior

Number of drinks in one hour	BAC	Effects
1 serving	.02–.03%	Inhibitions are lessened. Judgment and reasoning begin to be affected.
3 servings	.05–.09%	Unable to think clearly. Judgment and reasoning are not reliable. Muscular coordination is impaired
4 servings	.10–.12%	After four drinks, hearing, speech, vision, and balance are affected
5 servings	.13–.15%	Most behaviors are affected. Body parts seem to "not work together." Walking without stumbling is difficult. Unmistakable intoxication.

Take these actions to encourage friends not to drink:

- Get them involved in activities other than drinking.
- Encourage them to decide on a limit of drinks in advance and stick to it.
- Ask them to avoid drinks with a high concentration of alcohol.
- Suggest that they leave part of a drink in the glass. An empty glass invites a refill.
- Encourage them to sip a drink very slowly.
- Suggest that they not drink more than one alcoholic beverage in an hour.
- Make them aware of their physical and emotional conditions.

Controlling Impairment

Alcohol is absorbed into the body very quickly, but it is very slow to leave. Alcohol continues to circulate throughout the body until it is oxidized and removed by the liver. A very small amount of alcohol is also removed by the kidneys, breath, and sweat glands.

How much time is needed after drinking to be fit to drive again? A person's system oxidizes, or burns, alcohol at the rate of approximately three-fourths of a standard drink in one hour. A person who has one drink needs about one hour and fifteen minutes to rid the body of the alcohol in that drink. After consuming three drinks in an hour, a person needs over four hours for the body to oxidize and eliminate most of the alcohol. A person should not drive during those time periods. *Only time can reduce the body's BAC and that person's degree of impairment.*

A person's BAC increases when intake and absorption rate of alcohol is greater than the body's ability to oxidize and eliminate the alcohol. BAC continues to increase even after the person stops drinking. Note in the chart on the next page that alcohol remains in the body for about ten hours after the person stops drinking. This person's BAC reached 0.15 percent.

People who make the decision to drink can do the following to help control alcohol impairment:

- Limit the number of drinks.
- Space drinks at least one hour apart.
- Be aware of loud talk, unsteady coordination, and other signs of alcohol impairment.
- Know and respect individual limits.

Myths About Alcohol

Many people do not realize that these ideas about alcohol are *not* true:

- **I can burn off alcohol by strenuous activity.** Only time can reduce the effects of alcohol. Even very strenuous activity is ineffective in reducing BAC because the sweat glands release only a small amount of alcohol.
- **I can sober up by drinking black coffee and taking a cold shower.** The stimulation of black coffee and a cold shower cannot reduce BAC. The person might seem more alert after coffee or a shower, but BAC is not reduced.
- **I will not be affected because I am only drinking beer.** A 12-ounce bottle or can of beer contains as much alcohol as an average cocktail.
- **Alcohol will not affect me because I have built up a tolerance to it.** Even before a person's BAC level reaches .10 percent, that person is intoxicated and cannot expect to be able to drive safely.

- **I can drive better after a few drinks.** This mistaken reasoning might occur after a person has been drinking, and judgment and reasoning are already affected.
- **A young person cannot become a problem drinker.** Some young people have become problem drinkers even though most of their drinking is done on weekends.

Reducing Driving Risk

The surest way to eliminate the risk of driving under the influence of alcohol is to not drink and drive. Some people think they can drink and still drive safely. However, they cannot be sure that their judgment and responses are totally unimpaired.

Most people realize that driving after drinking is not a responsible act. However, some drivers take a risk and drive after drinking. Alcohol has reduced their inhibitions and impaired their judgment and decision-making ability.

Collision risk increases greatly as drinking increases.

The chances of a driver with a BAC of .05 being involved in a collision is more than double that of a sober driver. A driver whose BAC is .10, the legal level of intoxication in some states, is six times more likely to have a crash.

As a responsible driver, you can take steps to help reduce the risk of drinking and driving. Always refuse to ride with drivers who have been drinking. Make every effort to keep your friends from driving if they have been drinking. The risk of drinking and driving can also be reduced by appointing a person to be a **designated driver.** A designated driver is a person who abstains from drinking alcoholic beverages at a social function. Many establishments provide non alcoholic beverages at no charge for designated drivers or others who choose not to drink. Some establishments provide transportation for customers who might have drunk too much.

Review It

1. Which abilities are first affected by alcohol?
2. How can alcohol affect a driver's seeing abilities?
3. What is meant by blood-alcohol concentration?
4. What factors affect blood-alcohol concentration?
5. What are six myths regarding alcohol?

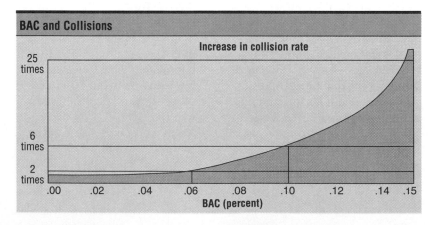

BAC and Collisions

Other Drugs and Driving

When you hear the word "drugs," you might think of hard drugs, such as marijuana or cocaine. A drug is any substance that changes the way the body works. Medicines are drugs, and over-the-counter and prescription medicines contribute to society's drug problems.

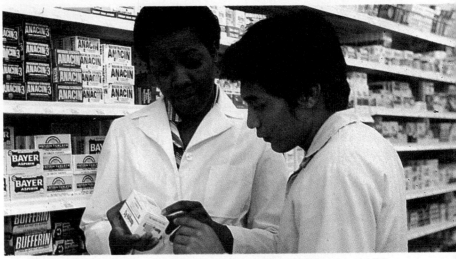

Learn about possible side effects of a medicine by reading its label. Ask the pharmacist if the medicine could impair your driving performance.

Types of Drugs

Most drugs are classified according to the effects they have on the central nervous system and bodily functions. Some drugs depress, or slow down, the central nervous system; others stimulate it, or speed it up. Other drugs can alter a person's thinking process and personality.

When legal drugs are taken in moderate amounts and for the right reasons, they are relatively safe. However, any drug can become dangerous if it is taken in excess or otherwise misused or abused. Any drug can produce unwanted side effects.

When buying any medicine, check the label for warnings of how the drug might affect driving performance. The labels of most medicines list their possible side effects. When a label says, "Might cause drowsiness or dizziness," do not use the drug before driving. Some labels might even say, "Do not drive after using." As a responsible driver, do not ignore such cautions.

Over-the-Counter Medicines
Drugs that can be obtained legally without a doctor's prescription can affect a person's driving abilities. Such medicines, called **over-the-counter** (OTC) medicines, are widely advertised.

Many OTC depressant medicines provide relief from colds, hay fever, allergies, and headaches. Side effects from OTC drops, sprays, syrups, and pills can include drowsiness, dizziness, slowed reaction time, and poor judgment. OTC medicines can increase driving risks and reduce a person's ability to drive safely. These medicines can be harmful because their effects on driving are often unexpected.

Prescription Mediciness
A drug that can be purchased legally only when ordered by a doctor is a **prescription medicine.** Most prescription medicines are stronger than OTC medicines. Ask your doctor how a prescription medicine might affect your driving ability.

A person who takes medicines prescribed by more than one doctor should make sure that each doctor knows about the other's prescriptions. Some medicines taken in combination with others might produce an unwanted, unexpected effect.

Depressants

A **depressant** is a drug that can slow down, or depress, the central nervous system. Some people use depressants to relieve tension, treat high blood pressure, and calm nerves.

A depressant slows down both mental and physical processes. A depressant's effect is similar to the effect of alcohol, which is a depressant. Reflex actions are slowed and coordination becomes clumsy. A driver can become very relaxed, lose inhibitions, and have difficulty identifying, predicting, deciding, and executing.

Stimulants

A **stimulant** is a drug that speeds up the central nervous system. At first, a stimulant can give a feeling of energy and alertness, and can prevent sleep. However, this effect does not last long, and the person can become nervous and irritable. A driver using a stimulant can develop a false sense of alertness and self confidence, thus increasing driving-related risks.

Marijuana

Marijuana is a powerful mind-altering drug that enters the bloodstream quickly and affects the brain and other parts of the central nervous system. Marijuana comes from the hemp plant, *Cannabis sativa*, and is commonly called "pot," "grass," or "weed."

Depressants	Stimulants	Hallucinogens	Marijuana
alcohol	amphetamines	LSD	marijuana
barbiturates	cocaine	PCP	hashish
codeine	crack	mescaline	hash oil
heroin	crank	peyote ("buttons")	
methadone	"ice"	psilocybin	
morphine	freebase	("mushrooms")	
sleeping pills			
tranquilizers			

A marijuana user can become easily distracted. The drug can impair judgment, memory, depth perception, and coordination. All these are basic abilities required for safe driving. The impairment from marijuana can last a long time. Unlike alcohol, which the body can eliminate in hours, chemicals in marijuana can remain in the body for weeks. It takes about one month for the chemicals from one marijuana cigarette to leave the body. A marijuana user might feel that the effects have worn off and safe driving is possible after a few hours. In reality, driving abilities remain impaired for a very long time.

Hallucinogens

A **hallucinogen** alters a person's thinking, awareness, perception, vision, and other senses. LSD and PCP are strong hallucinogens. They cause a user to see, hear, feel, or smell things that do not exist. Users become confused and unable to concentrate or think clearly. Use of any type of hallucinogen can distort a person's sense of direction, distance, and time.

Combining Drugs

Using two or more drugs at the same time can be very dangerous. You should not take more than one OTC or prescription medicine without first consulting your doctor or a pharmacist.

Using alcohol while taking medicine is especially dangerous. If a person uses alcohol while taking an antihistamine for a cold, the nervous system can be slowed down much more than by using either drug alone. When other drugs are combined with alcohol, the effects of both drugs are multiplied, rather than just added together.

While most alcohol-drug combinations increase driving risk, some combinations can be fatal. Combining depressants like alcohol and barbiturates can slow down the nervous system so much that death results.

Review It

1. Name three ways in which drugs can affect a person.
2. Why is combining alcohol and other drugs dangerous?

15–3

Traffic Laws Governing Alcohol and Drug Use

All fifty states have become uniform in requiring a person to be 21 years of age before legally buying or consuming alcoholic beverages. This uniformity has eliminated the problem that existed when a state in which the minimum age was 21 bordered a state that had an under-21 law.

Alcohol-related vehicle accidents among teenagers dropped after the drinking age was raised to 21. However, teenage drinking and driving is still a major problem.

Many state officials are concerned that young people who cannot legally drink in public

This new driver knows that he can lose his license if he refuses to cooperate with an officer who requests a drug test.

places are drinking illegally in cars. Partly for this reason, most states have made it illegal to have open containers of alcoholic beverages in vehicles.

Remember that drivers ages 15 through 19 are more likely to be alcohol-impaired than those in any other age group. Almost 40 percent of fatally injured teenage drivers were found to have been drinking prior to their crash. Everyone has the responsibility to adhere to the laws governing drinking, and to do whatever they can to influence their friends to support these laws.

Implied Consent Law

All states have an **implied consent law** for drivers. Anyone who is awarded a driver's license automatically consents to be tested for BAC and other drugs if arrested on suspicion of driving under the influence of drugs.

The new driver in the picture is being tested for his first driver's license. Part of his responsibility for receiving this license is the understanding that if he is stopped for suspicion of drug use while driving, he will consent to being tested. If he does not cooperate with the officers and refuses to be tested for BAC, his license can be suspended. The license can be suspended even if he is not convicted of driving under the influence of alcohol.

Safe Driving Tips

Persons under the age of 21 who buy and consume alcoholic beverages illegally are putting both their lives and their future reputations in danger. If you think friends are going to be drinking illegally while in a vehicle, do not join them. You risk getting arrested and having a police record if you are in a vehicle with illegal alcoholic beverages. Penalties for use of alcohol by underage drinkers are far more severe than for persons of legal drinking age.

Levels of Intoxication

Most states have set the level of intoxication at a BAC of .10 percent. A driver with this BAC could be charged with **driving while intoxicated** (DWI). Other states have set the legal level of intoxication at .08 percent. When a DWI charge is made, a driver can be convicted on the basis of the BAC. In some states, a charge of **driving under the influence** (DUI), can be made if the driver's BAC is between .05 and .09 percent. Some states make no distinction between DWI and DUI.

A charge of DUI can also refer to driving under the influence of any drug. A person can be convicted of DUI with just a trace amount of an illegal drug in the blood.

The intoxilyzer uses infrared light to help determine BAC.

Penalties for Conviction

Driving while intoxicated and driving under the influence are both very serious offenses. Arrests and convictions can be embarrassing and costly.

Penalties for DUI and DWI convictions vary from state to state. The most common penalty is suspension of the person's driver's license for a specified period of time. In many states the license is suspended for a minimum of one year for the first DUI or DWI conviction. In some cases, the results of conviction are both a fine and a prison term.

Penalties are more severe if an intoxicated driver is involved in a collision. If a fatality results from the collision, the driver could be found guilty of manslaughter.

Drivers who are convicted of a second DUI or DWI offense usually receive much harsher penalties than for the first conviction. Licenses can be revoked for as long as three years. Prison terms can be longer and fines more costly. A driver who has been convicted of DUI or DWI will also pay a much higher premium for automobile insurance for many years. Some insurance companies stop insuring drivers who have been convicted of driving while intoxicated.

Tests for Intoxication

Law enforcement agencies place a high priority on enforcing DUI and DWI laws. They also place an increased emphasis on training officers to recognize impaired drivers. Several tests can be used to evaluate a person suspected of DUI or DWI. Tests can be given in the police station or on the roadside.

Chemical Testing Chemical analysis of blood, urine, or breath can accurately determine BAC. The breath test is a widely used and simple analysis.

The breath-test machine most often used for determining BAC is an **intoxilyzer**. The person breathes into the intoxilyzer's tube. Then the intoxilyzer determines BAC by the amount of infrared light absorbed. Finally, the person's BAC is indicated on both the intoxilyzer's screen and on a paper printout.

Field Sobriety Testing Law-enforcement officers in many states can give a **field sobriety test** when they suspect a driver of DUI or DWI. Field sobriety testing includes a series of on-the-spot, roadside tests which help an officer detect driver impairment. In many cases the tests can indicate whether the impairment is caused by alcohol or by other drugs.

Roadside tests might include a variety of procedures. Some states might include only one or two tests, while other states include several tests. A variety of coordination tests and eye checks might be included. In many states, DWI convictions can be based on field sobriety test results.

One such test is the horizontal-gaze nystagmus test. The term **nystagmus** refers to the involuntary jerking of the eyes as the person gazes to the side. Most people show some nystagmus as their eyes track from straight ahead to the side. The horizontal-gaze nystagmus test determines the point where the jerking begins. As a person's BAC increases, the jerking begins at an earlier point. An officer properly trained in nystagmus testing can estimate a person's BAC that will be accurate to within .02 percent of chemical test readings.

Other roadside tests demonstrate both physical and mental impairment. Balance, coordination, the ability to follow simple instructions, and the ability to perform two tasks at once may be tested. The inability to perform two tasks at once is called divided attention impairment. Divided attention tests are given widely since it is evident that both physical and mental tasks are required to operate a motor vehicle safely.

A simple divided-attention test might require the driver to walk heel to toe a certain number of steps, while at the same time giving an oral count of the steps taken. This procedure not only tests the person's ability to follow instructions, it also tests both balance and counting abilities. The inability to complete this task successfully indicates divided-attention impairment.

If You Are Stopped by a Police Officer

In some communities, highway officers can stop vehicles at random to perform safety checks. At the same time, they might look for signs of drug use.

When a driver sees the flashing lights of a police car in the rearview mirrors, it is usually a signal to stop. If you see such a signal, slow down until you are sure the officer is signaling for you, not someone else. Pull to the right and stop as soon as it is safe to do so. You might need to pull into a parking lot or a side street to be out of the way of moving traffic.

Stay in your car and follow the instructions the officer gives you. You will be required to show your driver's license, and in states with mandatory insurance laws, you will need to show your certificate of insurance. Tell the officer first if you need to reach into the glove compartment or under the seat for your license. Some states require drivers to carry their vehicle registration form .

Regardless of the circumstances, be courteous and answer the officer's questions as honestly as you can. Make sure you know what documents your state requires drivers to have with them whenever they are driving.

This driver is taking a divided attention test.

Review It

1. What age must a person be before legally buying or consuming alcohol?
2. What is the implied-consent law for drivers?
3. What is divided attention impairment?
4. What is the first thing a driver must do when being signaled by a police officer?

Peer Pressure and Drugs

Cheering a friend on to win a game is an example of positive peer pressure.

As a young adult, you are making many important decisions about how you want to live your life. People your age continue to develop personal values, principles, and beliefs they want to live by. Pressure from other individuals or groups can cause you to have conflicting and unsure feelings about many decisions you will need to make. Influences and pressures from many sources directed at young people are very often difficult to cope with or resist.

Understanding Peer Pressure

The influence of others of a similar age is called **peer pressure.** One's peers can greatly influence how a person thinks and acts. Peers have strong effects on each other because people naturally tend to want to belong to a group. Peer relationships are very powerful forces in shaping a person's future.

Peer pressure can be positive or negative. When peers exert pressure on you in a positive way, they want to be helpful or encouraging. Talking a friend out of drinking alcoholic beverages or using drugs at a party is an example of positive peer pressure.

Negative peer pressure occurs when others encourage you to do something that you believe is wrong or dangerous. When peers exert negative pressure, they do not have your best interests in mind. However, some people worry a great deal about what others think of them. Because some people might have an excessive need to belong to a certain group, negative pressure might result in them doing things that are against their beliefs.

Some people also submit at times to indirect peer pressure. This type of pressure often occurs when a person *feels* pressure to use alcohol or other drugs just to fit in with a group. There is no direct pressure exerted by others.

You might think that you always can make decisions without being affected by negative peer pressure. However, acting independently can be difficult when several members of a group belittle you or put you down. Try to remember that strong, mature people are guided by their own beliefs and values, and do not give them up for group approval. Refusing to do things that you believe to be wrong and being able to say no without fear of losing friends indicates responsible behavior. Mature, independent thinking is especially important if you face peer pressure to use alcohol or other drugs when you will be driving.

Ways to Say No

People who are confronted with negative peer pressure often find it difficult to say no without the fear of hurting others. The following steps, and examples of ways to apply them, can help you to say no. Use these steps to ask questions when faced with peer pressure to use alcohol or other drugs before driving. These steps can help you identify potentially difficult situations, understand the consequences, and take actions to protect yourself.

1. Question the action. "Do they have my best interests at heart?" "What type of pressure is being used?"
2. State the problem. "I would be doing something illegal that could be harmful." "This pressure could be interfering with my right to decide what is best for me."
3. State the consequences. "If I give in, I could get in trouble, and even be arrested. I could harm myself or someone else."
4. Suggest alternatives. "I've got a better idea; let's go get a pizza."
5. Leave and encourage others to join you. "I have to leave. If you change your mind later, you can meet me at the pizza place."

Saying no to negative peer pressure can be critically important for your safety. At the same time, *how* you say no is also very important. You can tactfully decline or refuse without attacking the other person or sounding unsure of yourself. When people respond in an assertive manner, they calmly and firmly state a decision or a position while being respectful of the rights of others. Responding assertively when saying no helps get your decisions accepted. Assertive responses usually do not make others feel angry or threatened.

Making Responsible Decisions

Making responsible decisions, like learning how to make safe-driving decisions, is a skill that a person can learn and develop. Learning how to make responsible decisions can help you feel more in control of your life.

A decision-making process that consists of five steps offers

a plan that will help you make difficult decisions. The steps of this process are listed in the chart. Always remember you must be willing to face up to and live with all the possible consequences of whatever decisions you make.

Deciding About Drinking

Almost every person is in a situation at some time where alcohol is available. Each person must make his or her own decision whether or not to drink. The best decision a person can make is not to drink.

Individuals who decide not to drink alcoholic beverages never need to worry about alcohol impairing their driving performance. However, nondrinkers must share general concern about those people who do drink and then drive. Nondrinkers also might need to decide to not ride with a driver who has been drinking.

Steps for Making Responsible Decisions
1. Recognize that a decision is needed.   Realize that you need to make a decision from among several choices.
2. Consider the choices.
3. Consider the consequences of each choice and ask yourself these questions about each choice.   ▪ Is it safe and healthy?   ▪ Is it legal?   ▪ Would my parents and other family members approve?   ▪ Does it show respect for myself and others?
4. Decide which choice is best. Act according to your decision.
5. Evaluate your decision.   If your choice has not worked out as you expected, you have learned what does not work. You might do things differently next time. Know that you made a responsible decision.

Peer Education

Many schools have organized student programs for **peer education.** Peer education is a process in which young people help other young people make decisions and determine goals. Peer programs may be known by many other names, including peer counseling, peer helpers, or peer facilitators. Regardless of the name, the purposes and goals of such programs are the same.

Peer education programs help young people influence one another in a positive way. Many persons your age are more sensitive to the thoughts and opinions of your peers than to the thoughts and opinions of adults. Teenagers are often more willing to deal with issues like alcohol and driving with the help of someone who shares the same concerns.

Peer groups have properly trained peer leaders who can be more than a friend or a considerate listener. Peer leaders learn specific skills for helping others deal effectively with problems or concerns.

Training of peer leaders is supervised by teachers, counselors, or other professionals. Peer leaders learn communication skills, referral skills, and problem-solving skills. Basic to the training of leaders is the development of abilities to listen attentively, to ask questions, to share areas of concern, and to respond with understanding.

In this peer education group, students are trained to become peer group leaders or peer group counselors.

Most peer counseling sessions are informal group discussions.

Other Influences

Various aspects of today's society can affect a young person's values and beliefs. TV, radio, movies, music, billboards, and newspaper and magazine advertisements create images of excitement and fun as they encourage the use of alcohol. Products are shown in the most positive way and the message usually appeals to a person's need to belong to a group.

To prevent these messages from influencing you, try to recognize the way the product is promoted. Ask yourself, "What negative effects can this product have that they are not telling me about?"

Family viewpoints and religious beliefs continue to be strong influences when young people are confronted with pressures and decisions regarding alcohol and other drugs.

Organizations have formed to influence people about the harmful effects of drugs, as well as the problem of drinking and driving. Some of these include Mothers Against Drunk Drivers (MADD), Alliance Against Intoxicated Motorists (AAIM), and Students Against Driving Drunk (SADD). If your school does not have a SADD program, you might want to help organize such an activity.

Responsibility to Others

When people are in situations where alcoholic drinks are served, their first responsibility is for their own actions. However, a person's responsibility increases when the situation involves drinking and driving.

If anyone at a party is drinking, the host must remember that alcohol first affects judgment and reasoning abilities. People who are drinking might not have the ability to judge the effects the alcohol is having on themselves. Most people who have had too much to drink do not realize it, and rarely admit it.

To what extent should a person take responsibility for the actions of others? Some people feel that doing so is interfering in other people's lives. However, most people wisely realize that they are being caring friends when they prevent friends from driving after drinking. All drivers must understand what a hazard a drinking driver can be to other roadway users.

Everyone should accept the responsibility of trying to keep a drinker from driving. The drinker has the prime responsibility of not driving after drinking. Anyone who serves alcoholic beverages carries the next greater responsibility. Concern must be not only for the drinking driver, but also for others who might be injured or killed as a result of the actions of a drinking driver. In some states, a person who *serves* alcohol is legally responsible in case someone is injured or killed as a result of the actions of the drinking driver.

You must be able to recognize signs of too much drinking in order to share the responsibility for friends who drink. Since alcohol affects different people in different ways, no set pattern can determine a person's impairment. Look for these signs of impairment:

- walking unsteadily or stumbling
- slurred, unclear speech
- talking louder than usual
- inability to gain eye contact with others
- losing track of time or day of week
- any behavior that is the opposite of normal behavior for that person.

FRIENDS DON'T LET FRIENDS DRIVE DRUNK

Remember that only one drink can cause a person's BAC to reach .03 percent. Driving abilities can be impaired even at that BAC. Collision risk increases greatly as drinking increases.

A responsible person makes assertive efforts to encourage friends to make responsible decisions about alcohol use and driving. Keeping a drinking person from driving is the responsibility of everyone.

The host of any party has the responsibility of providing a variety of food, soft drinks, and activities.

What You and Others Can Do

A nondrinker has decisions to make about keeping drinking friends from driving. A responsible person does not let friends drive drunk. A friend will help to get a friend home.

A nondrinker might also have to decide whether or not to ride with a drinking driver. Try to persuade the drinker to let you drive. If you cannot prevent a drinker from driving, refuse to ride with him or her. Try to find other transportation to get home safely. Stay where you are if necessary.

When friends plan parties, encourage them to refrain from serving alcoholic beverages. If you know that some people will bring alcoholic drinks, consider not attending the party.

Some adult groups implement a designated driver program. A designated driver is appointed or volunteers not to drink before anyone in the group begins to drink. The best action is to volunteer to be the designated driver yourself.

The effects of alcohol are harmful, if not deadly, especially when operating a motor vehicle. Heavy drinkers are the major cause of alcohol-related collisions that result in death or injury. However, social drinkers share the responsibility for alcohol-related collisions. Responsible drivers should decide not to become a part of the drinking-driving problem, but to contribute to its solution.

Review It

1. How might negative peer pressure affect a young person's decision about drinking?
2. What are five ways to say no to drinking and driving?
3. What is peer education?
4. What decision might a nondrinker need to make about a friend who has been drinking?

Sometimes the best action is to call a taxi to take a friend home.

DECISION MAKING

1. Several passengers are trying to prevent a friend from driving after drinking. If the friend does insist upon driving, what choices do the passengers have to protect their own safety?

2. This driver has been stopped by the police for suspicion of driving while intoxicated. What types of tests might the officer request the driver to take? What can these tests detect and measure?

3. These two people have just left a party where each drank several cans of beer. The driver plans to pass the car ahead. What effects might the beer have on the driver's ability to pass safely?

4. The person above has just received a driver's license for the first time. What has this new driver automatically consented to do by receiving this license?

CHAPTER 15 REVIEW

Review Chapter Objectives

15–1 Effects of Alcohol on Driver Performance
1. How does alcohol affect the mental and physical abilities needed for driving? (294-297)
2. What is meant by blood-alcohol concentration? (298)
3. What factors affect blood-alcohol concentration? (298)
4. What are six myths about the use of alcohol? (300)

15–2 Other Drugs and Driving
5. How can depressant, stimulant, and hallucinogenic drugs affect a driver? (302)
6. What are the effects of combining alcohol with other drugs? (302)

15–3 Traffic Laws Governing Alcohol and Drug Use
7. What are implied-consent laws? (303)
8. What is meant by levels of intoxication and how can these levels be measured? (304-305)
9. What should a driver do when signaled by a patrol officer? (305)

15–4 Peer Pressure and Drugs
10. How might peer pressure affect a person's decision about drinking and driving? (306)
11. What are the steps to follow when faced with peer pressure to use alcohol or other drugs? (307)
12. Why should everyone share the responsibility of preventing friends from driving after drinking? (309)
13. What are ways for keeping drinking friends from driving? (310)

Check Your Knowledge

Multiple Choice   Copy the number of each sentence below on a sheet of paper. Choose the letter that best completes the statement or answers the question.

1. Forces that restrain impulsive behavior are called (a) physical impairments. (b) inhibitions. (c) hallucinogens. (d) reflexes. (295)
2. The amount of alcohol in 12 ounces of beer compared to $1^1/_2$ ounces of liquor is (a) about the same. (b) much less. (c) much more. (d) somewhat more. (297)
3. How much time does the human body need to rid itself of the alcohol in one drink? (a) about 24 hours. (b) about 1 hour and 15 minutes. (c) 3 hours. (d) 45 minutes. (299)
4. A drug that speeds up the central nervous system is called a (a) depressant. (b) prescription drug. (c) downer. (d) stimulant. (302)
5. The term nystagmus refers to (a) peripheral vision. (b) depth perception. (c) jerking of the eyes. (d) visual acuity. (305)

Completion   Copy the number of each sentence below. After each number, write the word or words that complete the sentence correctly.

6. The area of the brain first affected by alcohol is the area that controls _____ . (295)
7. A feeling of well being which may make people think they can do anything is called _____ . (297)
8. The percent of alcohol in a person's bloodstream is that person's _____ . (298)
9. A person who voluntarily abstains from drinking at a social function in order to drive home safely is a _____ . (300)
10. A drug that slows down the central nervous system is called a _____ . (302)
11. With supporting evidence, a driver in some states can be convicted of _____ with a BAC of .05 percent. (303)
12. An on-the-spot roadside test is called a _____ . (304)
13. Friends your age trying to influence how you think or act is called _____ . (306)

Check Vocabulary

Copy the number of each definition in list A. Match the definition in list A with the term it defines in list B.

List A
14. a medicine that can be purchased legally without a prescription (301)
15. driving with a BAC of over .10 percent (303)
16. process in which young people help other young people make decisions and set goals (308)
17. computerized machine that analyzes and determines BAC in breath (304)
18. medicine that can be purchased legally only when ordered by a physician (301)
19. permission to be tested for BAC if arrested for suspicion of DUI (303)
20. Drug that distorts visual perception and other senses (302)

List B
a. peer education
b. hallucinogen
c. over-the-counter medicine
d. intoxilyzer
e. prescription medicine
f. implied-consent law
g. peer pressure
h. driving while intoxicated (DWI)

Check Your Understanding

Write a short answer for each question or statement.

21. What factors influence how a person reacts to alcohol? (297-298)
22. What age group is more likely to be alcohol impaired when driving than any other age group? (294)
23. What are five ways to say no when you are faced with peer pressure to use alcohol or other drugs? (307)
24. Why are divided attention tests an important part of a field sobriety test? (305)
25. How can you help friends control the amount they drink? (299)

Think Critically

Write a paragraph to answer each question or statement.

1. Imagine you are babysitting for a family several miles from home. You have been sitting for this family for several years and the pay is very good. On this night, the couple arrives home quite late and both have clearly had too much to drink. When one of them says, "Ok, I'll drive you home." What do you say and what do you do?

2. Explain what is meant by the statement: "The depressive action of alcohol is progressive."
3. A group of friends have spent the day in a park. They have been playing games, eating food and drinking beer. They have decided it is now time to go home. Assuming everyone has a driver's license and is a skillful driver, what is the best way to decide who should drive home?

Projects

1. Interview your local police to determine alcohol-related collision and fatality statistics during the last year in your community. Develop a chart by age groups involved and present it to your class for discussion.
2. At a drug store, read the labels on twenty different packages of medication. List those that warn against driving after taking or using the medication. **Write** a report and present it to the class.
3 Organize a committee to develop a SADD program in your school. Write to the following address for materials: Students Against Driving Drunk (SADD) P.O. Box 800, Marlboro, MA 01752.

Chapter 16

RESPONSIBILITIES OF OWNING A VEHICLE

You're the Driver!

Many young people look forward to owning a car of their own. Many types of vehicles are available. How can you select one that best meets your needs? Should you have an automatic transmission? air conditioner? other optional equipment?

How much does a car cost? How much does it cost to operate a car for a year? How are you going to pay the costs of owning a car? Where should you buy the car? What is a fair price to pay for the car?

What kinds of insurance do you need? Does your state require insurance? How much does insurance cost?

This chapter discusses the financial and social responsibilities of owning a car. The chapter also deals with insurance and environmental concerns related to owning and using a vehicle.

Objectives

Section 16–1   Buying a Vehicle
1. Describe the responsibilities of owning a vehicle.
2. List the costs of owning and driving a vehicle.
3. Explain how to select a used vehicle.
4. Describe the steps to take when buying a used vehicle.

Section 16–2   Insuring a Vehicle
5. Explain how auto insurance works.
6. Explain what is covered by each kind of insurance: liability, collision, comprehensive, medical, uninsured motorist, and no-fault.
7. List factors that affect the cost of insurance.

Section 16–3   Environmental Factors
8. Describe how vehicle use affects the environment.
9. Discuss ways to moderate the effects of vehicles on the environment.

Buying A Vehicle

Owning a vehicle allows you to come and go on your own. Owning a vehicle also includes responsibility for the vehicle's purchase, maintenance, insurance, and fuel expenses.

Do You Need A Vehicle?

Is your present need for transportation great enough that you should own a vehicle now? Are there alternatives to buying a vehicle? Answers to these questions can help you decide if your reasons for buying a vehicle justify the expense of owning one.

Students who own a vehicle probably have to work many hours to pay for this expense. Working reduces the time available for family, study, sports, and social activities. A student who works to support a vehicle might earn lower grades. Vehicle ownership also reduces the money available for education, gifts, or clothes. Thus, you and your family might decide that you should not buy a vehicle at this time.

Cost of Owning a Vehicle

The actual cost of owning and driving a vehicle might be more than you expect. When careful records are kept, the total annual cost can be identified. Some of the major expenses include:

- **Purchase Price** The price of a vehicle is the amount of money the owner is willing to accept for it. Newspaper ads are a good way for you to check the cost of different types of vehicles.
- **Depreciation** The value of a vehicle drops steadily whether you use the vehicle a lot or little. This decrease is called **depreciation.** Usually, the newer the vehicle, the greater the depreciation.
- **Other Costs** Operating costs include fuel, oil, tires, repairs, and replacement parts. Tolls and parking fees should be added to the list. The cost of licensing, registration, insurance, taxes, and interest on the car loan should be considered. Saving to buy the vehicle without a loan eliminates the expense of interest on the loan.

A small car gets good gas mileage.

Some cars look sporty but are expensive.

These expenses can increase each year. Your cost depends on how many miles you drive, where you drive, and fuel mileage. A $2,000 used vehicle can cost you $3,000 or more each year if you drive 10,000 miles annually. These costs are estimates. Your yearly cost could be lower or higher.

What Kind of Vehicle to Buy

If you decide you need and can afford a car, what type should you buy? Think about your answers to the following questions when deciding what kind of vehicle to buy.

- What will the vehicle be used for?
- Is the vehicle intended for one or two passengers and some packages, towing a trailer, or for additional purposes?
- How many miles will you drive each year?
- Will the vehicle be used for long trips or mainly for short trips?

Vehicle Size

The size of the vehicle is an important factor in your decision to buy a vehicle. Consider these factors:

- A smaller vehicle often gets higher mileage than a larger one. However, smaller, lighter vehicles offer less protection in a crash than larger, heavier ones.
- A smaller vehicle might not give as comfortable a ride as a larger vehicle.
- A larger vehicle has a greater capacity for carrying passengers and parcels than a smaller vehicle has.

Engine Size and Type

A small engine in a small vehicle usually is economical. If you select a vehicle with air conditioning, power steering, and other options that require power, a small engine might not be the best choice. But remember, a large engine uses more fuel than a smaller engine.

Options that increase the power of the engine, such as a turbocharger or multiple valves per cylinder, increase the cost of buying the vehicle. These options also can result in increased repair costs. In some instances, fuel mileage can suffer from these options.

You might need to drive over rough terrain or tow a trailer.

A minivan can carry large articles or many passengers.

Transmission

An automatic transmission is nearly as fuel efficient as a manual transmission. While the cost of repair for an automatic transmission is usually higher, automatic transmissions usually require fewer repairs than manual transmissions.

Vehicles That Save Fuel

Many smaller vehicles are called "economy" vehicles because they are fuel efficient. One vehicle might deliver 25 miles per gallon (mpg); another vehicle, usually lighter in weight, might deliver 45 mpg. If you drove 12,000 miles annually, the first vehicle would use 480 gallons of fuel, while the second vehicle would burn 267 gallons. At $1.50 per gallon, the vehicle using the extra 213 gallons of fuel would cost its owner $319 more to drive per year.

Buying a Used Vehicle

If a new vehicle costs too much, you might consider buying a used vehicle. Used vehicles are available from private owners and car dealers.

Buying from a private owner can cost less. You can talk to the owner and try to learn about the history of the vehicle. A private owner will seldom repair the vehicle or provide a warranty. A **warranty** is a written guarantee that the seller will repair the vehicle for a stated

Monthly Payments (3 Years)				
Amount Borrowed	Interest Rate Charged			
	12%	14%	16%	18%
$2,000	$66.43	$68.36	$70.31	$73.30
$3,000	$99.64	$102.53	$105.47	$108.46
$4,000	$132.86	$136.71	$140.63	$144.61
$5,000	$166.07	$170.89	$175.79	$180.76

Total Cost of Car Loans				
Amount Borrowed	Total Amount Paid (Loan Amount Plus Interest on Loan)			
$2,000	$2391.48	$2460.96	$2531.16	$2602.80
$3,000	$3587.04	$3691.08	$3796.92	$3904.56
$4,000	$4782.96	$4921.56	$5062.68	$5205.96
$5,000	$5978.52	$6152.04	$6328.44	$6507.36

period of time. A private sale is final in nearly all cases.

Used-car dealers usually have a variety of vehicles available. Some used-car dealers do not have repair facilities. They might not provide a full warranty.

New-car dealers usually have a good selection of good used vehicles from those traded in for new cars. The new-car dealer's price might be higher than other sources. However, a warranty is usually included.

A car dealer must post a warranty statement in the window of each vehicle. The warranty specifies which parts are guaranteed and for how long the parts are guaranteed.

How Much Should You Pay?

Publications known as *blue books* list prices for used cars. The **blue-book** price of a vehicle is the average price paid to dealers for that type and age of vehicle.

The price actually paid for each vehicle depends on its condition. If a vehicle is in excellent condition, a dealer might charge more than the blue-book price. If the vehicle has high mileage or is in poor condition, a dealer usually will charge a lower price.

Additional Vehicle Expenses

Vehicle ownership involves unexpected expenses. Regardless of the initial cost of a used vehicle, be prepared to set aside at least $500 for repairs during the first year of ownership.

Remember to budget the costs of insurance, licensing, taxes, and interest on the loan if you borrow money to buy a vehicle. The chart shows that interest on a loan can significantly increase the cost of owning a vehicle.

Choosing a Used Vehicle

Selecting a used vehicle takes time. When you find a vehicle you like, check further to see if it is in good condition. You should not buy on impulse or be pressured into buying a vehicle.

A vehicle's outward appearance can differ from its operating condition. Be suspicious of a late-model vehicle that is priced very low. The vehicle might have been in a collision. It might have been a taxi or a police car with high mileage and hard use.

A seller might have turned back the odometer in a vehicle, even though it is illegal to do so. When possible, talk to the previous owner to verify the odometer reading and condition of the vehicle. Some states require dealers to provide a mileage disclosure statement, certifying that the odometer reading is accurate.

When you are considering a used vehicle, you should check it on the outside, inside, and under the hood. Following is a list of checks you should make.

Outside and Inside Checks

Walk around the vehicle and perform the following checks:

- All doors should open and close from inside and outside. Doors should not sag. Locks should operate on all doors.
- Paint color should be uniform on all parts of the vehicle.
- Rust should not appear around fenders, under trim,

Carefully check a used vehicle before you buy it, including the tires and the body near them.

around headlights, or at the bottom of doors.
- The vehicle should not lean to one side.
- A spare tire and working jack should be in the trunk.
- Check under the hood and in the trunk for collision damage to inner fenders and frame.
- Check for fluid spots under the vehicle, and for leaks from the engine or transmission.
- The seat should feel firm when you sit on it. Worn upholstery might indicate high mileage or hard use.
- Check pedals. Worn pedals or very new pedals might indicate high mileage.
- Turn the steering wheel. With unassisted steering, the

steering wheel should have no more than two inches of "play" (steering wheel movement that does not turn the front wheels). The steering wheel in a car with power steering should have no play when the engine is running.
- Check that accessories work. These items include heater, defroster, rear window defogger, radio, windshield wipers and washers. If power seats, power locks or windows, cruise control, or air conditioning are included, make sure they work.
- Check that all lights work.
- Firmly press the brake pedal. There should be no loss of firmness as you continue to press the pedal.
- Check the parking brake.

Checks Under the Hood

Open the hood and look for the following items:

- Check the radiator and fan for signs of collision damage.
- Check for leaks around hoses and around the radiator.
- Check the condition of belts when the engine is off.
- When the engine is cool, remove the radiator cap. The radiator should be filled with coolant. There should be no oil or corrosion on the bottom of the radiator cap.
- The battery and its cables should be free of corrosion. The battery should have no cracks.
- Start the engine. Listen for strange noises. Check for water or oil leaks while the engine is running.

Check under the hood when the engine is cool and when it is running.

Test Drive the Vehicle

Test drive any vehicle you are considering buying. If the owner refuses to let you test drive the vehicle or demands a deposit, look for another vehicle.

Make these checks during the test drive:

- Turn the ignition switch on. Check that all warning lights and signals work.
- Start the engine. It should start easily each time you turn the key. Warning lights should go out in a few seconds.
- Drive at low speed and test the brakes several times. The vehicle should stop smoothly and straight.

- Turn some corners. The vehicle should steer easily without play in the steering wheel.
- Accelerate moderately. The vehicle should accelerate smoothly, and without hesitation from 0 to 40 mph.
- Test the brakes at various speeds. Brakes should not pull to one side or grab.
- Drive at 25 mph on a rough road. The vehicle should not rattle or feel very unstable.
- Note any indication of low oil pressure, overheating, or other warnings from lights or gauges.

Check by Mechanic   If the vehicle passes your tests, have a mechanic make a final check. A car clinic or diagnostic center will check the vehicle for a moderate fee.

Repairs to Consider When Buying a Used Vehicle

If the seller will not repair any defects, you will need to fix the vehicle. Some repairs are very expensive, while others might not be too costly. Consider the costs of repairs as you determine the actual purchase price.

Least Expensive Repairs

The following repairs might not add too much to the purchase price of a vehicle:

- Replace a dirty air filter.
- Replace corroded battery cables; battery fluid level might be low.

- Fix chipped paint and small rust spots on the body.
- Replace frayed or worn fan belts.
- Replace cracked or soft hoses.
- Change oil and replace oil filter.
- Replace faulty thermostat.
- Add transmission fluid if the level is low.
- Replace hard or worn wind-shield wiper blades.
- Replace bulbs for head lights, tail lights, or brake lights.

Moderately Expensive Repairs

Repairs in this group will add a considerable amount to the price of a vehicle:

- Acceleration is uneven; vehicle hesitates.
- Vehicle body is damaged.
- Vehicle leans to one side due to a broken suspension part.
- Doors, hood, or trunk do not open and close smoothly.
- Engine is hard to start or idles roughly.
- Shock absorbers need to be replaced.
- Brakes or wheel bearings need repair or replacement.
- Hood, trunk, or doors do not fit properly.
- Ignition wires need to be replaced.
- Jack and/or spare tire are missing.
- Paint is faded or worn through.
- Large rust spots are present.
- Radiator leaks, needs cleaning, or should be replaced.
- Tires are worn and should be replaced.

- Upholstery needs cleaning or repair.
- Windows are broken, chipped, or do not operate smoothly.

Repairs Too Expensive

Do not consider buying a vehicle that needs any of the following repairs. These repairs are so expensive that you should look for another vehicle.

- Transmission does not shift smoothly; you feel a jerking motion or hear strange noises when shifting.
- Automatic transmission slips when accelerating.
- Brakes grab or pull to one side.
- Clutch slips or chatters.
- Engine smokes when acceler-ating or braking.
- Gears make noise when slow-ing, accelerating, or turning.
- Heater or air conditioner does not operate properly.
- A great deal of oil leaks from the engine or transmission.
- Radiator contains oily water.
- Seats sag.

Before You Close the Deal

If possible, pay for the vehicle in cash. If you must borrow money, shop as carefully for a loan as you did for the car. Talk to various **lending agencies,** such as banks, credit unions, or savings and loan associations. If you are buying from a dealer, the dealer might offer a loan. Bargain for a lower purchase

price if the dealer's interest charge is higher than at a lending agency.

If the seller is going to make repairs, do not close the deal unless you get a written agree-ment that the repair will be done. Have the repair work written into the sales contract.

Review It

1. What are some responsibili-ties of vehicle ownership?
2. What are some of the costs of owning a vehicle?
3. What should you consider when choosing the kind of vehicle to buy?
4. What steps should you take when buying a used vehicle?

Insuring a Vehicle

If you are involved in a collision, you may find that the largest expense in owning a vehicle is paying for damages you cause. Each state has a **financial responsibility law.** This law requires you to prove that you can pay for damages you cause that result in death, injury, or property damage. In some states, you can prove your ability to pay for damages by depositing cash or by posting a bond.

Most people protect themselves by purchasing insurance. Some states have mandatory insurance laws that require every licensed driver and vehicle to be insured. These states do not allow you to post a bond or deposit cash. In many cases, you can be subject to severe penalties, including the loss of your license, if you have a crash and cannot prove financial responsibility.

What Is Vehicle Insurance?

Insurance is financial responsibility. You buy insurance from an insurance company by paying a **premium,** a specified amount of money, to the company. A **policy** is a written agreement or contract between you (the policyholder, or insured) and the insurance company. Some insurance materials are shown here.

If you are involved in a collision, you pay the **deductible**, a set amount of the cost of damage to your vehicle, as stated in your policy. Your insurance company agrees to pay the balance (up to specified limits) of the costs of injuries to persons and damage to property.

Kinds of Insurance

The most important type of coverage is **liability insurance.** One type of liability insurance, bodily-injury coverage, protects the driver who is at fault against claims to pay the costs related to injuries to other people.

A second type of liability insurance, property damage coverage, protects the driver who is at fault against claims for damage to another person's property. Liability coverage is only good for others when you are at fault in the crash. The chart summarizes other types of insurance that protect you and your passengers from other expenses.

No-Fault Insurance

In most cases, the insurance company of the driver at fault pays for injuries and property damage to others. Sometimes, though, it is not clear who is at fault in a collision. A court might take years to determine blame.

In some states, insurance companies offer **no-fault insurance,** a type of insurance that does not raise the question of fault. No-fault insurance eliminates much of the need for legal suits. Under no-fault insurance, the insurance company provides its policyholder coverage (up to specified amounts), regardless of who is at fault.

Insurance documents include bills for premiums, coverage descriptions, and policies.

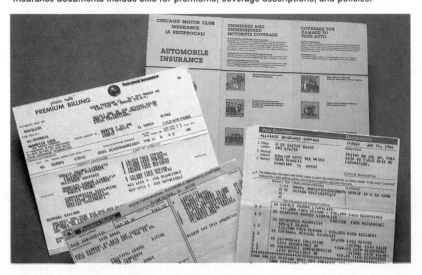

Car Insurance

Kind of Insurance	Coverage	Claim Includes	Minimum Amount	Notes
Bodily-injury liability	Pays claim against owner if someone is killed or injured and owner is at fault.	Hospital and doctor bills Legal fees Court costs Loss of wages	States normally specify minimum: $10,000–$15,000 for one person; $20,000–$30,000 for several persons.	Required in many states. Needed by all car owners. Minimum coverage required is generally too low.
Property-damage liability	Pays claim against owner if property of others is damaged and owner is at fault.	Other car and possessions in car. Damage to house, telephone pole, and traffic light.	States normally specify minimum: $5,000–$10,000.	Required in many states. Needed by all car owners
Uninsured-motorist*	Pays for injuries to you and your passengers in case of hit-and-run collision or uninsured motorist.	Hospital and doctor bills Legal fees Court costs Loss of wages (Does *not* cover property damage.)	Usually same as bodily–injury liability.	Required in many states. Needed by all car owners.
Collision (usually requires comprehensive coverage along with collision)	Pays cost of repairing or replacing owner's car when owner is at fault or when owner cannot collect from person at fault.	Repair or replacement of any car driven by owner or with owner's permission.	Insures for depreciated value of car. Owner decides on $100 to $500 deductible to reduce cost of premium.	Important for new or expensive car. Drop after 7-10 years of ownership or when value of car no longer justifies cost of coverages.
Comprehensive	Pays cost of repairing or replacing owner's car.	Fire Earthquake Theft Storm Flood Riots Wind Vandalism	Insures for depreciated value of car, usually with $100 to $500 deductible to reduce cost of premium.	Important for new or expensive car. Drop after 7 to 10 years of ownership.
Medical-payments	Pays medical costs for you and your passengers injured in any collision, regardless of fault.	Pays all immediate medical costs (generally in addition to other medical insurance).	Insures for $500 to $5,000 per person.	This insurance does not require a legal process to determine fault, while bodily-injury coverage usually does.
Towing	Pays cost of towing or minor repair to disabled car.	Dead battery Out of gas Flat tire Accident (regardless of cause or fault).	Usually pays amount validated by towing company.	Good to have. Not needed if owner belongs to automobile club with towing service.

*Note that uninsured-motorist insurance covers collision-related injuries only, not property damage.
Some states now allow insurance companies to offer uninsured-motorist property damage insurance.

Medical Payment Insurance

This insurance pays medical costs for the driver and passengers injured in a collision. It also covers family members injured or killed while riding in someone else's vehicle.

Medical coverage will pay if the policyholder or members of the family are injured as pedestrians, while riding bicycles, or as passengers in a bus or a taxi. Medical payment insurance does not depend on who is at fault in a collision. This type of insurance pays for medical, hospital, or funeral expenses up to stated amounts.

Comprehensive Insurance

This type of insurance pays for damage to your vehicle that is caused by something other than a collision. It can pay for repair or replacement of the depreciated value of the vehicle, minus the amount of deductible stated in the policy.

When a vehicle is about seven years old, it has depreciated so much that it usually is best to not buy comprehensive coverage.

Uninsured Motorist Insurance

This type of insurance is required in some states. It covers medical expenses if you are injured by a hit-and-run driver, or are in a collision with a driver who does not have liability insurance. This coverage is similar to the coverage provided by bodily injury insurance if you hurt someone else.

Part of the procedure you should follow if you are involved in a collision is to exchange insurance information with the other drivers.

Insurance Rates

Premium rates are determined by the amount paid out in claims. Each state regulates rates to assure fair costs for insurance coverage.

How Rates Are Determined

The premium you pay for insurance depends on the following factors:

- **Collision and Violation Record** A driver with recent convictions for moving violations tends to have more collisions so pays higher premiums.
- **Age of Principal Driver** The principal driver is the person who drives the vehicle the most. A principal driver under the age of 25 pays higher premiums. Insurance records show that young drivers have more collisions, in proportion to their numbers, than older drivers. Drivers age 16 to 24 represent about 16.5 percent

of all licensed drivers. However, these same drivers are involved in 31 percent of all collisions, and 28 percent of all fatal crashes. For the number of miles driven, young drivers have nearly twice as many fatal crashes as drivers over 25. Since young drivers average only half as many annual miles as older drivers, the actual collision rates for young drivers are as much as four times greater.

- **Miles Driven** The greater the mileage, the more the vehicle is exposed to the possibility of a collision.
- **Gender of Driver** The chart shows that young male drivers pay higher premiums because they drive more, have more collisions, and their crashes tend to be more severe than those involving young female drivers. Recently, the gap based on gender of the driver has narrowed.

- **Marital Status** A driver who is married tends to have fewer collisions than an unmarried driver.
- **Where the Driver Lives** Premiums are generally higher in cities than in rural areas.
- **Type of Vehicle** Premiums on expensive or sporty cars are higher because they are more expensive to repair and they are involved in more crashes.
- **Driver's Claim Record** Higher and more frequent claims, especially for collision and comprehensive coverage, result in higher premiums.

Reduced Premiums

Some insurance companies reduce premiums for a driver who:

- has had no claims or moving violations for three years.
- has more than one vehicle insured by the same company.
- has a car with an air bag.
- has successfully completed a driver education course.
- is a student and maintains a "B" grade average.

Assigned-Risk Insurance

An insurance company might cancel the policy of a driver who has had a serious collision or several traffic violations. Revocation or suspension of the driver's license can also result in policy cancellation.

A driver whose insurance has been canceled might not be able to get coverage at standard rates from another company. A high-risk driver might have to buy **assigned-risk insurance.** This type of insurance provides minimum bodily injury and property damage liability coverage to a high-risk driver for a higher premium. After a specified number of years of collision-free and violation-free driving, the driver can apply for standard insurance coverage at regular rates.

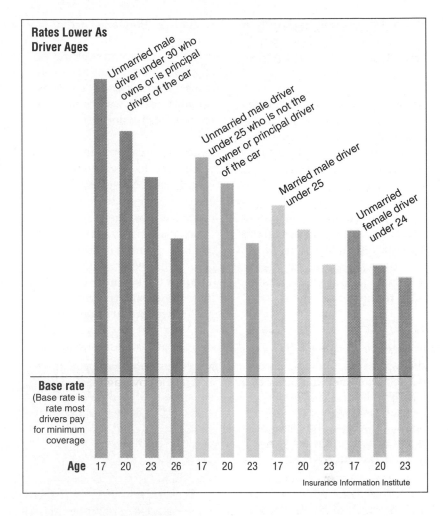

Rates Lower As Driver Ages

Unmarried male driver under 30 who owns or is principal driver of the car

Unmarried male driver under 25 who is not the owner or principal driver of the car

Married male driver under 25

Unmarried female driver under 24

Base rate (Base rate is rate most drivers pay for minimum coverage)

Age 17 20 23 26 17 20 23 17 20 23 17 20 23

Insurance Information Institute

Review It

1. What is the purpose of vehicle insurance?
2. What are the different types of insurance?
3. What factors determine vehicle insurance premiums?

Environmental Concerns

Owning and driving a vehicle places other responsibilities on you. One of these responsibilities is being aware of how vehicles affect our environment. The **environment** consists of the surroundings we live in. Any change in the environment affects us all. Vehicle use affects the environment in many ways. Each driver needs to behave in a way that causes the least harm to the environment.

How Do Vehicles Affect the Environment?

An obvious effect of vehicle use is the creation of engine exhaust. Some of the gases in exhaust harm the air we breathe and ourselves.

Exhaust Gases
Engineers have made today's engines more efficient than older engines. Newer engines deliver more miles per gallon and produce smaller amounts of harmful gases in the exhaust.

Carbon Dioxide   Carbon dioxide (CO_2) is one of several gases in vehicle exhaust. Large amounts of this gas throughout the atmosphere produce a "greenhouse effect," which warms the earth. Too great an increase in warming would

result in a change in earth's climate.

Maintaining your vehicle's engine so that it runs at top efficiency, burning as little fuel as possible, is one way of being a responsible owner.

Lead   A small amount of lead was added to gasoline until recent years. Most vehicles built after 1976 are made to run on unleaded gasoline.

Lead is a heavy metal that can be present in exhaust gases. Over many years, it has become a part of the soil near highways. It can seep from there into groundwater that enters the

drinking water supply. People can take lead into their bodies by breathing it in or by consuming it in food or water. Lead stays in the body, where it can harm the kidneys and nervous system.

Responsible drivers would not use leaded fuel, regardless of whether or not they have a "no-lead" car. Using leaded fuel adds to lead pollution of air. In addition, leaded fuel adds other pollutants to air because lead "poisons" the catalyst in your car's catalytic converter that converts some harmful exhaust gases into less harmful ones.

Many communities require emissions tests of the gases in each car's exhausts.

Refrigerant recovery systems keep CFCs from escaping into the atmosphere.

Abandoning a car is not a responsible way to dispose of it.

CFCs Air conditioners contain a gas to help cool air. Chlorinated fluorocarbons (abbreviated CFCs) are the types of gases used most often for this purpose. They work very effectively in air conditioners, but if these gases are released into the air when the air conditioner leaks or is being repaired, they wear away the ozone layer of earth's atmosphere. The ozone layer shields earth from some of the harmful ultraviolet rays from the sun. If the ozone layer continues to disappear, an increase in diseases such as skin cancer can result.

Vehicle repair shops are required to purchase a refrigerant recovery system to recover the CFCs when air conditioners are being repaired. These systems prevent the gases from escaping into the atmosphere. New types of refrigerants are being developed to replace CFCs. As a responsible driver, make sure that if your air conditioner needs repair, you would bring it to a mechanic who uses such a recovery system.

Vehicle Disposal

Vehicles, like all machinery, eventually wear out. They must be disposed of in a way that is not too costly or that will not harm the environment. Ugly piles of old vehicles, rusting and providing a home for rodents and insects, are not an environmentally acceptable solution to the problem.

Many of the materials in vehicles can be recycled. The plastics, when separated from other materials, can be recycled. Used tires and glass can be used as paving materials.

Stacks of old tires can provide a breeding ground for mosquitoes. Thus, some states regulate storage of used tires to eliminate this problem.

Vehicle owners have a responsibility for disposing of their vehicles in ways that do not harm the environment.

How Can Drivers Help the Environment?

Each person can utilize transportation, and yet keep from harming the environment. In many areas, one or more types of **mass transportation** are available. Mass transportation consists of several methods of moving larger numbers of passengers than individual vehicles do. These methods are safe, efficient, and environmentally responsible. They include small buses, city and suburban buses, intercity buses, rail trams, and urban rapid transit rubber-tired or steel-wheeled trains, including subway systems in several cities.

Using a mass transportation system reduces the cost per passenger mile, decreases exhaust gases, is safe, and does not require parking fees.

Another method of being environmentally responsible is **carpooling.** In this system, several workers or students commute to work or to school in one vehicle. To encourage carpooling, some highways have special lanes for buses or vehicles with three or more passengers.

Some companies support an employee ride-sharing program. The company provides a van or small bus for an employee to drive to and from work. Those employees who live on a route are picked up, taken to work, and later driven home. This method reduces the number of vehicles on the road, fuel used, exhaust produced, and the amount of parking space needed.

Similar forms of transportation are available in some communities for handicapped or senior citizens. These "on demand" programs provide environmentally sound and cost-efficient transportation.

Communities also can use traffic lights to control the flow of traffic. Traffic lights can be coordinated so that fewer stops are required. When vehicles wait at a red light, gas mileage suffers. Traffic light coordination helps fuel efficiency and makes driving safer and more enjoyable. When permitted, turns at a red traffic light also can help save fuel.

We all share the same environment. We must all do what we can to make the environment a better place in which to live.

Carpooling reduces the number of vehicles on the roads.

Review It

1. What are some ways vehicles affect the environment?
2. How can we dispose of old vehicles without harming the environment?
3. How can individuals and communities become more environmentally active?

DECISION MAKING

1. You are a high-school student working part time to save for college. What are the arguments for and against buying a car?

2. Newspaper ads display the same year used-car model at similar prices from a private owner, a used-car dealer, and a new-car dealer. How would you decide which of the three cars to buy?

3. How would you recommend that your community deal with this environmental problem?

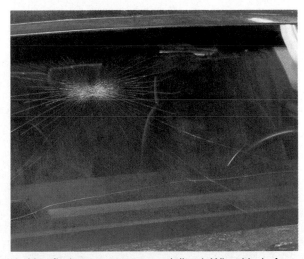

4. You find your car was vandalized. What kind of insurance will cover the repairs?

CHAPTER 16 REVIEW

Review Chapter Objectives

16–1 Buying a Vehicle
1. What are some of the responsibilities of owning a vehicle? (316)
2. What are the costs of owning a vehicle? (316)
3. What methods can you use to select a used vehicle? (318)
4. What steps should you take when buying a used vehicle? (319–320)

16–2 Insuring a Vehicle
5. What is auto insurance and how does it work? (322)
6. Describe the coverage of these kinds of auto insurance: liability; collision; comprehensive; medical; uninsured motorist; no-fault. (323)
7. What factors affect the cost of insurance? (324–325)

16–3 Environmental Concerns
8. How does vehicle use affect the environment? (326)
9. Describe several ways to reduce the effects of vehicles on the environment. (328)

Check Your Knowledge

Multiple Choice   Copy the number of each sentence below on a sheet of paper. Choose the letter that best completes the statement or answers the question.

1. The decrease in a vehicle's value is its
   (a) cancellation (b) deductible (c) depreciation (d) efficiency (316)
2. The general relationship between vehicle size and fuel mileage is
   (a) larger size, higher mpg (b) larger size, lower mpg (c) smaller size, lower mpg (d) size doesn't affect mpg (317)
3. A written document stating that a dealer will repair defects in a vehicle for a stated period of time is a
   (a) policy (b) warranty (c) liability (d) receipt (318)
4. A seller might make a vehicle appear less used than it really is by illegally
   (a) turning back the odometer (b) repairing defects (c) replacing tires (d) cleaning the interior (319)
5. Repairing this item would make a vehicle too expensive to buy:
   (a) cracked battery (b) fan belts frayed or worn (c) faded paint (d) engine smokes when accelerating (321)

Completion   Copy the number of each sentence below. After each number, write the word or words that complete the sentence correctly.

6. You buy insurance by paying a ____ to an insurance company. (322)
7. ____ insurance protects you from claims for damages you cause, up to stated limits. (322)
8. Records show that ____ drivers have more collisions than other drivers. (325)
9. Students who have completed ____ often pay a lower insurance premium. (325)
10. One way of reducing the effect of vehicles on the environment is to ____ the parts when the vehicle must be discarded. (328)

Check Vocabulary

Copy the number of each sentence in List A. Match the definition in List A with the term it defines in List B.

List A

11. miles per gallon (317)
12. listing of used vehicle prices (318)
13. source of vehicle loan (321)
14. requires proof of ability to pay for damages (322)
15. protects driver at fault from claims (322)
16. driver's insurance company pays for damages, regardless of fault (322)
17. high-cost minimal insurance for problem drivers (325)
18. surroundings under which we live (326)
19. method of moving more passengers than private autos can (328)
20. written contract between you and insurance company (322)
21. amount you pay for damages (322)

List B

a. assigned-risk
b. blue book
c. mass transportation
d. deductible
e. lending agency
f. no-fault insurance
g. environment
h. mpg
i. financial responsibility
j. policy
k. liability insurance

Check Your Understanding

Write a short answer for each question or statement.

22. Why should you test drive a used vehicle before completing a deal? (320)
23. How can you keep insurance rates as low as possible? (324)
24. In what ways does vehicle use affect the environment? (326)
25. How do lead and CFCs relate to the environment? (327)

Think Critically

Write a paragraph to answer each question or statement.

1. How can you prepare yourself to buy a vehicle and reduce the chance of making a poor decision?
2. How will vehicles change in the future to protect the environment better and become even more fuel efficient?
3. Does vehicle size and efficiency relate to your chances of survival in a collision? Explain your answer.
4. Your vehicle struck another in a collision like the one shown. No one was injured. What type of insurance will protect you for claims brought by the other driver? How will you pay for repairs to your car?

Projects

1. Find out about companies that have a ride-sharing program. **Write** a report on how the program works.
2. Suppose you have bought a used vehicle that turns out to be a "lemon." **Write** a story describing what you do about it.

Chapter 17

MAINTAINING YOUR VEHICLE

You're the Driver!

A car is a complex machine made up of many parts and systems. Each part is important to the safe and efficient operation of the vehicle. All vehicles can break down. Repairs can be costly and inconvenient. Preventive maintenance can help to avoid breakdowns.

You can perform some preventive maintenance. In the picture, one person is checking the oil level while the other is filling the fuel tank.

Would you know how to check the oil level? battery and cables? coolant level? tire pressure?

How do you operate a gas pump?

Major service and repairs should be performed by a mechanic. Have you read an owner's manual to see what repairs an owner can make and what repairs require a mechanic? This chapter discusses how to respond to various warnings and how to plan repairs or service.

Objectives

Section 17–1   Maintaining Your Vehicle's Systems

1. Describe warning signs for repair, replacement, or service to keep these systems running:
   - power train
   - ignition and electrical
   - lubrication
   - steering and suspension
   - cooling
   - fuel and exhaust
   - brake
2. Tell how to start a car that has a dead battery.
3. Describe three types of tires and list guidelines for replacing tires.

Section 17–2   Preventive Maintenance

4. Define preventive maintenance.
5. List preventive maintenance checks to make before and after starting the car, while driving, when stopping for fuel, and when having the vehicle serviced.
6. Tell how to find a qualified mechanic.

Section 17–3   Improvements for Saving Fuel

7. Tell how car design can improve fuel economy.
8. Explain how to calculate miles per gallon of fuel consumption.

Maintaining Your Vehicle's Systems

Learning about the care your vehicle needs can help to give you confidence to handle problems as they occur. Regular servicing helps ensure that you will have fewer serious problems. Your car consists of several systems, each of which needs a special kind of care.

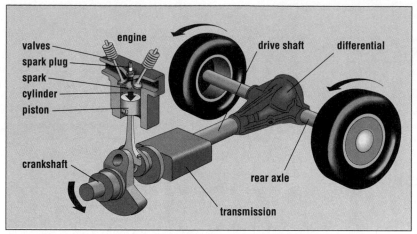

Transmitting Power in a Rear-Wheel Drive Car

Engine and Power Train

The engine burns fuel to provide the power that moves the vehicle. The power train transmits the power to the wheels.

How It Works

A spark produced by the **spark plug** ignites the air-fuel mixture in each combustion chamber or cylinder of the internal combustion engine. The resulting combustion forces the piston down the cylinder. The rods and crankshaft change the up-and-down motion of each piston into rotary motion which turns the car's drive wheels. Some cars are rear-wheel driven, while others are front-wheel driven.

The major parts of the drive train are the clutch (in a stickshift car), transmission, drive shaft (in a rear-wheel drive car), differential, and drive axles. The **transmission** has gears that enable the engine to

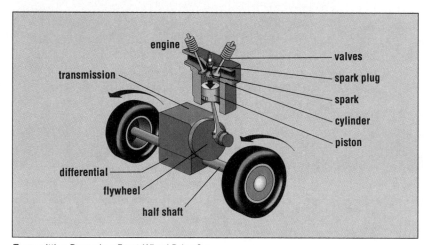

Transmitting Power in a Front-Wheel Drive Car

deliver power to the drive wheels. Lower gears let the engine turn faster; higher gears let the engine turn more slowly.

In a stickshift car, you shift gears by first pressing down on the clutch pedal. The clutch disconnects the engine from the transmission so you can select another gear. With an automatic transmission, you select the gear, but shifting is done automatically.

The **drive shaft** is a long metal rod in rear-wheel drive cars. The drive shaft carries power from the transmission to the **differential** in the rear of the car. The differential has gears which allow one rear wheel to turn faster than the other when turning a corner. In front-wheel drive cars, power is carried to the front wheels by two half shafts. The differential is located between the half shafts.

Keeping It Running

Until the engine is warm, drive at a moderate speed. This allows all engine parts to receive proper lubrication.

Check the **owner's manual** to find how often routine service should be performed on the car. This periodic **tune-up** might include cleaning or replacing spark plugs, and checking emission controls, fuel filter, and air filter.

Check the automatic transmission fluid level once a month. The owner's manual will show you how to check the automatic transmission fluid level. Warning signs of low fluid level include jerky shifting or a pause before the vehicle starts to move.

Ignition and Electrical System

The ignition system sets off combustion in the engine cylinders. The electrical system is involved in the ignition process and also runs the lights and accessories.

How It Works

Turning the ignition key sends an electric current from the battery to the electric starter motor that turns the engine. Once the engine is running, the **alternator** generates electric current that recharges the battery. A belt drives the alternator. Current from the battery powers the ignition system. This system delivers energy to each spark plug at the proper time to ignite the air-fuel mixture in each cylinder.

Keeping It Running

The battery must be kept in good condition because the starter, lights, and other electrical equipment depend on the electric power stored in the battery. Keep the battery cables tight and free of corrosion, especially where the terminals connect to the battery. See the owner's manual about servicing the battery.

Most batteries are sealed and do not need the fluid level checked. Others have vent caps and need to be checked regularly. If fluid is needed, carefully remove the caps and add distilled water as necessary.

A battery releases hydrogen gas, a very explosive material. Never expose a battery to an open flame or electrical spark. Never let battery fluid (a strong acid) touch your eyes, skin, or clothing. Severe injury can result. Wear eye protection and gloves when working with or around a battery.

If the alternator light comes on while you are driving, or the battery gauge shows strong discharge, the alternator is not generating electricity. The problem might be a broken or loose belt, or a defective alternator. Have repairs made promptly.

Cold weather makes starting the engine more difficult because the battery has less power when it is cold. In addition, engine lubricants thicken when they are cold. Keep the battery charged to avoid failure. If the starter does not turn the engine over quickly, have a mechanic recharge or replace the battery. By doing so, you can avoid having battery failure when you are not near a service station. During cold weather, if possible, park in a garage to keep the car warmer and easier to start. In extremely cold areas, you might install an electric engine-block heater to keep the engine warm at night.

Ignition and Electrical System

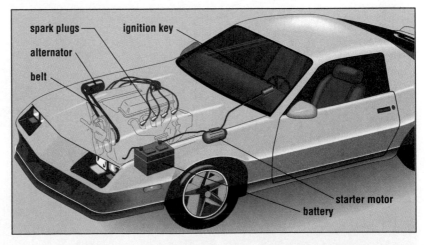

Lights

Headlights, tail lights, brake lights, and turn-signal lights can burn out. Check them by watching their reflection on a wall or garage door. Defective lights make your car hard to see.

Keep headlights aimed properly. Headlights aimed too high can temporarily blind an oncoming driver. Headlights aimed too low reduce your sight distance at night or during low-visibility conditions.

Starting a Car That Has a Dead Battery

If you turn the ignition key while in PARK or NEUTRAL and the starter makes no sound, the problem is usually a dead battery. In most cases, you can start the car by using jumper cables connected to a charged battery of the same voltage.

Check the owner's manual to verify the voltage of your battery (usually 12 volts). Before attempting to jump the battery, remove any vent caps to make sure that battery fluid is neither frozen nor too low. *Never attempt to start a car that has a frozen battery. The battery might explode.* Remove the frozen battery and place it in a warm area where the frozen fluid can melt.

Follow these steps to safely jump a dead battery:

1. Bring the two cars together so that the jumper cables can easily reach both batteries. Do not let the cars touch.
2. Turn off each engine and all accessories. Set the gears of each car in PARK or NEUTRAL. Set each car's parking brake.
3. Identify the terminals. They are usually marked on the battery with either a plus or minus sign, or POS or NEG.
4. Securely clamp the positive jumper cable (marked **+** or red) to the positive terminal of each battery.
5. Clamp one end of the negative cable (marked **—** or black) to the negative terminal of the good battery.
6. Clamp the other end of the negative cable to the engine block or chassis of the car with the dead battery. Do not clamp this cable to the dead car's negative terminal. You could cause a spark that might set off an explosion. Keep the jumper cables away from moving engine parts, such as the fan and belts.
7. Start the car that has the good battery first. Then start the engine of the car with the dead battery. Keep it running, but only at idle, until the jumper cables are removed.
8. Remove the cables in the opposite order from which they were attached. Store them for future use, if necessary.
9. Replace the vent caps, if necessary. Throw away any cloth used to wipe battery parts because it might have acid on it.

Car with dead battery   Car with good battery

Lubrication System

Lubrication is the use of oil and grease to reduce friction between a car's moving parts. Lubrication prevents damage from heat and friction. This system keeps the moving parts operating efficiently.

How It Works

When the surfaces of two moving parts rub against each other, friction and heat are created. If engine friction is not reduced, the engine will be destroyed. Oil helps the engine operate efficiently by reducing friction, carrying away engine heat, and keeping engine parts clean. Grease is used to lubricate other parts of the car, such as axles, suspension parts, and the steering components.

Notice that the **oil pump** forces the oil in the oil pan (bottom of the engine) through the oil filter. The oil then flows through the oil lines to the engine's moving parts. Oil is collected in the oil pan, and the cycle is repeated.

Keeping It Running

Your engine needs an oil change after being driven a given number of miles or months. Check the owner's manual for the service schedule set by the manufacturer for your vehicle. The used oil is drained and replaced with clean oil. The oil filter is usually replaced at the same time. If you drive mostly on short, local trips, or on dirt roads, you may need to change the oil and filter more often than recommended.

Cold weather thickens oil. Thick oil does not flow well. Your car will not start as easily as in warmer weather. Check the owner's manual for the type of multiweight or synthetic oil to use in the engine all year to lessen engine problems. Using unauthorized oil additives may void the manufacturer's warranty on the engine.

Environmental Issues

Many people change their motor oil themselves rather than have a service station drain and replace the oil. How they dispose of the used oil is very important. People should not dump oil down drains or put it into landfills. Incorrect disposal of used motor oil is very harmful to the environment.

Many states have used-oil recycling programs. People can put their used oil in leak-proof containers which they bring to collection centers, such as certain service stations and garages. Processors buy the used oil and re-refine it or make other lubricating products from it.

If the oil pressure warning light or gauge indicates low oil pressure while you are driving, pull over to the side of the road, stop and shut off the engine. *Do not drive your car until the low oil pressure problem is corrected.* Insufficient oil pressure will quickly and seriously damage the engine. Sometimes the problem is caused by low oil level. Check the oil level first. If the oil level is sufficient, have the vehicle towed to a mechanic for diagnosis and repair.

Your vehicle must be greased periodically. Check the owner's manual for a schedule of lubrication needs.

Lubrication System

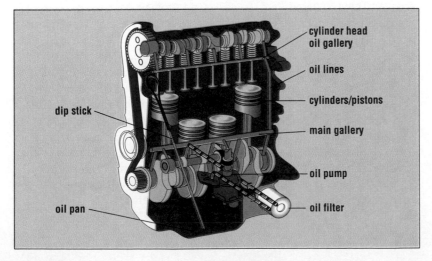

dip stick

oil pan

cylinder head oil gallery

oil lines

cylinders/pistons

main gallery

oil pump

oil filter

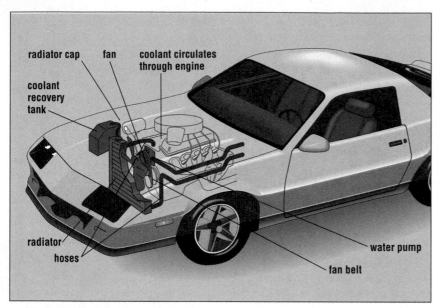

The Cooling System

steering has excess movement if there is more than 2 inches of "play."

- Steering is difficult even though tires are properly inflated. Check the owner's manual for the recommended tire pressure. A plate with this information is also on a door frame of some cars. There should not be a binding feeling in the steering wheel.

- You feel a "shimmy" or wobbling, or your car pulls to one side under normal driving conditions.

Cooling System

Although oil in the lubrication system removes some engine heat, the engine requires additional cooling. The cooling system provides that additional cooling ability. It also provides a source of heat for the car's interior in colder weather.

How It Works

The cooling system includes a fan, fan belt or electric motor, radiator, water pump, coolant recovery tank, thermostat, and hoses that connect the radiator to the engine. The **radiator** holds and cools the coolant, a mixture of antifreeze and water. The owner's manual indicates the correct mixture to use in your car. Except in emergencies, never use just water in the cooling system. Water without antifreeze might cause corrosion of metal parts.

Steering and Suspension Systems

The steering system is vital to safe car control. The suspension system contributes to car control, steering, and riding comfort.

How They Work

The steering system includes the steering wheel and steering column, steering gear, and connections to the front wheels. The steering column transmits your steering input to force the front wheels of the car to point where you choose. Some cars have **power steering** which uses a small hydraulic pump to make steering easier for the driver.

The suspension system consists of a series of rods, bars, springs, and other components which keep the wheels and tires pointed in the right direction and in contact with the roadway surface. The springs in the suspension system support the car to allow gentle up-and-down motion. A **shock absorber** or strut is located at each wheel to control hard bouncing and to keep the tire on the roadway.

Keeping Them Running

Steering problems may develop gradually and not be recognized. Any steering problem is serious and must be repaired immediately. Have a mechanic check the steering system if any of these problems occur:

- You feel "play" or excess movement in the steering wheel. For power steering, no "play" is acceptable while the engine is running. Standard

The water pump draws coolant from the bottom of the radiator and forces it through the engine's cooling passages. The fan draws air through the radiator, helping cool the coolant.

When the system's temperature is below the best operating level, the **thermostat** shuts off the flow of coolant to the radiator. When the temperature in the system rises to the correct level, the thermostat opens. Coolant then flows to the radiator and maintains a stable temperature.

Keeping It Running

Check your coolant level at least once each month. Check the coolant level in the recovery tank before starting the engine while the engine and coolant are cool.

Engine overheating can be caused by
- low coolant level
- loose or broken fan belt, or defective fan or water pump

- blocked radiator air flow
- frozen coolant in the system
- faulty thermostat.

Some cars use a computer to manage many engine systems, including the cooling system. A qualified mechanic with proper equipment can check the computer system for proper operation of the cooling system.

If the temperature gauge or warning light indicates overheating, it might be necessary to add coolant. *CAUTION: Never remove the cap from a hot radiator.* Hot fluid and steam can spurt out and burn you. Turn off the engine and let it cool. Pour the coolant in slowly while the cooled engine is running.

If you live in an area where weather can become very cold and very hot, your engine's cooling system must always work at top efficiency. Your engine can become damaged if coolant freezes in cold weather or boils out in hot weather. Check the owner's manual for a

recommended schedule for servicing the cooling system. The radiator should be cleaned and filled with the recommended amount of coolant to withstand the extremes of both winter and summer temperatures.

Never put engine antifreeze in the windshield washer tank; another liquid is needed for that system. Antifreeze is used only in the cooling system.

Fuel and Exhaust Systems

The fuel system consists of a fuel tank, fuel line, fuel pump, air cleaner, fuel filter, and carburetor or fuel-injection system. These components are shown in the picture. The exhaust system includes the exhaust pipe, catalytic converter, muffler, and tailpipe.

How They Work

The fuel pump draws fuel from the fuel tank through the fuel line. Fuel is then pumped to the **carburetor** or **fuel-injection system.** Air is drawn through the air filter and mixes with the fuel. The fuel-air mixture becomes a fine mist for combustion in the cylinders of the engine.

Exhaust gases leave the exhaust system through the tailpipe at the rear of the car. The muffler reduces noise from combustion sounds in the cylinders. The catalytic converter reduces pollution from the car's exhaust.

The Fuel System

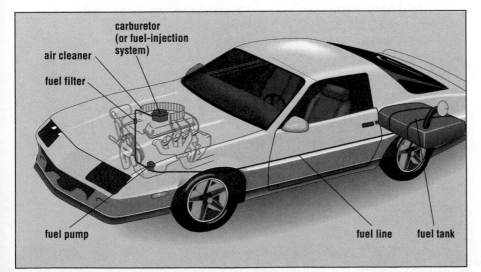

carburetor (or fuel-injection system)

air cleaner

fuel filter

fuel pump

fuel line

fuel tank

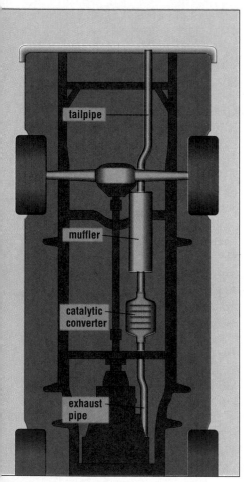

The Exhaust System

Keeping Them Running

A carburetor may need periodic cleaning and adjustment to remain efficient. A fuel-injection system needs little adjustment if good quality fuel is used. A tune-up usually includes a check of the air and fuel filters. Replace these filters according to the schedule in your owner's manual.

The exhaust system should be replaced when a part rusts out or is damaged. To protect the catalytic converter, use only unleaded gasoline.

Ignoring a defect in the exhaust system creates noise and increases the risk of carbon monoxide poisoning of the car's occupants. Carbon monoxide is an invisible, colorless, and odorless gas. It can cause headaches, nausea, coma, and death.

Brake System

Good brakes are an essential safety component in any motor vehicle. How long brakes last and how they perform depends on how you use and maintain them.

How It Works

The brake system's **master cylinder** contains two parts. Each part controls two wheels. Pressure on the brake pedal forces brake fluid from the master cylinder through the brake lines to each wheel's brake cylinder. The cylinder at each wheel forces the brake shoes or brake pads against a brake drum or disk. This pressure causes friction, which slows or stops the wheel.

Many cars have a **disk brake** on each front wheel, and a **drum brake** on each rear wheel, as shown in the pictures. Some cars have disk brakes on all four wheels. A disk brake works as fluid pressure squeezes the pads against the turning disk. A drum brake works as fluid pressure forces the brake shoes against the inside of the brake drum. Friction between the pads and disk, or between shoes and drum, slows and stops the turning wheels.

If a leak develops in the brake system, fluid will not reach one pair of wheels and the brake-warning light will illuminate. The dual master cylinder assures that the other two wheels will receive brake fluid under pressure, and the brakes on those wheels will still work. Stopping distance will increase, and handling may be erratic. The braking system must be checked immediately and repaired. *Never drive a car with a faulty braking system, regardless of the distance.*

The parking brake is a separate system. A steel cable connects the parking brake pedal or lever to a separate brake assembly on the rear wheels. The parking brake should be able to hold the car on a hill.

Keeping It Running

Both disk and drum brakes are self-adjusting. If the brake pedal goes too far toward the floor when you press the pedal hard, adjust the brakes by this procedure: Stop, back up, and press the brake pedal firmly. Repeat the sequence several times. If this procedure does not adjust the brakes, consult your owner's manual to see if another procedure is specified for your car. If the problem persists, have the brake system inspected promptly.

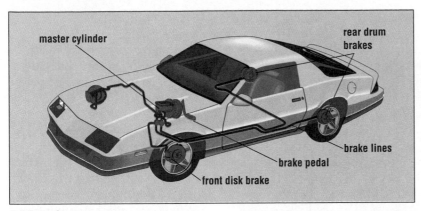

The Brake System

Drum Brake

wheel
cylinder

brake
shoe

brake
drum

Brake shoes are forced against hollow cylinder drum inside a wheel to stop the car.

Drum Brake

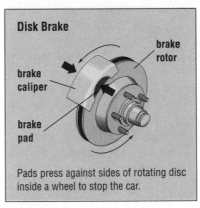

Disk Brake

brake
rotor

brake
caliper

brake
pad

Pads press against sides of rotating disc inside a wheel to stop the car.

Disk Brake

Keep the brake fluid in the master cylinder at the proper level, using the brake fluid specified for your car. Watch for these warning signs of brake trouble:

- brake-warning light is on
- low brake pedal (less than 2 inches from floor for power brakes; less than 3 inches for standard brakes when pressed firmly)
- "spongy" feel in brake pedal
- pulling to one side when stopping with dry brakes

- grabbing or uneven brake action
- squealing or chattering noises in the brakes
- a need to pump brakes or push brake pedal harder than usual to stop the car.

Tires

A tire is made of rubber reinforced by layers of cord material under the tread. Each layer, called a "ply," strengthens the tire and gives it shape.

Types of Tires

A **bias-ply tire** has cord layers that crisscross at an angle. Bias-ply tires offer less tread mileage, and are best suited to lower-mileage driving in local areas rather than long-distance driving. A **belted tire** has special cord layers added to the bias-ply tire for improved strength and mileage.

A **radial tire** has plies that run straight across under the tread, and strengthening belts of steel or other materials that circle the tire. Radial tires give improved tread mileage, traction, and fuel economy as compared to other tires.

Information about the tire's construction, size, and carrying capacity is clearly marked on the sidewall of the tire. New tires usually have a paper label with additional information.

Tire Construction

bias ply   belted   radial

A conventional bias-ply tire has no belt. All radial tires have belts, which improve mileage.

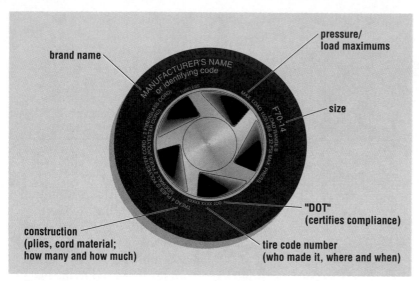

brand name

pressure/
load maximums

MANUFACTURER'S NAME
or identifying code

size

construction
(plies, cord material;
how many and how much)

"DOT"
(certifies compliance)

tire code number
(who made it, where and when)

Information on the Sidewall

Inflation and Tread

Maintain recommended air pressure in all tires. The owner's manual shows the recommended air pressure for tires on your car. Using the air pressure marked on the tire sidewall will yield maximum fuel and tire mileage. (On some cars, this information is also on a door frame sticker.) Too little air in even one tire can make a car difficult to control. Low inflation causes tires to wear quickly and can cause tire failure.

A puncture or faulty valve stem can cause a slow leak and deflate a tire, causing your car to act as if it had a blowout. Change the tire and have the leak repaired.

Keep a reliable tire gauge in your car and use it regularly. Check tire pressure when the tires are cool. Air pressure in a tire rises in warmer weather and falls in cooler weather. Air pressure increases when the car is driven, even for a short distance. Do not let air out of a warm tire to reduce it to the recommended reading; the tire will be underinflated when it cools .

Rotation and Alignment

Rotate your tires every 10,000 miles to promote longer tire life. Have them balanced periodically to promote even wear. The illustration shows some tire rotation patterns. Include the spare in the rotation pattern only if it is a regular full-size tire. See your owner's manual for the pattern recommended for your vehicle.

Wheels should be aligned when tires are rotated. Alignment is especially critical on front-wheel drive cars. Many cars need both front and rear wheels aligned.

Replacing Tires

Replace a tire when you see smooth bars across the tread. The wear bar shows that only 1/16 inch tread remains (out of the original 9/16 to 11/16 inch). A worn tire has poor traction, especially on a wet roadway, and is more likely to fail.

Replacement tires should be the same size and type as the original equipment. Never use radial tires with any other type of tire on the same car. Radial tires do not react the same as bias or belted tires. Oversize tires cause the speedometer and odometer to give inaccurate readings.

Tire Quality and Grading

All tires sold in the United States are rated with regard to two safety factors, traction and temperature resistance. They are also rated in regard to an economy factor, tread wear. A tire's performance is measured under controlled conditions on specific test surfaces and over a special test route.

Some Tire Rotation Patterns

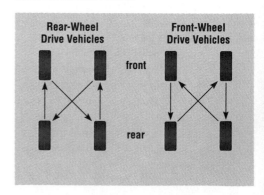

Rear-Wheel
Drive Vehicles

Front-Wheel
Drive Vehicles

front

rear

The white circle marks an area containing a wear bar across the tread.

Grades of Tires			
Tire Grading	Traction	Temperature	Treadwear*
Highest	A	A	200 190 180 170 160
	B	B	150 140 130 120 110 100
Lowest	C	C	90 80 70 60 50

* The higher the number, the greater the mileage from the tire. Tires with treadwear grading of 150 rating will give 50 percent more miles than one graded at 100.

For traction, measured by a tire's ability to stop on a wet surface, the grades are A, B, and C. An A-graded tire has the best traction performance. Temperature resistance is also graded A, B, and C, and indicates a tire's ability to withstand heat. A tire graded A is the most heat-resistant, and the least likely to suffer a blowout under the same conditions as a tire graded B or C.

Tread wear is graded on an index which indicates relative wear. A tire graded 150 should provide 50 percent more mileage than one graded 100. Under average conditions, each 50 points represents a life expectancy of about 10,000 miles. Some tires are graded as high as 400, or have a life expectancy of up to 80,000 miles. Keep safety in mind as you compare and decide which tire offers the best value for the kind of driving you do. The owner's manual can also give you information on the tires recommended for your car.

Other Tire Problems

Uneven wear often indicates problems in wheel alignment, balance, or inflation. A tire worn only in the center is usually overinflated. Worn edges often indicate underinflation. Wear on one edge only, or a "cupped" shape results from poor wheel alignment, worn shock absorbers, or defective struts.

You can extend the life of your tires by avoiding fast starts, stops, and turns. Check tires periodically. Look for weak spots, cuts, blisters, rocks caught in the tread, and uneven wear. Replace tires before they become unsafe.

Review It

1. What are warning signs for repair of the power train? the ignition and electrical system? the lubrication system? the steering and suspension system? the cooling system? the fuel and exhaust system? the brakes?
2. What is the sequence for trying to start a car with a dead battery?
3. How do the construction features of the three types of tires differ?
4. How can you judge the performance offered by a new tire?

Preventive Maintenance

The care you routinely give your car to avoid trouble later is **preventive maintenance**. This attention includes not only day-to-day care, but also the periodic servicing a car needs at the times listed in the owner's manual.

The schedule of service for maintenance jobs is important. The manufacturer's warranty might not stay in effect if service is not done at the scheduled times. Preventive maintenance saves money and is less expensive than repairs which result from lack of service.

Routine Checks

You should make it a habit to pay attention to the condition of your vehicle. Notice any changes in its condition before driving and while you drive.

Keep headlights clean so you will get the maximum light from them.

Before Starting the Engine

Before entering the car, note the condition of all tires. A slow leak in a tire can cause an emergency as you drive. It is easier and safer to change the tire at home than on a busy street or remote road.

Before starting the engine, clean the windshield, windows, and lights if they are dirty.

Check windshield wipers and, periodically, the windshield washer fluid level. Make sure all lights and the horn operate. When you turn the ignition on (without starting the engine) check that gauges and warning lights come on.

Once in a while, check under your vehicle for signs of leaking fluids. The color of any puddle on the pavement indicates the type of fluid that is leaking out. To make leaks easier to see, leave a large sheet of white paper under your car overnight. Check it in the morning. You should repair any leaking system before you have trouble.

After Starting the Engine

Check all instruments after the engine has started. All warning lights should be off. If the fuel gauge shows less than half, plan to fill the fuel tank soon. Test the feel of the brake pedal as you begin to drive. The pedal should feel firm, not soft or spongy, and should stay at least 2 or 3 inches away from the floor.

Colors indicate the type of fluid leaking out.

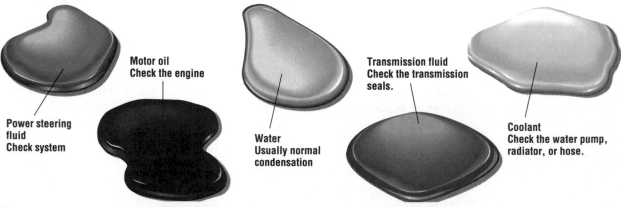

Power steering fluid
Check system

Motor oil
Check the engine

Water
Usually normal condensation

Transmission fluid
Check the transmission seals.

Coolant
Check the water pump, radiator, or hose.

1. Remove cap from tank.

2. Remove nozzle from pump.

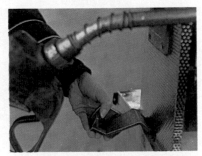

3. Turn pump lever on. Numbers will register zero.

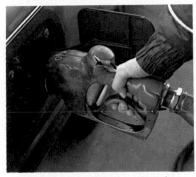

4. Place nozzle in gas tank. Squeeze nozzle.

5. Turn pump lever off. Hang up nozzle.

6. Put cap back on.

While Driving

Glance at the instrument panel to note any unusual readings or warning lights. Notice whether there are any unusual sounds, odors, vibrations, or other warnings. These signals indicate that something is wrong with your car. Have any change in steering, braking, handling, or acceleration checked promptly.

At A Fuel Stop

Many drivers fill their own fuel tanks at self-service stations. Operating instructions are displayed on or near the fuel pump. Smoking is not allowed around a fuel pump. Always turn off the engine while filling the fuel tank. These pictures show how to operate a fuel pump.

Type of Fuel To Buy The type of fuel delivered at the fuel pump is marked on the pump. If your car requires unleaded or diesel fuel, this information is marked on the instrument panel near the fuel gauge, around the fuel cap, and in the owner's manual. The octane rating of fuel necessary to prevent engine knocking or pinging during normal driving is noted in the owner's manual. Octane rating is shown on the fuel pump. Using higher octane fuel than your car requires costs more, but does not increase power or mileage.

Gasohol is a blend of unleaded gasoline and either methyl or ethyl alcohol. Gasohol sometimes has a higher octane rating than regular unleaded gasoline. Check the owner's manual to see if the manufacturer recommends use of gasohol. Gasohol is considered one method of reducing our dependence on foreign oil sources by substituting a natural resource grown in our country. Corn is the raw material for making ethyl alcohol.

The mechanics at this service station have taken special tests in order to earn this certificate.

Selecting a Qualified Mechanic

The safety and efficiency of your vehicle may depend on the judgment and skill of your mechanic. Select your mechanic *before* the car has trouble. If the car should break down unexpectedly, you might not have the time to make a wise choice in having the car repaired.

New car dealers and some independent repair shops display certificates earned by mechanics who pass specialized courses and tests. Many car dealers have the equipment necessary to service the new cars they sell. Family members, friends, neighbors, and an auto shop or driver education teacher might offer suggestions on how to find a qualified mechanic.

Scheduled Service

Cars need periodic service. The owner's manual includes a schedule that lists mileage or time intervals for tune-ups and other service. Keep records and receipts of all service, repairs, and replacement parts. You need complete records to have a proper maintenance history.

The owner's manual is the best guide for your car's preventive maintenance needs. Here is a time-based general schedule of preventive maintenance tasks. Severe driving conditions may require more frequent replacement of the air filter and checks of shock absorbers.

Mileage-Based Maintenance

Certain maintenance tasks should be done after you have driven a certain number of miles, regardless of time intervals. The chart lists a general schedule of preventive maintenance tasks based on miles driven.

Time-Based Preventive Maintenance Schedule

Weekly	Monthly	Semiannually	Annually
check oil level check washer fluid level check coolant level look for fluid leaks wash exterior clean interior, including all windows	check tires check belts for tension check hoses for leaks check battery level (note: maintenance-free batteries have an indicator) check level and condition of automatic transmission fluid check brake fluid level check power steering fluid level in winter months, run air conditioner briefly	check and clean battery cables and terminals wax exterior	check air conditioner refrigerant replace air filter check condition of brakes wash underbody flush radiator and refill coolant (see owner's manual) replace wiper blades check shock absorbers for leaks

State Inspections and Car Clinics

Some states require that each car periodically pass an inspection. Inspections can detect safety-related problems before they become hazards. Usually the owner must repair all serious defects and the car must pass inspection before it can be licensed. Some states require inspection before the car can be sold. Many cities and some states are attempting to attack the smog problem in the local environment by requiring inspection of emission control systems.

This diagnostic center has special electronic equipment to detect problems even before the driver is aware of them.

Automobile diagnostic centers or clinics test cars electronically and mechanically to detect problems. The car owner is given a report that lists all parts or systems that fail to work or meet acceptable standards. You or your mechanic can refer to the diagnostic report, and replace defective parts.

When selecting a diagnostic clinic, you might decide to select one that does not offer repair services. If the business does not profit from repairs, it will not try to sell you unnecessary parts or repairs.

Mileage-Based Preventive Maintenance Schedule

Interval	Maintenance tasks
Every 3,000 Miles	change oil and oil filter clean air conditioner condenser grille during months when it is in frequent use
Every 6,000 Miles	rotate tires lubricate chassis
Every 12,000 Miles	check exhaust system for leaks, excessive rust, and loose parts inspect underbody check for looseness in steering linkage, suspension joints, rust on frame, and underside of floor replace fuel filter check fluid level in differential check manifold heat valve and automatic choke if present check clutch pedal for excessive play
Every 25,000 Miles	check PCV (positive crankcase ventilation) system replace spark plugs check spark plug wires check ignition timing check/adjust engine valve clearance (if applicable) replace distributor cap back-flush cooling system replace belts and hoses, as necessary service automatic transmission check electronic ignition install new radiator cap have brake lines inspected for leaks service emission system inspect brakes and parking brake; replace parts or adjust as needed repack wheel bearings replace thermostat check battery and charging system
Every 50,000 Miles	replace spark plug wires check fuel pump(s) have fuel injector system serviced
Every 75,000 Miles	have radiator cleaned out inspect universal joints

Review It

1. What is preventive maintenance?
2. List some time-based preventive maintenance tasks.
3. List some mileage-based preventive maintenance tasks.

Improvements for Saving Fuel

Increases in fuel prices, government emission and mileage standards, "gas guzzler" taxes, and changing trends in the needs of car buyers have influenced the design of cars. Most newer cars are designed to increase fuel economy without decreasing comfort, handling, or usable space. Many design items, such as the design of wheel covers and shape of bumpers and headlights, can contribute to increased fuel economy.

Facts About Saving Fuel

Even though car design features help save fuel, drivers also need to follow certain practices to help conserve resources. When you consider these facts about energy conservation, think about the way you drive and the way you maintain your vehicle.

Control Your Speed
- Many cars use fuel most efficiently at a speed range of 35–45 mph. Above 45 mph wind resistance hinders the car. Newer cars with more efficient engines achieve peak fuel economy at 50–55 mph.
- For every 5-mph increase in speed above 55 mph, most cars pay a mileage penalty of 1.5 miles per gallon. Higher speed means more fuel used.
- One of the best ways to save fuel while driving in a city is to slow with your foot off the accelerator into all stops.
- Moderate acceleration to desired speed is a good way to save fuel. Fast starts and very slow starts waste fuel.
- You can cut wind resistance above 45 mph by keeping your windows closed.

Care For Your Engine
- If you have a choice, use a car with a warm engine. A warm engine is more fuel efficient than a cold one.
- The time of heaviest engine wear and highest gasoline consumption is the period immediately after starting the car with a cold engine.
- It is more fuel efficient to turn the engine off and then restart if you expect to idle for longer than one minute.
- With the air temperature at 78° F, a car with a cold engine normally takes about 15 minutes to reach its most efficient operating temperature. On colder days, you use more fuel.
- The most fuel-efficient way to warm a cold engine is to begin driving as soon as oil pressure reaches normal. If you let an engine idle, you waste fuel.
- Have tune-ups as often as your owner's manual recommends. Spark plugs can misfire if an engine needs to be tuned. Misfiring wastes fuel.

Watch Your Tires
- Keep your tires properly inflated. Check tire pressure regularly.
- Radial tires generally give the best gas mileage.

Calculating Miles Per Gallon

Most drivers are concerned with getting the most miles from each gallon of fuel. Checking fuel economy can warn you of possible mechanical problems. Follow these steps to calculate miles per gallon.

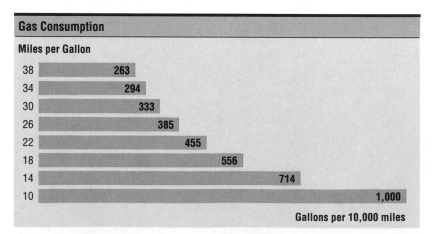

Gas Consumption

Miles per Gallon

Miles per Gallon	Gallons per 10,000 miles
38	263
34	294
30	333
26	385
22	455
18	556
14	714
10	1,000

Gallons per 10,000 miles

1. Fill fuel tank. Record the odometer reading. If your car has a trip odometer, set it at zero.
2. Drive normally until the fuel tank is about half full.
3. Refill the fuel tank. Record the odometer reading, or read the mileage on the trip odometer.
4. Subtract the first odometer reading from the second odometer reading, if you have not used a trip odometer.
5. Divide the number of miles driven by the number of gallons of fuel required to refill the fuel tank.
6. The result is miles per gallon (mpg).

For example:
- Second odometer reading is 17,703
- First odometer reading is 17,514
- Difference = 189 miles
- 7 gallons to refill tank
- 189 miles ÷ 7 gallons = 27 mpg

Obtain average mpg after refilling the fuel tank several times over a period of several weeks. Stop-and-go driving and short trips in city driving are less fuel efficient than driving at a moderate speed for a longer distance. Higher speed reduces fuel mileage.

Design Improvements

Cars are designed to use space efficiently. The design of many cars is streamlined to reduce

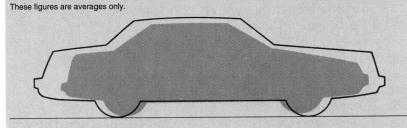

Streamlined, smaller, lighter-weight cars are more fuel efficient.

Past		Present
6 or 8 cylinders	**Engine**	4 or 6 cylinders
212 inches	**Length**	180 inches
77 inches	**Width**	67 inches
53 inches	**Height**	53 inches
4,100 pounds	**Weight**	2,900 pounds
14 to 22	**Miles per gallon**	20 to 30

These figures are averages only.

wind resistance. Aerodynamic design helps increase engine performance and fuel efficiency.

Smaller Size
Cars are generally smaller than they were just a few years ago. The smaller car weighs less and needs less power to move it. As a result, a smaller, lighter engine can be used to help increase fuel power. Some newer cars can carry five passengers in safety and comfort.

Front-Wheel Drive
Many new cars have front-wheel drive. That is, the front wheels provide the power that makes the car move. A car with front-wheel drive has good traction, especially on snow-covered roads. In front-wheel drive cars, the car is pulled by the drive wheels rather than pushed by the rear wheels.

Engine Improvements

Smaller engines are designed to produce sufficient power and fuel economy for small cars. Lightweight materials such as aluminum and plastics are frequently used on engines.

Electronic ignition and computer engine-management systems help engines use fuel efficiently under all driving conditions. The computer engine-management system helps the engine meet federal emission standards. Computer engine-management systems are not designed to be serviced by the owner. A highly qualified mechanic and special equipment are necessary for diagnosis and repair of the system.

Fuel-Injection System

Most new cars have an electronic fuel-injection system rather than a carburetor. This system delivers the exact amount of fuel to each of the engine's cylinders at the proper time to give maximum power and fuel efficiency. These systems also keep down the amount of pollution-causing gases. See your owner's manual for the proper starting procedure for your car.

Turbocharging and Supercharging

In a non-turbocharged engine, the engine exhaust gases are released into the atmosphere. A turbocharger is an engine-mounted rotary pump, powered by exhaust gas pressure. It is designed to force a greater fuel/air mixture into the engine under pressure. Under normal driving conditions, the turbocharger idles. When extra power is needed, such as accelerating to expressway speed from the entrance ramp, the turbocharger increases power. A supercharger provides a similar increase in power, but is powered by belts on the engine.

Multiple-Valve Engines

Most engines have two valves per cylinder . Some engines have more than two valves per cylinder. Such engines may be advertised as "16 valve engines," which means that the engine has four cylinders with four valves in each cylinder.

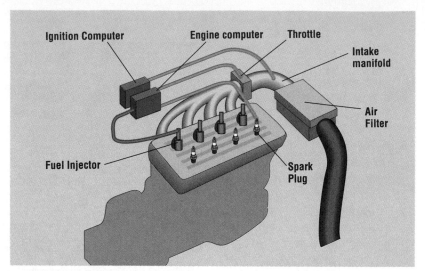

A Fuel-Injection System

Additional valves increase the efficiency of the engine. They increase power, and possibly increase fuel efficiency. Maintenance costs do not increase with multiple-valve engines, but repair costs do increase because there are more parts to replace. In the future, more engines will be multiple-valved because these engines are more efficient than conventional engines.

Transmission Improvements

The job of the transmission is to pass power from the engine to the drive wheels. Any power lost in the transmission system reduces fuel economy. A variety of transmission improvements have resulted in increased fuel economy.

Five- or Six-Speed Transmission

Many manual transmission cars have five forward gears; some have six gears. The highest gear (5th or 6th) is an **overdrive** gear. It lets the engine run more slowly at highway speed. Fuel economy is improved.

Automatic Overdrive

An automatic overdrive transmission lets the engine run more slowly at highway speed. When extra power is needed, such as for passing or entering the expressway, the transmission automatically shifts to a lower gear.

Review It

1. How have design changes in car shape, engines, and transmissions helped improve fuel economy?
2. Calculate fuel mileage in this situation. First odometer reading: 41,250; second odometer reading: 41,500. Gallons needed to refill tank: 10

DECISION MAKING

1. You are nearing this red light. As you step on the brake pedal, it goes very near to the floor. How can you correct the problem soon after leaving the light? What repairs could be essential before you continue driving your car?

2. One of your headlights is not working. What should you do to correct the problem?

3. These people are attempting to start a car that has a dead battery. What steps should they take to start the car safely?

4. You need a tire to replace one that has just failed. You do a lot of long-distance driving. What guidelines should you use in deciding what kind of tire to buy?

CHAPTER 17 REVIEW

Review Chapter Objectives

17–1 Maintaining Your Car's Systems

1. List warning signs for repair, replacement, or adjustment of each of the following systems: power train; ignition and electrical; lubrication; steering and suspension; cooling; fuel and exhaust; brake. (334–340)
2. How is each jumper cable marked? When trying to start a car that has a dead battery, which cable should be attached first? Which cable should be removed first? (336)
3. What is the construction of a bias tire? a belted tire? a radial tire? (341)

17–2 Preventive Maintenance

4. What is preventive maintenance?(344)
5. What preventive maintenance checks should you make before starting the car? when stopping for fuel? when having the car serviced? (344–345)
6. How can you find a qualified mechanic? (346)

17–3 Improvements for Saving Fuel

7. What car design changes have helped improve fuel economy? (349)
8. List steps you would use to calculate miles per gallon of fuel consumption. (348–349)

Check Your Knowledge

Multiple Choice Copy the number of each sentence below on a sheet of paper. Choose the letter that best completes the statement or answers the question.

1. How does cold weather affect a car battery?
   (a) increases power (b) decreases power (c) cold weather has no effect on the battery (d) causes the battery to expand (335)
2. When jumping a dead battery, which terminals are connected last?
   (a) positive terminals (b) negative terminals (c) both terminals on the dead battery (d) both terminals on the good battery (336)
3. The most common type of brake system on modern cars is:
   (a) disk brakes on front and drum brakes on rear. (b) drum brakes on front and disk brakes on rear. (c) 2- or 4-wheel brake system (d) brakes on rear only. (340)
4. At what speed do most cars use fuel most efficiently?
   (a) above 55 mph   (b) 10–20 mph (c) 20–30 mph (d) 35–45 mph (348)

Completion Copy the number of each sentence below. After each number, write the word or words that complete the sentence correctly.

5. The _____ ignites the fuel-air mixture in an engine cylinder. (334)
6. The _____ connects the transmission to drive wheels in a front-wheel drive car. (334)
7. The _____ has gears that enable the engine to deliver power to the drive wheels. (334)
8. The _____ is the best source of information about operating your car. (334)
9. Electric current from the _____ turns the electric starter motor. (335)
10. Service that includes cleaning or replacement of spark plugs, checking emission controls, air filter, and fuel filter is a _____ . (335)
11 A _____ is a precise system to deliver fuel to each of the engine's cylinders.(339)
12. A _____ uses brake pressure to squeeze brake pads on a turning metal disk. (340)

Check Vocabulary

Copy the number of each definition in List A. Match the definition in List A with the term it defines in List B.

List A

13. generates electric current (335)
14. older device for mixing fuel and air (339)
15. newer device for mixing fuel and air precisely (339)
16. tire with strengthening belts of steel (341)
17. stopping device in which pads squeeze a rotating steel disk (340)
18. device for cooling the engine (338)
19. container for brake fluid (340)
20. manufacturer's booklet with valuable information about your car (335)
21. device that regulates coolant temperature (339)
22. provides ignition in each engine cylinder (334)
23. periodic replacement of spark plugs and filters (334)
24. stops the car by forcing brake shoes against the inside of a rotating bowl-shaped metal piece (340)
25. a method of routinely taking care of car problems before they become serious (343)

List B

a. spark plug
b. owner's manual
c. tune-up
d. alternator
e. radiator
f. thermostat
g. carburetor
h. fuel-injection system
i. master cylinder
j. disk brake
k. drum brake
l. radial tire
m preventive maintenance

Check Your Understanding

Write a short answer for each question or statement.

26. What are the effects of cold weather on engine parts? (337)
27. What are the purposes of mandatory car inspection? (347)
28. What should you do about the radiator if you are in a situation like the one in the picture? (339)

Think Critically

Write a paragraph to answer each question or statement.

1. Suppose you need to buy some new tires. How can the markings on the side of a tire help you make a decision about which tire to purchase?
2. Write out a schedule of mileage-based or time-based preventive maintenance for your car, using the owner's manual as your source of information.

Projects

1. Interview the service manager at a new car dealership to determine how well the average car owner takes care of his/her car. **Write** an article about your findings for your school newspaper.
2. Find out about new design features planned for cars built over the next five years. Which features will improve fuel economy, increase safety and vehicle reliability, and improve air quality? How do these considerations interact with each other?

Chapter 18

PLANNING YOUR TRAVEL

You're the Driver!

You are the driver in the picture. You are at the wheel as you drive your family into Mesa Verde National Park in Colorado. It's taken lots of time, planning, and long, hard miles of driving, but now you're here.

What sort of things did you have to plan ahead of time? How did you prepare your car?

Who handled the navigation along the way? Did they know how to read maps?

What steps did you take to save fuel?

How did your car handle along the way? Did the preventive maintenance you had done on your car pay off?

These are just some things you would have to do and questions you would have to answer to make this major trip. When it's done right, a trip like this can be one of the great experiences in your life.

In this chapter, you will learn how to prepare for short and long trips. In addition, you will learn about special recreational vehicles and how to use trailers.

Objectives

Section 18–1   Local Travel
1. State two questions you should ask before making a short trip.
2. Describe three ways you can prepare in advance for a short trip.

Section 18–2   Long-Distance Travel
3. Demonstrate three ways you can use a road map to find the distance between two cities.
4. Tell how you can prepare in advance for a long-distance trip.
5. List emergency equipment you should keep in your car.

6. Name five things you should do to personally prepare for a long-distance trip.
7. Describe the best way to load your car for a long-distance trip.
8. Tell what techniques you can use to stay alert while driving.

Section 18–3   Recreational Vehicles and Trailers
9. Describe some potential problems you might have while driving a recreational vehicle.
10. Explain some of the special steps you need to take when pulling a trailer.
11. Tell how to back a trailer.

To make everyday local travel as safe and fuel efficient as possible, you will have to plan ahead. Arriving safely and on time are two important results of planning. If you are successful, you can have trouble-free driving and save money at the same time.

Short Trips

A short trip can be as simple as driving to your local shopping mall. Or, a short trip might mean you have to drive to the other side of a large city. Before starting a trip like this, pause and ask yourself these two questions:

Is This Trip Necessary?
Trying to conserve fuel should prompt each of us to ask this question before any trip. If the answer is "yes," ask yourself if there is a better way to make the trip. In some situations, you might be able to use public transportation, a bicycle, walk, or share a ride in a carpool.

Taking many short trips wastes fuel and shortens the life of the vehicle. A cold engine gets poor mileage and experiences excessive wear. When possible, plan ahead and combine your short trips into one slightly longer trip.

Do I Have Enough Time?
Once you have decided that the trip is necessary, think ahead again. How much time will it take to get there? To make an accurate forecast, think about these three things:

- **Leave on Time**   No matter how well you plan, if you don't leave on time, you obviously will not reach your destination on time. And, drivers who are in a hurry tend to make mistakes. Allow extra time for delays caused by poor weather or heavy traffic.
- **Listen to Weather and Traffic Reports**   Local radio and television stations in most cities will help you with weather and traffic reports. If the weather is bad, build in extra travel time for your trip. If your route is congested or blocked, change your route.
- **Choose the Best Time to Travel**   Traffic jams created by rush-hour traffic waste fuel and time. In large cities, your travel time can double in morning or evening rush-hour traffic. When possible, travel at an off hour.

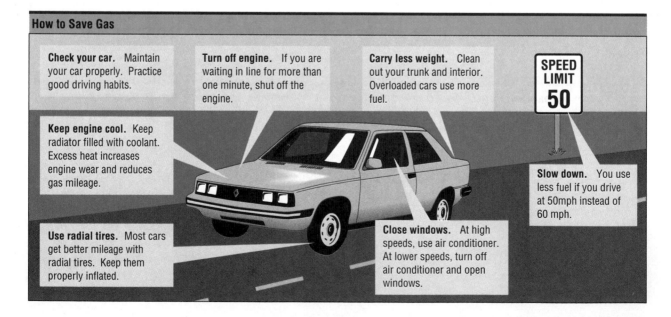

How to Save Gas

Check your car. Maintain your car properly. Practice good driving habits.

Turn off engine. If you are waiting in line for more than one minute, shut off the engine.

Carry less weight. Clean out your trunk and interior. Overloaded cars use more fuel.

Keep engine cool. Keep radiator filled with coolant. Excess heat increases engine wear and reduces gas mileage.

Use radial tires. Most cars get better mileage with radial tires. Keep them properly inflated.

Close windows. At high speeds, use air conditioner. At lower speeds, turn off air conditioner and open windows.

SPEED LIMIT 50

Slow down. You use less fuel if you drive at 50mph instead of 60 mph.

Your passenger can help you plan a route.

Planning Ahead

To avoid trouble, plan ahead. If your car is prepared and your route is planned, you will get to your destination economically and on time.

Vehicle Preparation Running out of windshield washer fluid, driving on an underinflated tire, or having a turn signal light fail might not sound like a big deal. But, each of these small problems can trigger an accident.

Each time you drive, make a routine pre-driving check of the tires, lights, and controls. If you detect any problem before or while driving, have the problem fixed as quickly as possible.

Make a routine check under the hood of your car each time you fill the fuel tank. All fluids should be maintained at the right level. Make sure you are a fuel-efficient driver by following the fuel-saving tips mentioned throughout this book.

Route Selection Select a route that will give you the shortest travel time and the lowest number of hazards. Routes with uncontrolled railroad crossings or uncontrolled intersections might save time, but they can also increase the risk of a collision. When possible, plan to use routes with intersections controlled by STOP signs or traffic lights. Reducing hazards is more important than saving time. And, you will enjoy driving the easier route too.

Know Streets and Addresses Have you ever been with a driver who was really lost? Such an experience is not fun, and can be frightening. Plan your route ahead of time. Write down the names of the streets and route numbers you will need to use. A passenger can act as a copilot by calling out directions as you drive to your destination. If you miss a street, do not make a last second turn or stop. Drive around the block and look for the street sign or house number a second time.

Review It

1. What two questions should you ask yourself before starting a short trip?
2. What are three things you can do to prepare in advance for a short trip?

Long-Distance Travel

A well planned trip can provide you and your companions with a pleasant, memorable experience. To manage costs and avoid unnecessary delays and surprises, plan each detail.

Map Reading

When you plan a long trip, you will need a map of the states and cities you intend to visit. Maps are available from state and city offices of promotion and tourism, chambers of commerce, motor clubs, book stores, and some service stations.

A map usually contains a **legend** or a chart that explains the markings and symbols used on the map. Most maps also include a mileage chart, town and city index, and large-scale maps of major cities.

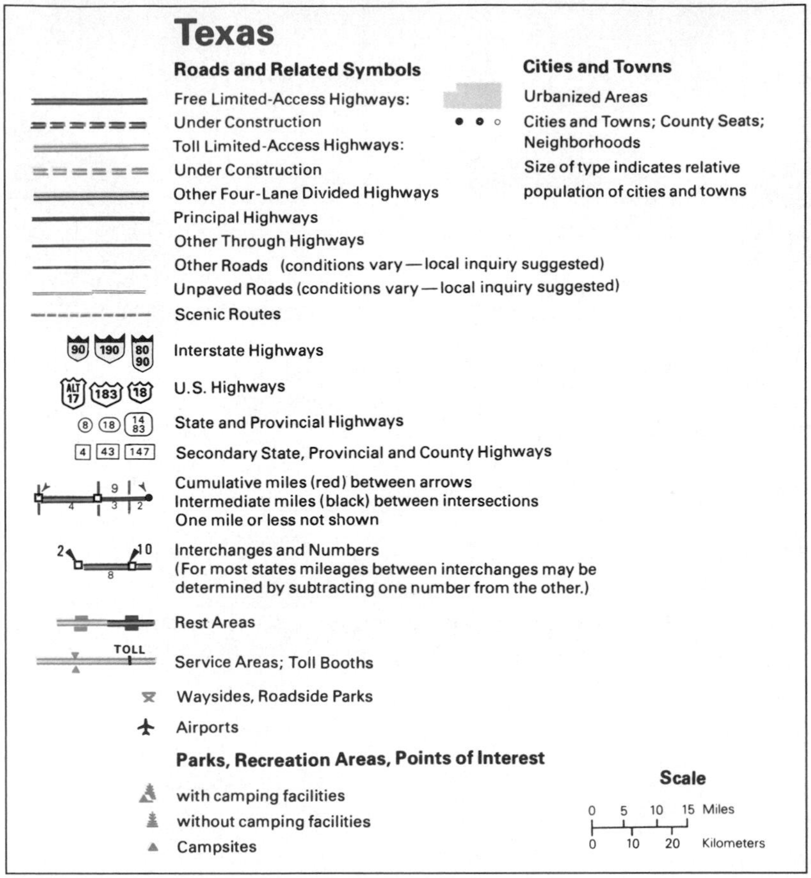

Finding Towns and Cities

Most maps contain an index. To find a city, note the letter and number that follows it in the index. The letters and numbers correspond to the letters and numbers around the edge of the map.

For example, to find San Antonio (O-5), locate O on the left of the map and 5 on the bottom. Next, draw an imaginary line across to the right from the O. Then strike an

imaginary line up from the 5. San Antonio is near the point where your two lines cross.

Determining Distances

Here are three ways you can use a map to estimate distances:

Map Scale   Use the **map scale** to estimate distances between towns and cities. On this map, one inch equals about 30 miles.

Mileage Chart   The mileage chart lists the distances between cities. Run your eyes across and down the columns listing two cities. The distance between

them will be printed where those two columns meet.

Colored Symbols   Colored numbers indicate distances between cities, towns, or points of interest marked with like colored symbols. On the map of Texas, red numbers indicate the distance between red arrowheads. If you follow Interstate 10, you will notice that San Antonio is 37 miles from Seguin. Black numbers indicate the distance between major intersections. You can add numbers to determine the mileage between two distant points.

A map's legend explains its marks, symbols, and distance scale.

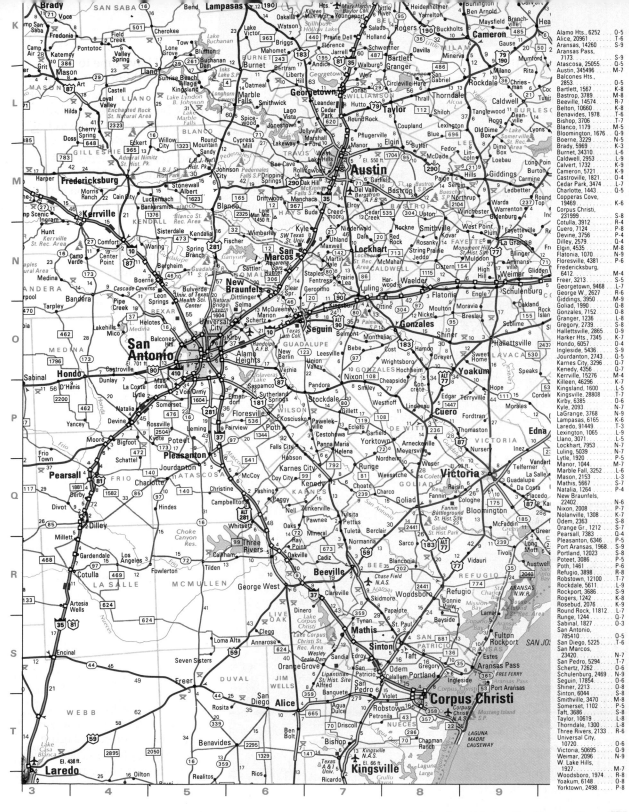

Vehicle Loading

A great deal of added weight will affect the way a car handles. In addition, your headlights might shine higher than normal if the rear of your car is loaded excessively. A heavily loaded car will be especially hard to handle in an emergency maneuver or in high cross winds.

Use the following guidelines when loading your car:

- Avoid heavy loads if possible.
- Check and *do not exceed* the highest load your tires can carry.
- Use the highest tire pressure listed in your owner's manual.

- Place the heaviest objects in the bottom of your trunk.
- Do not put heavy objects in a roof carrier. This will make your car top-heavy.
- Do not place objects on your rear-window shelf. These objects can block your rear view. They also could fly forward in a sudden stop and hit the occupants.
- Do not carry a filled fuel can.

Enjoying Your Travel

To make the most of your long-distance travel, you need to use the following practices. By doing so, your trip will be enjoyable.

Navigation   Following a route by reading a map is called **navigating**. *Never try to read a map while you are driving* . If you are driving alone, pull off the road and stop before you read your map. If there are others in your car, let one of your passengers navigate. Ask your navigator to plan ahead and give you directions well in advance. You then will be able to avoid making snap decisions and taking quick actions. If you are lost, stop and ask for directions.

Staying Alert   Use these techniques to stay alert during a long trip:

- Take a break every two hours, especially if you are traveling alone. Get out of your car and stretch.

Put the heaviest items in the bottom of the trunk.

Even in daytime, a vehicle is more visible if the headlights are on.

What if there was a device on all cars that could reduce daytime traffic accidents by up to 20 percent? Would we use it to save hundreds of lives, avoid thousands of collisions, and save millions of dollars?

Since 1989, all new vehicles sold in Canada have been equipped with a device that turns on their headlights day and night. Just like new motorcycles in the United States, more and more Canadian cars have their headlights on whenever the engine is on.

The reason this program works is simple to see. Both oncoming cars in the picture on this page are at the same distance. But the car with its headlights on is much more visible. This same visibility principle works in city traffic.

Do you have to wait to use this technique? No—any time you feel that being more easily seen would be safer, just turn on your low-beam headlights.

- If you are traveling with another licensed driver, take turns driving and navigating.
- Keep your eyes moving, scanning the mirrors and sides of the road. This ongoing effort will help you avoid being "hypnotized" by long hours of monotonous driving.
- Help other drivers stay alert by keeping your headlights on. Notice how much more visible your car is with its headlights on, even in daylight hours.
- Adjust your seat for greater comfort.
- Keep air moving through your car. Use the air conditioner or open the windows and vents.

Refreshments What you eat and drink on trips will affect your alertness. Avoid overeating when traveling. Avoid foods that are high in salt and excessive sugar. These foods can make you thirsty or jittery.

To maintain complete control of your car, do not eat or drink while driving.

Concentration Follow these steps to help you concentrate on driving:
- Maintain at least a 2-second following distance. This will help you keep alert for possible trouble well down the road.
- Read road signs aloud.
- Watch for mile markers to check the accuracy of your odometer.

Do whatever you can to think about your driving task. At the same time, enjoy the company of your companions and enjoy your trip.

Review It

1. What are three ways you can use a road map to find distances between two cities?
2. How should you prepare in advance for a long trip?
3. What guidelines should you use when loading your car for long-distance travel?

Recreational Vehicles and Trailers

At some time, you might have a chance to drive a recreational vehicle, or you might need to drive a rented truck. Your car might have to pull a trailer. In these driving situations, you will have to apply a different set of rules to your regular driving habits.

Recreational Vehicles

A **recreational vehicle** is a vehicle that is used primarily for fun and travel. A camper on a pickup truck or a large motor home are both examples of recreational vehicles. Recreational vehicles handle differently than cars. They accelerate, brake, and maneuver slower. And, they are hard to back safely because of limited rearward visibility.

Seeing   The minute you get behind the steering wheel of a recreational vehicle, you will notice that visibility is different than at the wheel of a car. Because you are higher up, you can see much farther ahead. You can project your path of travel better. You can search the road ahead with fewer things to block your line of sight. This single advantage can help you use the IPDE process much better. But do not forget, your

How does the view ahead from a recreational vehicle compare with the view from a car?

How much of the rear can you see from the right mirror of this recreational vehicle?

braking and maneuvering distances will be greater too.

Looking to the rear is completely different. Look at the picture of the view from your right rearview mirror. This is your only visual connection to things happening on your right. Is your blind spot bigger? Can you understand how other drivers can help the drivers of recreational and other large vehicles by giving them extra room?

Backing   Before you back your vehicle, walk around it to make sure nothing is behind it. When backing, get another person to stand beside your vehicle and guide you. Whenever possible, avoid backing by going around the block or turning around in a large, open parking lot.

Maneuvering   Accept the fact that because of your vehicle's size and weight, you will not

be able to maneuver it as you would a car. Take it easy when turning, braking, and accelerating.

Cross Winds   Since they have large flat sides, recreational vehicles will react more to cross winds. When driving in winds, slow down or, in extreme cases, stop in a sheltered area. Be prepared for wind gusts when driving out of a protected area like a tunnel.

Imagine you are driving a rented truck and are planning to enter this drive-through. Can you predict any possible conflicts?

Remember Your Size Hitting an overhead object like a service station canopy is one of the most frequent accidents experienced by novice rental truck drivers. They simply forget they are driving a tall vehicle. Always take the larger size into consideration when you project your path of travel into tight spaces.

Following Distance Your following distance should be at least 4 seconds in a recreational vehicle. This distance will give you more time to see and respond.

Fatigue It takes more energy to drive a recreational vehicle than a car. Their ride can be rough and they can be noisier than cars. You probably will tire more easily, so plan for rest stops and shared driving more often than when driving a car.

Trailers

Pulling a trailer puts a strain on a car. When you pull a trailer with your car, you can count on:
- doubling the time you need to accelerate and brake
- cutting your fuel economy almost in half.

When you use a trailer, you need to take the following steps.

Prepare Your Vehicle Make these checks before pulling a trailer:
- Inspect your engine oil and transmission fluid levels. Then check them regularly during the trip. Also check your radiator coolant. Some fluids, such as your transmission fluid, may have to be changed more frequently.
- Make sure fuel, air, and oil filters are serviced more frequently than normal.

Make sure you know how to properly hook up all attachments when towing a trailer.

- Increase rear tire pressures to the maximum recommended limit.
- Examine all car and trailer lights to make sure they work.

Study your owner's guide for any additional special steps you need to take before pulling the trailer.

Equipment You will need a solid hitch, safety chains, and mirrors on both sides of your car before pulling a trailer. **Safety chains** are used to hook the trailer to your car and will hold the trailer in case the hitch breaks. Check to make sure your car and trailer brakes and running lights are working. Make sure you know how to hook up and adjust all your equipment before leaving.

Load   Take these steps when loading your trailer:
- Place heavy items low over the trailer's axle and evenly distribute them to the left and right.
- If your loaded trailer weighs more than 1,000 pounds, you need special trailer brakes.
- Make sure about 10 percent of the trailer's weight is on the tongue where it hooks to your trailer hitch.
- Secure the load with ropes or tie-downs.

Special Towing Techniques

When pulling your trailer, keep the "two times" rule in mind. Remember it will take you about twice as long to pass, stop, accelerate, and turn. Follow these rules when towing a trailer:
- Use a 4-second following distance.
- Do not exceed any posted trailer speed limit.
- Make turns slow and wide. Your inside trailer tire will follow a tighter arc when turning.
- If your trailer starts to sway or "fishtail," steer toward the center of your lane and gradually slow. If your trailer has a separate set of brakes, use them first while accelerating slightly. When the trailer stops swaying, use your car brakes carefully. Check your load to make sure it has not shifted.
- Allow twice as much distance to pass.
- Anticipate it will take you twice as long to stop.

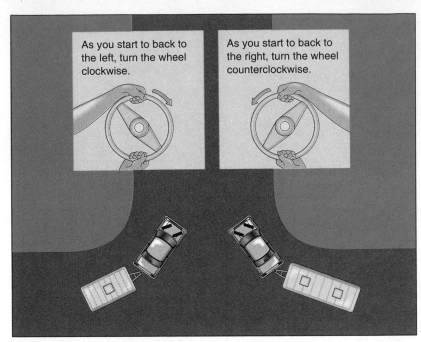

Steering while starting to back a trailer

- Shift to a low gear before going up or down a hill.
- Avoid traveling in high winds.
- Never carry passengers in a trailer. This is not only unsafe, it is illegal in most states.
- If your car starts to overheat while pulling a trailer, turn off your air conditioner and turn on your heater to help cool your engine.

Backing   Before backing a loaded trailer, practice backing an empty trailer in a parking lot. Look at the picture on this page to get a "feel" for what it is like to back a trailer. To steer while backing, put your left hand on the bottom of your steering wheel. Turn the wheel clockwise to *start* backing left. Turn the wheel counterclockwise to *start* backing right. Once your turn is

started, move back slowly and make small steering corrections as you go. You will need to use your outside rearview mirror and a person outside your car to help guide your backing.

Hazards   If you pass, or are passed by another large vehicle, be ready to adjust for any cross winds created by the other vehicle.

Review It

1. What are three special problems you might have while driving a recreational vehicle?
2. What special steps should you follow when towing a trailer?
3. What procedure should you use when backing a trailer?

DECISION MAKING

1. How can you find out in advance how weather and traffic conditions might affect your trip?

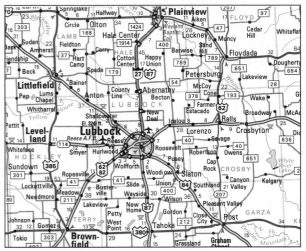

2. What main route would you take to go from Lubbock to Tahoka, Texas? How far is it and how long will the drive take? What other routes are available?

3. What common driving problem is this driver trying to fight? What else would you do?

4. What is the problem in this picture? What is the probable cause? How might the problem have been prevented?

CHAPTER 18 REVIEW

Review Chapter Objectives

18-1   Local Travel
1. What two basic questions should you ask yourself before making a short trip? (356)
2. What three ways can you prepare in advance for a short trip? (357)

18-2   Long-Distance Travel
3. What three ways can you use a road map to find the distance between two cities? (358)
4. How can you prepare in advance for a long-distance trip. (360)
5. What emergency equipment should you keep in your car? (361)
6. What five things should you do to personally prepare for a long-distance trip? (361)
7. What is the best way to load your car for a long-distance trip? (362)
8. What techniques can you use to stay alert while driving? (362–363)

18-3   Recreational Vehicles and Trailers
9. What potential problems might you have while driving a recreational vehicle? (364–365)
10. What are some of the special steps you need to take when pulling a trailer? (366)
11. How should you back a trailer? (366)

Check Your Knowledge

Multiple Choice   Copy the number of each sentence below on a sheet of paper. Choose the letter that best completes the statement or answers the question.

1. Which of these factors does *not* help to make a local trip easier for you?
(a) leaving on time (b) allowing enough time
(c) traveling during rush hour (d) listening to weather reports (357)
2. Before making a long-distance trip, you should
(a) have your car checked and serviced. (b) take an extra pair of gloves. (c) load a complete tool chest. (d) put a 5-gallon container of fuel in the trunk. (360)
3. How should you read a map during a trip?
(a) Rest it on the steering wheel. (b) Glance at it quickly while driving. (c) Stop or have a passenger read it. (d) Hold it to your side window. (363)
4. What special rule should you remember when pulling a trailer?
(a) "go slow" rule (b) "two times" rule (c) "take time" rule (d) "tire check" rule (366)
5. When backing a trailer, you should
(a) use your outside mirror and ask another person to direct you. (b) look over your shoulders. (c) use mirrors and some markers. (d) look over your shoulders and ask another person to call out directions. (366)

Completion   Copy the number of each sentence below. After each number, write the word or words that complete the sentence correctly.

6. To save fuel, combine several ____ . (356)
7. A ____ can help you locate towns and cities on a map. (358)
8. Have your car serviced about ____ before a long-distance trip. (360)
9. Inflate tires to the ____ recommended pressure before carrying heavy loads in your car. (362)
10. On a long trip, eat ____ than usual. (363)
11. Recreational vehicles are less stable than cars in ____ . (364)
12. You need ____ time to pass, turn, stop, and accelerate when pulling a trailer. (366)
13. To back a trailer to the right, turn the bottom of the steering wheel to the ____ . (366)

Check Vocabulary

Copy the number of each definition in List A. Match the definition in List A with the term it defines in List B.

List A
14. in a map legend, a line that indicates measurement in miles (358)
15. boxed area on a map that explains markings and symbols (358)
16. using maps to guide a driver (363)
17. large vehicle used for fun and travel (364)
18. holds trailer if the hitch breaks loose (365)

List B
a. legend
b. map scale
c. navigating
d. recreational vehicle
e. safety chains
f. trailer

Check Your Understanding

Write a short answer for each question or statement.

19. Describe some ways to reach a close destination if you cannot drive there. (356)
20. Of the three ways to estimate distance with a map, which one do you prefer? Why? (358)
21. Suppose you were planning to take a trip to the area in the picture. List some of the special equipment you would want to pack for the drive. (361)
22. Describe some of the special steps you would take to keep alert on a long trip. (362–363)
23. Explain how you would correct for a "fishtail" sway while pulling a trailer. (366)

Think Critically

Write a paragraph to answer each question or statement.

1. When taking a long trip, many drivers choose to use an auto or travel club to prepare their trip plan. Why do you think they make this choice? (360)
2. When you travel with an atlas map that shows large areas on a single page, why do you think it would be good to have isolated maps showing nothing but small towns or cities? (358)

Projects

1. To learn how complex and expensive a long trip can be, completely plan a trip that is at least 1,000 miles long. If possible, seek advice from a local auto or travel club. **Write** a report about your plan.
2. Riding in a large recreational vehicle is a unique experience for any new driver. Seek out a local recreational vehicle dealer or owner and ask if you can sit in the driver's seat. Imagine how demanding it is to drive one of these vehicles.

State Highway Patrol Officer

Duties: Supervising drivers on major highways is the main function of the highway patrol. These officers help keep traffic flowing in a safe and orderly manner. They help roadway users in trouble, investigate collisions, issue warnings and citations, and testify in court.

Training: Most state highway patrols require at least a high-school education, plus specialized courses in police science that many community colleges and universities offer. Recruits attend an intensive training program at the state's highway patrol academy.

Opportunities: Competition for most law-enforcement positions is expected to remain high. The outlook is best for those candidates with some college training in law enforcement. Opportunities for advancement include promotion to higher levels of command.

Career Information: Contact the State Police headquarters in your state's capital.

Highway Engineer

Duties: Highway engineers design and oversee the building, repair, and maintenance of roadways and bridges. They consider the geology of the area, as well as the environmental and social impact of any proposed roadway construction. Their duties can include presenting their plans to governmental committees, outdoor field work, and supervising construction crews.

Training: A college degree in civil engineering is required. Courses in mathematics, science (physics and geology), environmental management, and computer technology are highly recommended. Good drafting skills are necessary.
New engineering graduates often work as assistants to experienced engineers. Many engineers get a master's degree to increase their earning potential or become eligible for promotion. State licensing is usually required since the public's safety can be affected.

Opportunities: Employment opportunities are expected to improve for civil engineers. Some highway engineers can rise to administrative positions in federal, state, and local government agencies. Other engineers can become executives in engineering firms. Although most highway engineers work in urban areas, jobs in rural areas, foreign countries, or jobs involving frequent travel are also available.

Career Information:
American Society of Civil Engineers
345 E. 47th St.
New York, NY 10017

Driver-Education Teacher

Duties: Both high schools and privately owned driving schools employ driver-education teachers. These teachers use classroom instruction and in-car instruction to teach people how to safely operate a motor vehicle.

Training: Most driver-education teachers work in public high schools that require a four-year college degree as well as a teaching certificate. Some private high schools and privately owned driving schools do not require a teaching certificate. However, some states require a special teaching license for teachers in privately owned driving schools.

Opportunities: The need for driver-education teachers is expected to remain steady. Some driver-education teachers work as consultants for government and private organizations.

Career Information:
American Driver and Traffic Safety Education Association
239 Florida Ave.
Salisbury, MD 21801

Paramedics and EMTs

Duties: Paramedics and emergency medical technicians (EMTs) need excellent driving skills to reach emergencies as quickly and safely as possible. Paramedics administer first aid to the sick or injured, and transport them to a nearby medical facility. Paramedics often work in a mobile intensive-care ambulance under the direction of fire department or hospital personnel.

Training: Admission to training programs usually requires a high-school diploma or equivalent education. An emergency medical technician course is followed by a 3- to 5-month training program.

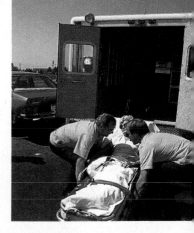

Opportunities: The demand for paramedics is increasing. Salaries of publicly employed paramedics are similar to those of police officers and firefighters. Benefits are usually good.

Career Information:
National Association of Emergency Medical Technicians
9140 Ward Parkway
Kansas City, MO 64114

Route Driver

Duties: Route drivers use panel or light trucks to deliver products. A route driver collects payments from customers and attempts to interest them in the company's new products or services.

Training: A route driver must have orderly work habits and must be able to work without direct supervision. In most states, a route driver must qualify for a commercial driver's license.

Opportunities: Sales supervisor and route supervisor are two opportunities for advancement. As the population continues to move toward suburban areas, there will be an increased need for route drivers.

Career Information:
International Brotherhood of Teamsters, Chauffeurs, Warehousemen and Helpers of America (Ind.)
25 Louisiana Ave., N.W.
Washington, DC 20001

Automotive Mechanic

Duties: A mechanic diagnoses automotive problems and estimates the cost of both parts and labor for repairs. A mechanic also repairs vehicles, using a wide variety of tools and skills.

Training: Some high schools, trade schools, and community colleges offer courses and certification in automotive repair. Some auto dealers and large, independent repair shops offer 3- or 4-year apprenticeship programs. Such a program combines on-the-job experience with classroom instruction.

Opportunities: The need for qualified automotive mechanics is expected to be excellent since many people keep their cars for long periods of time. Advancements in automotive technology should also increase the demand for qualified mechanics.

Career Information:
Automotive Service Industry Association
444 N. Michigan Ave.
Chicago, IL 60611

Sales Representative

Duties: Sales representatives usually need a car to present their company's products to local and out-of-state customers. In addition, they usually must complete an extensive amount of paperwork such as reports, expense accounts, and lists of prospective clients. Sales representatives must also devote study time and have self-discipline in order to study new products, read about the competition, and learn about new developments in the field.

Training: High-school graduates are sometimes hired as sales trainees for some companies. However, up to two years could pass before the trainees actually start working as sales representatives. Sales of some products (medical supplies and chemicals, for example) can require college degrees in biology, chemistry, or pharmacy. Some companies require that sales representatives be college graduates with degrees in business or other related fields.

Opportunites: Travel is often a part of the sales representative's job. Foreign travel is a possibility with some companies. Although compensation varies a great deal, a successful sales representative can often advance to regional or national sales management positions.

Career Information:
Sales and Marketing Executives International
Statler Office Tower
No. 458
Cleveland, OH 44115

Automotive Engineer

Duties: Automotive engineers design vehicles to make them safe, efficient, comfortable, and salable. Automobiles are complex machines made of many different systems. Automotive engineers work to make sure systems work together in the complete vehicle.

Training: Entry-level positions usually require a college degree in engineering. Most automotive engineers must be skilled in using computer-assisted design techniques.

Opportunities: Most automotive enginners work for large car-manufacturing corporations. While advancements in automotive technology continue, the economy and export and import patterns affect the availability of jobs in this field.

Career Information:
National Society of Professional Engineers
1420 King St.
Alexandria, VA 22314

Engineering Technician

Duties: Engineering technicians work with automotive engineers to design and produce prototypes of new automobiles. They can aid engineers in preparing design layouts or models. Other duties include making computations, performing laboratory tests, or working at a car manufacturer's proving-ground facilities.

Training: Required training varies. Some technicians need a diploma from a public vocational or technical high school with thorough training at a technical institute or junior college. Others need a college degree in science or mathematics.

Opportunities: While career opportunities are increasing, this field depends upon the state of the economy and automotive sales in general.

Career Information:
Engineers Council for
Professional Development
345 E. 47th St.
New York, NY 10017

Trailer-truck Driver

Duties: Trailer-truck drivers haul goods and materials over long distances in gasoline- or diesel-powered tractor-trailers.

Training: A long-distance truck driver must meet certain federal standards. Truck drivers must pass written tests on safety regulations and road tests on the type of truck they drive. Most states require drivers of large trucks to have a commercial driver's license (CDL), for which they must pass special examinations. Certain driving schools and some colleges offer truck-driving training.

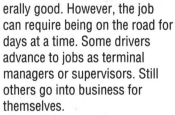

Opportunities: Pay for truck drivers is generally good. However, the job can require being on the road for days at a time. Some drivers advance to jobs as terminal managers or supervisors. Still others go into business for themselves.

Career Information:
American Trucking
Associations, Inc.
2200 Mill Road
Alexandria, VA 22314

Speed

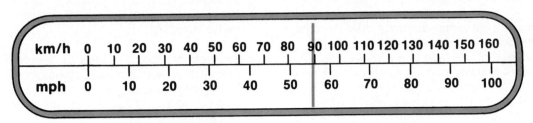

Distance

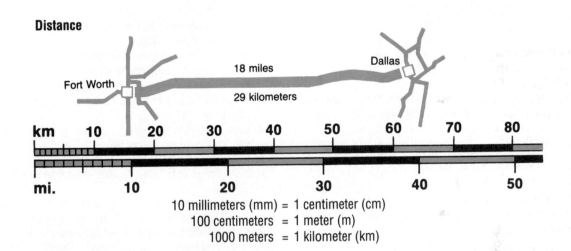

10 millimeters (mm) = 1 centimeter (cm)
100 centimeters = 1 meter (m)
1000 meters = 1 kilometer (km)

Volume

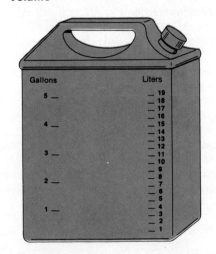

1 cubic centimeter (cm^3) = 1 milliliter (ml)
1000 milliliters = 1 liter (l)
1000 cm^3 = 1 liter (l)

acceleration lane lane that permits drivers entering an expressway to accelerate to the speed of expressway traffic (207).

accelerator pedal that controls the flow of fuel to the engine to regulate speed (41).

active restraint safety belt that a person has to buckle (93).

advisory speed limit maximum safe speed on a curve under ideal conditions, posted on a square, yellow sign (20).

alternator device that produces the electricity to recharge the battery and operate electrical equipment in a vehicle (335).

alternator warning light or gauge on the instrument panel that indicates that the alternator is not making enough electricity and the battery is being drained (39).

angle parking parking a car diagonally to the curb (109).

antilock braking system computer-controlled braking system that helps prevent skidding during emergency braking (239).

assigned-risk insurance type of insurance that provides minimum bodily-injury and property damage liability coverage to a high-risk driver for a higher premium (325).

automatic choke valve that opens and closes automatically to control the air flow through the carburetor (41).

backup lights white lights at the rear of a vehicle that signal that the vehicle is backing (45).

banked curve curve that is sloped down on the inside and up on the outside to overcome a car's tendency to tilt toward the outside of the curve (87).

basic speed law law stating that you should not drive faster than is safe and prudent for existing conditions, regardless of posted speed limits (20).

belted tire tire constructed with a combination of cord layers crisscrossed at a slight angle, and cord strips circling the tire (341).

bias-ply tire tire constructed with cord layers, or plies, crisscrossed underneath the outer material (341).

blind spot area that rearview mirrors cannot show (42).

blood-alcohol concentration (BAC) percentage of alcohol found in the bloodstream as measured by chemical tests of blood or urine (298).

blowout sudden loss of tire air pressure while driving (248).

blue book book that lists the average price paid to dealers for various makes and models of used cars (318).

brake fade loss of braking effectiveness caused by overheating of the brakes after long, continuous, hard braking (250).

braking distance distance traveled from the time the brakes are applied until the vehicle stops (90).

braking skid sliding of wheels that are locked because of braking too hard (237).

carbon monoxide colorless, odorless, and poisonous gas found in the exhaust fumes of gasoline engines (286).

carburetor part of the engine that mixes air and gasoline in the proper proportion and sends it to the combustion chambers as a fine mist (339).

carpooling several workers or students commuting to work or to school in one vehicle (328).

center of gravity point around which all of an object's weight is evenly balanced (82).

central vision three-degree, cone-shaped area in which you can see clearly while looking straight ahead (72).

chronic illness ailment that lasts for several years (288).

clutch pedal pedal in a stickshift car that enables a driver to shift gears (41).

collision contact between two or more objects, as when two cars crash into each other (9).

color-blindness inability to tell colors apart (272).

common speed speed used by most drivers on an expressway (213).

compromise space reduce risk by giving as much space as possible to the greater of two or more hazards (74).

controlled-access highway expressway that permits vehicles to enter or leave only at interchanges (204).

controlled braking technique of applying the brakes to slow or stop quickly without locking the wheels (238).

controlled intersection intersection at which traffic-control signs or signals assign the right of way (120).

controlled railroad crossing railroad crossing controlled by flashing red lights and/or crossing gates (130).

countersteer steer in the opposite direction in order to keep a car going straight (257).

covering the brake taking the foot off the accelerator and holding it just above the brake pedal, ready to apply pressure if needed (168).

crossbuck large, white X-shaped sign located beside a railroad crossing (130).

cruise control device that allows the car's speed to be set automatically for highway or expressway driving (43).

deceleration lane extra lane that permits drivers leaving an expressway to slow down without obstructing traffic on the expressway (217).

decide third step of the IPDE process in which the driver selects the best actions as well as when and where to take them to avoid conflicts (7, 64).

deductible the amount an insurance policyholder pays for damages in a collision (322).

defensive driving protecting yourself and others from dangerous and unexpected driving situations (7).

delayed green light traffic light that remains red while oncoming traffic proceeds; the delayed light turns green later (122).

depreciation decrease in the value of a car as a result of its increasing age (316).

depressant drug that slows down or depresses the central nervous system (302).

depth perception ability to judge distance between you and other objects (72, 274).

designated driver person who abstains from drinking alcoholic beverages in order to prevent drinkers from driving (300).

differential arrangement of gears allowing one wheel to revolve faster than the opposite wheel during turns (334).

disk brake type of brake that applies friction by pressing brake pads against a rotating steel disk attached to the wheel (340).

downshifting shifting from a higher to a lower gear (52).

drive shaft long, metal rod turned by the transmission that transmits power to the differential at the rear of the car (334).

driving task all the skilled actions a driver must take to drive safely (6).

driving under the influence (DUI) level of intoxication in some states in which a driver's blood-alcohol concentration is between .05 and .09 percent and driving ability is reduced (303).

driving while intoxicated (DWI) level of intoxication in most states in which a driver's blood-alcohol concentration is .10 percent or higher (303).

drum brake type of brake that applies friction between brake shoes and a steel drum or hollow cylinder attached to the inner side of the wheel (340).

emergency flares devices that burn with bright, red lights to warn approaching traffic of a hazard on the roadway (221).

emergency flasher device that flashes front turn-signal lights and taillights to warn others the vehicle is a hazard (42).

emotion strong feeling of any kind, such as joy, grief, fear, hate, love, anger, and excitement (279).

energy of motion kinetic energy or the energy an object has because it is moving (83).

entrance ramp ramp leading onto an expressway (207).

environment everything that surrounds us (10).

escape path place to go in case of unexpected conflict (59, 185).

euphoria alcohol-induced feeling that a person can do anything (297).

execute fourth step of the IPDE process in which a driver performs proper car control responses to avoid possible conflicts (7, 66).

exit ramp ramp leading off an expressway (217).

face shield clear, plastic device attached to a motorcycle helmet that protects the face and eyes from particles of dust, dirt, and insects (141).

field of vision all the area that a person can see while looking straight ahead (72, 273).

field sobriety test roadside tests given by police officers to detect driver impairment (304).

financial responsibility law law requiring drivers to prove their ability to pay damage claims resulting from a collision (322).

fishtailing swerving of the rear of a vehicle from side to side (248).

flash flood sudden rush of water, usually in desert areas, caused by heavy rain that can wash out roadways (198).

flashing signal red or yellow traffic light that flashes on and off to indicate stop (red) or caution (yellow) (26).

foot-brake pedal pedal that turns on the brake lights and causes the car to slow to stop (41).

force of impact force with which one moving object hits another. Force of impact varies according to speed, weight, and distance between impact and stop (92).

fresh green light traffic signal that has just turned from red to green (120).

friction resistance to motion between surfaces that touch (84).

friction point in a stickshift car point where the engine begins to turn the transmission and move the car as the driver releases the clutch (51).

front brake brake on a motorcycle that is operated by the lever on the right handlebar (140).

fuel-injection system fuel-combustion system (replacing a carburetor) in which vaporized fuel is pumped under pressure to the engine cylinders (339).

full stop a complete stop as required at a stop sign or red light (19).

gap distance between approaching cars in which a driver can cross an intersection or join traffic (126).

glare recovery time time required to regain clear vision after being temporarily blinded by a strong light (275).

glare resistance ability to continue seeing when looking at bright lights (275).

gravity force pulling all objects toward the center of the earth (82).

ground viewing making quick glances to the roadway in front of a vehicle as you drive (60).

guide sign sign that gives direction, distances, services, points of interest, and other information (18).

hallucinogen mind-altering drug that tends to distort a person's perceptions of time, distance, and the shapes or colors of objects (302).

hand-over-hand steering method of turning the steering wheel in which one hand pulls the steering wheel down while the other hand crosses over to pull the wheel farther down (103).

head restraints padded supports on the backs of front seats that minimize whiplash injury to front-seat occupants in a rear-end collision (42).

helmet protective device worn by motorcyclists to prevent or reduce head injuries in the event of a collision or upset (141).

highway hypnosis dulled or drowsy, trancelike condition caused by concentration on the roadway ahead and monotony of driving (220).

highway transportation system (HTS) complex system made up of people, vehicles, and roadways (4).

hood release lever under instrument panel on left side that releases the hood lock (43).

hydroplaning condition in which the tires of a moving vehicle ride on the surface of water, resulting in loss of steering and braking control (232).

identify first step of the IPDE process in which the driver locates potential hazards (7, 58).

ignition switch switch operated by a key which starts or stops the engine (40).

implied-consent law state law providing that a driver must give up the driver's license if he or she refuses to consent to take a chemical test for intoxication if arrested on suspicion of driving under the influence of alcohol (303).

inhibitions inner forces of personality that restrain a person's impulsive behavior (295).

international symbols symbols used on traffic signs that give a message without using words (24).

intoxilyzer computerized machine that analyzes and determines the blood-alcohol concentration through the amount of infrared light absorbed by breath (304).

IPDE process organized system of seeing, thinking, and responding that includes the steps of identifying, predicting, deciding, and executing (7, 58).

jack hand-operated device for lifting one corner of the car, generally used when changing a tire (249).

joining traffic fitting into a gap in the flow of traffic (126).

lane signal signal, usually overhead, that designates whether a lane can or cannot be used at a specific time (27).

legend boxed area on a map containing explanations of the symbols and markings on that map (358).

lending agencies institutions that lend money, such as banks, savings and loan associations, credit unions, and finance companies (321).

liability insurance insurance coverage that pays for bodily injury and property damage to others in a collision caused by the insured (322).

lug nuts small pieces of hardware that hold a wheel to a car (249).

map scale line an inch or more long appearing in the legend of a map, indicating a measurement in miles or kilometers for distances on that map (358).

master cylinder device in the brake system from which brake fluid is forced to the wheel cylinders when a driver steps on the brake pedal (340).

mass transportation methods of moving larger numbers of people than cars can carry (328).

median strip area that separates two-way traffic on a divided, multilane highway (186).

merging area stretch of roadway at the end of an acceleration lane on an expressway where cars join the flow of traffic (207).

minimize a hazard reduce risk by increasing space between a vehicle and a single hazard (73).

minimum speed limit lowest legal speed a car may travel on certain roadways under good conditions to prevent wide differences in speed among vehicles (20, 213).

moped a two-wheeled vehicle that has an engine and can be pedaled (146).

motor scooter a two-wheeled, engine-powered vehicle that is more powerful than a moped but less powerful than a motorcycle (146).

mpg miles per gallon, a measure of the fuel-efficiency of a vehicle (318).

navigating process of reading a map and following routes to reach a destination safely and efficiently (362).

night blindness condition of not being able to see well at night (274).

no-fault insurance insurance that provides the policyholder with medical coverage (up to specified limits), regardless of who is at fault (322).

nystagmus rapid, involuntary movement of the eyes as a person gazes to the sides (305).

odometer device on the instrument panel showing the total number of miles a car has traveled (39).

oil pump device that forces oil from the oil pan to parts of the engine that need lubrication (337).

orderly visual search pattern process of searching or scanning critical areas in a regular sequence (58).

overdrive gear that allows an engine to run more slowly at speeds of 40–45 mph (45, 350).

overdriving headlights driving at a speed in which the stopping distance exceeds the area lit by the headlights (230).

oversteer turning the steering wheel too much (100).

overtake approach and pass a slower-moving vehicle ahead in your lane (171).

over-the-counter (OTC) medicine drug that can be legally obtained without a doctor's prescription (301).

owner's manual manufacturer's booklet containing valuable information about a vehicle (335).

parallel parking parking the car parallel to the curb (110).

parking brake lever primarily used to hold a parked car in place; also used to slow a vehicle when the foot brake fails (41).

passive restraint device, such as an air bag or automatic seat belt, that works without action by car occupants (42, 94).

pedestrian signal traffic signal or symbol for the use of pedestrians, usually reading walk and wait, or walk and don't walk (28).

peer education type of counseling that uses peer leadership to help others make decisions and determine goals (308).

peer pressure influence of friends on a person's actions (306).

perception distance distance a car travels during the time a driver sees and identifies an object or situation ahead (90).

perception time time it takes a person to become aware of an object or situation ahead (90).

peripheral vision side-vision area to the left and right of central vision (72, 273).

perpendicular parking parking at a right angle to the curb (109).

point of no return point beyond which a driver can no longer stop safely without entering the intersection (167).

policy contract or agreement between a vehicle owner and an insurance company specifying the amount and type of insurance coverage for which a premium is paid (322).

power skid spinning of tires during acceleration (237).

power steering device in some vehicles to make steering easier (338).

predict second step of the IPDE process in which the driver foresees where possible conflicts can occur (7, 62).

premium specified amount that a policyholder pays for insurance coverage (322).

prescription drug drug that can be obtained legally only with a doctor's prescription (301).

preventive maintenance care given to a vehicle to keep mechanical problems from developing (344).

protected left turn left turn made on a left-turn light, green arrow, or delayed green light while oncoming traffic is stopped (122).

protective equipment special equipment such as helmet, face shield or goggles, and heavy clothing which a motorcyclist should wear to prevent or reduce injury in the event of an upset or a collision (141).

pull-out area safe stopping area on narrow roadways where slow-moving vehicles can pull over to permit faster traffic to proceed (196).

radial tire tire constructed with plies running straight across the tire from one side to the other and encircled by nylon or steel reinforcing material (341).

radiator part of the cooling system in which the coolant that circulates around the engine is cooled by a current of air (338).

reaction distance distance the car travels during a driver's reaction time (90).

reaction time time it takes a driver to respond to a driving hazard once it has been identified (90).

rear brake brake on a motorcycle that is operated by a foot pedal (140).

recreational vehicle large vehicle, such as a camper or motor home, used for fun and travel (364).

regulatory sign sign that informs highway users of traffic laws or regulations and indicates requirements to perform in a certain manner (18).

restraint device device designed to hold a car occupant in the seat during a collision (93).

riding the brake driving with a foot on the brake pedal so that the brake lights remain on and the brakes are partially applied (168).

riding the clutch driving with the left foot resting on the clutch pedal (50).

right of way privilege of immediate use of the roadway (19, 128).

right-turn-on-red turning right when the red signal is on unless specifically prohibited to turn (26).

risk-taking behavior taking chances when the consequences can be dangerous (278).

roadway marking lines, words, or figures painted on the roadway that give drivers a warning or direction (29).

roadway users people who use the HTS by walking, driving, or riding (4).

rocking the car means of loosening a car's wheels from snow, mud, or sand by alternately putting the car in low gear and moving ahead, and then shifting to reverse and moving back (233).

rumble strips sections of rough pavement intended to alert drivers of roadway construction, approach to a toll booth, or other traffic condition ahead (222).

safe path of travel path that is free of hazards and conflict (71).

safety chains chains linking a vehicle and a trailer being towed, to give extra protection if the hitch loosens (365).

scanning glancing continually through an orderly visual search pattern (60).

school zone portion of a street or highway near a school that is subject to special speed limits (18).

selective seeing selecting and identifying only those events and clues that pertain to the driving task (59).

selector lever device in an automatic transmission car used to select forward or reverse gears (40).

separate the hazards process of adjusting the speed of a vehicle to handle one hazard at a time when two or more hazards threaten a driver (73).

shift indicator device on a car that shows the different driving gears and the one being used (45).

shock absorber device that absorbs the bouncing action of a wheel (338).

sideways skid sliding of the rear of a vehicle to the left or right (237).

sight distance distance a person can see ahead (71).

slow-moving vehicle farm or construction vehicle that cannot reach highway speeds, usually identified by an orange triangular sign at the rear of the vehicle (193).

space cushion open area all around a vehicle consisting of adequate following distance between it and the cars ahead and behind, plus swerve paths to left and right (64).

spark plug device in the cylinder of an engine which produces a spark to ignite the fuel-air mixture (334).

speed smear blur and distortion of objects on the sides as speed increases (276).

springs devices that support the vehicle to allow and help control up-and-down bouncing (338).

stale green light traffic signal ahead that is green at the time it is first noticed and about to turn yellow (120, 167).

stimulant drug that speeds up the central nervous system (302).

switchback series of sharp turns on a mountain roadway (196).

tailgating following a vehicle too closely (164).

thermostat automatic device for regulating temperature of the coolant in the cooling system (339).

tire chains devices placed over the tire tread to increase friction when driving on roadways covered with snow and ice (233).

total stopping distance total distance it takes to stop a car, including perception distance, reaction distance, and braking distance (90).

tracking steering a car in its intended path (47).

traction friction or gripping power between a tire and the roadway (84).

tractor semitrailer tractor that pulls one trailer, commonly called an "18-wheeler" (151)

tractor trailer truck that has a tractor that pulls a separate trailer (151).

traffic signal any signal used to control the movement of traffic (25).

transmission mechanism that transmits power from the engine to the drive wheels (334).

tread grooved surface of a tire that grips the roadway (84).

tune up process of checking, repairing, and adjusting various parts of the ignition and fuel systems to obtain maximum engine performance (335).

tunnel vision very narrow field of side vision (273).

turnabout maneuver for turning the car around to go in the opposite direction (105).

uncontrolled intersection intersection at which there are no traffic-control signals, signs, or roadway markings to regulate traffic (118).

uncontrolled railroad crossing railroad crossing which has no signals or crossing gates (130).

understeer not turning the steering wheel enough (100).

unprotected left turn left turn made at an intersection that does not have a special turn light (121).

vapor lock condition in which fuel in a gaseous form in the fuel line near the hot engine prevents the engine from starting (197).

vehicle code organization of federal and state laws that regulate the HTS (5).

velocitation condition of unconsciously driving too fast as a result of driving for long periods at high speeds (220).

visual acuity ability to see objects sharply and distinctly, both near and far away (272).

warning sign yellow or orange sign with black symbols or lettering that informs drivers of possible danger ahead (18).

warranty written guarantee that the seller will repair the car for a stated period of time (318).

wolf pack group or formation of vehicles traveling on an expressway (213).

yield allow another vehicle or other roadway user to proceed first (19,128).

INDEX

stop-swerve situations, 258
traffic signals, 120
uncontrolled intersection, 119
urban traffic, 160–161, 172
vehicle capabilities, 88–89
visibility, 228–231
wind blast, 240
winter driving, 242

Jack, 249
Jogging areas, 147, 148
Joining traffic, 126–127
Judgment
    effects of alcohol, 295
    and prediction, 62
    distance and fog, 230
    time, distance, size of gap, 126–127

Kinetic energy, 83

Lane signal, 25, 27
Lanes
    blocked, 61, 215
    car position, 65, 170, 173
    changing, 102, 170
    expressway, 215
    lines, 30
    multilane road, 186–187
    one-way street, 173
    reversible, 27
    signal, 25, 27
    urban areas, 170
    width change, 61
Lap belt, 94
Large vehicles, 89
Lead, 326
"Leave yourself an out," 59, 64
Leaves, 235
Leaving car, 49
Left turn
    arrow, 27
    from one-way street, 173
    in front of motorcycle, 137
    joining traffic, 125
    LEFT TURN SIGNAL, 122

light, 122
    on red light, 123
    protected, 122
    unprotected, 121
    yielding right of way, 12
Legend, map, 358
Lending agencies, 321
Liability insurance, 322
License plates, handicapped symbol,
    288
Licenses, 316, 318
Light switch, 43
Lights, 43, 65
    See also Headlights
Lights, backup, 65
Limited-access highway, 204
Lines
    broken white, 30
    broken yellow, 29
    center, 165
    solid white, 30
    solid yellow, 29
Load
    and braking distance, 91
    and car performance, 87
Loading vehicle, 362
Loans,costs of, 318
Locked wheels, 237, 238
Lodging, 360
Low-beam headlights
    as communication, 65
    dawn and dusk, 228
    day and night, 263
    in bad weather, 229, 230, 231
    sand or dust storms, 198
    with sun glare, 228
Low gear
    on hills, 82
    on slippery road, 242
    when pulling trailer, 366
Low gear positions (automatic), 45
Lubrication system, 337
Lug nuts, 249

MADD (Mothers Against Drunk
    Driving), 308

Maintenance, 206, 334–347
Manual transmission, 40, 50–52, 318
    backing, 101
    downshifting before curve, 103
    mountain driving, 196–197
Map reading, 358–359
Map scale, 358
Marijuana, 302
Markings, roadway, 29–32
    raised roadway markers, 31
    white line, 30
    yellow line, 29
Mass transportation, 328
Master cylinder, 340
Mechanic, selecting, 346
Median strip, 186, 187
Medical payment insurance,
Medicines, 286, 287
Meeting other vehicles
    city, 165
    headlights, use of, 229
    motorcycles, 138
    reduced visibility, 229
    rural roads, 194–195
    trucks, 152
Merging area, 207, 208, 210
Mid-size vehicles, 89
Miles per gallon (mpg), 318, 348–349
Minimize hazard, 73
Minimum speed limit, 20, 213
Mirrors, 42, 365
Moisture on windows, 228
Moped, 146, 230
Mothers Against Drunk Drivers
    (MADD), 308
Motor home, 364
Motor scooter, 136, 146
Motorcycles
    conflict-reducing strategies, 142–143
    and expressway entrance on left, 210
    handling traits, 140–141
    interaction with cars, 136–143
    protective equipment, 141
    where to look for, 137–138
Mountain driving, 5, 196–197, 361

ACKNOWLEDGMENTS

Unless otherwise acknowledged, all photographs are the property of ScottForesman. Page abbreviations are as follows: (T) top, (C) center, (B) bottom, (L) left, (R) right, (INS) inset. ScottForesman photographs by Jack Demuth, John Moore, Allan Landau.

iv	Courtesy Chrysler Motor Company
vii	Grant Heilman Photography
1–2	David Young-Wolf/Photo Edit
4	David Young-Wolf/Photo Edit
5(T)	Kent Knudson/West Stock
6	Data source: Valvoline Oil Co. survey
7	Data source: Massachusetts Institute of Technology and University of California at Berkeley, 1990
15	Milt & Joan Mann/Cameramann International, Ltd.
20	Courtesy United States Department of Transportation, Federal Highway Admininstration
22	Courtesy United States Department of Transportation, Federal Highway Admininstration
23	Courtesy United States Department of Transportation, Federal Highway Admininstration
27	Martin R. Parker & Associates, Inc.
55	Jan Halaska/Uniphoto
78–79	Don and Pat Valenti
80–81	Courtesy Chrysler Motor Corporation
97	Courtesy Insurance Institute for Highway Safety
112	Robert Clay
113(R)	Ray Hunold
156–157	Don and Pat Valenti
158–159	Dan Noble/FPG
198	Peter Menzel/Stock Boston
204	Barrie Rokeach
205 (all)	Grant Heilman Photography
226–227	Murray & Associates/Tony Stone Worldwide
230	Frank Cezus/Tony Stone Worldwide
233	Alex Duncan
241	R.P. Kingston/Stock Boston
242	Phylane Norman/Nawrocki Stock Photos
261	Eric Carle/Shostal/Superstock
268–269	Milt & Joan Mann/Camermann International, Ltd.
272	Russ Kinne/Photo Researchers
294	Data source: *Accident Facts,* 1990 edition, National Safety Council
325	Data source: *A Family Guide to Auto & Home Insurance,* © Insurance Information Institute
326	Milt & Joan Mann/Cameramann International, Ltd.
327 (all)	Milt & Joan Mann/Cameramann International, Ltd.
329 (BL)	Tony Freeman/Photo Edit
354–355	Jim Markham
358–359	© Copyright by RAND MCNALLY & COMPANY, R.L.86-S-12
361	J.H. Burnett/Shostal/Superstock
367(R)	© Copyright by RAND MCNALLY & COMPANY, R.L.86-S-12
369	Bob Daemmrich
370 (BL)	Bill Gillette/Stock Boston
370 (BR)	Bruce Roberts/Photo Researchers
371 (R)	Ellis Herwig/Stock Boston
372 (T)	Don & Pat Valenti/Tom Stack & Associates
373 (T)	Rene Burri/Magnum
373 (B)	Andrew Sacks/Tony Stone Worldwide
374 (T)	Brownie Harris/The Stock Market
374 (R)	Hay/Daemmrich